gardening

a commonsense guide

gardening
a commonsense guide

Compiled and edited by
Geoffrey Burnie
Adapted by Alan Toogood
Photographs by Lorna Rose

bay books

CONTENTS

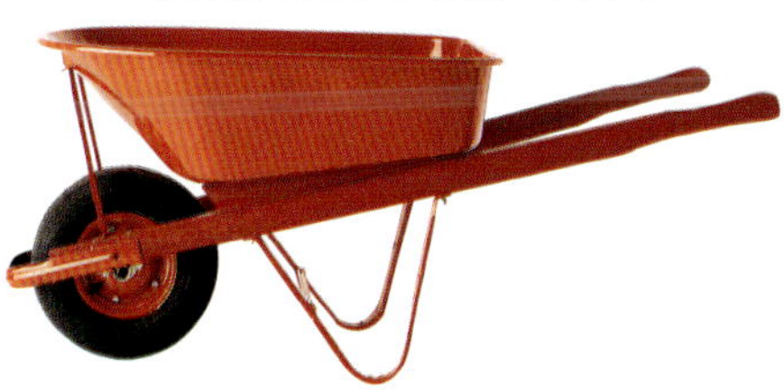

USING THIS BOOK

Gardening: A Commonsense Guide offers you sound, practical advice from a team of expert home gardeners and includes an extensive color dictionary that will show you some of the best, most successful plants for your garden.

GENERAL INFORMATION

In the first twelve chapters you'll find practical advice on a broad range of gardening topics. There are chapters on garden design ideas, on soils and how to improve them, on composting and weed control, and there are easy-to-follow instructions on how you can save money by creating your own plants at home. Also included are a color dictionary to help you quickly identify and learn how to control common garden problems before they get out of hand, a handy guide to the most useful tools and a chart to consult when you need a plant for a special purpose. In fact, in the first twelve chapters you'll find answers to most of the common day-to-day gardening questions.

IDENTIFYING YOUR CLIMATE

Because climates vary and can have a big effect on plant performance, we've made a special effort to identify your climate and the plants that should suit it. The first chapter of the book discusses climate and includes maps from which you can identify your particular climate zone. Remember your zone number when you refer to the plant dictionary and you'll find that choosing plants for your garden has been made easy.

THE PLANT DICTIONARY

From Chapter Thirteen on, the book is arranged as a plant dictionary. It describes and illustrates hundreds of plants our team of gardeners have found to be most successful. To make them easier to find, they're arranged

USE THE NOTES on climate zones to choose plants that grow well together.

SO MANY PLANTS but which to choose? The color dictionary makes the decision simpler by describing and illustrating hundreds of popular plants. All these are in the book.

in chapters—everything from trees and flowers to vegetables, herbs and fruit.

Each chapter begins with a useful introduction. It outlines the broad principles involved in growing the type of plant and gives advice on how to make the best use of them and avoid common mistakes. Each plant is described under the same headings, and so comparison is easy.

In each entry you'll find a heading "Climate". Plants are described as good for your particular climate zone, not suitable or just possible. "Possible" means you'll have to go to some trouble for that plant or find a particularly favored spot for it.

Other headings in the plant entries describe the important features of the plant, but don't forget that the chapter introduction may have some additional information that applies to all of the plants in that chapter.

FINDING YOUR WAY AROUND

- If you want to know about a particular subject, check the Index first, as everything is covered in it.
- If it's more general information you seek, go to the Contents and look up a specific chapter.
- If you come across a term you don't understand, look up the Glossary, which covers most of the terms commonly used in writing and talking about gardening.

YOUR RESULTS

Finally, use *Gardening: A Commonsense Guide* with confidence. The information it contains is the result of direct gardening experience, but remember also that it is just a guide. Your soil, your local climate, your aspect, your exposure and your gardening behavior will all influence the results you achieve in your particular garden.

Act on the information given here but compare what it says with the results you achieve. If there is a difference, ask yourself why. The answer you come up with will help you better understand the possibilities and limits of gardening where you live. We'd be very interested in hearing from you.

IN A COOL CLIMATE plants grow more slowly and gardeners are more easily able to maintain a neat, clipped style of garden. Deciduous trees and shrubs, herbaceous perennials and spring bulbs are well suited to the climate.

•CHAPTER ONE•

YOUR CLIMATE

If you know your climate and choose plants that suit it you are well on your way to a beautiful, easy-care garden. Plants that like your climate won't be stressed by unfamiliar conditions and so will remain healthier and less troubled by pests.

Consider palms and other plants from warm climates. They struggle to live in areas that are a little too cold for them and will die when an unusually cold winter strikes. Even if they survive in a marginal climate, they won't look lush and well. The reverse is also true. Plants that expect a cold winter just don't thrive where winters are mild or warm. In Florida, for example, where winters are mild, many conifers and other cold climate plants are short lived. Weakened by the too warm and humid climate, they are susceptible to attacks by pests and diseases.

VITAL STATISTICS

It is helpful to know the following statistics for your area: total annual rain and when it falls, the average monthly maximum and minimum temperatures and, most importantly, the extreme winter minimum you can expect. Knowing the extremes, even though they may occur only once every hundred years, will help you avoid costly and disappointing losses. For example, if your average winter minimum is, say, 28°F but your area has, in the past, experienced 21°F, it could do so again. If major elements of your garden are plants that die in temperatures below 30°F, you will be in trouble when an extreme low inevitably returns.

IN WARM CLIMATES constant growth makes for lush, full, exuberant gardens.

RAINFALL

Rainfall and humidity are also important in determining which plants grow where. We all know that plants need water to live but turning on the sprinkler every few days may not be the answer and doesn't ensure success. If, for example, you live in an area where summers are hot and dry and you choose to grow Japanese maples, all the water in the world won't stop them from browning off when hot, dry winds blow. The plants are native to cool, mountainous areas where the air is always humid, and summer rains are frequent.

Another important factor to consider is the seasons when rain falls. In some places the year's rain falls mostly or only during the cooler months; summers are hot and dry. For example, a Mediterranean climate, typical of California, has a weather pattern like this. Elsewhere a lot of rain may fall during the summer with far less in winter. In North America, a humid climate such as that found in the south-east (including Florida) has this pattern. Rain falls relatively evenly throughout the year, often in summer, in a cool continental climate, typical of a large part of North America. In the arid and semi-arid areas of the south-west United States, rainfall is unpredictable.

Seasonality of rainfall has an impact on the plants of each region and on gardeners who grow them. If you get summer rain it can be hard to grow plants from the winter rainfall zones, even if the temperatures are similar. The plants often die suddenly, usually during a rainy summer, a time when they are expecting dryness.

ZONAL MAP OF THE UNITED STATES AND CANADA
The planting zones shown on this map correspond to the United States Department of Agriculture planting zones, which are based on mimimum winter temperatures.

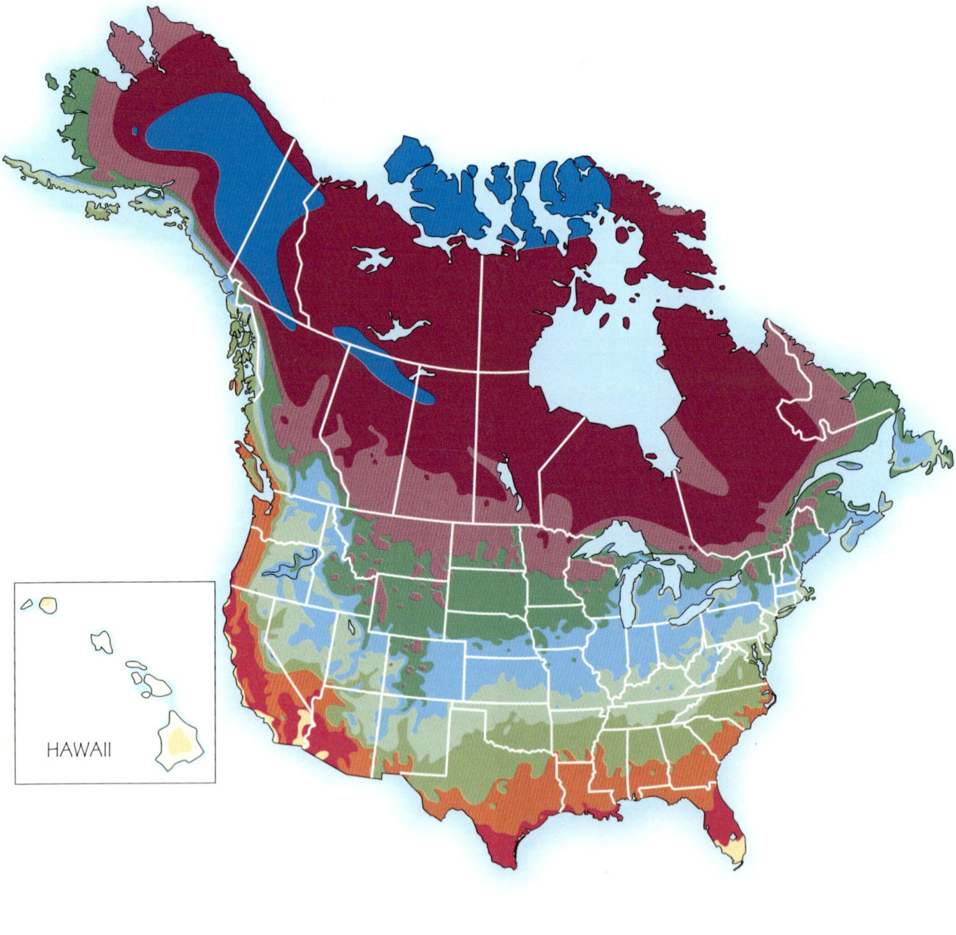

Key to zones

Zone 1	Below -50°F
Zone 2	-50°F to -40°F
Zone 3	-40°F to -30°F
Zone 4	-30°F to -20°F
Zone 5	-20°F to -10°F
Zone 6	-10°F to 0°F
Zone 7	0°F to 10°F
Zone 8	10°F to 20°F
Zone 9	20°F to 30°F
Zone 10	30°F to 40°F
Zone 11	Above 40°F

CLIMATE ZONES

The climate of North America and Canada varies tremendously, from sub-polar to subtropical, and even tropical in the Hawaiian Islands. Northern Canada has a subpolar climate, which has short summers, long winters with a great deal of snow, and low light intensity, especially during the winter. Part of western Canada has a high-altitude climate with short summers, very long and very cold winters with a great deal of snow, and high light intensity. These climates are home to the huge range of dwarf and prostrate, including montane, plants.

Much of southern Canada and the north and central regions of the United States have a cool continental climate with long cold winters with the possibility of much snow and severe frosts (classified as a cool temperate climate). The spring is short and warm and the summers long, and warm or very hot. The falls are short. There is rainfall all the year round, often in summer. This climate is suitable for growing a vast range of hardy plants from all over the world. The climate of the eastern coast is usually less extreme than that of the interior.

The further south you go the warmer the climate becomes. The south-east of the United States, including Florida, has a humid climate, which is subtropical or warm temperate. There is rainfall all the year round but particularly during the summer when the weather is hot and warm, thus creating a humid atmosphere. The winters in this region are generally mild, but sometimes they can be cold. Such a climate supports a large and extremely diverse range of plants, including subtropical kinds. Palms, for example, are a particular feature of this region.

To the west of the United States are the arid and semi-arid areas, the deserts, which are home to many drought-tolerant plants. The former is very hot dry desert with cold seasons, and sparse, unpredictable rainfall. The semi-arid areas are still hot but they are not quite so extreme and have more rainfall. Therefore these areas support a wider range of plants.

California has a Mediterranean climate which is warm temperate, characterized by warm or hot summers with little or no rain, and cool wet winters. Such a climate supports a large and varied range of plants, including citrus fruits. Further north along the Pacific Coast the climate becomes cooler and moister but the winters are still mild and wet and the summers dry.

In Hawaii the climate is tropical but the temperature and humidity vary little through the year because of the influence of the Pacific Ocean. Some mountainous areas have extremely high rainfall and are among some of the very wettest regions of the world.

So pick plants to suit your climate. It makes gardening so much easier. If they do not suit your climate plants may need protection, such as a greenhouse for heat and humidity, or a shade area to protect them against too much sun. Some will simply not grow—for example, high-altitude plants will not thrive at lower levels, and cool-temperate plants are not suited to the tropics.

THE PLANT HARDINESS ZONE SYSTEM

The Plant Hardiness Zone System devised for North America and Canada helps gardeners to choose the most suitable plants for their particular areas. It was devised by the US Department of Agriculture, Agricultural Research Service. In this system the country has been divided up into 10 climatic zones, as shown on the map and key on pages 10 and 11. Zone 11 applies to Hawaii. The zones represent the approximate range of average annual minimum temperatures. The coldest is zone 1, where the temperature can fall to below –50°F. The warmest includes zone 10 where the average annual minimum temperature is 30–40°F. In zone 11 the temperature is always above 40°F.

This system has proved so popular and easy to use that it has been adapted to other parts of the world, and many gardening dictionaries and encyclopedias worldwide give zone numbers for plants.

All the plants in this book have been given an appropriate zone number, so making it easy for you to choose plants for your particular area. The plant should thrive in that particular zone and in zones with higher numbers (and therefore higher minimum winter temperatures).

Remember, though, that plants from low zone numbers and therefore cool or cold climates may not be happy or may not thrive in much higher zone numbers. In this book we have indicated this wherever possible in the plant lists. Also bear in mind local variations in climate in each of the zones. No system dealing with hardiness in plants can be one hundred per cent accurate.

•CHAPTER TWO•

GARDEN DESIGN

It isn't hard to design an attractive garden that will fit your needs and lifestyle, even if you know next to nothing about gardening. In working out a design, you should first consider how you and your family will want to use and enjoy the garden.

First, forget all about plants. Thinking of a garden just in terms of what plants to grow is like designing a house by first choosing the curtains. Just as you consider a house in terms of its rooms—kitchen, den, bedroom and so on—you can imagine your garden as a sequence of outdoor living rooms. Their "walls" are made of trees and foliage, the floor is the soil, carpeted with grass or paving, the ceiling is the branches of trees or the open sky, and it's all decorated with flowers and such furniture as you might use. The particular plants you choose are not important at all at this stage. Instead, think about the overall look you want to achieve.

A PAVED AREA for outdoor living, a lawn for games, a cutting garden for the house and a kids' play area make this backyard a safe and enjoyable place for all the family.

LUNCH IN THE GARDEN becomes much more enjoyable and easy to arrange when you have a private, sheltered patio or deck that you've designed for the purpose. If you decide what you want in the garden, its ultimate layout and contents will become clearer.

PLANNING THE GARDEN

Assess your needs

Begin your planning by sitting back and daydreaming a little. Does the idea of breakfast in the sun on a Sunday morning appeal? Or dinner under the stars, in the cool of a summer evening? Then you probably need a sheltered and private patio.

Do you need space to build a boat, work on the car, or pull a motorbike to pieces? Do you long for a swimming pool—maybe not now, but when you can afford it? Do you want to grow vegetables and fruit or lots of flowers for cutting?

If you enjoy entertaining, think about whether you should build a permanent barbecue and whether you need parking space for your guests. If you, or the children, like kicking a football around or if you have a dog that likes to romp, you'll need unencumbered space, surrounded by tough plants that are able to withstand the punishment.

It pays to think ahead a few years. If the children are still at the tricycle-and-sandpit stage, you might want to create a special space for them, but one that can be transformed when they grow out of it. Planning for it now will mean less disruption later.

Finally, think about whether you want to spend much of your free time at home. If you're a reluctant gardener, enthusiasm may develop as the garden grows and you begin to see the results of your labors, but it's wise not to plan a garden that will demand more time than you're prepared to give it. All gardens are work and the more elaborate the layout and contents, the more work there will be. If you enjoy gardening, you'll think of it as a hobby, but if you'd rather be sailing or golfing or doing other things, you won't have the time or inclination to maintain big beds of flowers or vegetables, or for a lot of shrubs that need annual pruning or regular spraying.

Assess your site

Before you start transforming your garden into what you would like, take stock of what you have. Whether you're faced with bare soil and the debris of a just-departed builder, or an established or partially established garden, look around critically—it's surprising how the process will throw up ideas to get you going.

Start with the house. If you have big windows looking straight out onto the street or at the neighbor's windows, so that you have to keep your curtains drawn for privacy, a screen of foliage might be called for. Not necessarily a dense mass—a clump of airy trees or shrubs will usually be enough to take away the fish-bowl feeling and allow you to look out.

A group of birches might lead you to a woodland theme for a garden or palms to an evocation of a tropical wilderness with a path winding through it to the door. Always position screening shrubs and trees as far away from the place to be screened as possible. This creates an area between you and the screen that can be gardened into a pleasant outlook, and it also minimizes the loss of light.

Sloping sites

A sloping site may call for some juggling of earth to create level areas for outdoor living, with retaining walls and steps to link it all together. But remember that earthworks will mean either money to a contractor or back-breaking work—a level site is easier to develop.

On the other hand, a strongly sloping hillside site might well have fine views, and you will want to ensure that your plants frame them while at the same time masking distractions such as the neighbors' houses and electricity poles. A two-

IT'S RARE for a house to stand alone without neighbors. In the average street, you're likely to have no less than five properties adjoining your own. Their houses, sheds and trees affect your landscape and need to be taken into account in your plans for the garden.

SEPARATING SPACES

Different parts of the garden can be assigned different functions. You could have a play area for the children, an outdoor living area, a place to grow vegetables and flowers, a utility area for the clothes line or compost heap. These separate spaces can be physically marked off, making the garden more interesting to look at and be in. To divide space you can use:

1. *SHRUBS—densely foliaged to the ground for total separation.*

2. *TREES—which allow you to see under the branches.*

3. *LOW PLANTING—for a gentle division, maybe with a climber-covered pergola overhead.*

4. *A SCREEN, FENCE OR WALL—perhaps softened with creepers, shrubs or tall flowers.*

5. *A CHANGE OF LEVEL, with steps as a link, and associated planting creates a separate, upper room.*

6. *A CHANGE OF LEVEL, without dividing plants or structures, keeps the spaces separate but open.*

storey house may have views from upstairs, too, and so make sure the garden looks good from there.

Trees and paving

Nothing can give the garden a head start like established trees, and you should think very carefully before deciding to remove any. Even if a tree is a bit scruffy now, a few years' care will probably see it grow to beauty, although judicious pruning may be needed to reveal handsome trunks and branches. If you have doubts about the safety of a tree, seek expert advice from a professional tree surgeon.

Paths and pavements are another matter. If they fit your purposes, fine, but if they don't, the cost of replacing them will be well spent.

The soil

If the soil is not the ideal deep, crumbly loam, don't worry—beautiful gardens have been made on all soil types. It's almost always better to work with what you have than to import topsoil (unless your builder has carried away your topsoil or buried it irretrievably under subsoil and rubble). Any soil can be improved out of sight by cultivation and the addition of as much organic matter—compost and the like—as you can manage.

DESIGN FOR THE CLIMATE

It's always pleasant to sit in the sun in winter, but in summer a retreat to the shade is safer and more comfortable. A usable garden needs a balance between sun and shade, through the day and through the year, and once you know which way your property faces—where north is—you can plan for it easily.

We all know that the sun rises in the east, sets in the west and is at its highest at noon. However, it's never quite overhead—in the northern hemisphere it's somewhere to the south. This is why the south side of the house gets the sun and the north side is in its own shade for most of the year. In the southern hemisphere, the north is the sunny side.

In summer, though, the northern sunrise and sunset are quite a bit to the north of an east-west line so that at midsummer the hot afternoon sun will hit your "shady" north-side patio at about three o'clock and stay there for the rest of the day. Conversely, the winter sun moves to the south and doesn't rise so high; shadows are longer, and the spot you chose in summer for the vegetable garden because it was so sunny may turn out to get little sun during the fall, winter and spring. The same is true in the southern hemisphere except that north and south are reversed.

The ideal aspect

The ideal aspect for outdoor living is the sunny side of the house (south or south-east in the northern hemisphere, north or north-east in the southern hemisphere). Paving here reflects warmth to the house, but you'll need shade for the summer. You could rig up awnings or umbrellas but the shade of trees is cooler. Deciduous trees let the winter sun through their bare branches; plant them on the east to let through the early winter sun. Evergreens can go to the south, and in hot areas where the afternoon sun is rarely welcome plant them on the west side also.

Shading the house

Shading the roof can make quite a difference to your comfort inside, and large areas of glass cry out for shade. Remember, once heat gets in, it's

NO VERANDAH is able to keep out the afternoon sun, which just shines straight under it. An awning of vines (trained on one or two wires) provides a solution. It's cooler than canvas, too, both because it lets any breeze in and doesn't trap hot air, and because transpiration from the leaves cools the air that blows through.

TREES THAT OVERHANG and shade the roof will keep the interior of the house many degrees cooler in summer. Deciduous trees, such as Robinia pseudoacacia *"Frisia", are best since they allow the sun's free heat to warm the roof space in winter.*

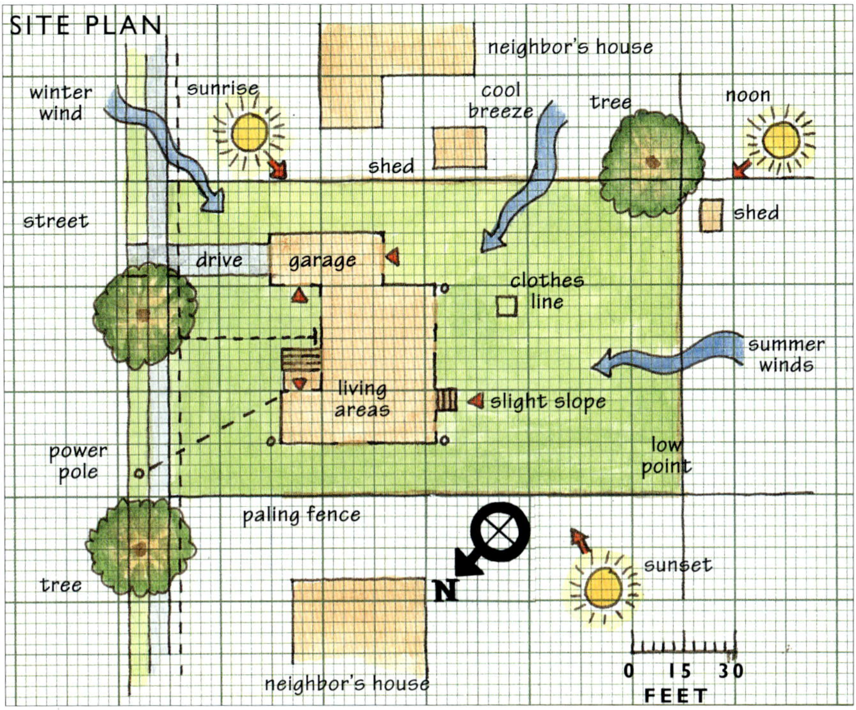

THE FIRST STAGE in making a design is to assemble a plan of the property as it exists. Builders' plans can serve as a basis, but you'll still need to measure fences, trees, sewer lines and such. Show everything that might affect your design. Graph paper helps to keep everything in scale (1:100 is usual).

hard to get out. If shade trees will dominate the garden too much don't forget the ancient climate-control device of the vine-covered pergola.

In sunny climates, it is better to err on the side of too much shade than too little; most trees will put up with a bit of judicious pruning and thinning if they get too dense.

PUTTING THE PLAN ON PAPER

Now that you've made an objective assessment of your needs and your site, it's time to think about what you want the garden to look like. Perhaps you'd like to look onto an English-style garden of flowers and lawns, or a slice of prairie might be more to your liking. Japanese-style gardens are lovely, but maybe a more formal, European plan would suit you better. A garden based on lush, tropical-looking plants can be attractive but you might prefer the stark lines of dry climate plants.

Once you've decided on the look you want, it's much easier to plan the garden layout and contents and that's the time to start drawing. It doesn't matter if you can't draw very well. As long as you can understand your own doodles, drawing a range of ideas, just roughly at first, will help you to gather your thoughts together.

Once you've decided which of your rough doodles you like the most, draw it up on a larger scale using graph paper (above), make an enlarged photocopy or lay a piece of tracing paper over your original site plan and transfer the doodle to it. Work out your ideas in detail, checking the measurements to make sure paths are wide enough, there is room for screening shrubs and you've allowed for steps between the patio and the lawn. Make sure you haven't forgotten anything important. Resist the temptation to elaborate the design—remember the art of all art is knowing when to stop.

Think of the third dimension

A plan can be deceptive, as it gives an exaggerated emphasis to things such as paving patterns, and it flattens out the third dimension of height. We draw trees and shrubs as circles on a plan, but that's not how we see them in real life. You can plot perspective drawings, but perspective needs considerable artistic skill. It's much easier to simply tilt the plan at an angle and draw in the trees and structures at their measured height. This gives you a sort of bird's eye view (it is technically known as an "axonometric projection"), and though the heights tend to look a bit exaggerated, it can be a great help at all stages of making the design.

THE RULES OF GOOD DESIGN

Works of art—and beautiful gardens—aren't created from rule books but there are some general principles that most gardeners would agree on. A successful design is balanced and harmonious, neither so complex that it will seem overdone and fussy in reality, nor so over-simple that it will be boring. (But remember that plants will bring beauty as their birthright, and so it's best to err on the side of simplicity—you can always add more features later.)

A theme unifies a design

It always helps to have a theme for a design. The three doodles shown opposite, based on the site plan on page 19, use circles and straight lines (doodle 1), rectangles (doodle 2) and triangles (doodle 3).

Making doodles on a small scale is the heart of the design process—if it doesn't look good in a small doodle, it won't when it's built—but sooner or later you'll come up with an idea that seems to incorporate all the things you want. Then you can lay tracing paper over your original

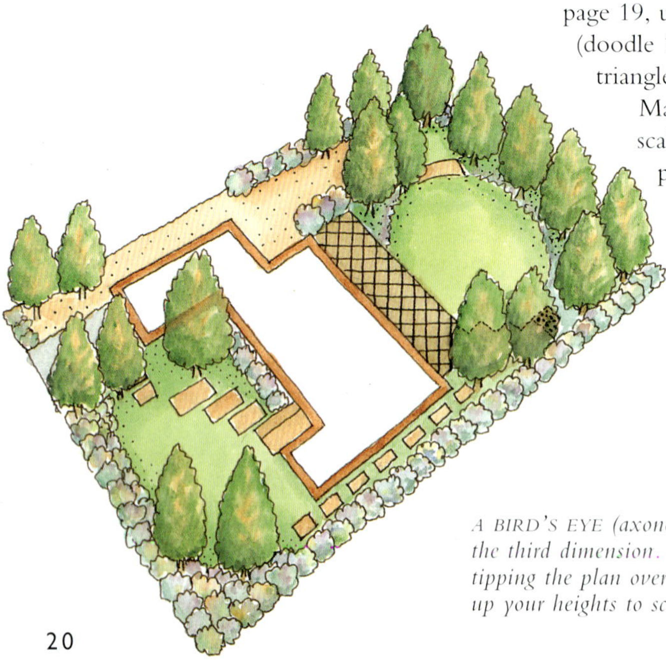

A BIRD'S EYE (axonometric) view helps you see the third dimension. You make it by simply tipping the plan over at an angle and carrying up your heights to scale.

Doodle 1, based on circles and straight lines

Doodle 2, based on rectangles

Doodle 3, based on triangles

USE SIMPLE DOODLES based on themes to develop layout ideas for your garden. These three doodles show how you can give an overall theme to your design—and how you can change the overall character of your garden.

DESIGN AND PLANNING CHECKLIST

Have you thought about:

- summer shade, winter sun
- windbreaks
- blocking undesirable views, providing privacy
- washing line, compost heaps
- storage for garden equipment and furniture
- steps and/or retaining walls where there are changes in level in pavements and lawn
- lighting
- letterbox, house number
- drainage
- easements, overhead lines, drains and/or sewers
- widths of paths, gates and steps
- position of outdoor living areas
- size of pavings and patios
- shape of lawns and ease of mowing them
- the ultimate size of trees and the effect of their shade on your and your neighbors' properties
- security, especially for swimming or other pools
- space for children's games, herb and vegetable gardens and other special projects
- access for the car
- access to the garden during construction and afterwards
- comfortable access to the house
- enough space for planting, so that plants won't outgrow themselves and need constant cutting back
- official approval for fences, structures and pools, and for planting on the street
- building the garden in stages, if necessary

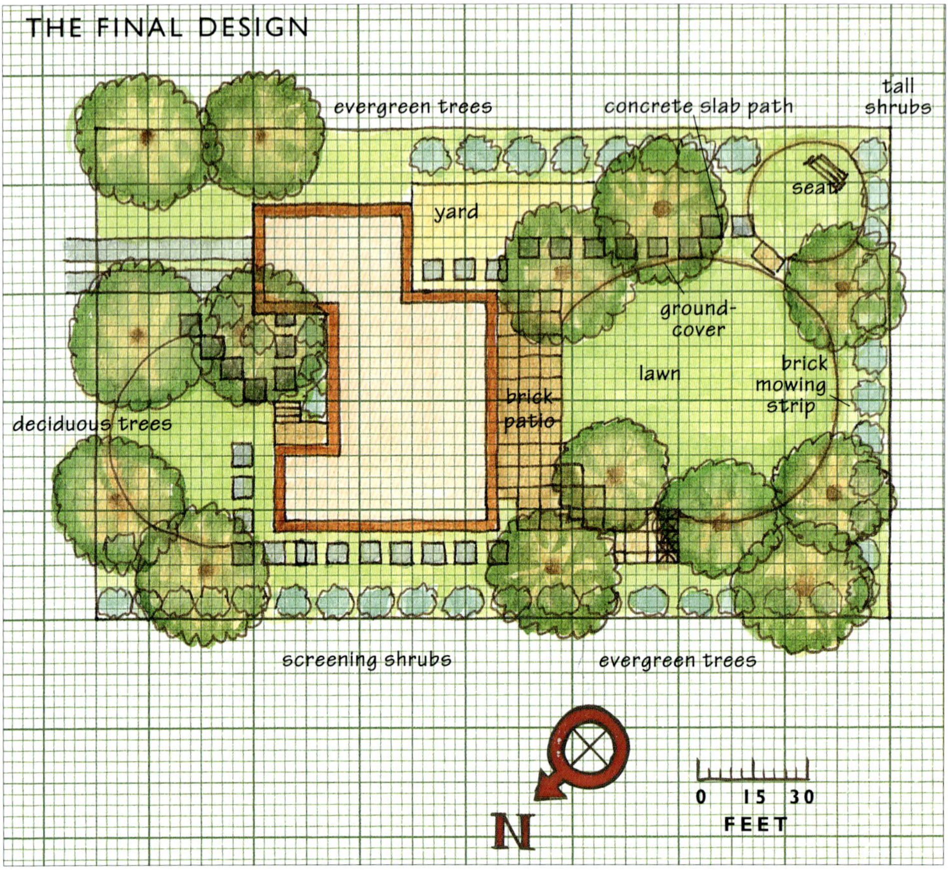

THE FINISHED DESIGN, elaborated from doodle 1 on page 21, based on circles. It was traced onto graph paper and more details were added. If you like, you can nominate which plants will go where or simply buy plants that fit the description on the plan.

site plan and transfer the doodle to it. The result might look like the plan shown above, based on the doodle with circle theme. You still have to decide on the specifics but you now have a design that will provide a framework for your thinking.

Getting down to specifics

Now, as you get close to your final layout, you can begin to think in terms of materials and specific plants. Decide whether the patio will be brick, concrete or stone; whether those screening shrubs, which you see in your mind's eye as evergreen and six to ten feet tall, will be camellias, shrub roses or rhododendrons; what those groundcovers will be and whether there will be spring bulbs among them. Think about how the colors and textures of foliage will blend. Ideally, you should ask what the best plant for a spot is rather than where you can put a particular plant.

There's no need to try to work out all your planting details on paper—half the fun of gardening is improvising, playing with planting schemes and changing things around, all within the framework that your overall design has created.

•CHAPTER THREE•

GARDEN SOIL

Soil is the foundation of your garden. Its quality makes all the difference to how plants grow. Most experts agree that the ideal soil is deep, friable or crumbly, fertile, well drained and rich in organic matter—but few garden soils fit that description.

WHAT IS SOIL?

Soil is a complex mixture of minerals and organic matter. The minerals come from disintegrated rock, the organic matter from decomposed plant and animal matter. Mixed in with this is water, air and numerous living organisms. The main functions of soil are to provide plants with nutrients, water, oxygen and anchorage for root systems.

Soil is not static. Changes in physical, chemical and biological properties take place all the time, caused by both nature and human beings. In nature, the weather, plants themselves, insects, worms, bacteria and fungi change soil. The changes we make are numerous and far-reaching: just digging over the soil can change its character. Adding fertilizers, chemicals and mulches can completely alter the type of soil.

Most virgin soils fall into two major categories, "heavy" or "light", depending on the amount of clay or silt (fine particles) or sand (coarse particles) they have.

Clay is made up of very fine particles that pack together closely, thus hindering the downflow of water and air—both essential for plant roots. When clay soils finally do get wet, they stay wet and roots can literally drown as water fills and remains in the spaces between clay particles. Clay soils are physically heavy and they are hard to dig because they are sticky when wet and set hard when dry.

Sandy soils are "light" because they are much easier to dig whether wet or dry. With a greater proportion of large

BIGGER PARTICLES of sandy soils have more air spaces between them. When water is applied, it drains through freely.

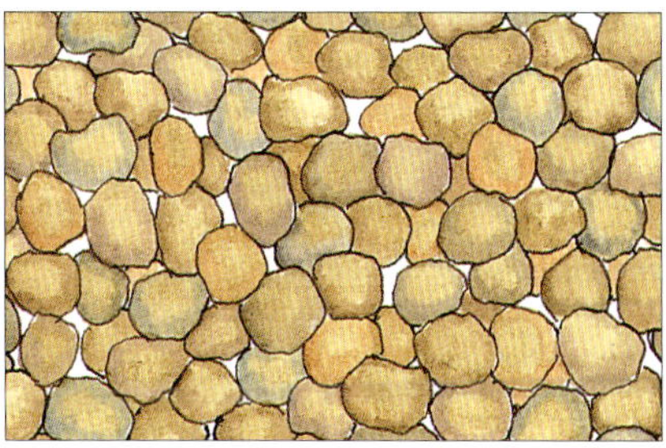

FINE PARTICLES of clay soils pack together closely, excluding air and making penetration of water slow and difficult.

HOW TO IDENTIFY YOUR SOIL TYPE

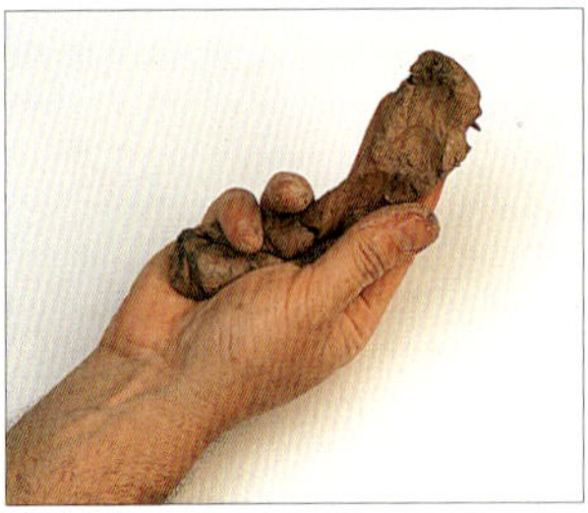

Moist clay

Sandy soil

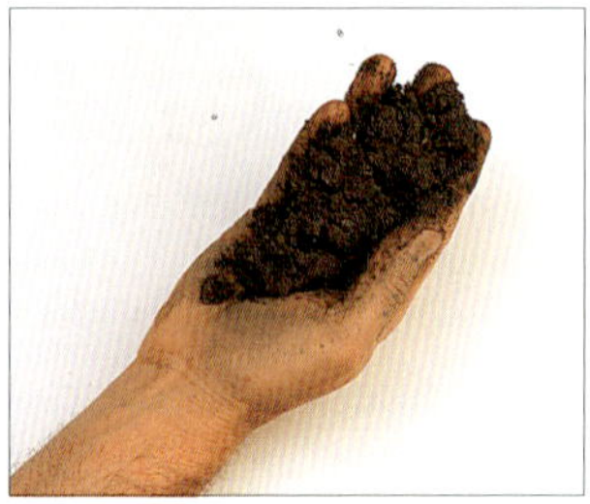

Loam

CHECKING YOUR SOIL TYPE. Moist clay has a consistency like modeling clay and can be formed into a long, thin ribbon. Sandy soil is crumbly and will not form any length of ribbon. Loam has big crumbs and clumps together. It may form a short ribbon if it contains a high proportion of clay.

soil particles than clay, sandy soils drain fast, which is good for most plants, but it also means they can dry out fast. Sandy soils must be watered more frequently than clay soils and they must be fertilized more often, too, because nutrients are washed out by the frequent watering.

The ideal soil, "loamy", falls between these two extremes. Aim for it, but first identify the soil you have.

IDENTIFYING YOUR SOIL TYPE

Just feeling the soil can teach you a great deal about it. Take a handful of your topsoil when it is moist and squeeze it gently to form a lump. Soil with a high clay content will form a tight, sticky ball, while the sandy type will lose its shape and fall readily from the hand. Soil of good, friable or crumbly texture will hold its shape but break away easily when further squeezed or prodded.

IMPROVING SOIL QUALITY

Fortunately extremes of both clay and sandy soils can be greatly improved by adding one important ingredient—organic matter. This may take several forms, such as old farmyard manure, compost, peatmoss, leaf-mould or composted sawdust. Laid on top of the soil or lightly dug in, these natural substances are further broken down by useful soil organisms such as bacteria, fungi and earthworms. In the process,

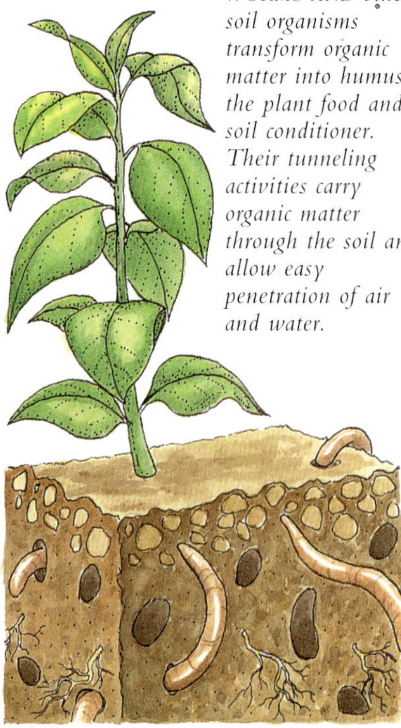

WORMS AND other soil organisms transform organic matter into humus, the plant food and soil conditioner. Their tunneling activities carry organic matter through the soil and allow easy penetration of air and water.

a nutritious, fibrous material called humus is formed. Over time, and with repeated applications of rotted organic matter, the activities of a booming population of soil organisms distribute the organic matter through the top layers of soil, opening up clays and making sands more water retentive and rich.

Organic matter

But where do you get all this organic matter? If you live in a leafy area, you can sweep up bagloads of fallen leaves from the streets, and riding schools or stables will usually give you as much horse manure as your trailer will carry. You can buy bulk quantities of composted organic matter from landscape supply companies and some garbage dumps. Best of all is to make your own compost from your kitchen and garden waste (see pages 28–31).

Don't use organic matter when it's fresh. When it comes to organic matter, the older and more rotten, the better. That's because the process of decomposition uses up nitrogen and, if green matter or fresh manure is dug into the soil, the nitrogen needed will come from the soil. Nitrogen is one of the most important plant foods, and so while you'll be improving your soil you'll be starving your plants. Get around this by using only rotten organic matter or composting fresh matter first.

HOW SOIL pH AFFECTS PLANT GROWTH

The pH of anything is a measure of its acidity and that level is determined on a scale of 1 to 14. A pH of 1 would be extremely acid while a pH of 14 would indicate extreme alkalinity. Seven is neutral, being neither acid nor alkaline. Most plants prefer

GYPSUM IMPROVES SOME CLAYS

Gypsum is a mineral that, when added to clay soil, can cause the fine particles to clump together into bigger particles, thereby opening up the soil and improving its drainage. However, it doesn't work on all clays and you should carry out this test before you buy and apply it. The test originated in Australia (devised by CSIRO).

1. Drop a 1/4 in fragment of dry soil into a glass of distilled or rain water and let it stand for twenty-four hours. Don't shake or stir it.
2. If the water turns cloudy around the fragment, your soil will be improved by the addition of gypsum. The more obvious the discoloration, the greater the improvement will be.
3. If there is no discoloration, repeat the test with moist soil of a malleable soft consistency.
4. If the water then turns cloudy, adding gypsum will help prevent wet weather damage to your soil.

Add gypsum at the rate of 16 oz per square yard but don't dig in.

THE SIMPLE TEST described above indicates whether or not gypsum will improve your clay soil.

slightly acid soil and do well where the pH reading is 6–7. Some, such as azaleas, rhododendrons, camellias and magnolias, like quite acid soil with a pH of 4.5–5.5, but only a few plants could tolerate the strongly acid soil of pH 4 or less. Those plants that prefer alkaline soils generally do best with a pH of 7.5–8.

The pH of soil affects the level of nutrients available to plants. Thus, if you grow a plant native to alkaline soils in quite acid soil, it will have overdoses of some nutrients and shortages of others. The result will be poor growth, yellowing leaves and/or eventual death.

You can test the pH of soil with a simple electronic meter or a soil testing kit. The latter, available from garden centers, is usually more reliable. Over-acid soil (less than pH 5) can be made less acid with the addition of lime. Excessively alkaline soil can be acidified with flowers of sulfur. Apply at the rate of a handful to the square yard and lightly dig in, then water the treated area deeply.

Don't try to make large changes in the pH suddenly or you may shock your garden to death. Instead, apply the appropriate remedy as described above. Let the soil lie for two months, test it again and make another application if necessary. Repeat at two monthly intervals until the correct pH is achieved.

SOIL DRAINAGE

Only aquatic plants or those native to swamps or boggy areas can survive having their roots in sodden soil for long periods. Dry land plants, and that includes virtually everything commonly grown in gardens, must have air in the soil around their roots or they will drown.

If all or part of your garden is poorly drained, you can either accept it and grow only the plants that will tolerate those conditions or, and this is a far better solution, install subsurface drainage to take the excess away.

How do you tell if your soil is badly drained? Dig holes in a few places about 20 in deep. Fill them with water, allow the holes to drain completely and then refill them. If, after the second filling, some water still remains twenty-four hours later, your soil is not well drained and the more water in each hole, the worse the drainage problem.

Another way to determine the need for drainage is to observe what happens after rain. Does water lie in pools for long periods or does the soil remain sodden and squelchy? If so, subsurface drainage will remedy the problem and allow you to grow a much wider range of plants. If the

SUBSURFACE DRAINS are often laid in a herringbone pattern across the fall of the slope. If this pattern does not suit your site, use one that catches most water.

poor drainage is restricted to a small area, an alternative to drainage is to raise the area about 12 in above the natural level using retaining walls. Fill the area behind with good quality, weed-free topsoil bought from a landscape supplier.

How to install drainage

Subsurface drainage involves the laying of conduits in trenches dug to catch the maximum amount of water seeping through the soil. The trenches are dug 12–18 in deep across the fall of the land. A herringbone pattern, where angled side trenches feed into a central main trench, is an efficient layout but you should determine your own layout based on the topography of your land.

Two types of soil drainage conduits are commonly sold: plastic pipes perforated to allow water to enter (agricultural drains) and drainage strips that consist of a flat, plastic, egg-carton-like core wrapped up in a non-rottable cloth. Both are laid in a similar way—buried in trenches which must be dug with sufficient fall to carry the water to an approved outlet such as a stormwater drain. You may not direct a stream of water onto a neighbor's property or into the sewer, which is not designed to cope with stormwater.

To install subsurface drainage, lay a drainage strip or pipe in the trench. Drainage strips are laid vertically, not flat. Perforated pipes are usually laid on a bed of gravel but this is not necessary with drainage strips.

Refill the trench. Perforated pipes are first covered with more gravel to prevent soil particles from blocking the fine perforations and then the trench is topped up with soil.

Replace the turf, if any.

Dig a trench the same depth and width as the spade.

Lay the perforated pipe in the trench.

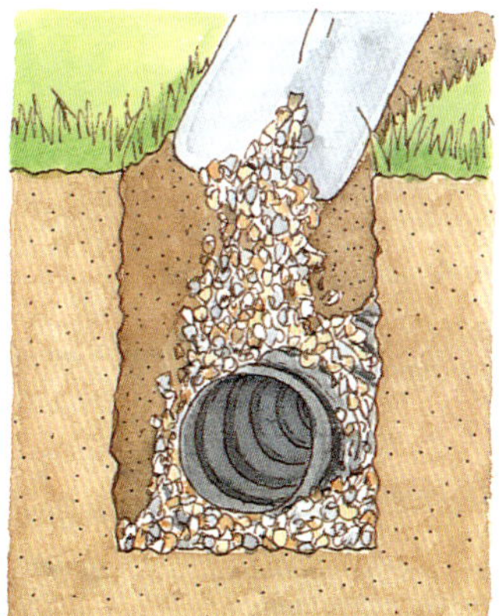

Refill the trench.

THE METHOD used to lay subsurface drainage is essentially the same for both drainage strips and perforated plastic pipes (shown).

•CHAPTER FOUR•

COMPOST

Anything that was once alive rots and, in doing so, enriches the soil. By composting organic wastes you can accelerate this process and produce a soil-improving tonic that can reduce your use of both water and fertilizer, and suppress weeds too.

Compost improves the structure, fertility and drainage of all soils. It causes soil particles to cling together in bigger crumbs and this improves drainage and aeration. It feeds plants, earthworms and useful soil organisms, retains moisture, makes digging easier, stabilizes the pH of soil and suppresses harmful bacteria and fungi.

WHAT TO COMPOST

Anything organic can be composted. A typical house and garden could probably contribute:

- grass clippings
- fallen leaves
- weeds
- prunings
- vegetable and fruit peelings
- food scraps
- coffee grounds
- tea leaves
- vacuum cleaner contents
- faded cut flowers

If you have free access to them, straw, sawdust, manure, seaweed or waste from food processing plants, such as pea trash, rice hulls and nut shells, can also be added.

Thick, woody prunings from trees and shrubs make good compost but they must be shredded first. If you produce enough of this waste each year, consider hiring or buying a mulcher. Thin, sappy stems can be cut up with a rotary mower before they are added to the heap.

THE CARBON TO NITROGEN RATIO

Just piling up shredded garden waste won't necessarily make good compost quickly. It is important that there is a correct balance between the amount of carbon and the amount of nitrogen in the heap. There should be 25–30 times more carbon than nitrogen. Woody items such as branches, sawdust, hay, paper and fallen leaves are very high in carbon, whereas ingredients such as grass clippings, green plants, old flowers, manure and vegetable and fruit waste are quite high in nitrogen.

If you think you have an excess of carboniferous matter (and most gardeners will) add sulfate of ammonia, urea or manure, or water the heap occasionally with a high nitrogen, soluble fertilizer. The total nitrogen content will be on the pack: over 20 per cent nitrogen is high. A small amount of superphosphate added from time to time helps speed up the composting process.

COMPOSTING BINS

THIS PURCHASED composting bin can be taken apart for easy removal of the compost when it is ready.

AN UPTURNED garbage bin makes an efficient compost bin. Cut out the bottom and use the lid over the hole.

WORM FARMS are a good way to make compost, especially if you have only small amounts of waste.

THIS WOODEN BIN has removable doors and two compartments; when one is full but not ready, use the other.

APPROXIMATE COMPOSITION OF SOME ORGANIC MATERIALS

Material	*Carbon:nitrogen ratio*	*Carbon oz per 1/4 lb*	*Nitrogen grains oz per 1/4 lb*
Lawn clippings	20:1	1/4	5
Weeds	19:1	1/4	5
Leaves	60:1	1	7
Paper	170:1	1 1/4	3
Fruit wastes	35:1	1 1/4	3
Food wastes	15:1	1 1/4	8
Sawdust	450:1	1 1/4	1
Chicken droppings	7:1	1	1/8 oz
Chicken litter	10:1	3/4	39
Straw	100:1	1 1/4	7
Cattle droppings	12:1	3/4	27
Human urine	0:1	0	14 (per 5 fl oz)

The chart above (originally devised in Australia by the CSIRO) shows the carbon:nitrogen ratios of typical ingredients of compost heaps. You can see that sawdust has 450 times more carbon than nitrogen, leaves sixty times more and chicken manure only seven times more. The optimum carbon:nitrogen ratio is 25–30:1, so that if you want to compost shredded, woody prunings, you will need twelve times the weight of the prunings in lawn clippings in order to make the composting process work quickly and most efficiently.

Weeds, leaves and lawn clippings in the proportions 3:1:2 make excellent compost. Here are some other mixtures with good carbon:nitrogen ratios. The proportion of one to the other is shown in brackets.

- lawn clippings and sawdust (12:1)
- leaves, sawdust and cow manure (2:1:2.5)
- fruit waste and lawn clippings (2:1.5)
- weeds, paper and chicken litter (4:3:1)
- leaves, weeds, paper, chicken droppings and urine (3:3:1:0.5:1)

HOW TO BUILD A HEAP

The easiest and cheapest way to compost garden and kitchen waste is to pile it up in a heap. If you have enough material to make a big heap (5 x 5 x 5 ft), good quality compost can be produced in three weeks. Heaps that are built up over time work less well but they can still produce a satisfactory result. If you produce only a small amount of organic waste, a compost bin is a good alternative to a heap, or try a worm farm (see the description on the following page).

Building up a heap in thin layers of different ingredients helps distribute carbon and nitrogen evenly. Apply a very light sprinkling of nitrogen-rich fertilizer and superphosphate at intervals. Try to build the heap to at least half a cubic yard immediately or it won't have enough bulk to generate the heat necessary. As a large pile of organic matter begins to rot, it generates heat which, in a well-composed heap, is hot enough to destroy pests, diseases and weed seeds.

Moisture is essential for good composting and you should aim for a heap that feels evenly damp but never sodden. During rainy weather, cover your heap, but when it's hot and dry, spray it regularly.

Adding lime

Don't add lime to heaps that are turned regularly or to tumblers as it can reduce the amount of nitrogen available to plants in the end product. Compost produced in unventilated bins, however, will be quite acid. Adding a small amount of lime from time to time will help to counteract the acidity.

MICRO-ORGANISMS DO THE WORK

Successful composting depends on billions of micro-organisms inside the heap. They do most of the work for you but they'll only continue to do so if you turn the heap every three days for two weeks. This lets air into the center and helps mix the ingredients. You should do this whether you have a free-standing heap or one that is contained. In the third and final week no turning is necessary.

If you do not turn a large heap often, the combination of increasing heat and lack of air in the center kills the microbes that are doing the composting and the process stops.

WORM FARMS

Worm farms are ideal for turning the small amounts of kitchen waste most households produce into a nutritious plant food or potting compost. The system harnesses the natural capacity of compost worms to consume green waste, the by-products being worm castings and a liquid manure that may be applied to all plants.

Worm farms can be bought from garden centers. Bought worms are added to an organic medium in one of the chambers of the farm. Food scraps are placed on top and as the worms consume them, more food is added. The bulk of material eventually grows and another chamber is added. When food is placed in the second chamber, the worms migrate to it and begin the process again. When all the chambers are full, the first can be emptied onto the garden or into pots. If water is occasionally poured into the farm, it filters through the worm castings and can be collected via a tap in the bottom. This liquid manure is a wonderful natural fertilizer for all garden and container plants.

IF YOU don't see plenty of worms when you dig in the garden, your soil is lacking organic matter. Add more compost.

• CHAPTER FIVE •

FERTILIZERS

Fertilizers can make the difference between success and failure in the garden but how much fertilizer you need to apply and how often you need to apply it, depends on whether you use nature's own, free, miracle food—compost.

WHY PLANTS NEED FERTILIZING

Plants exist by converting water and minerals from the soil into stems, leaves and flowers. In the wild, those minerals are constantly replaced: leaves, twigs, fruit and bark fall to the ground and every animal deposits plant food in its droppings. Nature is in perfect equilibrium—what goes up (into plants) must come down (and go back into the soil).

In gardens, however, things are different. The plants are not an eco-system but an unrelated mixture of species from a wide variety of habitats and soils. Each may have different nutrient needs. More importantly, there is no build up of fallen vegetation and few animals to enrich the soil. Gardeners sweep up fallen leaves, and dead plants are removed before they can rot. The result of all this tidiness is a gradual but steady impoverishment of the soil.

The answer is not to stop sweeping and clearing up, but it is helpful if the sweepings are composted and returned to the soil. Compost has virtually all the nutrients plants need and it also does the soil good by creating humus, a vital natural ingredient, present in all fertile soils.

Unfortunately, the average suburban garden does not produce enough compostable matter to supply all the garden's needs, but if you compost what you can and distribute the product around, you will not need anything like the fertilizer an uncomposted garden requires.

MAJOR PLANT FOODS

The elements nitrogen, phosphorus and potassium (usually abbreviated to their chemical symbols NPK) are considered to be the major plant foods and are the main ingredients of all complete plant foods.

All are essential, although nitrogen (N) stands out as the single most important. It is responsible for the growth of healthy leaves and is also present in chlorophyll and many other plant parts. If plants lack nitrogen, leaves gradually turn yellow, and new growth is stunted.

Without any phosphorus (P), photosynthesis is not possible and there will be no new roots, shoots and flower buds. Insufficient phosphorus causes stunting, spindly growth and blue-green leaves, but an excess can also be harmful, even toxic to many of the ornamental and fruiting plants that we grow in our gardens.

Potassium (K) regulates and aids chemical reactions within plants and promotes stem growth. Shortage of this element causes leaves to turn a lusterless gray-green, perhaps with yellow spots. Affected leaves often brown at the edges, die and fall.

Packaged complete plant foods usually include percentages of calcium and sulfur as well as the three main elements. Magnesium, the sixth important element for plant growth, is normally present in sufficient quantities in the soil. A garden fed with complete plant food should not lack any major nutrients. The minor ones are a different story.

MINOR PLANT FOODS

Trace elements are vital to all plants and are usually present in well-composted soil. In other soils, deficiencies can occur because plants use up the supply or because other plant foods are applied too generously. For example, iron is abundant in most soils, yet plants can suffer deficiencies if too much lime has been applied. But there are other causes of discoloration and poor growth, such as too much or too little water, attacks by pests and diseases, salty soils, misuse of poisons, too much or too little shade or an inappropriate pH reading in the soil.

SOME SYMPTOMS OF NUTRIENT DEFICIENCIES

Symptoms	*Possible deficiency*
Older leaves with uniform yellowing, often with reddish tints; premature maturity; retarded growth; excessive leaf loss	NITROGEN
Stunted growth; blue-green or bronze tonings on older leaves	PHOSPHORUS
Leaf margins scorched; spotting surrounded by pale zones on leaves	POTASSIUM
Patchy yellowing on older leaves with dark green triangular pattern at base of leaf; excessive leaf loss	MAGNESIUM
Distorted stems; curling and mottling of older leaves	MOLYBDENUM
Yellowish or light green areas between veins on both younger and older leaves	MANGANESE
Yellowing of young leaves with veins remaining green; reduction in leaf size and early leaf fall	IRON
Reduced leaf size; twisted foliage; creamy-white to yellow blotches on young citrus and grape leaves	ZINC
Tip curling, blackening and early shedding of young leaves	CALCIUM
Yellowing leaf margins; dimpled apples; hollow stems in cauliflower; distorted leaves on beetroot	BORON
Twisted and curling foliage; tips of young leaves wilt and die; leaves darken to blue-green color	COPPER
Yellowing on young leaves; reduction in size and failure to mature	SULFUR

MAGNESIUM DEFICIENCY in plants shows up as yellowing between leaf veins. Watering with Epsom salts cures it.

ZINC DEFICIENCY appears as yellow mottling between main veins and can cause stunted or twisted foliage.

MANGANESE DEFICIENCY in plants is usually seen on the younger leaves first. Yellowish markings appear between veins and affected leaves may wither.

IRON DEFICIENCY causes young leaves to yellow but the veins remain bright green. It can be induced by the overuse of lime, the alkalinity of which locks up iron.

If none of these apply to an affected plant, then suspect a trace element deficiency. However, they are not called "trace elements" for nothing. Only a tiny amount is needed and it is vital that they be applied strictly as directed, as overdoses are fatal. Balanced mixtures of all the trace elements can be bought at nurseries and may be needed in gardens not regularly mulched with rotted organic matter. Apply trace elements annually or as directed on the pack.

TYPES OF FERTILIZER

Complete plant foods

Plants have evolved on all types of soils, from extremely fertile to almost barren, and so they do not all need the same nutrients. "Complete" plant foods cannot, therefore, suit all plants. They are too rich for some plants and too mild for others, but they are just right for many. Moreover, although complete plant foods all contain nitrogen, phosphorus and potassium, some do not contain calcium, magnesium and sulfur or the trace elements which they would need to be truly complete. Other types of fertilizers have been developed to fill these gaps.

Slow-release fertilizers

Many chemical fertilizers quickly release all their nutrients into the soil. This gives plants a sudden boost but rain or frequent watering soon washes the nutrients out of the soil and into rivers and another dose of fertilizer is needed. To counter this, slow-release fertilizers have been developed. These react with water and temperature to exude a continuous supply of nutrients for up to a year. They are expensive but do provide a constant food source. Dig in if possible.

Superphosphate

"Super" provides plants with an instantly usable source of phosphorus and a hefty dose of calcium and sulfur as well. It is good for peas (including sweet peas), beans, lupins and all other legumes, and most annual and perennial flowers. A little is good, a lot can be toxic.

Blood and bone

A natural slow-release fertilizer, blood and bone is mild enough to use on all plants. It contains nitrogen and phosphorus, sometimes calcium and a very small amount of potassium.

Sulfate of ammonia

High in nitrogen, sulfate of ammonia is soluble and rapidly produces lush, new growth in lawns, shrubs, palms and flowers. Water in immediately and use very sparingly as it not only acidifies the soil, it is also harmful to earthworms.

Animal manure

Animal manure is organic matter. All types contain plant nutrients but some are richer than others. Horse manure is fairly mild, cow manure is a little stronger, and pig and chicken manure are both extremely strong. All fresh manures should be piled up and allowed to rot for at least a month before use or you may kill the plants around which they are applied.

Complete plant food

Blood and bone

Slow-release fertilizer

Milled cow manure

Pelletized chicken manure

Soluble fertilizer

• CHAPTER SIX •

WATER & MULCH

Water is the foundation of all life but every day we use and pollute more and more as if it were endless. It isn't, and gardeners, as big users, can do a lot to conserve water while still being surrounded by the plants they love.

There's a golden rule that all gardeners should follow and it is this: only water when your plants actually need it, and then water thoroughly.

HOW MUCH WATER?

Soils vary in the way they accept water. Clay takes it in only slowly but dries out slowly too; sand takes it in very quickly but dries out fast. Loam is the ideal, but all soils will have their water holding capacity improved with the addition of organic matter.

You might need to do a bit of experimenting to work out how much water you need for a thorough soaking. When the soil is dry, try putting the sprinkler on, or holding the hose for a timed period of ten minutes. Then, when any puddles have disappeared, dig down to see how far the water has gone (wet soil looks different from dry). If it's wet to, say, 4 in, then you'll know that you probably need to water for half an hour to get the water down to 12 or 15 in, which is where you want it.

Weeds are water thieves

All plants consume and transpire water. In fact, far more moisture is lost from the soil by transpiration from plants than by evaporation from the soil itself. A simple way to reduce your garden's water needs is to reduce the number of unwanted plants—the weeds. It makes no sense at all to allow plants you don't want to rob water from those you do.

HOW OFTEN TO WATER?

You don't want to waste water by watering more often than you need, but you do want to keep your plants happy. If they get really parched, they'll wilt, but if you watch carefully you'll learn to recognize the advance warnings: leaves and flowers look limp and lustreless; grass loses its springiness and retains footprints. It doesn't take long to develop the sixth sense that says, "That plant looks thirsty". Don't be deceived by the surface soil looking dry; if you're in doubt, dig down a little to check.

Of course, you'll need to water more often when it's hot. But try, unless it's an emergency, not to water in the heat of the day, when much of your precious water will evaporate at once. As a general rule, it's better to get the water directly to the soil, but don't apply it faster than it can be absorbed or you'll not only lose water from run-off, you'll also run the risk of compacting the surface which will further reduce water penetration. On clay and silty soils this may mean that you can't turn the hose on full, so just be patient and keep it on for longer.

SELECT PLANTS CAREFULLY

You can save a lot of water if you design a garden that will flourish on your local rainfall. Plants do not all need the same amount of water and if you've filled the garden with species that come from a much cooler and/or wetter climate than yours, you'll have to pour on the water just to keep them going. A better idea is to garden with plants that could survive in your climate without you. Those that are native to your area are a good starting point, but you don't have to be restricted to them. You'll find that there are many other places in the world that have a climate like yours and plants from those places will have a good chance of success in your garden. You can still have thirsty favorites, but don't dot them around the garden. Instead, group them all together because plants that have similar watering needs usually look best that way. They can also be watered more easily.

WATERING LAWNS

It has been estimated that lawns take nearly 80 per cent of garden water, and that half of it is usually wasted in run-off or unnecessary application. Even in the hottest weather, a well-managed lawn shouldn't need more than 3/4 in of water a week (including rainfall), and it only needs half that in cool climates or in winter. If the soil under your lawn is deep and fertile, apply the water in one dose. On poorer soils, give 1/2 in twice per week. To measure the amount of water you are applying, place several straight-sided containers at various distances from the sprinkler. Turn the tap on, noting how many times you turn it, and then time the period it takes for 3/4 in to accumulate in the containers. Next time you water you will know how long to leave the sprinkler going. If run-off occurs, slow the rate of application as every drop that runs off is a drop wasted.

You may also be wasting water if your lawn is unnecessarily large, if you have more lawn than you use. Your garden might look better and be much less thirsty if part or all of the lawn were replaced with groundcovers or shrubs, or even with paving or gravel. Lawns are not essential to good garden design.

MEASURE THE WATER you apply by placing straight-sided containers at various distances from the sprinkler.

WATERING SYSTEMS

A watering system with micro-jet sprays or drippers uses a lot less water than conventional sprinklers or hand watering. That's because these systems deliver small amounts of water directly to where it is wanted. There is less wastage from run-off and evaporation, and they can be operated by timers that switch them off in case you forget. On the downside, they can be tricky to install in established gardens and it is not always easy to achieve total coverage. Nevertheless, properly installed they do save water and they are very convenient for the gardener.

Holding the hose can be very enjoyable and relaxing and a good way to see what's going on in the garden. But to water deeply, the way you should, you'll have to stand there for a long time and few gardeners do this. Better to put the sprinklers on for a much longer period, less often.

MULCH SAVES WATER

Applying mulch to all garden beds regularly is the best way gardeners can save water. Recent research in Australia (for the Sydney Water Corporation) has revealed that gardeners who kept their gardens mulched can reduce water consumption by as much as 25 per cent. A layer of mulch shades soil from the sun and shelters it from drying winds. This keeps moisture in the soil by reducing the rate of evaporation.

Mulch has other benefits as well. It improves the structure of soil which leads to better aeration and drainage, and an ability to hold more moisture for longer. It encourages beneficial soil organisms such as earthworms which, in turn, improve the fertility and aeration of the soil. Mulch also suppresses weeds by smothering seedlings as they germinate, evens out the temperature of the soil, which can lead to a longer growing season, and reduces erosion during heavy rain, which means water soaks in to where it is needed rather than running off.

What is mulch?

Mulch is a layer of material spread evenly over the soil, 2–4 in thick. Organic mulches are best because they actually benefit the soil. Inorganic mulches conserve moisture but do not condition or feed the soil.

Organic mulches

Organic mulches were once alive. They slowly rot, releasing valuable plant foods. Typical organic mulches include compost, rotted manure, dry grass clippings, straw, hay, leaf litter, composted sawdust, peatmoss, pine bark, pine needles, wood chips and shredded prunings.

Inorganic mulches

Inorganic mulches were never alive and do not rot into soil-enriching humus. Stones, gravel, crushed rock or coarse sand may all be used, as can black plastic and even aluminium foil.

ADDING ORGANIC MATTER at every opportunity keeps the soil fertile.

Ten good organic mulches

- Compost adds humus to the soil and helps improve soil structure. It allows good moisture penetration.
- Grass clippings are high in nitrogen and other nutrients. Dry them before use and mix with leaf mould or manure for easy air and water penetration. Used alone they may make a water-repellent mat.
- Pine bark is a low nutrient, dense, acidic mulch that may be slightly water repellent. Slow to rot, it is a good mulch for paths.
- Leaf litter is attractive and quick to break down into a rich humus. Shred it before use and reapply annually.
- Woodchips are attractive, natural looking and long lasting but they do not add much to the soil.
- Cocopeat is made from waste coconut fiber. Apply it moist in a thin layer 1–2 in thick. It is a good substitute for peatmoss which is a non-renewable product.
- Sawdust is useful if used carefully. It must be composted before use as sawdust that is too fresh or comes from pine wood could rob the soil of nutrients. Mix it with blood and bone or old poultry manure and apply it thinly. Applied too thickly, it prevents moisture penetration. It is good for paths and between rows of vegetables.
- Rotted cow manure is one of the best mulches. It is an excellent soil conditioner as well as being high in nutrients. Don't use it fresh as the ammonia may burn plants.
- Seaweed is a high nutrient mulch that rapidly enriches sandy soil. Wash it before use to remove surface salt.
- Mushroom compost is potentially a very good mulch but quality varies with the worst being too alkaline for good garden health. Test the pH of a sample before buying it.

Compost

Woodchips

Coconut fiber peat

Chopped lucerne hay

Gravel

Processed seaweed

•CHAPTER SEVEN•

Weed Control

Not just unsightly, weeds take space, light, water and food from wanted plants. They can also harbor pests and diseases. Your garden will never be free of weeds, but they're easier to control if you adopt the approach of "a little weeding often".

CONTROLLING WEEDS

Weeds are colonizers that invade and thrive in disturbed soil. To prevent them settling in, replant cleared areas immediately and mulch around the young plants with clean compost. As the new plants grow, pull out anything else as soon as you see it, for young weeds are always easier to remove than mature specimens. If you plant thickly, so that there is no bare earth when your plants are mature, most weeds are crowded out and any that do grow are easily pulled.

To control established weeds effectively you need to understand the life cycle of the weed and when control measures are best applied. Annual weeds reproduce by seed each year. Perennials live longer than two years and reproduce from their underground stems as well as from seeds. Some perennial weeds with bulbs or corms are especially difficult to control as many develop small bulbils underground. These can detach from the parent bulb and form new plants. Some bulbous weeds, such as nut grass, also produce many seeds. Weeds may also be shrubs, trees or climbers.

In all cases it is best to remove weeds when they are young and definitely before they flower and set seed. Once you have cleared the garden of weeds, they need never again become a major problem, as long as you make it a habit to pull new weeds as soon as you see them.

WAYS TO CONTROL WEEDS

Manual methods

Hand pulling, hoeing and chipping are the best methods of controlling weeds. Hand weeding is preferable in small spaces, especially where weeds have come up among wanted plants. A garden fork and trowel will help you remove the whole of the root system. Always hand weed when the ground is moist.

A Dutch hoe is a useful tool with a long handle and flat blade. The blade cuts off weeds just below the surface of the soil and the tops die off and provide mulch. A sharp hoe is one of the best cultivators for small gardens. Early and frequent hoeing will control most weeds in flower beds and vegetable gardens.

Chipping is a fast way to remove weeds in lawns, paving, walkways, fencelines and garden beds. A chipper is a thin and narrow blade on a long pole. It works with a slicing action and you needn't bend down to use it.

Mulching

Mulching is a good way to keep the garden free of weeds. Applied thickly, mulch will smother most weed seedlings. Any that do poke through are easily cut. Should you pull a large weed from the mulch, make sure to re-cover any exposed soil. You'll find more on mulching on pages 38–39.

Groundcovers

As all weeds need light to live, an easy way to suppress them is to cover them with thickly foliaged, evergreen plants. Small shrubs that are densely leafy to the ground are ideal. Plant them so that when mature, they form a complete cover over the soil. Any weeds that germinate underneath will struggle to live in the very low light. A few may survive but, as long as the shrubs are taller than the weeds, you won't see them and the weeds definitely won't thrive.

Weed mats

Woven weed mats are made of plastic mesh similar to shade cloth and they effectively control weeds while allowing air and water to penetrate to the soil and root zone. The weed mat can be worked around existing plants but is best spread over an unplanted area. You can set new plants in the ground through holes cut in the weed mat. The mat is then hidden with a topping of organic mulch.

Solarization

Solarization is a technique that will totally clear a weed-infested area. It traps the heat from the sun and raises the soil temperature by several degrees, thereby killing weed seeds, roots and bulbs in the ground. It will also eradicate soil nematodes and some diseases, such as verticillium

Dandelion

Oxalis

Bermuda grass

Annual meadow grass

Ground elder

wilt. Solarization only works during hot, dry weather when temperatures are above 78°F. It involves stretching a sheet of clear or black plastic over soil that has been stripped of weeds and then dug over. The soil must also be deeply moistened before covering. Ensure that the edges of the plastic are sealed down with soil and that the plastic covers the soil surface. For maximum effect, keep the plastic on for at least four weeks and pray for continuous hot, sunny weather. As soon as the plastic is removed you can plant directly into the treated soil.

SAFETY WITH HERBICIDES

- Always read the label. It states the product's uses and lists the safety precautions. Mix strictly according to the directions—more does not make the product more effective and can be damaging.
- Don't mix up more than you need right now as the diluted product will not keep.
- For weeds in lawns, choose a herbicide that is safe to use on your particular grass. Some grasses will be damaged by any use of herbicide and not all lawn weeds can be controlled by selective herbicides.
- While spraying wear shoes, long trousers, a long-sleeved shirt and gloves, and any other protective clothing specified on the label.
- Spray on a still day so as to prevent spray drift, which will damage wanted plants and can be dangerous to other people.
- Keep children, pets and adults out of the area while you spray and until the spray dries.
- Treat weeds when they are actively growing (usually the warmer months).
- Wash out spray equipment after use but be careful where you put the waste water—definitely not down drains.
- Don't use the same spray equipment to apply pesticides.
- Store herbicides in a cool place well out of reach of children.

Herbicides

Before using a herbicide it is important to identify the weed and to make sure that the herbicide chosen will kill it.

Most herbicides sold for home garden use are based on the chemical glyphosate. This herbicide is absorbed through the leaves and then circulated through the sap so that the entire plant dies. A glyphosate herbicide is most effective during the active growing season of the plant. As it is a non-selective chemical, take care not to let it touch wanted plants. It can be sprayed on or applied directly to the weed by dabbing or painting. Glyphosate is a relatively safe garden chemical to humans and the environment when it is used according to directions. It is not residual in the ground, but do remember it kills or damages anything it touches, and so if you are spraying, do so on a still day so as to avoid spray drift.

There are also selective herbicides that kill only certain types of weeds. They were developed for use on lawns, to kill the weeds without damaging the grass. Some of these are quite toxic and for general use around the garden, careful application of glyphosate is better. Glyphosate may not kill some woody weeds.

•CHAPTER EIGHT•

PESTS & DISEASES

Robust, healthy plants have an ability to shake off pests and diseases when they occur on a minor scale. Large infestations are another matter. When these occur you may have to intervene with a chemical solution, but only as a last resort.

Nature gets along very well without sprays. Some gardeners find that they, too, can do without using any kind of chemical and still have a productive and thriving garden. Remember, every time you use a spray to control a pest you may also be killing its natural predators and predators of other pests.

If spraying does become necessary, use a chemical that is specific against the particular pest involved and use it strictly in accordance with the instructions. Never spray a chemical without knowing what it is for and without identifying the pest that is causing the problem.

BIRDS HELP keep many insect pests under control. Attract them to your garden by growing plants that feed and shelter them.

NATURAL CONTROLS

Beneficial insects

Not all insects are bad. Many feed on other insects and some help pollinate plants. Even pest insects aren't all bad. They only become pests when their populations get out of hand, and for the sake of the environment all gardeners should spare the sprays and learn to live with some degree of insect damage.

Birds and beneficial insects will often arrive shortly after the pests and clean up the problem for you. Insects such as ladybug beetles devour huge numbers of aphids, mites, mealy bugs and scales. Ladybugs, ground beetles, hoverflies, dragonflies, lacewings, parasitic wasps, certain capsid bugs, spiders and predatory mites are all working for you but can be killed by the overuse of chemical sprays.

Birds

A home garden is mostly designed for pleasure and one of life's small joys is seeing birds feeding off insects of various kinds on garden trees, shrubs and even lawns, and breakfasting on plant-damaging snails.

SEVEN-SPOT LADYBUGS feed on aphids.

THE LARVAE of ladybugs also feed voraciously on aphids.

VIOLET GROUND BEETLES feed on many soil-dwelling pests.

DRAGONFLIES eat mosquitoes, flies, small beetles and wasps.

Birds need gardens and gardens need birds for the control of insect pests. Birds are essential in helping to keep the balance of nature. They can deal with at least half your insect problems, but if you use chemicals they may eat the poisoned insects and die. Birds that eat sprayed insects and survive tend to lay infertile eggs. If you must spray, use the least toxic chemical for the job.

Bees

Bees are very important in the garden. Without them there would be no flower seeds for next year and many fruit and vegetables will set much better crops after being visited by bees. Most bees are busy during the warmer part of the day. To avoid wiping them out, the best time to spray insecticides is either early morning or early evening when bees are less active. Some insecticides such as dimethoate are highly toxic to bees and should not be used when plants are in flower.

Leafcutting bees look similar to honeybees but are chubby and covered in golden brown hairs. They cut neat, semi-circular "bites" from leaves to make nests but this damage is nothing to worry about.

USING CHEMICALS

You should begin your controls as soon as you notice an ailing plant or a lot of one particular insect. With early diagnosis it is sometimes possible to control a pest or disease by hand-picking or removing damaged material and destroying it before the problem spreads further.

On some occasions you may have to resort to the use of chemicals. Obviously it is wise to use the weakest chemicals whenever they will do a satisfactory job. It is important to identify the problem and then get good advice on solutions. There are government agricultural authorities where you can get information about gardening problems. Indiscriminate use of chemicals can damage plants and upset the balance of nature more than the pests or diseases the chemicals are designed to eradicate.

Read the instructions on the manufacturer's label before you buy the product. Container labels always carry a warning relating to the hazard of the product. Labels also state the withholding period. This is the minimum time that should pass between the chemical's last application and the harvesting of the plant. This is particularly important when fruit and vegetables are being treated.

COMMON GARDEN PESTS

Gardens are full of creatures that eat plants but they also contain at least one very efficient predator—the gardener. Whenever you are in the garden, if you make it a habit to squash snails and grubs as you find them, rub aphids out when you see them and despatch weevils if you catch them, you will have gone a long way towards controlling four major pests. Another way to keep pests at bay is to ensure that your plants are healthy and not stressed by lack of food or water or by an unsuitable climate. Insects are drawn to sick or weak plants and if you have something that seems constantly under attack, try to improve its growing conditions. If that doesn't work, is it worth persisting with a plant that brings pests into your garden? There are plenty of others that are rarely if ever troubled.

TIPS FOR SAFE USE OF SPRAYS

- Read the label carefully and follow the manufacturer's instructions exactly.
- Wear a long-sleeved shirt, long trousers, rubber gloves, goggles and any other protective clothing indicated on the label.
- Mix concentrated liquids in a well-ventilated place and avoid breathing fumes.
- Mix only as much spray as you need, measuring accurately. Overdosing does not give a better result and can be damaging.
- Don't leave spills or the chemicals around while you are spraying. Should you spill any concentrate or the solution on yourself, wash it off immediately.
- Choose a cool, calm day when no rain is expected.
- Keep people and pets well out of the way while you are spraying and until the spray has dried. Fish are killed by many pesticides and so ponds should be covered.
- Do not smoke or eat while using garden chemicals.
- Do not spray in confined places, such as a glasshouse, for any prolonged period. If this is essential, wear breathing apparatus approved for the job.
- Wash your hands and face straight after using chemicals.
- Wash out all spray equipment thoroughly when you have finished but don't tip the waste water down the drain.
- Store all chemicals in their original containers, preferably in a locked cupboard, and always well out of reach of children.

Ants

Ants found in gardens are a nuisance rather than plant pests. Often found on plants heavily infested with aphids and other sap-suckers, they collect the honeydew these pests produce. The main problems are heaps of fine soil in lawns and beds. These are created during underground nest making and can be a nuisance when lawn mowing They can also disturb small plants.

CONTROL: Ants cannot be eliminated from gardens but they can be kept under control. Destroy any nests causing problems by treating with proprietary antkiller dust.

ANTS DO NOT attack plants directly but underground nest-making activities may disturb roots of plants and result in heaps of fine soil in lawns.

Aphids (greenfly)

Aphids are tiny, soft, rounded insects. Most commonly green, they may also be pink, black or gray. All suck sap and feed in large groups, usually on new shoot tips and buds but sometimes on leaves and roots. They cause new shoots to die, distort flowers and can spread plant diseases.

CONTROL: There are many natural predators of aphids and gardeners can easily squash clusters of the pests by hand or squirt them away with a strong jet of water. Soapy water mixed with white oil is a non-toxic control and the pyrethrum or fatty acid based sprays, which are more effective, are among the safest to use. Aphid populations build up fast in spring and summer—check infested plants often.

WOOLLY APHIDS ON AN APPLE TREE. Aphids often cluster on flower buds and new growth. They are easily squashed by hand or they can be treated with a low-toxicity spray.

Cabbage white butterflies

Pieris rapae and *Pieris brassicae*

A serious pest of all members of the cabbage family, these destructive caterpillars are green with a faint yellow stripe down the back and along each side. They feed from under the leaf, starting on the outer leaves. They are small, no more than 1 in long, and infestation is worst in late summer and early fall. The white butterflies have three or four black spots on the tips of the wings and a wingspan of nearly 2 in.

CONTROL: Spray with permethrin or with *Bacillus thuringiensis* (a disease that affects only caterpillars), or use a contact powder such as derris or cabbage dust.

THE CATERPILLAR of the cabbage white butterfly attacks cabbages, cauliflower, broccoli, nasturtiums, stocks, wallflowers and watercress.

Capsid bugs

Lygocoris species

CAPSID BUGS damage many garden plants during feeding.

Several species of capsid bugs attack many plants including fuchsias, roses, dahlias, chrysanthemums, fruits and many more. Light green and about 1/4 in long, they suck sap from the shoot tips of plants, resulting in leaves in this area becoming misshapen and disfigured with numerous tiny holes. The flowers of plants such as dahlias and chrysanthemums may become distorted.

CONTROL: The main time of year for damage to occur is between late spring and late summer. Keep an eye on plants and if any damage or the pests themselves are seen spray the plants with an insecticide containing dimethoate or pirimiphos-methyl.

Cutworms

CUTWORMS OR moth larvae live in the soil where they feed on roots of plants, which can be fatal to seedlings and young specimens.

Cutworms are the caterpillars of various moths and they live in the soil where they feed on plant roots. Their feeding can result in the death of small ornamental plants and vegetables. Plants start off by wilting. The caterpillars eat through small roots or chew the bark of roots, just below soil level. They eat cavities in potatoes, carrots and other root crops. They also feed at night on the soil surface damaging the foliage of low-growing plants. Cutworms vary in appearance according to species. They may be light brown or green-brown and up to 1 1/2 in long.

CONTROL: Keep weeds under control. The caterpillars, especially older ones, are not easy to control with insecticides, but try pirimiphos-methyl or lindane.

Earwigs

Forficula auricularia

EARWIGS FEED on a range of garden plants causing ragged holes.

Earwigs eat plant tissue, creating unsightly ragged holes. Young leaves and flowers of a wide range of plants, especially dahlias and chrysanthemums, are favored. Earwigs feed by night and hide by day. They are brown, up to 1/2 in long, with rear pincers.

CONTROL: Loosely fill flower pots with straw and invert on bamboo canes level with the tops of plants. Earwigs hide in these traps by day, so inspect and destroy any earwigs daily. Spray plants in the evening with insecticide containing pirimiphos-methyl, fenitrothion or permethrin.

Fruit flies

Fruit flies attack many fruits and vegetables in warm and tropical climates. Eggs are laid into the fruit as it ripens and soon hatch into maggots. When mature, the maggots drop to the ground where they pupate to emerge as adult flies. The cycle takes about five weeks and several cycles can be completed in a year. Attacks start in spring, becoming worse as numbers build up through summer. Control is essential.

CONTROL: Collect fruit as it falls and seal it in a plastic bag left in the sun. Do not leave fruit on the ground for more than three days and never bury it. Control is almost impossible without spraying, which is done at fortnightly intervals from fruit set. Splash baits and traps only warn you that the fly is present.

FRUIT FLIES are very destructive insects in warm and tropical climates, attacking a wide range of plants.

Leaf miners

The larvae of various moths, flies, wasps and beetles tunnel inside the leaves of plants, leaving narrow, twisting trails. Many plants are attacked by leaf miners. Some species of the pest attack a specific plant while others may attack more than one.

CONTROL: If damage is minor, remove infected leaves and place them in the garbage. Because the larvae are protected by the leaf surface, it is necessary, if spraying, to use a systemic or penetrant spray such as dimethoate. A weak solution of white oil has also proved effective when used against the citrus leaf miner.

LEAF MINERS of various kinds attack a wide range of plants in the garden and under glass.

Mealy bugs

These small, oval insects are covered in mealy wax threads. They congregate on the undersides of leaves, in leaf joints and crevices, and on roots. They are sap-sucking insects and may cause severe wilting on soft young shoots. They attack a wide range of indoor plants, especially ferns, cactus, succulents, palms and vegetables. They also attack many trees and shrubs.

CONTROL: Spray with a systemic insecticide such as dimethoate or immerse potted plants in a malathion solution. Ladybugs, wasps and small birds are natural predators of mealy bugs, but as the pests secrete themselves in crevices and beneath the soil, chemical control is usually necessary.

MEALY BUG numbers build up fast and if you can see the pest, chances are there are many more in hiding.

Mites

Mites are related to spiders and ticks and attack a large variety of plants. They are often a serious pest of indoor plants and those in glasshouses. Most adult mites are so small that they are not visible to the unaided eye. Others, such as the two-spotted mite, can just be seen. Their attacks on plants are worst during hot, dry periods when the pest sucks the sap from the leaves.

CONTROL: Mites have several predators, including ladybugs, but the most effective is another mite—the predatory mite. These can be bought and released onto affected plants, but once released, toxic sprays will kill the predators. Acaricides are sold but are not always effective.

BRONZING OR MOTTLING of the leaves and very fine webbing are symptoms of attack by the two-spotted, or red spider, mite.

Nematodes

Nematodes, or eelworms, are microscopic worm-like creatures that live in the soil and mostly attack root systems and bulbs. Some species may also feed on stems and leaves. Symptoms are bead-like swellings or galls on roots or tubers, rot in bulbs, swellings and distortions on stems, and browning and drying of leaves. The above-ground parts of the plant may exhibit leaf yellowing and stunted growth.

CONTROL: Root nematodes thrive in light, sandy soils, and are discouraged by high levels of organic matter in the soil. Growing marigolds can clear an area of nematodes which are repelled by an exudate from the plant. In the worst cases, treat soil with a nematicide and in vegetable gardens practice crop rotation.

NEMATODE INFESTATION causes bead-like swellings on roots.

Sawflies

Similar to caterpillars, sawfly larvae feed on the foliage of various plants, which they may defoliate. They cluster on branches by day and spread out at night to feed. When disturbed, they defend themselves with a waving movement and eject a sticky yellow fluid. In the USA they attack numerous ornamental garden plants and also certain fruits such as gooseberries.

CONTROL: Large birds feed on the larvae and should keep populations down. Otherwise, remove infested twigs and squash the sawflies underfoot. If spraying is necessary, use derris.

SAWFLY LARVAE cluster together during the day and can be easily squashed or sprayed.

Scale

Scale are small, immobile bumps on leaves, branches and stems. They feed by sucking sap, hiding beneath a protective shield or under mealy or waxy secretions. Scale vary in size, shape and color and attack many types of plants. Severe infestations can cause weakening and death of parts of the plant. Sooty mould may grow on the honeydew secreted by the insects and, in turn, affect the vigor of the plant.

CONTROL: Small numbers can be washed off with a brush and soapy water. Spray larger infestations with an insecticide containing malathion, and in winter spray deciduous fruit trees with tar-oil winter wash.

SCALE MAY be black, brown, pink, white or red and may be hard or soft. They usually cluster on leaves or stems.

Snails and slugs

Most active during spring and fall after rain, snail and slug numbers can build up fast if not controlled. They feed, mostly at night, by rasping the surface from foliage, leaving a silvery trail of mucus behind.

CONTROL: Begin by cleaning up hiding places. Look under the rims of pots, under bricks and in the folds of dense leaves close to the ground. They can be collected on dewy early mornings and dropped into a bucket of salty water. To deter from particular places, encircle with a band of fresh sawdust or coarse sand or finely crushed stone. Commercial snail baits are very effective but are attractive and poisonous to dogs, and so they must be scattered thinly, never piled in heaps.

SNAILS ARE most active at night and numbers can build up fast in spring and fall. Collect by hand and drop into a bucket of salty water.

Thrips

Thrips are tiny, slender, fast moving insects just visible to the naked eye. They grow to around 1/32 in long and are black, light brown, or cream. Evidence of their attack is a silver streaking or blasted appearance on leaves and flowers. They attack a wide range of vegetables and ornamental plants and are more often seen during hot, dry conditions. The eggs of most thrips are laid within plant tissues and the nymphs and adults often shelter within partly opened blossoms.

CONTROL: Thrips are often hard to control as they are protected inside flowers or under leaves for most of their lives. Malathion and dimethoate control thrips. After a 10-day interval a second application of the chemical is recommended.

THRIPS DAMAGE on this camellia is severe, causing complete defoliation of some branches. Some flower buds have also failed to open.

Weevils

ONE OF the numerous kinds of weevil, this vine weevil is one of the most destructive. The grubs feed on roots and the adults chew leaves.

These are small beetles characterized by a long snout-like head. There are various kinds but the most serious as far as gardeners are concerned is the vine weevil. The dull black adult and the small cream, brown-headed grubs cause much damage to a wide range of plants. The grubs live in the soil and feed on roots, tubers and corms. The adults eat notches in leaf margins, and are especially fond of rhododendrons.

CONTROL: Biological control is best, using one of the pathogenic nematodes. Insecticides are not very effective but plants can be sprayed with pirimiphos-methyl or dusted with lindane in the evening. The soil can also be drenched with pirimiphos-methyl in an attempt to kill the grubs.

White curl grubs

WHITE CURL GRUBS vary in size but almost all feed on root systems.

These grubs are the larvae of scarab or cockchafer beetles and include Christmas and African black beetles. The whitish, fleshy grubs curl up like a "C" and have well-developed orange-brown heads. They feed on the root systems of a wide range of plants and can cause significant damage to container-grown plants.

CONTROL: Small numbers cause little damage and are often controlled by natural predators. Control measures are best aimed at the adult beetle, which can be collected and destroyed after they are dislodged from trees and shrubs. Infested container plants should be repotted after the grubs have been shaken out of the soil.

Whiteflies

WHITEFLIES ARE attracted to yellow and sticky sheets of yellow card are sold as non-toxic lures.

These sap-sucking, tiny white flies infest the undersides of foliage, causing yellowing and wilting. Sooty mould will also grow on the honeydew they secrete. When disturbed they rise in clouds, but they quickly resettle. They attack many plants and may be a big problem in glasshouses, especially on ferns and orchids.

CONTROL: An introduced parasitic wasp, *Encarsia formosa*, often keeps the numbers of whiteflies down. If spraying is necessary, use permethrin or dimethoate at fortnightly intervals. Commercial, non-poisonous, sticky, whitefly traps are available.

COMMON PLANT DISEASES

Plant diseases are caused by fungi, bacteria or viruses and may be spread by insects, by spores floating through the air, in the soil or in debris. Pruners, pruning knives and other gardening tools can also carry disease from one plant to another. Some non-pathogenic diseases may be due to environmental conditions, deficiencies in diet, chemical injuries and incorrect use of fertilizers or herbicides.

A healthy, well-fed plant, in a sunny, open position with good drainage and air circulation will always have a greater resistance to disease than those stressed by poor growing conditions or lack of water.

To reduce the spread of disease it is important to practice good hygiene. Use top quality potting mix, scrub all used pots and seedling trays, clean compost containers and remove plant debris. Dip pruners and other pruning tools in a fungicide solution after each pruning. Crop rotation will reduce the incidence of soil-borne disease in vegetable beds. Traditionally, as soon as gardeners noticed problems, they would cut off the diseased parts of the plants and destroy them: this is still the best method.

ABOVE: Discoloration of leaves can be a sign of plant disease: in this case it is a result of rose mosaic virus.

LEFT: Keep the garden clean and weed-free so as not to harbor disease-carrying insect pests.

Bacterial canker

Pseudomonas species

This disease attacks fruiting and ornamental prunus including cherries, plums and peaches. Sunken patches appear in the bark, which may exude amber-colored resin. Leaves shrivel and die and may be disfigured with a mass of tiny holes. Buds fail to open and branches are killed as the canker girdles them. This disease is most active during fall or spring. Trees can be infected through injured bark or pruning cuts.

BACTERIAL CANKER attacks the bark of ornamental and fruiting prunus, leading to the death of branches if measures are not taken to control it.

CONTROL: Cut out affected parts of plants in summer. Spray trees with a copper-based fungicide or copper oxychloride: once in late summer, again in early fall and finally in mid-fall. Grow varieties that have some resistance to the disease.

Black spot

Black spot is a fungus disease that affects a number of different plants, notably roses but also apples, pears, plums and quinces. It causes dark spots on the leaves which wither and fall prematurely, rendering the plant unsightly. Extensive defoliation can eventually kill a young plant. Black spot is usually worst when humidity is high or in tropical and subtropical regions.

BLACK SPOT is commonly seen on roses in warm, humid weather. To control it, use a general rose spray that includes a fungicide.

CONTROL: Collect all fallen leaves. Cut off and destroy infected leaves. Spraying may also be necessary. A number of fungicides, such as carbendazim, copper oxychloride and mancozeb control black spot. Ensure good air circulation by not overcrowding plants.

Botrytis

Botrytis cinerea

This widespread fungal disease affects many plants in the garden and under glass, particularly young plants and propagation material. Mild damp conditions will spread botrytis rapidly if it is uncontrolled. Gray fluffy fungal growth is found on all parts of plants, including flowers and fruits, causing rot. Spores spread by rain, irrigation water and wind can enter plants through wounds.

BOTRYTIS OR gray mould affects many garden and greenhouse plants.

CONTROL: Be scrupulously hygienic and prune affected parts of plants back to healthy tissue before infection occurs. Do not leave bits of plants lying around. Spray plants with a fungicide containing carbendazim.

Dollar spot

DOLLAR SPOT attacks in warm, humid weather but usually disappears in the cooler months.

Dollar spot is a common fungal disease in lawns. It leaves circular, dead patches about 2 in across. Bent grass and blue couch are particularly susceptible. The disease attacks both leaves and stems and occurs in late spring, summer and early fall when the weather is warm and humid. Brown patch is similar to dollar spot, causing irregular, straw-colored dead patches with a dark outer margin.

CONTROL: Regular doses of nitrogenous will keep the grass healthy. To control dollar spot or brown patch treat with a proprietary lawn fungicide as soon as discoloration appears.

Downy mildews

DOWNY MILDEW of grapes shows as yellow or dead patches on the upper leaf surface and as white down on the underside.

These mildews are a group of fungi that attack a wide range of vegetables, fruits and ornamentals. Small, yellow, pale green or brownish spots appear on leaves and cause portions of the leaf to dry out and die. In humid conditions, grayish downy patches develop on the undersides of the leaves under each spot.

CONTROL: Do not overcrowd plants and avoid overhead watering. Remove and burn affected leaves. Spray with a fungal spray such as mancozeb, wetting the undersides, too. If plants are being regularly infected, your climate is probably too humid for them.

Infectious variegation of camellias

SYMPTOMS OF infectious variegation will not appear on more than a few camellia leaves and is not usually considered a problem.

It is not known for certain but a virus infection is believed to be the cause of yellow marks or mottling on the foliage of camellias. Not all the leaves are affected and the plant will still produce good flowers, some variegated.

CONTROL: Only a few leaves are usually affected with the spotting and these can be cut off and then destroyed. A diseased plant should not be used for grafting and although the problem is not very serious in the home garden, if you grow a lot of camellias you should consider completely removing an infected plant to prevent any possibility of transmission of infectious variegation to other, healthy specimens.

Leaf curl

Taphrina deformans

LEAF CURL fungus affects various prunus including peaches and nectarines.

Leaf curl is a fungal disease affecting peaches, nectarines and almonds. Leaves pucker, swell, turn bright red or purple and drop before they mature. A powdery white layer appears on the surface. Peach leaf curl occurs in spring and early summer and can affect vigor and cropping of trees, especially if it occurs year after year.

CONTROL: Pick off affected leaves as soon as noticed. Between mid- and late winter spray trees several times with copper fungicide to protect them. Spray again in fall just before the leaves drop. Water and feed trees well.

Powdery mildew

SEVERE CASES of powdery mildew on roses infect stems and thorns. Infected canes may die back.

The powdery mildews are a group of fungi that coat leaves, young shoots, flowers and fruits with a conspicuous white or pale gray, ash-like film. It occurs on many plants including vegetables and ornamentals. Powdery mildew is more prevalent in warm, humid weather and spreads rapidly from plant to plant by wind.

CONTROL: Grow mildew-resistant varieties where possible. Remove and destroy affected foliage. Avoid overcrowding and overhead watering. At first sign of infection, spray with mancozeb or cardendazim at regular intervals.

Root rots

GOLDEN TOADSTOOLS are produced from the source of infection of armillaria root rot. The fungus may linger in the soil for years and so do not replant with woody plants.

Root rot is caused by various fungal diseases. One of the most serious is cinnamon fungus, *Phytophthora cinnamomi*. In hot weather a healthy plant may partially or completely wilt and die within a few days. Armillaria root rot spreads through the soil by means of flat, black cords that resemble shoelaces. Infected trees lose vigor, leaves yellow and branches die back from the tips. Clusters of honey- or golden-colored toadstools appear at the base of dead trees or from roots remaining in the ground.

CONTROL: There is no effective chemical cure available to the home gardener. Remove dead plants, including their roots. Do not replant with same subject nor any other woody plant. In future, grow plant species that are tolerant of cinnamon fungus.

Rose canker

Dark reddish lesions and cracking bark of rose canes are symptoms of rose canker. They are caused by a fungus that enters through pruning cuts or wounds to the shrub. Cankers can encircle stems and cut off the flow of nutrients and water to growth further up.

CONTROL: Prune off and burn diseased canes. Canker can be spread from plant to plant by infected pruners. Make a neat slanting cut to just above a good outward-facing bud and disinfect pruners often.

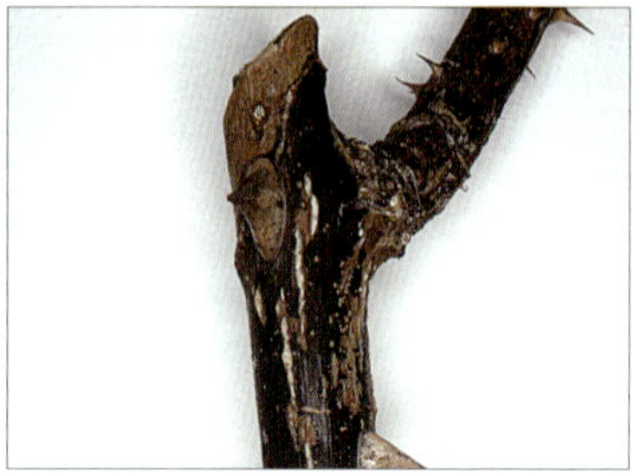

ROSE CANKER is usually the result of careless pruning or breaking of stems. Cut and trim diseased stems to a clean, sharp end.

Rusts

Rusts are recognized as small yellow or orange patches or spots, which appear mainly on the upper surfaces of leaves. On the underside, powdery, raised pustules appear under each spot. This disease can cause leaf fall and seriously weaken plants. Most rusts attack a specific plant or a small group of related plants and will not transfer from one host to another, but there are varieties for a broad range of plants.

CONTROL: As a preventative measure it is best to grow rust-resistant varieties of plants whenever possible. As different rusts affect a great many plants, appropriate treatment often differs. Spraying with mancozeb or myclobutanil is effective against most varieties of rust fungi. Clear away any fallen leaves to prevent a carry-over of the disease.

OLD-FASHIONED HOLLYHOCKS are particularly susceptible to rust. Remove and burn obviously infected foliage and spray with mancozeb.

Sooty mould

This dark fungal growth forms on the sticky secretions (called honeydew) produced by sap-sucking insects. It causes unsightly black mould to appear on leaves and stems but does not harm plants directly. Occasionally sooty mould will appear on shrubs growing under trees or palms infested with pests because their sugary secretions have fallen onto the leaves below.

CONTROL: If you remove the primary infection, such as the aphids, scale or psyllids, the sooty mould will disappear. Hose the plant with a strong spray to assist in the clean up.

THE SOOTY MOULD on these grapefruit leaves is growing on the secretions of an infestation of black citrus aphid. Controlling the insects will eliminate the mould.

•CHAPTER NINE•

PROPAGATION

Individually, plants aren't expensive but when you start a new garden, the numbers needed can cost big money. Propagating your own plants saves money, is fun even if slower and is often the only way to get something that's hard to find.

GROWING PLANTS FROM SEED

Growing seeds is simple in principle. Sow them in fine-textured soil, cover them to a depth equal to the size of the seed, and keep the soil moist until they come up. When the seedlings are big enough to handle, they are transplanted ("pricked out") into another pot or bed to give them more room until they are large enough to plant out in the final positions you have chosen for them.

Sowing seeds outdoors

Many seeds can be sown directly where they are to grow. Big, easy-to-handle seeds are usually sown this way. With direct sowing, it is important to have the bed cultivated to a fine tilth so that the soil won't cake over the emerging seedlings. You should also water very gently, with a fine mist. Put out snail bait, so that you won't lose your seedlings as soon as they come up. It's easiest to sow in rows, making a shallow furrow with a pointed stick. Big seeds can be sown at their final spacings, but smaller seeds are sprinkled along the furrow and the seedlings thinned to their correct spacings when they come up. For an even distribution of fine seeds, mix them with dry sand and sprinkle the mixture.

Sowing seeds in containers

The great advantage of sowing seeds in containers is that it gives you complete control of their growing conditions. This is especially an advantage with seed sown in spring, when cold snaps may be a problem. You can sow in the greenhouse if you have one, or on a sunny windowsill indoors, and the seedlings will be ready for transplanting earlier than they would have been if they had been grown outside.

The ideal container is wider and shallower than a flower pot. You need area rather than depth of soil, except for tree seeds for which depth is important. You can get wide, shallow seed trays from garden centers, or you

SOWING TIP

Don't plant seeds too deeply or they will never germinate. Fine seeds should be barely covered with very fine soil. Bigger seeds can be sown slightly deeper. Never allow the soil to dry out before seedlings have emerged.

can use egg cartons, flat plastic carry-out food boxes or even waxed paper trays or polystyrene boxes from greengrocers. Just make some holes in the bottom for drainage.

POLYSTYRENE BOXES covered with plastic wrap make warm mini-greenhouses which speed the germination of seeds and the rooting of cuttings.

Sow seeds thinly into seed-raising mix which is sold at garden centers. You can enclose small containers in a plastic bag, or spread plastic food wrap across the top of a bigger one to keep everything warm and moist, but be sure to uncover the containers as soon as germination is under way or the seedlings may go mouldy.

The time needed for germination varies. Most annuals and vegetables appear in ten days to a fortnight, but shrubs and trees may take much longer, so don't be in too much of a hurry to throw out a container of seeds that hasn't come up.

After germination, the seedlings will become overcrowded if you leave them long in the sowing container or bed. Once they have grown 1 1/2 in tall, they are ready to be pricked out. Be very gentle—lift them with a small, pointed stick, and either relocate them to a new container or a fresh part of the nursery bed, setting them about 2 in apart. Water them in, and provide shade for a few days. When they have settled in, they can be given some slow-release fertilizer, and once they have made three or four sets of leaves they are ready to go in their final positions. You may want to pot up trees, shrubs or perennials for a few months or a year until they are big enough for the garden.

VEGETATIVE PROPAGATION

Unlike seeds, which are the result of a combination of male and female flower parts, vegetative propagation doesn't involve sex. Plants reproduced vegetatively are an exact copy of one parent plant only.

Vegetative propagation is done in one of three basic ways: by removing a part of the plant that already has roots (by dividing a clump of perennials or bulbs), by removing a part that hasn't any roots and inducing it to make roots (by taking a cutting or making a layer) or by uniting a rootless piece with one that is already rooted and growing (by one of the several forms of grafting).

Division

Division is probably the simplest means of propagating—a plant multiplies itself into a clump and you simply lift it from the ground, separate it into several sections and replant each one.

Cut the clump apart with pruners or a sharp knife. The best propagations are almost always the young, strong growths from the outside of the clump. Don't try to break up the clump into smaller divisions than come fairly easily.

Division is most appropriate with perennials and bulbs, but some thicket-forming shrubs can be divided too, or you can detach rooted suckers.

PLANTS THAT expand into clumps can be easily propagated by dividing the clumps into smaller individuals. Lift and divide when they are dormant or, in the case of evergreens, when they are least actively growing. Perennials, bulbs, orchids and some shrubs can be divided.

Layer

Many trailing or running plants layer themselves, which means they form roots where their runners touch the ground. These rooted sections can be severed from the parent, dug up and then replanted.

Most shrubs with branches that can be bent low enough to touch the ground can also be layered—bend a suitable branch down, make a nick by cutting into but not through the lowest point, bury it, and when it has made roots in a few weeks or months, detach the new plant and transplant it. You need to hold the branch still, either by putting a brick on top of the buried section or, better, by staking the far end of your branch upright. Layering is particularly valuable with plants such as rhododendrons that root only slowly from cuttings, but any plant that will grow from cuttings can be layered.

Air-layering

If you can't bend a branch down to the ground you can take the soil to the plant, in what is called air-layering or marcottage. Select the point where you want roots to grow, make a nick in the stem there and pack some moist sphagnum moss or similar moss around it, tying it in place with a piece of polythene. When you see roots through the plastic, cut the

LAYERING

AIR-LAYERING

SELECT A suitable branch and cut part way through the stem, cutting on a fairly steep slant.

PROP THE CUT open with a matchstick, brush with hormone rooting powder and tie to a support.

PACK SPHAGNUM MOSS into a plastic bag; tie it around cut. Remove when roots push against the bag.

branch off and plant it (taking the plastic away, of course). Air-layering can be done to almost any shrub that will strike roots from a layer or cutting. Watch that the moss doesn't dry out, but if you seal it well inside clear plastic it won't.

Cuttings

Cuttings are made when you remove a part of the plant that has no roots and place it in soil in such conditions that it will be kept alive until roots develop and it can start to support itself. Normally, you take a piece of the stem, either one that is actively growing (softwood or tip cuttings), one that has stopped growing but is not quite mature (half-ripe or semi-mature cuttings) or one that is quite mature and firm (it may be dormant and have lost its leaves—mature or hardwood cuttings).

Most cuttings, of whatever type, make roots best from a node in the stem, the point from which a leaf arises, and that is where to cut. Remove all leaves that will be buried and cut the remaining leaves in half to reduce moisture loss. Always take a few more cuttings than you think you will need to allow for some failures. If you have a choice, take cuttings from young, more vigorous plants rather than from old, sedate ones, or at least from vigorous shoots—and always take

TAKEN IN late spring, this coleus cutting took only a month to form its own healthy root system.

BUDDING (OR SHIELD GRAFTING)

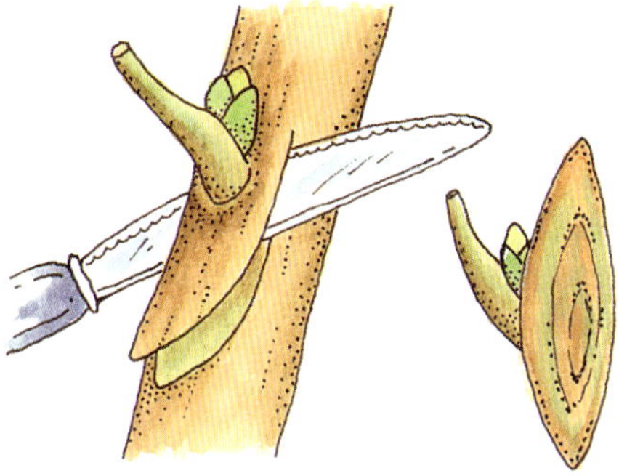

CUT THE BUD from the stem with a sliver of bark. Don't let it dry out.

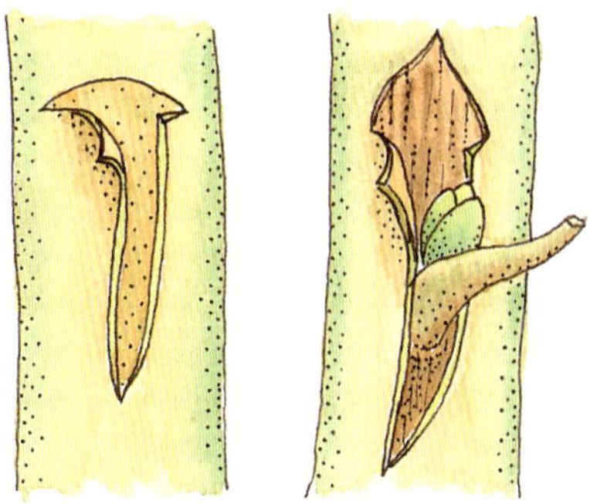

MAKE A SHALLOW T-cut in the bark of the understock and lift the flaps. If the bark is stiff, water heavily and wait a day or two. Slip the bud behind the flaps.

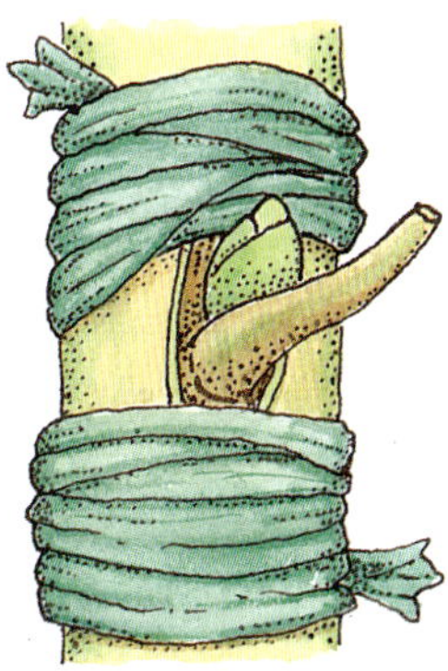

BIND THE FLAPS together with raffia or budding tape.

the cuttings from the choicest, healthiest plants you have. That way you have the best chance of success.

The length of time rooting takes varies with the species, but as long as the cutting hasn't died, the process is underway. You can speed it along by dipping the cut ends into fresh rooting hormone (the preparation loses its potency quickly, and an old or opened packet is useless).

Hardwood cuttings can be struck in the ground in the same sort of bed in which you would grow seeds, but soft and half-ripe cuttings need some protection. The simplest way is to put them up in pots of very sandy soil (three parts of sharp sand to one of regular potting mix), and enclose each pot in a plastic bag to keep the cuttings moist and humid.

Grafting

Grafting is the union of one plant (the scion) with the roots of another (the stock or understock). It is a more skillful process than other forms of propagation and most home gardeners will not need to master it. However, you may have a camellia that is too good to discard but has flowers that don't appeal—you can convert it to a plant you like by grafting, or you could try grafting several different varieties on it to create a multi-colored tree. Grafting is also used to change varieties on grape vines. Most often, however, grafting is used to control the growth of the scion, either by giving it the benefit of more vigorous roots than it would make for itself (as when roses are budded on wild rose roots) or, conversely, by using a less vigorous, "dwarfing" stock, a technique used especially with apples and pears to create smaller, more manageable trees.

CLEFT GRAFTING

CUT THE STOCK right across and trim scions to a long wedge to fit.

WEDGE THE CLEFT open. Insert scions on either side of cleft, matching green cambium layers exactly.

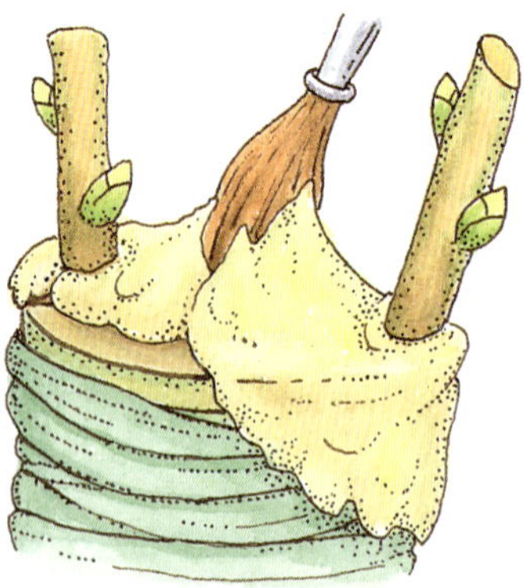

REMOVE THE WEDGE and bind tightly with raffia or plastic tape. Coat with grafting wax.

Although grafting isn't difficult, it does call for skill. What you are doing is making a wound on the stock plant and inserting into it a piece of scion (a cutting), in the hope that both stock and scion will callus together and grow as one. To do this, you must match the cambium layers, the green section of stem immediately below the bark, together perfectly. Use razor-sharp blades to make the cuts, and a steady hand to make the match precisely. Disinfect the blades after each cut so as to minimize the chance of transmission of infection.

The simplest form of grafting is budding (or shield grafting)—you lift a flap of bark on the understock (which has been grown from seed or a cutting), and slip in a growth bud from the scion, trimmed to give just a sliver of bark to support it. Cambium matching is automatic, and you bind everything together with raffia or plastic tape (see the diagram on page 61). Around midsummer is usually the best time for budding, and after it's done you let the stock grow, cutting it off just above the bud the following winter. Come spring, the bud will grow away to start the branches of a new plant on the more desirable roots of another species.

Cleft grafting is another method. With it you cut off the stock first, cleave it with a sharp knife and insert a scion in the cleft (or two, one on either side), matching the cambiums exactly. All the wounded surfaces are then covered with grafting wax and the graft is enclosed within a plastic bag to keep the scion moist. The best time for this process is towards the end of dormancy (early spring). The understock can be a young plant or a mature branch, which will need several grafts.

•CHAPTER TEN•

PRUNING

Pruning is the removal of part of a plant so as to encourage it to grow the way we want it to. Although it calls for artistry, it is not hard to master, and when you see the improvement it brings you may even look forward to this seasonal task.

HOW PLANTS RESPOND TO PRUNING

Whether the stem in question is a trunk, a branch or a twig, it is essentially a tube conveying sap, and if you cut it off, you divert the sap to some other stem, which will then grow more strongly.

A stem can be cut back to another, preferred stem or it can be cut back to a bud, from which a new stem will arise. On most plants buds can be seen as small nubs, either at the end of a stem (the terminal bud) or along the sides (the lateral buds). Lateral buds almost always grow in the axil ("armpit") of a leaf. Once a stem matures, the buds may lie dormant beneath the bark until pruning or injury removes the growth above them and provokes them into growth.

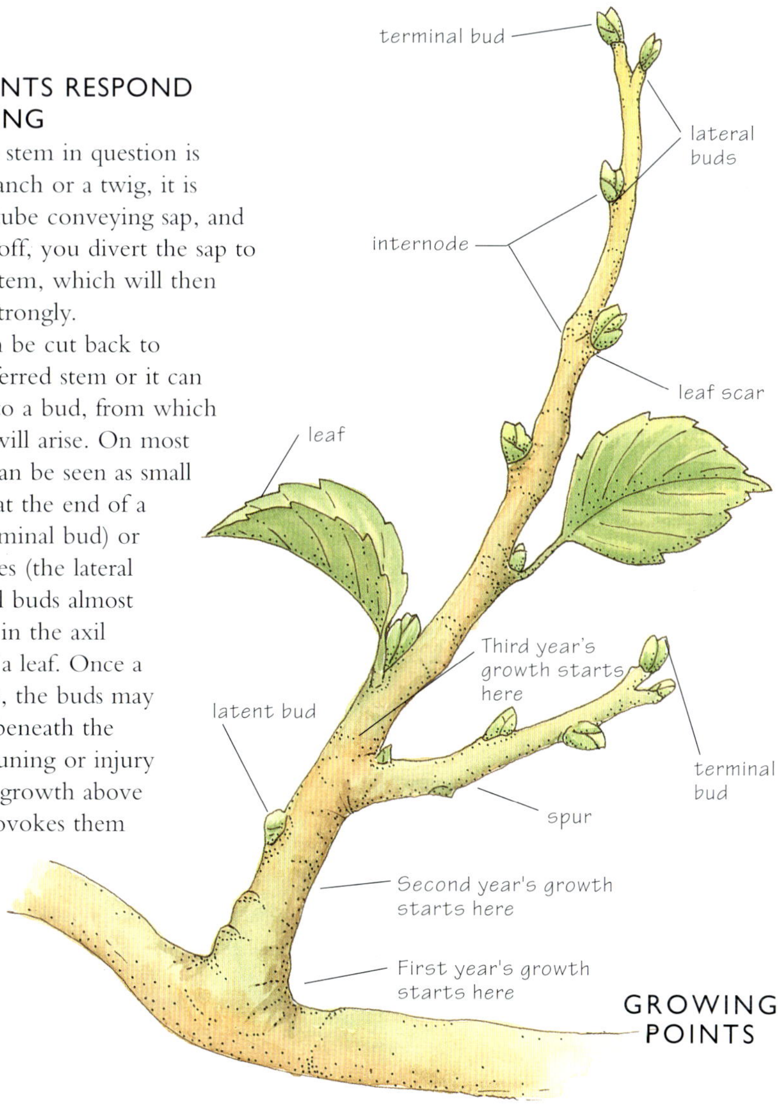

GROWING POINTS

When you cut a stem back, you remove the terminal bud, forcing the lateral buds to make side shoots. This usually makes the plant bushier. Conversely, you might choose to pinch back side shoots, diverting the plant's energy into the terminal bud to make the branch grow longer. And by cutting back hard into old wood, you may also force dormant buds into growth. But beware, not all plants will tolerate being cut back to old wood and may die as a result.

The way you prune a plant depends on the sort of growth that will come from each bud. If you are training a climbing rose, for instance, you might remove the ends of the long shoots to force the side shoots that will bear the flowers; if you are training a young tree to grow tall, you might well shorten the side shoots back to encourage the main shoot (the leader) to grow up faster.

PINCHING

SHEARING

HEADING BACK

PRUNING TECHNIQUES

If you decide to prune, there are four basic techniques you can use, depending on what you want to achieve and the way the plant grows. These techniques—pinching, shearing, heading (or cutting back) and thinning—all start the same way, with the removal of any dead and obviously weak and sickly branches or shoots. Sometimes that is all that is needed. Take a critical look at your plant before proceeding further.

Pinching

Pinching is the removal of the tip of a shoot, causing the lateral buds to begin growing. Repeated pinching will make many new shoots and give a compact, bushy plant. It can be used on annual flowers such as petunias and marigolds and also on bushy shrubs such as lavender. Usually you only need to pinch a plant twice, and you shouldn't pinch once the plant shows signs of wanting to flower and is large enough to do so (or you will be pinching off the flowers).

Shearing

Shearing is like pinching on a more drastic scale: you clip the outer parts of the plant to an even surface, using a pair of hedge shears. Repeated shearing destroys the plant's natural form, but that may be what you want. Shearing a hedge is the most obvious example, but you might also want to shear back a groundcover to make it grow lower and more evenly or to remove a multitude of dead flowers. Shearing is not suitable for plants with large leaves such as camellias—you will end up cutting a lot of the leaves in half, which can create an unpleasant sight. It is much better to trim these large-leaved plants by cutting back each shoot individually with pruners.

Heading back

Heading back shortens a branch without removing it entirely and thus forces growth from one or more lateral buds. You might head back to reduce the size of the plant, to encourage growth from lower down where it will be stronger or more productive of flowers or fruit, or to remove a part of a branch that has been damaged. Always head back to a point from which growth will come—to another branch or to a bud—and consider whether that growth is likely to go in the direction you want (it will grow the way the bud is pointing). Don't leave the stubs to rot, and always go easy when heading back. You can always cut off more, but you can't stick branches back on.

THINNING

Thinning

Thinning is the removal of whole stems, cutting them right back to their origin, with the aim of reducing the plant's bulk and bushiness but not making it any smaller. You might do this to let in more light and air, to reveal the lines of the branches or, by removing old and unproductive stems, to channel the plant's energies into younger and more productive ones. Often you will combine thinning and heading back, as in the pruning of bush roses where you cut out old branches and head back the rest.

CHOOSING A TECHNIQUE

Every plant is different and how you apply the basic techniques will vary from plant to plant but here are a few generalizations to guide you.

Trees

Some trees may need pruning when young to encourage them to develop into shapely adults. But training a young tree is not a hasty business and it is best to take several years over the initial pruning. An established tree usually needs only the removal of dead wood but it is often desirable to thin out the branches to allow more light to reach the garden beneath. This is almost always better than trying to reduce the size of a tree by cutting it back all over.

Go easy when pruning trees. Ideally, the results should not be obvious. First cut out weaker branches and then any that are growing immediately above or below others. Now stand back and take a look before cutting any more. If a tree is branching too low, you can cut out the lowest branches so as to raise the crown but it is better to do this over a few years than all at once.

Groundcovers

Groundcovers are a very mixed group: some, such as ivy, are climbers that trail along the ground for want of something to climb up; some, such as hypericum and vinca, are spreading herbaceous perennials; while others are prostrate, spreading shrubs. An occasional shearing or general heading back will keep all these types of groundcovers dense and low.

PRUNING A SHRUB

Shrubs

Shrubs fall into two main groups: those that have several permanent branches growing from a single, short trunk and those that form clumps or thickets of more or less evenly sized stems growing straight from the

CONVERTING A SHRUB TO A TREE

CONVERT A multi-stemmed shrub to a small tree by removing the lower limbs and excess stems.

ground. Shrubs with a trunk, such as daphne and most viburnums, are usually headed back, although you might want to thin out the occasional weak or badly placed branch to keep them from becoming too bushy. On the other hand, thicket shrubs such as philadelphus, abelias and spiraea are generally thinned by cutting a few of the oldest branches right to the ground. Large shrubs such as camellias and the bigger rhododendrons can be trained as small, multi-stemmed trees by removing the lowest branches. Not all will take being severely headed back into bare wood to make them smaller and in most cases it is usually better to begin pruning when shrubs are still young and flexible.

Conifers

Conifers range from creeping groundcovers to the world's tallest timber trees. With few exceptions,

CONIFERS

Random branching—juniper

Whorl branching—pine and spruce

they are evergreen and their leaves are needles: either long as in pines and cedars or short as in cypresses and junipers. They fall into two broad classes: those such as pines, cedars and firs that bear their branches in whorls,

RENOVATING A SHRUB

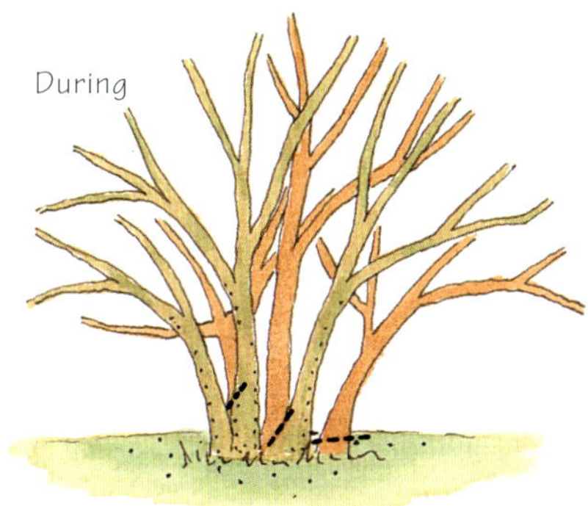

RENOVATE AN overgrown shrub over three years—each winter cut to the ground one-third of the oldest stems.

radiating out from the trunk or limbs like the spokes of a wheel, and those such as sequoias, cypresses and junipers that branch at random along the stem. This is not a commonly used distinction, but it is important when pruning, for while the random branches have dormant buds all along their shoots, so that you can cut anywhere and expect growth, the whorl branches have buds only at the points where the whorls arise—at the tips or the bases of new shoots. If you cut between them, there will be no growth and the cut branch will die back: cut only to a lateral or, if you can see it clearly, to the cluster of buds that mark the base of a year's growth. (See the diagram on page 67.)

Most conifers are naturally shapely, and if you choose a conifer to suit your situation, you should not need to prune. In any case, don't cut into bare wood—the dormant buds lose viability when the leaves finally fall and so it won't regrow. *Taxus*, the English yew, and *Podocarpus*, the plum pines, are notable exceptions, which is one reason why yew is so valued for hedging and topiary.

MAKING PRUNING CUTS

A plant is a living thing and pruning is a kind of surgery from which it has to heal itself. Properly made cuts will heal quickly; bad ones will heal only slowly, if at all, and the open wounds will invite infection and decay.

Except in shearing, all cuts must be made either where the plant will grow or where, if it will not grow, it can heal itself. Usually this means to just above a bud, just above another branch, or back to the main trunk or

WHERE TO MAKE CUTS

PRUNING CUTS

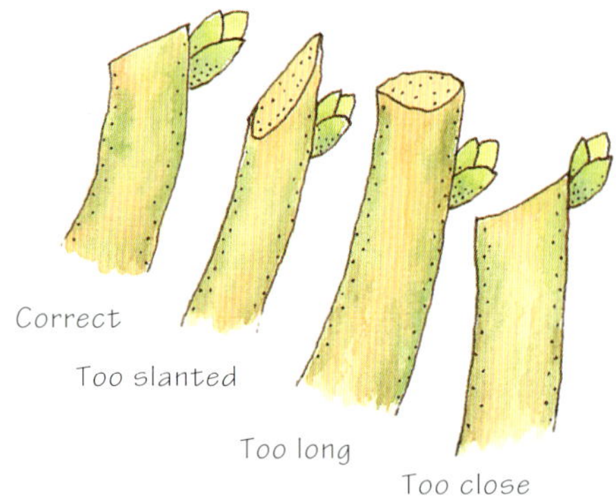

CUTTING LARGE LIMBS

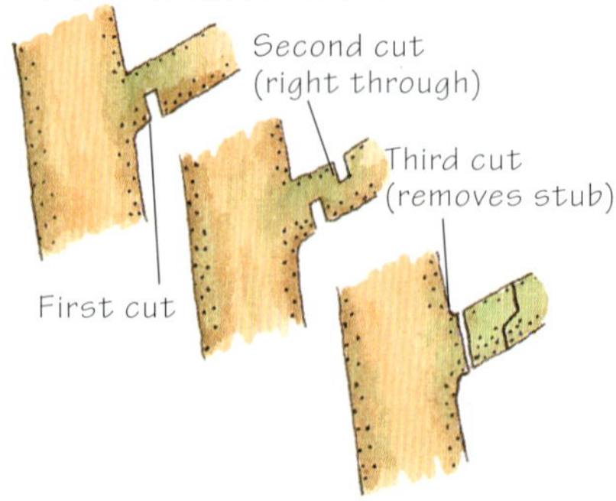

rootstock. If you leave a stub above a growing or healing point, it will die back and rot, and the rot can spread to the living tissue.

As important as placing your cut correctly is making it cleanly: a ragged wound won't heal. This means that your tools must be sharp.

WHEN TO PRUNE

A lot of minor pruning—pinching, removing dead wood, shortening that wayward branch—can be done any time you notice the need. But any major pruning of trees and shrubs is best done when the plant is dormant or least actively growing. For most plants, including many evergreens, this means in the winter but there is a large group of plants that flower in spring or early summer on stems that were produced during the previous summer. This is often referred to as "old wood". If you prune these in winter you will be cutting away the flower buds and will get nothing but leaf growth that year. Instead, prune them immediately after the flowers have finished but before the new season's growth is properly underway. If you like, you can combine pruning with cutting long branches of flowers for the house, taking the branches that you plan to prune out, and finishing off the job as soon as the rest of the flowers have finished for the year.

Summer and fall-flowering shrubs mostly bloom on the current season's growth (stems produced after winter and called "new wood") and can be pruned at any time from the end of fall until they show signs of growth in spring. You will never kill a plant by pruning it at the wrong time of year. At worst, you may lose that year's flowers or fruits.

THE MAIN PART of the branch has been cut off (note how the bark tore) and now the stub is trimmed close to the trunk.

PRUNING TOOLS

Most gardeners can get by with a pair of pruners and a pruning saw. You might also add long-handled loppers, which are pruners with long handles. Use them for higher stems and those branches that are too big for pruners but not quite big enough for a saw.

The most useful saw has a tapering, curved blade, which can get into tight corners. Bigger hand saws are useful for big limbs, and you can buy pruning saws with coarse teeth on one side, fine on the other. You can also buy the ordinary curved saw with a long handle to extend your reach. If you are faced with limbs large enough to call for a chain saw, get professional help: chain saws are dangerous in inexperienced hands.

Hedge shears are really just enormous scissors. There isn't much to choose in the various models, but lightness is always an advantage.

A ladder is useful when pruning as you can't cut precisely if you are reaching up on tiptoe. Be very careful with a stepladder; it needs firm footing to be stable. Always have another person hold the ladder steady.

TIE THE CANES *of climbing roses as horizontally as possible and you'll get flowers on short lateral branches all along the canes. Prune these laterals back in winter.*

PRUNING ROSES

Almost all roses send up vigorous new shoots from the base each year. After about three years, each of these has grown old. Fewer and fewer flowers are produced and the decrepit stems are easy targets for pests and diseases. By pruning out the oldest branches each year, right at the base, and cutting the younger ones back to a healthy bud, you make room for and encourage the fresh new stems that will carry masses of flowers.

When to prune

The right time to prune is governed by your climate. Pruning stimulates regrowth but frost will destroy the soft, new shoots. In frosty areas don't prune until frosts are finished or becoming less severe, which will be just before new spring growth appears. In a frost-free area, prune in the second or third month of winter.

How to prune

Using very sharp, clean pruners, cut out all dead, weak or spindly growth. Now decide which of the main branches to preserve. You should aim to keep three to seven healthy young stems, each growing upwards and outwards. Cut out all others completely, and then prune back the selected branches to any height desired. Cut the stems at an angle of 45° so that they shed water and prune fractionally above an outward pointing bud. Don't prune to an inward pointing bud or the plant will become congested in the center.

Any growths that appear below the graft union near the base of the plant should be removed when they are first seen. This can be done at any time.

Summer pruning

Summer pruning involves more than just snipping off the dead heads of faded flowers, or all you will get in the fall is a few short-stemmed blossoms clustered around the tip. A better idea is to cut about 12–16 in off each stem in late summer, even if the stem hasn't flowered and even if it has some flower buds. By doing this

PRUNING ROSES

AFTER A few years, twiggy sticks will crowd the main canes and flowering will be reduced. Prune the bush by reducing the main canes and shortening laterals to three sets of leaves.

you will encourage a mass of new growth, all bearing long-stemmed roses 6–8 weeks after pruning.

Pruning climbing roses

Climbing roses produce many long canes from their bases and these should be tied to their support horizontally. Flower stems will arise all along the tied-down cane. In the fall, take 10–12 in off each cane and, in winter, remove any old woody canes (there won't be any on newly planted climbers). Shorten new canes that have not yet grown long enough to tie down. Also in winter, shorten lateral branches from the tied-down canes that have flowered back to two or three buds from their bases. Those lateral branches that have not flowered should be tied down horizontally but not shortened.

CLIMBING ROSES

CLIMBERS produce long canes which should be tied horizontally to a support. Flower stems will appear along the length of the tied-down cane.

•CHAPTER ELEVEN•

GARDEN TOOLS

No gardener can function without the use of workable and appropriate tools. The selection of gardening aids available is immense, and so careful consideration is needed to make sure you spend your money wisely.

THE ESSENTIALS

Every gardener needs a spade, fork, trowel, hose and pair of pruners. Never buy hand tools too large or heavy for the user. Some firms make "lady's weight" items, which are lighter and smaller, and some tools are made for left-handers.

- *Spade*: Buy a spade, not a shovel. A spade has a straight blade and is used upright. It should have a sharp cutting edge and a handle of smooth, good quality wood. Spades are used for digging over soil and excavating planting holes: buy one with a flange on top of the blade to save the instep.
- *Fork*: A fork normally has four prongs, each 10–12 in long and almost straight. They should be thick and strong or they will soon become bent and useless. Use a fork to turn dug-over soil or compost heaps.
- *Trowel*: A trowel should be slightly scooped with a blade 6–10 in long. Ensure that the neck of the tool, where the blade meets the handle, is strong. Trowels are used for planting out seedlings and hand weeding.
- *Hose*: Hoses come in 60 to 100 ft lengths in various quality grades. The best are kink and split resistant and very supple, even in cold weather.
- *Pruners*: Pruners should have a removable blade that can be sharpened or replaced and well-shaped handles that feel comfortable. Pruners do a lot of work and it's worth spending more for top quality. Use them for cutting flowers and for pruning twigs and small branches. Don't use them to cut thicker branches or you will damage them. Use long-handled loppers or a pruning saw instead.

OTHER USEFUL TOOLS

Although not essential, these tools will make gardening easier for you.

- *Rake*: Buy a flexible plastic or bamboo rake for gathering fallen leaves or lawn clippings. A steel-tined rake is useful for preparing the surface of vegetable or flower beds.
- *Hoe*: Two types of hoe are used to break the soil surface and remove weeds. One is used with a chopping motion while walking forwards, the other, the Dutch hoe, is used with spade-like action, while walking backwards. Some hoes have interchangeable heads, others have dual heads with a straight blade on one side and prongs on the other. A hoe is one of the most useful tools for gardeners who grow vegetables or annual flowers in beds.

A SELECTION OF USEFUL TOOLS

- *Hand fork*: A hand fork is a small implement to loosen soil around seedlings and lift smaller plants. Use it while kneeling.
- *Weeder*: A weeder is a useful hand tool consisting of two prongs. It is used for lifting weeds, complete with their roots, out of the ground. It can be used among small, closely planted subjects and it is frequently used to remove single, deep rooted, broad-leaved weeds, such as dandelions, daisies and plantains, from lawns.
- *Shears*: Shears are used for cutting long grass or hedges. They resemble scissors, and the blades are easily replaced or sharpened. Edging shears have long handles so that you can use them to clip lawn edges without bending down.
- *Wheelbarrow*: Wheelbarrows are useful for carrying bulk mulch or topsoil, or for lugging heavy items around the garden. Don't buy one unless you are sure you will need it.
- *Watering can*: A watering can is handy for spot watering pots or for applying liquid or soluble fertilizers. Plastic ones are lightweight but don't leave them in the sun.
- *Portable sprayer*: A portable sprayer is used to apply garden chemicals. Some are pressurized for continuous spraying, others must be pumped. One or the other will be essential if you have fruit trees or other plants that need regular spraying. Smaller, hand-held models are for individual spraying chores.
- *Saw*: A pruning saw has a curved blade with coarse teeth; a bow saw is like a big hacksaw. Both are useful when pruning trees or big shrubs.
- *Sprinkler*: A sprinkler distributes water over a wide area with a rain-like spray. The simplest ones emit a fountain-like, circular spray while more sophisticated models can water in various patterns that you select to suit the shape of the area.

WATERING SYSTEMS

The correct hose, sprinkler or other system is vital if the garden is to be well maintained. The type depends on whether the garden is new or established. Some plants prefer overhead sprinklers (they aid pollination when the plant is in flower), others need a dribble or soaker system that keeps soil moist but flowers and foliage dry (so that fungus diseases are discouraged).

An in-ground sprinkler system will cut down your watering time considerably, but water restrictions

MAINTENANCE *DOS* AND *DON'TS*

Do

- store tools under cover
- keep tools clean (hose off, dry and give a quick rub over with an oily rag to prevent rust)
- have a spare spade handle ready in case you need to replace one that suddenly breaks
- be careful with sharp, inflammable or poisonous materials (store them out of reach of children and pets)

Don't

- poke an incinerator fire with a hoe handle
- leave the wheelbarrow outside with rubbish in it (it will rust)
- cut wire with pruners (use wire cutters)
- store a lawnmower with grass clippings in the catcher (empty them onto your compost heap)

apply in some areas. You need enough good quality hose to reach all parts of the garden, a variety of interchangeable sprinklers ("click" fittings are excellent) and a fixed or mobile hose reel.

TOOLS FOR THE LAWN

A motor mower is now a must for most gardens. Choose one that has the correct horsepower and a big enough catcher for your lawn. Hand-held trimmers, motorized or manual, make quick, light work of neatening rough areas along paths, around trees or next to fences.

TOOLS FOR SPECIAL PURPOSES

The following tools and garden accessories are only some of the many that have been developed to make gardening easier. Some will be suitable for your needs.

- Cut-and-hold tools are useful for those with physical difficulties. They incorporate a device for holding the pruning, flower, fruit or weed after removal: pruners and a type of weeder are available. The tool known as a flower gatherer will hold the flower once cut as well as remove rose thorns. It is suitable for left- and right-handed gardeners.
- A weeder will make planting large numbers of seedlings or bulbs easier and quicker.
- A device for disposing of dog waste consists of a durable container that is planted in the garden so that all you see above ground is a foot-operated lid and rim. Decomposition occurs quickly and naturally. The device comes with a special collector, which is a steel pan and pusher on a long handle, so that there is no need to stoop. This is ideal for those who have reduced mobility.
- Edgers, such as those that swivel in different directions, allow you to cut grass edges in difficult spots. They are designed to rotate into three different cutting positions, diagonally for tricky spots, horizontally for around trees and vertically for edges and paths. Easy-to-use cordless grass cutters powered by batteries are available.
- A greenhouse is ideal for people in cooler areas who want to grow plants that love warmth and humidity and so do not thrive out of doors. They are great for getting vegetables and flowering potted plants started early
- Hedge trimmers are a boon to those with large, formal hedges which require trimming a few times a year. Several companies have developed excellent hedge trimmers with good safety features such as a safety cutter bar, starting lock, enclosed handle and shield to protect the operator's hands.
- A hose director enables you to use the hose as a sprinkler by directing water to any part of your garden. They are good where space is limited.
- A kneeler is a lightweight, padded waterproof cushion with a handle either side to make kneeling and rising afterwards much easier and more comfortable.
- Knee pads keep knees warm and dry during winter. They are comfortable and let you kneel directly on hard and stony ground.
- Long-handled tools give greater leverage and increased reach, placing less strain on your back. Long-handled loppers give greater reach, long-handled vertical shears are designed to trim grass without stooping, long-handled spades provide greater leverage, and long-handled hedge shears give a wider cutting sweep.

•CHAPTER TWELVE•

SPECIAL PURPOSE PLANTS

The plants listed here are grouped according to some of the special purposes they can perform for you, in particular the difficult conditions under which they will grow. Each plant is included in the relevant chapter of this book—check the index to find out the page on which it appears.

PLANTS FOR COASTAL GARDENS

The plants listed here will grow at or near the coast as well as further inland. Some will take direct exposure to sea winds, others need a more sheltered location.

Agapanthus
Alexandra palm
Alyssum
Anemone
Angel's trumpet
Aurora daisy
Baboon flower
Baby's tears
Bottlebrush
Butterfly bush
Cabbage tree palm
California poppy
Californian lilac
Campion
Catmint
Coreopsis
Cosmos
Daylily
Dianthus
English box
Escallonia
Euphorbia
European fan palm
Everlasting daisy
Freesia
Gazania
Geranium
Globe amaranth
Golden barrel cactus
Golden cane palm
Grevillea
Harlequin flower
Hawthorn
Heath
Hibiscus
Holm oak
Hydrangea
Irish strawberry tree
Jade plant
Japanese fatsia
Jelly beans
Kalanchoe
Kentia palm
Lavender
Lily
Livingstone daisy
Mammillaria
Marigold
Mexican sunflower
Milfoil
Mondo grass
Mountain flax
Mountain pine
Nerine
Oleander
Ornamental onion
Ox-eye chamomile
Palmetto
Paper daisy
Perennial sunflower
Petunia
Pinks
Pittosporum
Plumbago
Port Jackson pine
Pygmy date palm
Red hot poker
Rock rose
Sage
Sallow thorn
Sea holly
Shasta daisy
Shore juniper
Shrubby groundsel
Snow-in-summer
Speedwell
Spider flower
Spiderwort
Statice
Stokes aster
Sturt's desert pea
Sun rose
Sunflower
Tea tree
Thorny elaeagnus
Thrift
Verbena
Wine palm
Zephyr lily
Zinnia

PLANTS THAT GROW IN SHADE

These plants can grow in various degrees of shade. Some prefer shade, others will tolerate it. Shade may be full shade or part-shade. Some of these plants prefer shade in hot areas but sun in cooler gardens.

Agapanthus
Alexandra palm
Astilbe
Azalea
Baby blue eyes
Baby's tears
Balloon flower
Balsam
Bamboo palm
Bear's breeches
Bedding begonia
Belladonna lily
Bellflower
Bergamot
Bergenia
Big blue lilyturf
Black cohosh
Blue bugle
Blue poppy
Bluebell
Camellia
Campion
Cardinal flower
Catmint
Cherry pie
Cinquefoil
Climbing hydrangea
Colchis ivy
Coleus
Columbine
Common snowdrop
Coral bells
Cosmos
Cranesbill
Creeping jenny
Cyclamen
Dahlia
Daphne
Daylily
Dead nettle
Delphinium
Dog-tooth violet
Dogwood
English holly
English ivy
Epimedium
Floss flower
Forget-me-not
Foxglove
Freesia
Geranium
Geum
Goatsbeard
Godetia
Golden cane palm
Grape hyacinth
Grevillea
Gunnera
Harlequin flower
Honesty
Hosta
Hydrangea
Jade plant
Japanese anemone
Japanese fatsia
Japanese hydrangea vine
Japanese maple
Japanese rose
Japanese spurge
Jonquil
Kentia palm
Kuma bamboo grass
Lady palm
Lady's mantle
Lenten rose
Lily
Linaria
Lobelia
Love-in-a-mist
Lungwort
Mahonia
Meadow rue
Michaelmas daisy
Mock orange
Mondo grass
Monkey flower
Nemesia
Nerine
Obedient plant
Orchid cactus
Ornamental onion
Pansy
Parlor palm
Pasque flower
Peony
Pieris
Plumbago
Polyanthus
Primrose
Pygmy date palm
Red hot poker
Rhododendron
Rose-of-Sharon
Sacred bamboo
Sage
Sedge
Shasta daisy
Shore juniper
Sour gum
Spider flower
Spiderwort
Spring starflower
Star jasmine
Stokes aster
Torenia
Tulip
Vinca
Virginia creeper
Wallflower
Yellow spotted dead nettle
Zephyr lily

PLANTS THAT GROW FAST

The plants listed here all grow fast to very fast. How fast they grow depends on your climate and the growing conditions. Often, plants will grow faster in a warmer climate. Annual and perennial flowers and bulbs are not included as they all grow fast.

Actinidia
Alexandra palm
Alpine snow gum
Angel's trumpet
Bamboo palm
Bottlebrush
Butterfly bush
Catmint
Cherry pie
Cotoneaster
Dragon-claw willow
Dutch woodbine
English ivy
Flowering quince
Golden hop
Golden robinia
Grevillea
Hibiscus
Himalaya honeysuckle
Honey locust
Hydrangea
Lavender
Oleander
Palmetto
Pin oak
Pittosporum
Port Jackson pine
Potato vine
Rock rose
Rose-of-Sharon
Shrubby cinquefoil
Shrubby groundsel
Siberian dogwood
Snow-in-summer
Spindle tree
Staghorn sumac
Tea tree
Tree mallow
Tree of heaven
Trumpet creeper
Vinca
Virginia creeper
Warminster broom
Weigela
Wisteria

PLANTS HARDY TO AT LEAST 14°F

These plants all accept winter lows of at least 14°F. Some take much lower temperatures but others, although they will survive 14°F, will be damaged.

Actinidia
Agapanthus
Alpine phlox
Anemone
Astilbe
Autumn cherry
Azalea
Baboon flower
Baby's tears
Balloon flower
Barberry
Beard tongue
Bear's breeches
Beautyberry
Belladonna lily
Bellflower
Bergamot
Bergenia
Big blue lilyturf
Black birch
Black cohosh
Blue bugle
Blue poppy
Bluebeard
Bluebell
Box elder
Bramble
Butterfly bush
Californian lilac
Camellia
Campion
Cardinal flower
Catmint
Checkered lily
Chinese cherry
Cinquefoil
Clematis
Climbing hydrangea
Cockspur thorn
Colchis ivy
Common snowdrop
Coral bells
Coreopsis
Cotoneaster
Crab apple
Cranberry bush
Cranesbill
Creeping jenny
Crepe myrtle
Daffodil
Daphne
Darwin's barberry
Daylily
Dead nettle
Dog-tooth violet
Dogwood
Dragon-claw willow
Dutch iris
Dutch woodbine
English box
English holly
English ivy
Epimedium
Escallonia
Euphorbia
European red elderberry
Fire thorn
Flowering quince
Fuschia-flowered gooseberry
Gaura
Geranium
Geum
Glory-of-the-snow
Goatsbeard
Golden hop
Golden robinia
Grape hyacinth
Gunnera
Hawthorn
Heath
Himalaya honeysuckle
Holm oak
Honey locust
Hosta
Hubei rowan
Hyacinth
Hydrangea
Irish strawberry tree
Italian alder
Japanese anemone
Japanese crab apple
Japanese flowering cherry
Japanese hydrangea vine
Japanese maple
Japanese rose
Japanese spurge
Jonquil
Judas tree
Juneberry
Kaffir lily
Kuma bamboo grass
Lady's mantle
Lenten rose
Lilac
Lily
Liquidambar
Lungwort
Mahonia
Maidenhair tree
Meadow rue
Mexican orange blossom
Michaelmas daisy
Milfoil
Mock orange
Mondo grass
Monterey cypress
Mountain pine
Nerine
Obedient plant
Oleander
Oriental poppy
Ornamental grape
Ornamental onion
Ornamental pear
Ox-eye chamomile
Paper-bark maple
Pasque flower
Pencil pine
Peony
Perennial phlox
Perennial sunflower
Pieris
Pin oak
Pink
Primrose
Red hot poker
Red valerian
Rhododendron
Rock rose
Rose-of-Sharon
Rowan
Sacred bamboo
Sage
Sallow thorn
Sargent cherry
Sea holly
Shasta daisy
Shore juniper
Shrubby cinquefoil
Siberian crab apple
Siberian dogwood
Silver birch
Small globe thistle
Smoke bush
Snake-bark maple
Snow-in-summer
Sour gum
Speedwell
Spindle tree
Spiderwort
Spring starflower
St John's wort
Staghorn sumach
Star magnolia
Stokes aster
Sun rose
Taiwan cherry
Thorny elaeagnus
Thrift
Tosa spiraea
Tree of heaven
Trumpet creeper
Tulip
Viburnum
Vinca
Virginia creeper
Warminster broom
Wedding bells
Weigela
Whitebeam
Winter jasmine
Wisteria
Witch hazel
Woolly willow
Yellow spotted dead nettle
Yulan

THIS HYBRID DAYLILY is hardy to 14°F.

DROUGHT TOLERANT PLANTS

The plants listed here will tolerate extended periods without water. How long they can go without water depends on your soil and climate. They won't all have the same degree of drought tolerance.

Agapanthus
Beard tongue
Belladonna
Big blue lilyturf
Bottlebrush
California poppy
Californian lilac
Campion
Coreopsis
English box
English ivy
Euphorbia
Freesia
Gaura
Gazania
Geranium
Golden barrel cactus
Grevillea
Italian alder
Jade plant
Jelly beans
Judas tree
Lavender
Livingstone daisy

RED HOT POKERS (such as Kniphofia caulescens*) are good for drought-prone areas.*

Mammillaria
Mexican sunflower
Oleander
Ornamental grape
Palmetto
Pencil pine
Petunia
Portulaca
Red hot poker
Red valerian
Sallow thorn
Sea holly
Sturt's desert pea
Sun rose
Thorny elaeagnus
Warminster broom
Whitebeam
Wine palm
Zinnia

FRAGRANT PLANTS

Plants with fragrant flowers or aromatic foliage may be lightly or strongly fragrant or they may have foliage that is aromatic on hot days or when brushed.

Actinidia
Angel's trumpet
Apple cactus
Belladonna lily
Bluebeard
Cherry pie
Cranesbill
Daphne
Dutch woodbine
Freesia
Gardenia
Golden robinia
Grape hyacinth
Hyacinth
Jonquil
Lavender
Lilac
Lily
Mahonia
Mexican orange blossom
Pink
Pittosporum
Polyanthus
Red valerian

LILAC produces trusses of sweetly perfumed flowers.

Star jasmine
Star magnolia
Stock
Sweet pea
Sweet William
Viburnum
Wisteria
Witch hazel
Yulan

• CHAPTER THIRTEEN •

TREES

A house without trees looks almost as unfinished as a house without a roof. By planting trees around your home, you will not only improve its appearance, you will also make it a more comfortable and pleasant place to live, thus adding to its value.

In time, the trees you plant will grow to dominate your block, so it's vital to position them carefully with their ultimate height and spread in mind. You should define the job that you want the trees to do (provide shade, privacy or wind shelter) and choose those that are most suitable. Trees planted just anywhere can become a nuisance and are expensive to remove.

LIVING SPACE

Don't overplant. Saplings look small but will soon be a thousand times bigger and trees planted too closely together may force each other to adopt unnatural, unappealing shapes.

Another factor to remember is the rights of your neighbors. Consider the shade your tree will cast on their property, the amount of their garden space its branches will invade and the litter it will drop. You wouldn't like to be adversely affected and neither will they. If, when grown, your trees are entirely within your property, you can't go wrong.

DANGER SPOTS

Don't plant under electric wires. It is dangerous and you will be charged with the cost of clearing them.

It is also unwise to plant trees near sewer lines, for if they ever leak, fine roots will enter. As roots grow, they thicken, widening the crack and

DAMAGE BY TREE ROOTS

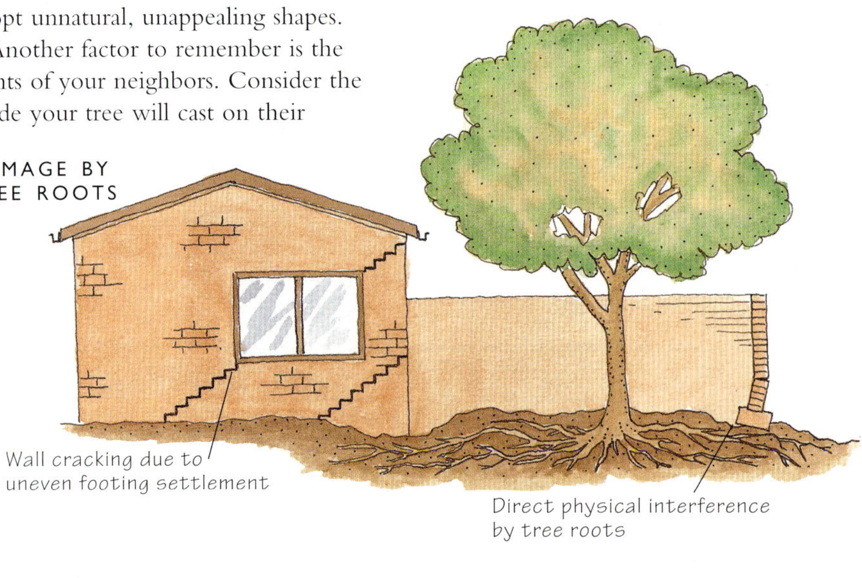

MAGNIFICENT, DOMINANT TREES have a place in every garden but where that place is needs to be carefully thought out with the mature size of the tree in mind.

allowing in more roots to penetrate until eventually they block the pipe. Roots can't enter good pipes and modern, plastic pipes laid in long lengths are less likely ever to be penetrated than old terracotta pipes with their many leaky joins.

Surface tree roots can crack and lift paths and paving if planted closer than about 16 ft. Roots can also cause cracking in houses. The problem is worst on clay soils. In dry spells, as the tree takes up water, the clay shrinks and houses crack as they settle. When it rains, clay expands causing further movement cracks. Sandy soils hardly shrink or expand at all. The greater the tree's potential height, the further from the house it should be planted, especially on clay soil.

WHEN AND HOW TO PLANT

Avoid the extremes of summer and winter. In the first year, water deeply to help the tree to grow deep roots.

To plant, water the tree in its pot. Dig a hole twice as wide as the pot, drop in a small amount of fertilizer and cover it with soil. Don't add compost or manure or the tree may keep its roots in the "pot" of good soil you have created.

Unpot the tree, untangle the roots, cleanly removing any that are too long. Place it in the hole, so that the soil level will be the same as it was in the pot. Backfill, pressing soil into air pockets, and water well. Top up with more soil if there is any settlement.

STAKING

Sooner or later trees must cope with wind. To help them make strong roots, do not stake them. If the wind bends the trees, then let them bend, that is how trees cope with wind. Only if young trees are in danger of blowing over should you stake, but aim to remove the stakes as soon as the trees are firmly rooted.

ALPINE SNOW GUM

Eucalyptus pauciflora subsp. *niphophila*

EVERGREEN

ORIGIN: Australia.
SIZE: One of the smaller-growing eucalypts with a height of up to 20 ft and a spread of about 14 ft.
FROST TOLERANCE: It tolerates a temperature down to 10°F and is perhaps the hardiest species of eucalyptus as it comes from mountainous areas.
APPEAL: All parts of this tree are handsome. It has smooth, whitish or grayish bark. This flakes off to reveal underbark in various colors, including yellow and bronze. The young shoots are covered in a waxy white coating or "bloom" and the older shoots are grayish green in color. The longish leaves are sickle shaped and grayish green as well.
CLIMATE: Zone 8. It needs a position in full sun and shelter from cold winds.
USES: Makes a striking focal point placed where its pale bark can be seen to advantage—for example, with a background of dark-leaved shrubs.

THE ALPINE SNOW GUM is both one of the hardiest eucalypts and also one of the most decorative.

AN INTOXICATING perfume oozes from the big, fleshy flowers of angel's trumpet.

ANGEL'S TRUMPET

Brugmansia suaveolens

EVERGREEN

ORIGIN: South-eastern Brazil.
SIZE: Grows to 16–20 ft with a crown that spreads almost as wide.
FROST TOLERANCE: None.
APPEAL: This exotic, tropical-looking tree has a very long summer and fall display of big, pendulous, trumpet-shaped flowers that are strongly and sweetly scented at night.
CLIMATE: Zone 10. It is advisable to grow angel's trumpet in a tub. This can then be placed outdoors during the summer, on a terrace perhaps, and then brought indoors to be overwintered under glass.
USES: Angel's trumpet is an eye-catching feature tree and an excellent shade caster for small or big gardens. Its night fragrance is too strong for some people and so it should be planted away from the house. All parts of the angel's trumpet plant are poisonous. Also note that the narcotic sap attracts caterpillars.

THE ORNAMENTAL CHERRY is almost unique, flowering in the fall and winter.

AUTUMN CHERRY

Prunus x *subhirtella* "Autumnalis Rosea"

DECIDUOUS

ORIGIN: This ornamental cherry is of garden origin.

SIZE: Suitable for a garden of average size, with a height and spread of 28 ft.
FROST TOLERANCE: A hardy tree, tolerating temperatures as low as 5°F.
APPEAL: This is one of the few ornamental trees that flower in the fall and winter. The semi-double pink flowers are carried on the bare branches mainly during mild periods.
CLIMATE: Zone 6 and above. This tree is best grown in positions that receive sun for most of the day.
USES: It is often grown in a mixed border with shrubs that have fall and winter interest, such as the witch hazel, *Hamamelis* x *intermedia*. A dark background, such as deep green evergreen shrubs or conifers, is needed for the flowers to show up well. Autumn cherry can be grown as a lawn specimen.

BLACK BIRCH

Betula nigra

DECIDUOUS

ORIGIN: Eastern North America.
SIZE: At around 128 ft, this is quite a tall tree. It is somewhat conical in form, with a spread of 42 ft.
FROST TOLERANCE: Very hardy, tolerating temperatures at least as low as 5°F.
APPEAL: Grown mainly for its attractive bark, it makes a change from the more common, white-stemmed silver birch. The bark is reddish brown and peels off. Older bark is blackish in color and quite rugged. Leaves turn an attractive yellow during the fall before they drop.
CLIMATE: Zone 6 and above. Positions in full sun or partial shade suit this tree equally well.
USES: Looks good when planted on the edge of a woodland garden. Alternatively, it can be displayed as a specimen tree on a lawn. If space allows, plant a group of three trees for a stunning effect. An alternative is to grow it as a multi-stemmed tree.

WITH BLACKISH bark, black birch makes a change from the usual silver birch.

ONE OF THE FEW trees with variegated leaves to create light in the garden.

BOX ELDER

Acer negundo "Variegatum"

DECIDUOUS

ORIGIN: The species comes from North America.
SIZE: It is quite a fast growing tree, attaining about 50 ft in height with a spread of 33 ft. It can also be grown as a shrub if pruned back at an early age.
FROST TOLERANCE: The box elder is extremely hardy, taking temperatures as low as – 38°F.
APPEAL: This tree is grown for its attractive variegated foliage. The leaves are broadly edged with white. The young shoots are also attractive, being grayish green.
CULTIVATION: Zone 3 and above. This tree will grow well either in full sun or partial shade.
USES: A fine specimen tree for a lawn but can also be included in a shrub border. It needs quite a dark background, such as deep green conifers or shrubs, to show up well.

CAMELLIA

Camellia japonica

EVERGREEN

ORIGIN: Japan, Korea and China.
SIZE: To 50 ft but often 35 ft or less tall and 20–28 ft wide. Final size varies with variety and growth is slow.
FROST TOLERANCE: Takes the odd extreme low of 9°F if sheltered among other evergreen trees. Better where winter lows are above 19°F.
APPEAL: Flowers for a long period in fall, winter or early spring. The flowers are single, semi-double, or double in white, cream and shades of pink or red. Trees are neat and compact with glossy, dark leaves.
CLIMATE: Zone 8 and above. Best in a moist climate with humus-rich, moisture-retentive soil, which must be acid.
USES: Ideal hedging plants which thrive in light shade. *C. japonica* tolerates full sun where summers are mild but prefers dappled shade.

BEAUTIFUL SMALL TREES, camellias are ideal for bushy, woodland-style gardens.

THE HANDSOME peeling bark of this cherry provides year-round interest.

CHINESE CHERRY

Prunus serrulata

DECIDUOUS

ORIGIN: Western China.

SIZE: This ornamental cherry has a height and spread of about 33 ft.

FROST TOLERANCE: It is very hardy and will take a temperature as low as 5°F.

APPEAL: This tree is of interest all the year round as it is grown mainly for its handsome peeling bark. This is reddish brown and shiny, showing up particularly well in winter when the tree has shed its leaves. In late spring there is a display of white flowers, followed by small red fruits.

CLIMATE: Suited to zone 7 and above. Best grown in a position that receives sun for most of the day.

USES: Often grown in woodland gardens but is equally at home in a mixed border. Make sure that the trunk can be easily seen. Alternatively use it as a lawn specimen.

COCKSPUR THORN

Crataegus crus-galli

DECIDUOUS

ORIGIN: Eastern North America.

SIZE: A broad-crowned tree growing to 28 ft, with a spread of 33 ft.

FROST TOLERANCE: An extremely hardy tree, tolerating temperatures as low as –20°F.

APPEAL: It is grown for its brilliant fall leaf color. The dark green, leathery leaves turn brilliant crimson before they fall. White flowers are produced in early summer followed by dark red, long-lasting berries. Beware of the vicious curved thorns which are 3 in long and generally hidden among the foliage.

CLIMATE: Zone 5 and above. Sun and limestone soils are best. It also copes with windy or exposed situations. Good for town gardens.

USES: A fine tree on a lawn. Makes a good windbreak mixed with other suitable subjects. Grow it also in a mixed or shrub border, ideally with other fall-interest subjects.

A SUPERB TREE for fall leaf color, but watch out for the thorns.

THIS IS ONE OF the most impressive trees for cooler gardens but note how much space the crab apple needs. It is an ideal lawn specimen but will eventually shade the grass out.

CRAB APPLE

Malus floribunda

DECIDUOUS

ORIGIN: This is probably a natural hybrid from Japan.
SIZE: Reaches 16–28 ft tall with a similar or greater spread. The outline is broad and rounded and branches may weep. It is fairly slow growing.
FROST TOLERANCE: Takes –9°F at least if sheltered from freezing winds.
APPEAL: This is one of the loveliest of all flowering trees, with reddish-pink buds opening in early spring into masses of white flowers blushed pink. They literally cover the bare branches, their weight causing the stems to droop and giving the tree its elegant, weeping shape. In late summer and fall a crop of yellow or red crab apples is produced. In cool climates the leaves color before falling.
CLIMATE: It is ideally suited to zones 5 and above. Crab apples need deep, fertile soil and do best in areas with regular rainfall. They don't thrive in hot, dry areas and have little tolerance for drought.
USES: This is a magnificent specimen tree sited in the open where it can develop its broad, weeping shape and where it can be seen from a distance. It is a romantic shade tree and very suitable for sitting under. Don't plant it within 16 ft of a path or drive.

GARDENER'S TIP

The crop of crab apples that drops in fall makes a tart jam or jelly. If you don't want to use them in this way, still rake them up and dispose of them carefully as they can harbor fruit flies.

CREPE MYRTLE

Lagerstroemia indica

DECIDUOUS

ORIGIN: Northern India, Burma, China and Japan.
SIZE: Reaches 20–28 ft tall with a spread of 14–20 ft. Crepe myrtle produces a short trunk which branches into a broad, vase-shaped crown. Dwarf and shrub-sized varieties are also available.
FROST TOLERANCE: If sheltered from cold winds and grown in full sun, crepe myrtle will tolerate 10°F but it generally performs better in areas no colder than 27°F.
APPEAL: Masses of white, pink, mauve or wine-red flowers appear from midsummer. In the fall there is a good display of foliage color in soft tones and the bark of the tree is attractive year-round.
CLIMATE: Zone 7, ideally zone 8 and above. In humid summers leaves may be attacked by powdery mildew, especially if the tree is partly shaded. Adequate soil moisture during the summer is essential. Provide shelter from cold winds if necessary.
USES: Use as a shade tree in small gardens, a lawn specimen or a screen.

OFTEN KEPT to shrub size, crepe myrtle is more useful and attractive as a tree.

ALTHOUGH IT blooms only briefly, the dogwood gives a bonus show in fall.

DOGWOOD

Cornus florida

DECIDUOUS

ORIGIN: Woodlands of the eastern United States.
SIZE: Reaches 14–30 ft with a similar or wider spread. Branches are layered and horizontal.
FROST TOLERANCE: Takes down to –22°F.
APPEAL: Pretty pink or white bracts appear on bare branches in mid-spring, followed by berries that ripen red in early fall with leaves turning yellow, orange or red later.
CLIMATE: Grows in zone 5 and above. Needs frosty or colder winters and warm summers. Year-round moisture and humidity are essential. They grow best in bright, dappled shade. Not for frost-free gardens.
USES: Grow as a feature tree or it can be grown in groups of three. In big gardens, plant in copses or under taller trees. It is a good street tree.

THE DRAGON-CLAW WILLOW, bizarre or beautiful, according to your taste.

DRAGON-CLAW WILLOW

Salix babylonica var. *pekinensis* "Tortuosa"

DECIDUOUS

ORIGIN: The species is Chinese but the variety is of garden origin.
SIZE: Fast growing, upright willow 50 ft high with a spread of 28 ft.
FROST TOLERANCE: A very hardy tree tolerating –20°F.
APPEAL: The branches and branchlets are spirally twisted, giving a very bizarre appearance, especially striking when it has dropped its leaves. The leaves are also twisted. Yellow catkins are produced in the spring.
CLIMATE: Zone 5. Avoid shallow limestone soils and try to provide moisture. Plant in full sun.
USES: Needs to be grown in isolation to appreciate its habit of growth. Therefore grow it alone on the lawn. It can also be grown in a container on a patio which will restrict its size.

ENGLISH HOLLY

Ilex aquifolium "Bacciflava"

EVERGREEN

ORIGIN: This is a garden variety, but the species is native to southern and western Europe, North Africa and western Asia.
SIZE: Forms a broad, dense, pyramid-shaped tree to 50 ft spreading 14 ft.
FROST TOLERANCE: Zone 7. Needs a moderate climate where minimum temperature is 0°F.
APPEAL: The yellow berries of "Bacciflava" are a welcome change from the more common red. A female needs a male plant nearby to ensure good crops of berries. There are many other equally good varieties of *Ilex aquifolium*.
CLIMATE: Zone 7 or above. Can be grown equally well in full sun or partial shade. Protect plants from wind in northern regions.
USES: Excellent in a woodland garden, shrub border or as an imposing lawn specimen. It will also make a good hedge or windbreak.

THIS YELLOW-BERRIED English holly makes a welcome change from the red.

GOLDEN ROBINIA

Robinia pseudoacacia "Frisia"
DECIDUOUS

ORIGIN: North America.
SIZE: Grows about 32 ft tall with a spread of around 25 ft. Relatively fast growing in good conditions.
FROST TOLERANCE: Takes 20°F while leafless. Spring frosts, after leaves have appeared, may damage foliage.
APPEAL: Beautiful foliage tree. New spring growth is bright lime-green and fall color a rich butter yellow. Fragrant flowers appear in spring.
CLIMATE: It is well suited to zones 5 and above, and is widely planted in temperate regions.
USES: Grow it as a single street or garden tree or in a group with other deciduous trees for an fall show. Prune it to a single trunk when young and remove the lower branches as the tree grows. Digging around the roots will cause extensive suckering (trees coming up everywhere). This is not a tree for small gardens: don't plant it within 32 ft of a sewer line.

BRILLIANT, BUTTER-YELLOW leaves are a feature of the robinia in fall.

THE HAWTHORN is a fine specimen tree, with masses of spring flowers.

HAWTHORN

Crataegus laevigata, "Paul's Scarlet", syn. *Coccinea plena*
DECIDUOUS

ORIGIN: Of garden origin, although widely distributed in the wild from Europe and North Africa to India.
SIZE: A distinctive, rounded tree which is very thorny, attaining a height and spread of 28 ft.
FROST TOLERANCE: Extremely hardy tree tolerating temperatures as low as –20°F.
APPEAL: Grown mainly for deep pink, double flowers which are produced in profusion in late spring.
CLIMATE: Zone 5 and above. Sun and limestone soils are best. It also takes windy and exposed situations in its stride and is good for town, city and coastal gardens. It will thrive in full sun or partial shade.
USES: Grow it as a specimen tree in the lawn, or work it into the design of a mixed or shrub border. Could make part of a windbreak.

HOLM OAK

Quercus ilex

EVERGREEN

ORIGIN: Native to south-west Europe.
SIZE: A large, rounded tree, grows to 80 ft in height with a spread of 70 ft.
FROST TOLERANCE: Tolerates a minimum temperature of 10°F.
APPEAL: Grown for its overall appearance. Makes a really handsome tree when mature or semi-mature. The smooth bark is dark gray and the shiny leaves, of variable shape, are very dark green with whitish, woolly undersides. As with other oaks, it produces acorns in the fall.
CLIMATE: Best attempted only in southern and warmer parts of the country, zone 8 or above.
USES: In mild regions and coastal areas it makes a very good windbreak. Otherwise grow it as a lawn specimen, provided the garden is large enough to take it. It can also be grown as a striking, formal hedge.

THE HOLM OAK, shown in bloom, can be grown as a tree or a hedge.

THE HONEY LOCUST is ideal for creating a light airy effect.

HONEY LOCUST

Gleditsia triacanthos

DECIDUOUS

ORIGIN: Central and eastern North America.
SIZE: The honey locust is a fast-growing tree reaching 100 ft and has a broad cone-shaped habit of growth, about 70 ft wide.
FROST TOLERANCE: The honey locust is fully hardy, taking temperatures down to 5°F, although as a young tree it may suffer from some frost damage to the young or new growth but it will recover from this.
APPEAL: This large tree is grown for its airy mid-green pinnate foliage which takes on yellow-colored tints in the fall. The trunk and branches are spiny.
CLIMATE: Suitable for zones 7 and above. Choose a position in full sun for the best growth.
USES: The honey locust is essentially a specimen tree and therefore should be grown in isolation—it could be a feature on a lawn, for example.

HUBEI ROWAN

Sorbus hupehensis

DECIDUOUS

ORIGIN: China (Hubei).
SIZE: A small tree suited to limited space, attaining about 28 ft in height and spread.
FROST TOLERANCE: A hardy tree, withstanding temperatures down to 5°F.
APPEAL: Grown mainly for its crops of white, pink-flushed berries which ripen in the fall and are generally left alone by birds. It is a good all-round tree, though, with attractive bluish-green pinnate leaves coloring red in fall before they drop, and heads of white flowers in spring.
CLIMATE: Zone 7 and above. Best results are achieved in acid to neutral soil. Ideally grow in full sun although it will thrive in light or partial shade. Good for town gardens.
USES: Grow as a specimen tree in the lawn, include it in the mixed or shrub border, or plant it on the edge of a woodland garden. The berries show up best against a dark background.

THE BERRIES of this small-growing sorbus are generally left alone by birds.

WITH THE Irish strawberry tree you get colorful fruits and pretty flowers together.

IRISH STRAWBERRY TREE

Arbutus unedo

EVERGREEN

ORIGIN: Southern Europe, Ireland.
SIZE: Grows 25–28 ft tall with a dense, rounded crown of dark green, leathery leaves. Slow to moderate growth rate.
FROST TOLERANCE: Takes 14°F and survives even lower temperatures with damage.
APPEAL: It has dark good looks with clusters of small, white, lantern-shaped flowers and red, strawberry-like fruits in fall. The stringy bark is an attractive reddish color and birds are drawn to the fruits. Neighboring trees produce more fruit than does a tree planted as a single specimen.
CLIMATE: Suited to zone 8 and above. This tree will take coastal exposure in mild areas. Grow under glass in pots in the north.
USES: This is a good shade and shelter tree of a size suitable for smaller gardens. It can be grown as a broad hedge or used as a windbreak.

THIS ALDER can either be an ornamental tree or an effective windbreak.

ITALIAN ALDER

Alnus cordata

DECIDUOUS

ORIGIN: Southern Italy, Corsica.
SIZE: A fast-growing, large, conical tree 80 ft in height with a spread of 20 ft, making it a suitable choice for the larger garden.
FROST TOLERANCE: It is a hardy tree, tolerating temperatures down to 5°F or lower.
APPEAL: This alder is grown mainly for its deep green glossy leaves and 3 in long yellowish-brown catkins which appear before the leaves in spring.
CLIMATE: Zone 6 and above. Alders like moist soil but even so it must be well drained and not lie wet. However, this species will also tolerate poor, dry soils. Provide a position in full sun for best results.
USES: This alder looks good planted near water such as a pool or stream, but this is not essential. It also makes an attractive lawn specimen in the larger garden and is ideal for creating a windbreak.

JAPANESE CRAB APPLE

Malus tschonoskii

DECIDUOUS

ORIGIN: Japan.
SIZE: It is an ideal tree for the average-sized garden as it has an upright rather than a spreading habit, reaching a height of 42 ft with a spread of 22 ft.
FROST TOLERANCE: It is hardy, taking temperatures as low as 5°F.
APPEAL: The main attraction of this ornamental cherry is the display of foliage tints in the fall—the leaves turn to fiery shades before they fall. In spring it has attractive white flowers flushed with pale pink.
CLIMATE: Suitable for zone 7 and above. This is an amenable tree, growing best in full sun although partial shade is tolerated.
USES: Grow it as a specimen tree, ideally with a dark background such as provided by a group of conifers with deep green foliage.

THIS JAPANESE crab apple is one of the best small trees for fall foliage color.

JAPANESE FLOWERING CHERRY

Prunus x yedoensis

DECIDUOUS

ORIGIN: Japan but is of garden origin, not known in the wild.
SIZE: A medium-sized, fast-growing tree growing to about 50 ft with a spread of 33 ft. Relatively short lived.
FROST TOLERANCE: It is hardy, taking temperatures as low as 5°F.
APPEAL: This is considered to be one of the finest flowering cherries and its appeal lies in the mass of pale pink single flowers that is produced in the arching branches in early spring before the foliage appears. The blossoms age to almost white before they fall.
CLIMATE: Zone 6 and above. For best growth and flowering grow in full sun.
USES: This is a fine specimen tree for the lawn. Try to provide a dark background so that the flowers show up well.

THE JAPANESE flowering cherry produces its blossoms early in the spring.

JAPANESE MAPLES will glow in fall when grown in cool, humid climates.

JAPANESE MAPLE

Acer palmatum

DECIDUOUS

ORIGIN: Korea, Japan.
SIZE: Grows to 25 ft, often less, with a similar spread. There are dwarf forms, too.
FROST TOLERANCE: Accepts –12°F at least.
APPEAL: The leaves of the Japanese maple are fresh, bright green in spring, turning deep reds and golds in fall. There are dozens of leaf shapes, colors and patterns.
CLIMATE: The Japanese maple is suited to zone 5 and above. Avoid hot dry climates as it likes cooler moist conditions. Fall color is most impressive only where nights are chilly and the plant grows in sun.
USES: It is suitable to grow in small gardens and can be pruned to a compact, artistic shape. It makes a good shade tree and is pretty in groups. Dwarf forms are lovely in pots.

JUDAS TREE

Cercis siliquastrum

DECIDUOUS

ORIGIN: Eastern Mediterranean and the Middle East.
SIZE: Reaches 25–38 ft with a rounded, relatively open crown of irregular shape.
FROST TOLERANCE: Takes –4°F at least, lower if sheltered.
APPEAL: Dark rosy-purple or, more rarely, white blossoms cover the tree in early spring with or before the new leaves. In drier climates, where fall nights are cold, foliage turns bright yellow before dropping.
CLIMATE: Suitable for zone 7 and above, it relishes a Mediterranean climate. Cool, drizzly summers usually reduce flower production in the following year.
USES: Plant it as a street tree or lawn specimen, or combine it with other early spring bloomers such as crab apples and flowering cherries.

THIS VERY IMPRESSIVE tree is said to be the one on which Judas met his end.

SPRING AND FALL color in abundance are provided by this versatile small tree.

JUNEBERRY

Amelanchier lamarckii

DECIDUOUS

ORIGIN: Unknown but it has naturalized extensively over Europe.
SIZE: A small tree with a rather upright habit of growth, it reaches a height of 33 ft with a spread of 42 ft.
FROST TOLERANCE: It is extremely hardy and will withstand temperatures as low as –31°F.
APPEAL: The appeal is the showy white blossom in spring and the leaf tints in fall—the foliage turns to brilliant fiery shades before it falls. There are various other similar species grown, many native to the USA. This species is often confused with some of them, including *A. canadensis* and *A. laevis*.
CLIMATE: Zone 4 and above. Amelanchiers generally must have acid or lime-free soil but will be happy in full sun or partial shade.
USES: A good tree for a woodland garden or in a mixed or shrub border. Underplant with colchicums (fall "crocuses") for a pleasing fall picture.

COLD WINTERS are essential for the golden laburnum to be this spectacular.

LABURNUM

Laburnum anagyroides

DECIDUOUS

ORIGIN: Central and southern Europe.
SIZE: This slender, short-trunked tree grows moderately fast into a vase-shaped small tree 19–25 ft tall.
FROST TOLERANCE: Takes –4°C.
APPEAL: In spring it has masses of golden yellow flowers dripping from the plant in long, pendulous bunches similar to those of related wisterias.
CLIMATE: Zone 6 or the coldest parts of zone 5. Needs a cool to cold climate with plenty of rain. Does not do well in frost-free areas.
USES: Laburnum is a striking single specimen tree and very effective in odd-numbered groups. Pliable branches can be trained over metal arches to create a spectacular tunnel of golden flowers, or it can be espaliered against a wall.

LIQUIDAMBAR

Liquidambar styraciflua

DECIDUOUS

ORIGIN: Eastern United States from Maine to the Mexican border.
SIZE: Growing 64–96 ft tall and 19–25 ft wide at the base of its foliage canopy, it usually develops a straight trunk and a pyramidal outline.
FROST TOLERANCE: Tolerates lows of –20°F.
APPEAL: The liquidambar has a pleasing shape and a spectacular fall foliage display. In frost-free areas, the fall display varies from tree to tree and is not usually as striking as in cooler districts.
CLIMATE: Grows well in zones 5 and above. Its native climate is rainy and fairly humid year-round. The liquidambar needs a plentiful supply of water in the spring and summer and it will not tolerate drought conditions.
USES: Makes a lovely specimen but leaf and seed litter must be raked from lawns regularly. Suits large gardens; don't plant within 48 ft of sewer pipes.

GIVE THE stately liquidambar plenty of space and don't plant it near sewer lines.

MAGNOLIA

Magnolia x soulangiana

DECIDUOUS

ORIGIN: Hybrid of Chinese parents.
SIZE: Reaches 19–25 ft tall with a spread of 16 ft.
FROST TOLERANCE: Takes −20°F, especially if well sheltered from freezing winds.
APPEAL: The magnolia is grown for its magnificent display of big, fleshy, goblet-shaped flowers which appear on bare branches in middle to late winter. The flowers are white inside but various shades of purple outside.
CLIMATE: Zones 5 and 9 are suitable. The magnolia tree is hardy in the north of the country and is very common in cultivation.
USES: A spectacular lawn specimen or good, small courtyard tree, this magnolia can also be grown in a large tub. Protection from wind is essential or the flowers will be blown away.

MAGNOLIA FLOWERS bring color and beauty to the midwinter garden.

FOSSIL LEAVES of the maidenhair tree date back to the time of the dinosaurs.

MAIDENHAIR TREE

Ginkgo biloba

DECIDUOUS

ORIGIN: China.
SIZE: This is a narrow, erect tree 48–80 ft tall with a spread of around 22 ft. Slow growing.
FROST TOLERANCE: Accepts −13°F at least.
APPEAL: This tree is a relic from the dinosaur age and quite primitive in the world of trees. As such it has curiosity value but it is also attractive in itself. Its leaves, like those of a maidenhair fern, open a soft lime-green in spring and turn a rich buttery yellow before dropping in fall.
CLIMATE: It is hardy throughout zone 5 and above. The ginkgo loves a long, hot summer but also needs regular rain or water then. Extended hot, dry times will dry out the leaves.
USES: A good city tree as it tolerates air pollution well but its ultimate size makes it an unwise choice for very small gardens. It is a lovely specimen tree and is ideal in a woodland grouping of deciduous trees such as nyssa, liriodendron and liquidambar.

THE YELLOW Monterey cypress will brighten up a garden in mild regions.

MONTEREY CYPRESS

Cupressus macrocarpa "Golden Pillar"

EVERGREEN

ORIGIN: The species is native to Monterey County, California.
SIZE: This coniferous tree forms a narrow cone shape or column to a height of 16 ft or more, with a spread of about 16 ft.
FROST TOLERANCE: The Monterey cypress is recommended only for mild climates, with a minimum temperature of 10°F.
APPEAL: "Golden Pillar" is one of several varieties of Monterey cypress. It is very distinctive with its yellow leaves and shoots which impart a sunny atmosphere to any garden.
CLIMATE: Zone 8. To obtain the best color grow this variety in a position that receives sun for most of the day. Provide shelter from cold winds.
USES: This conifer makes a fine focal point in the garden and is generally grown in the lawn. A pair of these conifers could be used to flank an entrance to a driveway.

MOUNTAIN PINE

Pinus mugo

EVERGREEN

ORIGIN: Central and south-eastern Europe.
SIZE: Slow growing, its size varies from a stunted, tree-like shrub to a tree 80 ft tall. Poor, rocky soil and exposure to cold winds stunt it.
FROST TOLERANCE: Very hardy. Will accept –40°F and freezing winds.
APPEAL: Grown for its dark green, fairly dense foliage. With age, may develop a twisted, windblown shape of great character.
CLIMATE: It can be grown in zone 3 as well as higher zones. It grows well in coastal or windy regions.
USES: It is a good privacy screen or part of a windbreak and looks good by big ponds. It can be trained to shape and is an excellent bonsai subject. It must have full sun all day or growth will be poor.

BENT AND WINDBLOWN, mountain pine is a good choice for cold, exposed gardens.

ORNAMENTAL PEARS are not often considered for gardens but are fine trees.

ORNAMENTAL PEAR

Pyrus calleryana

DECIDUOUS

ORIGIN: China.
SIZE: It is a conical tree attaining about 50 ft in height and spread.
FROST TOLERANCE: This is a very hardy tree which will take temperatures down to –9°F.
APPEAL: Ornamental pears are not often planted in the garden, yet they are fine, handsome trees and well worth considering. Their main attraction is the handsome foliage, which turns red in the fall before it drops. The spring flowers are white followed by round brown fruits which are not very decorative.
CLIMATE: Zone 6 and above. Choose a site that receives full sun for best results.
USES: A good tree for town gardens and resistant to fireblight. It makes a fine specimen tree for the lawn but could also be grown in a shrub or mixed border.

PAPER-BARK MAPLE

Acer griseum

DECIDUOUS

ORIGIN: Central China.
SIZE: A smallish ornamental tree at around 33 ft in height and spread. Its slow growth rate makes it ideal for the smaller garden.
FROST TOLERANCE: It is a hardy tree, tolerating temperatures down to at least 5°F.
APPEAL: Its unusual and attractive bark is bright orange-brown and peels off in strips. In the fall the lobed leaves take on fiery tints before they fall. It is most conspicuous in winter once the leaves have fallen.
CLIMATE: Zone 6 and above. Grows well in any reasonable fertile, moisture retentive yet well-drained soil in full sun or partial shade.
USES: Good in a large container, it also makes a fine lawn tree. Include it in a shrub or mixed border but make sure the trunk is not hidden.

THE PEELING BARK of this maple makes it a fine subject for the winter garden.

PENCIL PINES make an ideal accessory for a Mediterranean-style house and garden.

PENCIL PINE

Cupressus sempervirens "Stricta"

EVERGREEN

ORIGIN: Greek and Mediterranean islands, Turkey and Iran.
SIZE: Grows 32–64 ft tall with a very narrow, columnar habit.
FROST TOLERANCE: Accepts 14°F and possibly a little lower.
APPEAL: Pencil pine is grown for its formal, vertical shape and very dark green foliage. The nuts may attract seed-eating birds.
CLIMATE: Grows best in zone 8 and above. It is not well suited to and can be short lived in humid, rainy places. A Mediterranean climate is the ideal.
USES: Use it as a vertical accent tree, in avenues in formal gardens, in windbreaks or boundary plantings. It is ideal where space is restricted or where a Tuscan look is wanted. Scattered specimens look good and very Italian on dry hillsides.

PIN OAK

Quercus palustris

DECIDUOUS

ORIGIN: Forests of the eastern United States and Canada.
SIZE: Grows 64–112 ft tall into a pyramidal tree with low branches and dense foliage. Relatively fast growing.
FROST TOLERANCE: Accepts –12°F at least.
APPEAL: It has brilliant red fall foliage and an attractive shape.
CLIMATE: Tolerates town and city conditions and indeed is often planted as a street tree. It is happy in zone 5 and above and enjoys a warm or hot summer but needs a cool to cold winter. The foliage will not color well unless fall nights are chilly.
USES: This is a fine specimen tree, especially in bigger gardens, and is good in copses where space permits. Grow it with maples and other deciduous trees for a brilliant fall display. After coloring, the leaves hang on the tree through winter, dropping when new leaves appear.

COOL SUMMER SHADE, brilliant fall color: the pin oak gives plenty of both.

PITTOSPORUM

Pittosporum species

EVERGREEN

ORIGIN: Asia, Australia, New Zealand, South Africa and Hawaii.
SIZE: 16–80 ft. *P. tenuifolium* is one of the tallest although in gardens it is often less than 30 ft high, and half as wide. Fast growing when young.
FROST TOLERANCE: Species vary from frost hardy to frost tender. The species shown is frost hardy down to 23°F. Give young trees overhead protection from frosts in their first winter.
APPEAL: Some species are grown for their leaves and habit, others for their fragrant flowers. *P. tenuifolium* has glossy foliage and black twigs.
CLIMATE: Mostly zone 9. Grow the species shown in zone 8 in a sheltered spot with full sun or partial shade.
USES: A good plant for a lawn or border. In mild coastal areas use as a good screen or hedge.

THE FLOWERS of Pittosporum tenuifolium *are honey-scented.*

GOOD SCREENING and windbreak trees, Port Jackson pines have an Italian look.

PORT JACKSON PINE

Callitris rhomboidea

EVERGREEN

ORIGIN: Eastern and southern Australia.
SIZE: Grows 16–25 ft tall with a narrow, upright habit perhaps 6 ft wide. Fairly fast growing.
FROST TOLERANCE: Accepts 23°F with ease and may take rare extremes as low as 10°F if it is not exposed to freezing winds.
APPEAL: It has a formal-looking, columnar habit with dense foliage from the ground up. The seed pods attract seed-eating birds.
CLIMATE: It is useful in the arid regions of zone 10, but nevertheless should ideally be watered well. Will also survive in zone 9.
USES: It is an ideal hedge, privacy screen or windbreak. Its columnar habit can give the garden a formal look and the tree is a good choice for lining drives or defining entrances. It is a top tree for the coast.

ROWAN, MOUNTAIN ASH

Sorbus aucuparia

DECIDUOUS

ORIGIN: Europe and Asia.
SIZE: This tree grows to a height of 50 ft and has a spread of about 22 ft.
FROST TOLERANCE: A very hardy tree, tolerating a temperature at least as low as 5°F.
APPEAL: Grown mainly for its crops of orange-red berries in the fall which, unfortunately, may be taken by birds. In spring the white flowers are also attractive, and the pinnate foliage turns red or yellow in fall before it drops. There are several cultivars with variously colored berries.
CLIMATE: Can be grown in a zone as low as 2. Best results in acid to neutral soil. Ideally grow in full sun although it will thrive in light or partial shade. Good for town gardens.
USES: Generally grown as a specimen tree in a lawn, but looks good also in a mixed or shrub border, ideally associated with fall-interest plants.

THE ROWAN is a good fall-berrying tree, provided the birds leave the fruits alone.

THE SARGENT CHERRY is grown mainly for its fiery fall foliage color.

SARGENT CHERRY

Prunus sargentii

DECIDUOUS

ORIGIN: Russia, Japan and Korea.
SIZE: A fairly large tree at 70 ft in height with a spread of 50 ft, it would be suited to the medium-sized garden.
FROST TOLERANCE: The Sargent cherry is fully hardy, taking a temperature at least as low as 5°F.
APPEAL: This is one of the finest ornamental trees for fall leaf color. Before they fall, the leaves turn bright orange-red and really glow when the fall sun shines on them. In the spring it produces attractive light pink flowers followed by deep red cherry-like fruits.
CLIMATE: Zone 5 and above. Very intolerant of smog. This cherry is best grown in full sun.
USES: This is a specimen tree. Ideally plant it in a lawn, or include it in a mixed border with shrubs and hardy perennials. Ideally a dark background is needed for the fall tints to show to advantage.

SIBERIAN CRAB APPLE

Malus baccata

DECIDUOUS

ORIGIN: Eastern Asia.
SIZE: This vigorous tree develops a rounded habit and will reach a height and spread of 50 ft.
FROST TOLERANCE: The Siberian crab apple is very hardy and will take temperatures as low as 5°F and below.
APPEAL: This is considered to be one of the best ornamental fruiting trees for gardens, as it produces huge crops of red or yellow crab apples in the fall and they generally persist into winter. White flowers are produced in the spring and are quite attractive.
CLIMATE: An extremely hardy tree surviving in zone 2, and up to zone 9. Best growth and fruiting in full sun though partial shade is tolerated.
USES: Essentially a specimen tree, for example in a lawn. Also makes a good addition to the mixed border, particularly when associated with fall-interest shrubs.

THIS CRAB APPLE produces heavy, long-lasting crops of ornamental fruits.

THE WHITE TRUNKS of the silver birch look best planted in groups.

SILVER BIRCH

Betula pendula

DECIDUOUS

ORIGIN: Europe and western Asia.
SIZE: Reaches 70–100 ft as a tall, narrow, open tree.
FROST TOLERANCE: Accepts –40°F.
APPEAL: Silver birch has a graceful shape and open foliage. Its silver trunk brings brightness to the winter garden. Its characteristic, peeling, curling white bark is particularly attractive when the tree is bare during the winter months.
CLIMATE: Can be grown in zones as low as 2. Also happy in higher zones, up to zone 8. However, it needs a cold and frosty winter to do well.
USES: In small gardens, plant as feature trees or in a triangular group of three, 5 ft apart. Close planting may help keep these trees to a suitable height. They make a good screen against much taller buildings. In bigger gardens, plant them in avenues or use them as view framers.

THE UNUSUAL snake-like bark makes this maple one of the most distinctive species.

SNAKE-BARK MAPLE

Acer davidii

DECIDUOUS

ORIGIN: A native of China.
SIZE: A spreading tree, around 50 ft in height and width.
FROST TOLERANCE: It is a hardy tree, accepting down to 5°F or below.
APPEAL: Unusual bark is its main attraction, resembling the skin of a snake. The bark is green, striped with white. In the fall the lobed leaves take on orange and yellow tints before they drop.
CLIMATE: Zone 6 and above. Grows well in any reasonably fertile, moisture retentive yet well-drained soil, in full sun or partial shade.
USES: Looks good in a shrub or mixed border with winter-interest shrubs such as witch hazel, *Hamamelis* x *intermedia*. Often grown as a lawn specimen or in a woodland garden, it can also be grown in a large container but this will restrict its size.

SOUR GUM

Nyssa sylvatica

DECIDUOUS

ORIGIN: Eastern North America, in moist, humid places.
SIZE: Grows 70–100 ft tall in woods, usually much less in open situations.
FROST TOLERANCE: Takes 5°F at least.
APPEAL: It has an attractive habit with layered, horizontal branches. In the fall the leaves turn a brilliant, glossy scarlet before falling.
CLIMATE: Grows best in zone 7 and above. Fall foliage color will always be disappointing unless fall nights are chilly.
USES: Tolerates shade, and so is a good addition to woodland gardens. It is lovely near water and makes a nice partner for other fall foliage trees, such as the maidenhair tree or the maples. It can be used alone but looks better with other deciduous trees.

THE SOUR GUM is a beautiful, water-loving tree but needs cold to color well.

THE EARLIEST of the flowering cherries to bloom, this grows well in warm areas.

TAIWAN CHERRY

Prunus campanulata

DECIDUOUS

ORIGIN: Taiwan and islands of Japan.
SIZE: Reaches 20–28 ft tall with a spread of 15–16 ft.
FROST TOLERANCE: Tolerates 14°F but does better where winter lows remain above 23°F.
APPEAL: It has a compact, upright habit and a generous display of pinky-red flowers. These appear on bare branches around the middle of winter in frost-free areas, a little later in cooler climates. Where fall nights are cold enough, the Taiwan cherry gives a remarkable fall display.
CLIMATE: Zones 8 and 9. It needs cool nights in the fall for the foliage to color well. In hot and dry areas extra summer water and shelter from hot winds will be needed.
USES: The Taiwan cherry is a lovely lawn specimen and grows well in big tubs on sunny patios. It is a good avenue tree for formal gardens or for lining long drives. It is also a good street tree.

TREE OF HEAVEN

Ailanthus altissima

DECIDUOUS

ORIGIN: Western China.
SIZE: A fast growing, wide-spreading tree reaching 80 ft in height and a spread of 50 ft.
FROST TOLERANCE: A very hardy tree that has become naturalized in most of North America except the extreme north. It takes a temperature as low as –31°F.
APPEAL: Grown mainly for its bold pinnate foliage. In summer it bears green flowers and these are followed by reddish-brown winged fruits. Male and female plants needed for fruits.
CLIMATE: Suitable for zone 4 and above. It makes a good town and city tree as it resists smog. Also, it is not troubled by pests and diseases. Grow it in sun or partial shade. A hot summer is needed for best flowering and fruiting.
USES: Widely planted as a garden and street tree. It makes a particularly good lawn specimen. It can be grown as a shrub by annual hard pruning.

THE TREE OF HEAVEN can be grown as a shrub if space is limited.

USE THIS WHITEBEAM if a light-colored effect is needed in the garden.

WHITEBEAM

Sorbus aria "Lutescens"

DECIDUOUS

ORIGIN: The species is a native of Europe.
SIZE: This is a fairly compact tree, reaching a height of 33 ft with a spread of about 28 ft.
FROST TOLERANCE: It is very hardy, accepting as little as 5°F.
APPEAL: Grown mainly for its large, oval leaves which are silvery gray in color but later change to gray-green. In the spring the tree produces heads of white flowers which are followed by deep red fruits.
CLIMATE: Zone 6 and above. This sorbus is especially good for dry, chalky soil and will also grow in acid conditions. Best growth is achieved in full sun but it can be grown in light or partial shade. Good for town gardens as it tolerates a polluted atmosphere.
USES: Primarily grown as a specimen tree, for example on a lawn. Also grown in woodland gardens.

YULAN

Magnolia denudata

DECIDUOUS

ORIGIN: Southern China.
SIZE: Grows to around 35 ft tall with a rounded crown about 22 ft wide. Moderate growth rate.
FROST TOLERANCE: Takes –4°F but likes some shelter.
APPEAL: There is a magnificent floral display in late winter when big, white, tulip-shaped flowers appear on bare branches. They have a sweet, citrus-like fragrance.
CLIMATE: Zones 6 to 9 suit this magnolia well. It likes regular rainfall, especially during spring and summer, and deep, moist soils that contain plenty of rotted organic matter. Shelter from wind is essential during flowering. It is not suitable for exposed coastal gardens.
USES: Yulan is mostly seen as a lawn specimen where its rounded shape and gorgeous flowers can be fully appreciated. It is a good small shade tree for courtyards.

THE FLOWERS of the yulan are big and waxy and emit a glorious citrusy perfume.

• CHAPTER FOURTEEN •

PALMS

Never too big for even the smallest yard, palms bring a tropical ambience to the garden and are ideal for shelter or privacy screens. They are widely used indoors in both warm and cold regions and many can be grown in pots for years.

Palms are classified by their trunks and their fronds. Trunks may be single (solitary) or numerous (clumping) and fronds may be fan- or feather-shaped. Among the oddities in the palm world are some with underground trunks, some that climb and a very few with a branching habit.

Most young palms like a shaded or semi-shaded aspect. In their natural habitat, young plants grow up beneath the shelter of mature palms. Most adult palms have at least their heads in the sun and many grow well in quite open positions, but it is best to provide shade for seedlings and very young plants.

SOIL AND PLANTING

Most palms prefer a well-drained soil that contains plenty of organic matter and, generally, the better the soil, the better the results. Sandy soils should be improved by the addition of decayed manure or compost several weeks before planting and the planted palms should always be well mulched. Heavy clay soils can be made more friable with the addition of gypsum at a rate of about 9 oz per square yard and copious amounts of organic matter. Sometimes it may be better to plant the palm on a mound so that there is no danger of creating a water-holding well or sump in the clay.

Potted palms can be planted out at almost any time of year but in cooler areas it is best to avoid planting in winter as there will be little or no root growth until the soil warms and the days lengthen. Dig a good wide hole, about three times as wide as the top of the pot. Thoroughly water the palm in its pot an hour or two before planting. If you have improved the soil with organic matter ahead of time you can simply remove the plant from its pot and position it in the hole. Backfill the hole and firm the soil around the plant so that the finished level is the same as it was in the pot. Give the area a good watering, and then mulch around the base. You can add slow-release fertilizer or blood and bone to the base of the hole before planting but be sure to cover it with soil so that the roots do not come into contact with the fertilizer.

WATERING AND FEEDING

Once established, many palms are very drought tolerant but all will do and look better if given regular, deep soakings during dry periods in the warmer months. Keeping the root zone well mulched will retain soil moisture and improve growing conditions around the roots.

Palms like to be fertilized during the warm months of the year when they are actively growing. Make sure the soil is well watered before applying fertilizer. You can use any complete plant food, blood and bone, rotted manure, slow-release or soluble or liquid fertilizer. Apply the fertilizer to the root area under the canopy of the palm and then water well again.

PRUNING

Palms cannot be reduced in size by pruning. They die if the top is removed and often recover only slowly if green leaves are cut from them. When the lower fronds die, some palms shed them and others retain them, but either way you can remove the fronds once they have gone quite yellow.

IN REGIONS UNSUITABLE for growing palms outside, consider growing them in containers in a conservatory. They could be stood outside for the summer.

PROPAGATION

Clumping palms can be propagated by cutting off a suckering growth so long as it has already formed its own roots. Cut it from the clump using a sharp knife or spade and replant or pot it up at once. Keep the new division in a very sheltered, shaded situation until you can see it is thriving. This method of propagation often fails, usually because the sucker has too few roots, but it is worth a try if the original clump is well developed.

Palms are also grown from seed, which should be sown as fresh as possible. Fruit ripeness is generally indicated by color change or the dropping of ripened fruits. Remove the fleshy exterior of the fruit, a process that will be easier if you place the moistened fruit in a plastic bag, seal it and keep it in a warm place out of sunlight. After a week or two the outer pulp comes off easily.

Seeds are best sown in small pots of seed-raising mix. Sow them at a depth twice the diameter of the seed. Water carefully and cover the container with a sheet of glass or enclose it in a plastic bag. Place it in a warm, light place but not in direct sun. It is important to keep the seeds moist at all times, but not wet. Inside a plastic bag they may not need watering for a long time but should be checked often. Palm seeds need high temperature and high humidity to germinate and these conditions are not easy to achieve outside tropical regions. Some palms, such as kentias, have very erratic germination and may take anywhere from six months to two years to germinate, while others may germinate within six to eight weeks. Once the seeds have sprouted they should be transferred into individual pots as soon as possible.

ALEXANDRA PALM

Archontophoenix alexandrae

SOLITARY, FEATHER-LEAVED

ORIGIN: Coastal areas of Queensland from sea level to over 3,500 ft.
SIZE: Grows 50–70 ft high in tropical gardens, elsewhere it may not exceed 35-42 ft. Fast growing.
APPEAL: It is long lived and attractive, especially in flower or fruit. Trunks are ringed and new foliage has a bronzy cast. A very elegant palm.
CLIMATE: Zone 10 only and needs plenty of summer water. Also recommended is the related Bangalow palm (*A. cunninghamiana*) which is also suited only to zone 10.
ASPECT: Young plants need shade but like to grow into the sun.
GARDEN USES: It looks lovely grown in odd-numbered groups or in formal avenues. For a screen or dense shade, underplant alexandras with the lower growing kentia palm for a two-tiered canopy.
INDOORS: Grow in a conservatory.

ALEXANDRA PALMS have ringed trunks and an elegant, self-cleaning crown.

SLENDER AND ELEGANT, bamboo palm grows in pots or in the ground in shade.

BAMBOO PALM

Chamaedorea seifritzii

CLUMPING, FEATHER-LEAVED

ORIGIN: Mexico.
SIZE: Usually 7–10 ft tall but can grow up to 14 ft in ideal conditions. Clumps spread slowly to less than 4 ft across at the base. Moderate growth rate.
APPEAL: The elegant, slender trunks are lightly foliaged with short, glossy green fronds and a pleasing, clumping habit. A very appealing small palm.
CLIMATE: Zone 10. It can take more sun than most other species of chamaedorea. Keep it moist and humid in the summer.
ASPECT: Best in bright shade or dappled sun. Plants bleach in sun and may be attacked by two-spotted mites.
GARDEN USES: This is a good screening or enclosure palm and ideal for narrow spaces such as the gap between houses. It is also a good understorey plant in shady, rainforest-style gardens and makes a beautiful tubbed specimen for patios or decks.
INDOORS: Good indoors but needs a very bright room.

SMALL SPECIMENS of the Burmese fishtail palm make excellent houseplants.

BURMESE FISHTAIL PALM

Caryota mitis

CLUMPING, FEATHER-LEAVED

ORIGIN: Burma to Malaysian Peninsula, Indonesia and the Philippines.

SIZE: Grows 10–40 ft tall.

APPEAL: This is a particularly distinctive palm. It has clusters of stems and large deep green pinnate leaves. The individual leaflets resemble fish tails in shape, hence the popular name. Mature or well-established plants produce cream flowers in summer.

CLIMATE: Must be frost free: zone 10. This palm is suitable for growing outdoors all the year round only in the warmest parts of the USA. The Burmese fishtail palm is particularly well suited to Florida.

ASPECT: Outdoors this palm likes a bright open position; however, it appreciates shade during the hottest part of the day.

GARDEN USES: The fishtail palm is much planted in the tropics. It makes a good and distinctive specimen tree and also looks good in containers on a patio or decking area.

INDOORS: When grown in a conservatory or glasshouse provide bright light, but shade from direct sun, and high humidity.

CABBAGE TREE PALM

Livistona australis

SOLITARY, FAN-LEAVED

ORIGIN: Coast of eastern Australia from southern Queensland to southern New South Wales, with some isolated colonies in Victoria.

SIZE: Can grow 100 ft high but usually only about half that in gardens. Slow to moderate growth rate.

APPEAL: Neat, globular crown of glossy, dark green fronds sits atop a smooth, gray trunk. This was a popular palm in various parts of the world in Victorian times and is still worth growing, especially in historic gardens.

CLIMATE: Zone 10. The related palm *L. mariae*, a native of Central Australia, accepts the odd 23°F when it is established and is therefore suited to zone 9.

ASPECT: Young plants prefer shade for their first few years but tolerate sun early if gradually introduced to it.

GARDEN USES: Attractive if used formally in rings or rows or included in a rainforest planting. Plants develop a broad crown before the trunk rises and the leaf stems are spiny.

INDOORS: Can be used indoors when young but needs bright light.

CABBAGE TREES ARE attractive fan-leaved palms that look lovely in groups.

EUROPEAN FAN PALM

Chamaerops humilis

SOLITARY OR CLUMPING, FAN-LEAVED

ORIGIN: Mediterranean region of Europe and North Africa.
SIZE: Grows to 10–20 ft, the clumping forms reaching the same width. Slow to moderate growth rate.
APPEAL: Its compact size, neat head of stiff, gray-green leaves and attractive, rough trunk make this a good feature palm. It is also among the most cold tolerant of all palms.
CLIMATE: Zone 9. Ideally suited to a Mediterranean-type climate.
ASPECT: Grows in full sun or semi-shade. Must have good soil drainage.
GARDEN USES: An excellent lawn specimen, but also very striking in big tubs. Its form is very variable, some varieties having shiny green fronds while others are more gray-green. The bases of the fronds are armed with very sharp spines.
INDOORS: Not suitable.

THE EUROPEAN fan palm is the palm for anyone who is normally incapable of growing palms.

GOLDEN CANE PALMS only keep their golden color where they can be grown in the sun. Old leaves are self-shedding.

GOLDEN CANE PALM

Chrysalidocarpus lutescens

CLUMPING, FEATHER-LEAVED

ORIGIN: Madagascar.
SIZE: Grows 16–30 ft tall, taller in tropical areas. Moderate to fast growth rate, fastest in the tropics.
APPEAL: A dense cluster of smooth, golden trunks are topped with long, arching fronds that are a glossy mid-green. Good size for smaller gardens.
CLIMATE: Widely grown outdoors in the tropics and subtropics. Zone 10. Will also thrive in the warmest parts of zone 9 provided there are no frosts, which it will not accept. This palm likes humidity and mild to warm winters. If necessary keep it sheltered from hot dry winds which will burn the fronds.
ASPECT: Some sun is essential or the golden color will disappear. Out of the tropics grow it in the warmest place, sheltered from cold winds.
GARDEN USES: This good screen or feature palm is very attractive by pools. Suitable for containers.
INDOORS: Lovely indoor palm but must have very bright conditions. Good in humid conservatories.

KENTIA PALM

Howea forsteriana

SOLITARY, FEATHER-LEAVED

ORIGIN: Lord Howe Island.
SIZE: Grows 28–35 ft tall with an elegant crown of drooping, dark green fronds. Slow growing.
APPEAL: Always popular, the kentia has a very attractive crown and a pleasing, ringed trunk that never grows too tall. It can be grown for many years in a large pot.
CLIMATE: It is grown outdoors in the warmer parts of zone 9, especially in California, and is also suited to zone 10. Widely grown in the tropics and subtropics. This palm likes summer humidity and shelter from hot winds. It can be especially recommended for planting near the coast.
ASPECT: Prefers shade when young but accepts sun after a few years.
GARDEN USES: Grow them as understorey palms or in a forest on their own. They make fine tubbed plants for patios or decks.
INDOORS: One of the best indoor plants, tolerates fairly dim conditions.

AN IDEAL CHOICE for the warm, non-tropical garden, kentias never grow so tall you are left with just trunks to look at.

LADY PALMS eventually form dense thickets ideal for privacy or shelter screens.

LADY PALM

Rhapis excelsa

CLUMPING, FAN-LEAVED

ORIGIN: Southern China.
SIZE: Reaches 5–10 ft tall, slowly spreading into dense clumps. Very slow growing.
APPEAL: Very elegant appearance with dark, glossy green leaves atop slender, hairy, black trunks.
CLIMATE: Zones 9 and 10. Has for long been grown as clumps or hedges in southern California and southern Florida. This palm likes humidity and rainy summers but not tropical heat. Accepts 27°F.
ASPECT: Dappled or full shade is essential. The lady palm bleaches badly in bright sun.
GARDEN USES: Makes a feature palm, especially in courtyards or narrow spaces, or use it as a privacy screen. It is an excellent long-term choice for big containers. When clumps become dense, they can be thinned for a pleasing, open, Japanese-style appearance.
INDOORS: A very attractive and desirable indoor palm which can tolerate fairly dim light for some time if the position is airy.

THE BEAUTIFUL BARK of the palmetto is formed by the remains of old leaf bases.

PALMETTO

Sabal palmetto

SOLITARY, FAN-LEAVED

ORIGIN: Central and southern east coast of the United States.
SIZE: Grows to 80 ft in its habitat but is usually smaller in gardens. Fast growing in good conditions.
APPEAL: Resistant to drought and cool temperatures, this palm has interesting, criss-cross bark and a neat foliage crown. An outstanding characteristic of the palmetto is the twisting of the large fan leaves on their sturdy stems.
CLIMATE: Zones 9 and 10. Likes to be kept well watered in the summer. Once established, this palm accepts 27°F at least if winter days are mild.
ASPECT: Tolerates both full sun or partial shade. It will also tolerate some exposure to salty wind.
GARDEN USES: An impressive lawn specimen and attractive in avenues or groups. The trunk is quite a feature. Palmettos prefer good drainage but tolerate permanently moist soil as long as it is not heavy or waterlogged.
INDOORS: Not suitable for indoor use. Needs full sun.

PARLOR PALM

Chamaedorea elegans

SOLITARY, FEATHER-LEAVED

ORIGIN: Mexico and Guatemala.
SIZE: Usually seen under 4 ft tall but in ideal conditions it may grow to twice that height. Moderate to fast growth rate.
APPEAL: Its small size, attractive appearance and shade tolerance make this a useful palm indoors or out.
CLIMATE: One of the most commonly cultivated palms, it is suited to zone 10. The parlor palm appreciates summer humidity and should be sheltered from hot winds.
ASPECT: Must have dappled or full shade. Leaves burn in hot sun.
GARDEN USES: This is a good groundcover for shady places, especially under taller palms, and is lovely beside shaded water features. Seedlings crowded together in a wide pot make an attractive patio feature.
INDOORS: One of the best indoor palms for bright, airy rooms.

LOW-GROWING parlor palms look good in pots or massed in shady areas.

PYGMY DATE PALM

Phoenix roebelenii

SOLITARY, FEATHER-LEAVED

ORIGIN: Tropical east Asia.
SIZE: Grows to 6–10 ft tall with a broad crown of arching leaves. Slow to moderate growth rate.
APPEAL: A slender, elegant palm with fine, dark green fronds and a textured trunk. Its compact size makes it very useful in small gardens.
CLIMATE: This palm can be grown outdoors in the warmer parts of zone 9, plus zone 10. Plenty of summer water, humidity and shelter from hot winds are important.
ASPECT: It will grow in sun or part or full shade. In sun, it needs plenty of water or leaves will bleach. Shelter from strong wind is desirable.
GARDEN USES: A fine lawn specimen, especially effective in groups of three, or use it beneath taller palms or under trees. It is fine in big tubs or by pools. The lower ends of the fronds are armed with long, very sharp spines.
INDOORS: This is a good indoor palm in a brightly lit, airy room, but beware of the spines.

USE THESE pygmy palms for fence height screening or grow them in groups.

THE HANDSOME wine palm is even more decorative when carrying its ripe red fruit.

WINE PALM

Butia capitata

SOLITARY, FEATHER-LEAVED

ORIGIN: Argentina, Brazil, Uruguay.
SIZE: Grows 16–20 ft tall with a big crown of arching, light gray fronds. Slow growing.
APPEAL: Very attractive, silvery-gray foliage on a short, stout trunk makes this an unusual and eye-catching palm either singly or in groups.
CLIMATE: A relatively hardy palm that will grow in sheltered sites in zone 8. Also suitable for zones 9 and 10. It accepts 19°F at least.
ASPECT: The wine palm does best in an open, sunny position.
GARDEN USES: Grow it as a lawn specimen or feature palm. It is attractive with other dry climate plants and can be grown in a pot for years.
INDOORS: Not suitable.

•CHAPTER FIFTEEN•

SHRUBS

A lovely garden can be created almost entirely from shrubs. They are the plants that give the garden form and definition and much of its color and texture, too. With careful planning you can have shrubs in flower every month of the year.

Shrubs are usually defined as perennial woody plants. They are frequently multi-stemmed but not always, and the line between tall shrubs and small trees is rather vague. Shrubs may be evergreen or deciduous and because they come in such a range of shapes and sizes there's one to suit every situation. When you are planning your garden, select shrubs to suit the particular position. Will the shrub thrive in full sun or does it prefer shade? Consider how high and wide it will grow. Don't buy a large-growing shrub for a small space thinking you will keep it pruned. You will get tired of pruning and end up removing it. Having the right plant in the right place makes for a low-work garden.

CHOOSING A SHRUB AT THE GARDEN CENTER

When buying shrubs, biggest is not always best. Look for plants that are well shaped and have a good cover of healthy leaves. Avoid shrubs that have woody roots protruding from the drainage holes, those that are too tall for the pot size and those that have knobbly, thickened bases to their stems. All these signal that the shrub is pot bound, which means its roots will be so tightly packed they may never spread out after planting. Sometimes you can tease out the roots of a pot-bound shrub before planting but some shrubs resent this and die. Better to buy a plant that's not pot bound.

SOIL PREPARATION

As most shrubs are long lived and form the permanent framework of the garden, it is worth putting some effort into soil preparation. Few shrubs tolerate heavy, waterlogged soil. If drainage is poor, consider raising the planting area or installing subsoil drains (see page 27). Heavy clay soils can be improved by the addition of gypsum (see page 25) at the rate of 7–10 oz per square yard and by working in large quantities of well-rotted organic material. Organic matter should be dug in well ahead of planting time, perhaps two or three weeks ahead in summer and six weeks or so in winter. Sandy soils with poor water and nutrient retention benefit greatly from the addition of large amounts of organic matter before planting. All plants and soils benefit from mulching. Organic mulches such as rotted animal manure, compost, leaves, straw or decayed grass clippings give the most benefit as they help form humus.

PLANTING CHECKLIST

- Container-grown shrubs can be planted out into the garden at almost any time of the year except in areas that experience very heavy frost in winter. There it is best to avoid planting anything other than dormant deciduous plants during winter.
- Check that the position you have chosen for your shrub suits its requirements in terms of sun or shade, shelter, drainage and area available for growth.
- Dig a hole at least twice as wide as the potted plant and about the same depth. Loosen soil in the bottom of the hole but don't dig down into a clay layer or you may create a well in which the plant roots will drown.
- Do not put compost or manure in the hole. Blood and bone or slow-release fertilizer may be sprinkled in the bottom of the hole but it must be covered by 1–2 in of soil so that the roots do not come into contact with it.
- Thoroughly water the plant in its pot, loosen by tapping the base and sides of the pot, and then slide the plant out gently.
- Place the plant in the hole so that the soil level is the same as it was in the container. Backfill the hole with soil you have dug out and firm soil in well, but don't compact the soil and crush the roots by stamping around.
- Water thoroughly again to eliminate air pockets and settle the soil around the roots.
- Mulch the area around the shrub but keep the mulch well clear of the stem.

MAINTENANCE

Keep newly planted shrubs moist but not soggy. When established, slowly decrease the frequency of watering. Some shrubs will go for two or three weeks without watering, depending on the soil and weather conditions, but those from cool, moist, rainy climates, such as azaleas or fuchsias, may always need watering more than once a week. If you look carefully at your plants, you will see the subtle changes in leaf color and gloss that occur before wilting point is reached. When you see these signs, it's time to give a deep soaking.

Wait four or six weeks after planting before you begin feeding the plants. Complete plant foods, blood and bone or pelleted poultry manure are suitable for most shrubs, but avoid using poultry manure for acid-loving plants such as azaleas, camellias, gardenias and daphnes. Some plants, especially South African and Australian shrubs such as grevilleas, are sensitive to fertilizers, particularly phosphorus. If you consider it necessary to feed these plants, choose a fertilizer that is low in phosphorus. The best bet, though, is to give them a permanent mulch of organic matter such as leafmould.

PRUNING

Pruning is not done as a matter of course and many shrubs will never need it unless it is to rejuvenate very old plants or to remove the odd wayward stem. However, if you want or need to prune, do so immediately after flowering. The only exception is for plants that are grown for their berries which form after the flowers, but these rarely need pruning. For more detailed information on pruning turn to page 63.

FEED AZALEAS after they bloom but never in fall or winter. Shear azaleas right after they bloom and again in late summer.

AZALEA

Rhododendron hybrids

EVERGREEN AND DECIDUOUS

TAKES SHADE

ORIGIN: Azaleas are derived from various species of rhododendron and are among the most widely hybridized plants on earth.

SIZE: Height varies with type from about 20 in to 8 ft tall with a similar spread. Slow to moderate growth rate.

FROST TOLERANCE: Its tolerance depends on type chosen. The deciduous Mollis azaleas need a cold winter and are only successful in zones where minimum temperatures range from 21°F to –9°F. Most of the evergreen azaleas will generally accept a temperature down to –9°F. It all depends on the breeding.

APPEAL: Grown for the glorious spring blooms, azaleas are definitely one of the world's most spectacular shrubs. They are easily shaped by shearing and look good that way.

CLIMATE: Azaleas love rainy, humid places where summers are not too hot. They are not a success in the tropics or hot subtropics, neither do they like places where summers are hot and dry. Zones 6 to 8 are ideal for them but any higher and they may not perform so well. Being shallow rooted, they need frequent rain or watering.

PRUNING: Immediately after azaleas have flowered pick off all the seed heads. Any over-long shoots can be cut back in order to maintain shapely plants.

ASPECT: Although there are azaleas sold as "sun hardy", generally they do better in bright shade or where they get shade from about late morning. Where summers are mild and conditions often cloudy, they will take more sun. Growing in the shade simulates their forest homelands. Raise local humidity by surrounding them with other shrubs and trees.

BARBERRY

Berberis wilsoniae

SEMI-EVERGREEN

ORIGIN: Western China.
SIZE: It reaches 3 ft in height and forms a very dense mound of growth.
FROST TOLERANCE: Takes a low of at least 5°F.
APPEAL: This is a very spiny shrub which carries pink fruits on its arching branches in the fall. These are preceded in the spring by pale yellow flowers. Another attraction is the fall foliage tint. The leaves turn to brilliant flame shades before they fall.
CLIMATE: Zone 6 and above. This berberis will thrive in northern states provided the climate is not too severe.
ASPECT: It performs best in full sun but good results are also possible in partial shade.
PRUNING: Prune lightly after flowering to maintain shape. Do not prune too hard or berries may be lost and it may not flower the next year.

THIS BARBERRY has a crop of striking yellow flowers in the fall.

THE ATTRACTION of the beautyberry is the remarkable berry color.

BEAUTYBERRY

Callicarpa bodinierei var. *giraldii*

DECIDUOUS

ORIGIN: Western and central China.
SIZE: An upright, very bushy plant reaching a height of about 10 ft.
FROST TOLERANCE: It may tolerate a low of –9°F.
APPEAL: Prized for its bright violet berries which are very freely produced in the fall. The fruits are preceded by small pink flowers in the summer, which are not particularly attractive. Must be planted in groups for berries to be produced, unless an hermaphrodite variety is chosen. Beautyberry makes a welcome addition to the shrub border with its late display.
CLIMATE: Survives in zone 5 but is better in zone 6 and above. Needs a long hot summer to fruit well.
ASPECT: Full sun or dappled shade.
PRUNING: In early spring cut back the previous year's shoots to a permanent framework of older wood.

BLUEBEARD

Caryopteris x clandonensis

DECIDUOUS

ORIGIN: Garden origin.
SIZE: Forms a dense mound of growth to a height of 3 ft.
FROST TOLERANCE: This is not one of the hardiest shrubs and will tolerate a low of only 0°F.
APPEAL: Appreciated for its late flowering season—late summer and early fall. The flowers are blue or purplish blue and the gray-green foliage is aromatic. Grow this small shrub at the front of a shrub or mixed border in association with other late-flowering plants such as asters (Michaelmas daisies) and sedums.
CLIMATE: Zone 6. Not fully hardy out of doors in the north but can be grown in pots in the greenhouse. Suitable for outdoor culture in the southern states.
ASPECT: Needs a spot in full sun. A position against a warm, sunny wall would be ideal.
PRUNING: In early spring each year the old stems should be cut back close to the base.

BLUEBEARD IS A small shrub valued for its late flowering season.

EASILY GROWN, shrubby bottlebrushes can be used as informal hedges.

BOTTLEBRUSH

Callistemon species

EVERGREEN

ORIGIN: Australia, usually in wetter areas or by streams.
SIZE: Height varies with species from less than 3 ft to about 12 ft. There are also trees. Fast growing.
FROST TOLERANCE: All tolerate light frosts while some accept lows of 21°F. In frosty areas, check hardiness before choosing a species.
APPEAL: Bottlebrushes may be weeping or upright but all produce magnificent, mostly spring flowers which attract birds. Flowers are usually bright red but may also be pink, burgundy, cream or green.
CLIMATE: Ideal for growing in California and other mild Pacific Coast areas. Bottlebrushes grow in a wide range of soils. Although they tolerate dryness, they grow and look better where rainfall is reasonably generous and reliable.
ASPECT: Best in full sun. They tolerate coastal exposure.
PRUNING: Prune by removing faded flowers. Some cutting back helps to keep growth compact. Old, open shrubs can be cut back quite hard in spring for rejuvenation.

BOX

Buxus species

EVERGREEN

ORIGIN: Mediterranean region, central and east Asia and Japan.
SIZE: Ranging from about 20 in to nearly 16 ft. Moderate growth rate.
FROST TOLERANCE: Both English box and Japanese box will tolerate frosts of –4°F at least.
APPEAL: Box is grown for its dense foliage which can be clipped into formal hedges or used for topiary.
CLIMATE: Grows best zone 6 and above, but English box (*B. sempervirens*) is not really recommended for warm climates—there try Japanese box (*B. microphylla* var. *japonica*) instead. Neither is suited to the tropics.
ASPECT: Needs full sun to maintain compact growth habit.
PRUNING: Can be clipped at any time to maintain a formal shape. If growing box as a formal hedge or a topiary shape, use hedge clippers instead of trying to cut each stem with pruners.

USE ENGLISH box for taller hedges and the smaller Japanese box for low borders.

BUTTERFLY BUSHES have a wild, loose exuberance ideal for background plantings.

BUTTERFLY BUSH

Buddleia davidii

DECIDUOUS

ORIGIN: Japan and China.
SIZE: Grows to 10 ft tall and wide.
FROST TOLERANCE: At least –9°F.
APPEAL: This shrub has an old-fashioned charm. The light purple flowers appear spring and summer. Named cultivars are available with flowers in white, rose, purple, dark blue or magenta.
CLIMATE: Suitable for zone 5 and above. It has become naturalized in parts of California. It is not suitable for tropical gardens.
ASPECT: Performs best in full sun.
PRUNING: Flowered canes can be shortened back in late winter, and any thin, weak growth can be cut out. You may also cut back immediately after flowering if you prefer.

CALIFORNIAN LILAC

Ceanothus species

EVERGREEN AND DECIDUOUS

ORIGIN: Western North America.
SIZE: Prostrate to shrubs 13–16 ft tall.
FROST TOLERANCE: Most of the Pacific Coast species are not hardy in areas with temperatures below 10°F. Other species can tolerate –9°F.
APPEAL: Most varieties have blue flowers, the color varying from pale powder blue to deep violet, in mid-spring. Out of bloom they are densely foliaged with glossy, dark green leaves.
CLIMATE: Zone 8 and above, but not warm subtropical or tropical climates. Some species are suitable for zones 5 to 7.
ASPECT: They must have full sun and plenty of good air circulation.
PRUNING: Not strictly necessary but a light trim after blooming produces a more compact plant.

IN BLOOM, Californian lilac is one of the most remarkable blue shrubs of all.

CAMELLIAS AND azaleas are perfect partners. Both like the same conditions.

CAMELLIA

Camellia species

EVERGREEN; TAKES SHADE

ORIGIN: China, Japan, subtropical Southeast Asia.
SIZE: This varies with type within a range of 3–20 ft, occasionally up to 33 ft. Shrub has a slow to moderate growth rate.
FROST TOLERANCE: This depends on the species but the most widely grown such as *C. japonica* and *C.* x *williamsii* varieties will take a low of 10°F.
APPEAL: Glossy green foliage and showy flowers are produced on the various species from fall, through winter into spring. Flowers may be single, semi-double or double in white, pink, deep rose or deep red with many combinations of these colors. Camellias make ideal garden plants for almost any situation provided that soil and climatic conditions are suitable. Use as hedges, espaliers, pot specimens, lawn specimens or in mixed shrub borders.

CLIMATE: Camellias are popular shrubs in the south-east and on the Pacific Coast. Zones 8 and 9. Provide camellias with shelter from hot dry winds. They are native to rainy, humid forests and are therefore not suited to tropical areas.
ASPECT: A position among other big shrubs or beneath lightly foliaged or high branching trees is ideal. Most grow well in filtered sun although some varieties take full sun. Sasanquas tolerate more sun than most other camellias and reticulatas need full sun for part of the day. Some cultivars of *C. japonica*, such as "The Czar", "Great Eastern", "Moshio" and "Emperor of Russia", take full sun.
PRUNING: Cutting blooms for the vase is usually enough to keep plants compact. However, any thin, spindly, unproductive growth can be cut from the centre of the shrub at almost any time. Old, overgrown camellias can be rejuvenated by quite heavy pruning as long as cuts are made directly above a leaf or leaf bud.

SASANQUA CAMELLIAS start the season, blooming as early as late summer.

CHERRY PIE

Heliotropium arborescens

EVERGREEN

ORIGIN: Peru.
SIZE: Grows to 3 ft or more tall with a wider spread.
FROST TOLERANCE: Does not tolerate frost.
APPEAL: A fragrant flowered, neat rounded shrub with either very dark green or golden foliage. Flowers are produced over a long period from spring to fall and may be in shades of mauve or violet. The flower fragrance is reminiscent of vanilla.
CLIMATE: Zone 10. In other regions grow as a pot plant, which can be overwintered in a cool greenhouse or conservatory and stood outdoors for the summer.
ASPECT: Full sun is best for the plants to flower well. Protect from hot drying winds. Plants under glass will need shading from strong sun.
PRUNING: A light shearing all over in early spring promotes bushiness.

GROW CHERRY PIE and you get months of color for very little effort.

DAINTY BELLS deck the lovely Chinese lantern plant for months on end.

CHINESE LANTERN

Abutilon x hybridum

EVERGREEN OR PART-DECIDUOUS; TAKES PART-SHADE

ORIGIN: Hybrid.
SIZE: These open, arching shrubs reach 6–10 ft.
FROST TOLERANCE: Grows best in frost-free gardens but accepts the odd light frost if sheltered from cold winds. It will lose some leaves in cooler areas.
APPEAL: It has a graceful habit and virtual year-round pendulous, bell-shaped flowers which may be white or shades of pink, yellow or red. Use as an addition to a mixed shrub planting or as a background to lower shrubs or flowers.
CLIMATE: Zone 9 and above. In other zones grow as a pot plant and overwinter under glass. Stand outside for the summer.
ASPECT: Full sun produces the most flowers over the longest period. This plant accepts quite a lot of shade but foliage will be more sparse.
PRUNING: Prune back to a compact shape in late winter.

COTONEASTER

Cotoneaster "Cornubia"

SEMI-EVERGREEN

ORIGIN: Garden origin.
SIZE: A very vigorous shrub needing lots of space, with an arching habit of growth to a height of 20 ft.
FROST TOLERANCE: Hardy to at least 0°F.
APPEAL: The main attraction of this shrub is the heavy crop of brilliant red berries which are borne in the fall. These are preceded in the summer by heads of white flowers. The deep green leaves turn bronze in winter. If space permits, grow it in a shrub border. It can also be grown as a specimen shrub in a lawn and it makes a very good screen.
CLIMATE: Zone 6 and above.
ASPECT: Thrives in full sun or partial shade. Always protect from cold drying winds.
PRUNING: No regular pruning is needed. Any over-long shoots can be trimmed in spring.

THE COTONEASTER is noted for its huge crops of berries.

CRANBERRY BUSH

Viburnum opulus "Compactum"

DECIDUOUS

ORIGIN: Europe, North Africa and northern Asia but the variety is a garden selection.
SIZE: A compact bushy slow-growing shrub, ideal where space is limited, attaining a height of 5 ft.
FROST TOLERANCE: Very hardy, taking a low of –38°F.
APPEAL: A popular ornamental shrub grown mainly for its fall color. In late spring it produces flat heads of white flowers which are followed by clusters of bright red berries. The lobed maple-like leaves turn red in fall before they drop. Ideal for a shrub border or woodland garden, best grown in a group of three or more.
CLIMATE: Zone 3 and above.
ASPECT: Full sun or partial shade.
PRUNING: None required except cutting back any overlong shoots if necessary to maintain a shapely plant.

IDEAL FOR limited space, this cranberry bush produces clusters of berries.

DAPHNE HAS one of the best loved floral fragrances of all.

DAPHNE

Daphne odora

EVERGREEN; NEEDS SHADE

ORIGIN: China.
SIZE: Grows up to 3 ft with a similar or wider spread. Slow to moderate growth rate.
FROST TOLERANCE: Takes 5°F for short periods.
APPEAL: Grown for its sweet fragrance, so plant it close to the house or beside a path. Flowers are star-shaped, pink or white, and are borne in clusters on the stem ends or in leaf axils in late fall and winter.
CLIMATE: Can be grown in zone 7 and above but is not suitable for tropical gardens and does not really care for hot dry summers. In colder regions it can be grown as a pot plant under glass.
ASPECT: Prefers a position where it will receive morning sun, midday and afternoon shade, and shelter from strong drying winds. Filtered sunlight is also suitable.
PRUNING: Pruning is not necessary, but cutting sprigs of flowers for the house will keep the bush compact.

DARWIN'S BARBERRY

Berberis darwinii

EVERGREEN

ORIGIN: Chile and Argentina.
SIZE: This is a fairly slow-growing shrub which eventually reaches a maximum height of 7 ft.
FROST TOLERANCE: Low of 5°F.
APPEAL: Grown mainly for its eye-catching display of orange-yellow flowers in the spring, followed by bluish-black berries. It has attractive deep green spiny foliage. This shrub can be grown as an informal flowering hedge, in other words, it will not need regular trimming.
CLIMATE: It will thrive in zone 7 and above and is suitable only for the south and California. This barberry is not hardy in northern states.
ASPECT: It performs best in full sun but good results are also possible in partial shade.
PRUNING: After flowering carry out any light pruning to maintain a shapely plant—just the odd over-long shoot, for example. Do not prune hard or it may not flower the following year.

DARWIN'S BARBERRY can be grown as a shrub or an informal, flowering hedge.

ESCALLONIAS ARE grown for their long flowering season, often into fall.

ESCALLONIA

Escallonia "Apple Blossom"

EVERGREEN

ORIGIN: This is a hybrid of garden origin but the species of escallonia come from South America.
SIZE: A compact, bushy shrub reaching a height of 8 ft.
FROST TOLERANCE: It will take a low of 10°F.
APPEAL: This hybrid flowers very freely over a long period in summer, the blooms being light pink and white, reminiscent of apple blossom, hence the varietal name. The leaves are dark green and shiny and make a good background for the flowers. Grow it in the shrub or mixed border, against a wall or as an informal flowering hedge.
CLIMATE: Zone 8 and above. Escallonias are planted mainly in California where they bloom into the fall and winter. They are good for coastal gardens.
ASPECT: Provide a position in full sun and shelter from cold winds.
PRUNING: No regular pruning needed. Just cut back any over-long shoots to maintain a shapely plant. Dead flower heads can be cut off.

EUPHORBIA

Euphorbia characias subspecies *wulfenii*

EVERGREEN

ORIGIN: Balkan region of Europe.
SIZE: Reaches about 3 ft tall with a similar or wider spread. Fast growing.
FROST TOLERANCE: Accepts lows of 10°F, lower if sheltered.
APPEAL: This is a good contrast plant as the foliage is a very soft gray green and the lime-green "flowers" (really bracts) make a great foil for other colors. Use in a mixed shrub border, as a background planting to annuals or perennials or as a feature on its own. Flowers are produced during winter and early spring. The milky sap is caustic, and so take care when cutting stems. It is very drought tolerant once well established.
CLIMATE: This euphorbia is suitable for zones 8 and 9 where it will grow strongly and flower well.
ASPECT: Full sun is essential. Takes coastal exposure.
PRUNING: Immediately after bloom, cut back stems that have flowered to promote growth of new stems that will flower the following year.

EUPHORBIAS ARE decorative for several months over winter and spring.

THE EUROPEAN red elderberry is best in its golden yellow variety.

EUROPEAN RED ELDERBERRY

Sambucus racemosa "Plumosa Aurea"

DECIDUOUS

ORIGIN: This species is native to Europe and western Asia.
SIZE: A bushy shrub reaching 10 ft.
FROST TOLERANCE: Takes temperatures down to −20°F.
APPEAL: This is essentially a foliage shrub, valued for its finely cut golden-yellow pinnate leaves. Grow it in a shrub or mixed border or as a lawn specimen. Ideal for a container on a terrace.
CLIMATE: Hardy in the north. Zone 5 and above.
ASPECT: Likes a rather moist soil. Full sun for best foliage color, although it may be scorched by very hot sun. The color is retained for a longer period if the plant is grown in dappled shade.
PRUNING: Cut back the stems to within two or three buds of their base in early spring. Alternatively, if you want a taller plant allow a permanent woody framework to build up and prune back to this.

FIRE THORN

Pyracantha coccinea "Lalandei"

EVERGREEN

ORIGIN: The species is a native of south-east Europe to the Caucasus.
SIZE: A vigorous, dense, bushy shrub growing to a height of 20 ft.
FROST TOLERANCE: Takes a minimum of 0°F.
APPEAL: A thorny shrub with creamy white flowers in early summer and persistent, showy, orange-red berries in fall and winter. Grow in a shrub border or as a hedge. Espalier or train to other shapes, such as on a wall of the house. There are other varieties of *P. coccinea* which are worth growing.
CLIMATE: Fairly hardy in the central states. Zone 7 and above.
ASPECT: Full sun or partial shade. Needs shelter from cold drying winds in frost-prone areas.
PRUNING: Free-standing shrubs need no regular pruning. Trim hedges and wall-trained plants in midsummer after flowering. The harder you trim fire thorn bushes, the less berries they produce.

THE FREE-BERRYING fire thorns can be trained into many different shapes.

THE FLOWERING quince is valued for its early flower display.

FLOWERING QUINCE

Chaenomeles speciosa "Simonii"

DECIDUOUS

ORIGIN: China.
SIZE: This is a very vigorous spiny shrub with a spreading, semi-horizontal habit of growth. It grows only about 3 ft in height.
FROST TOLERANCE: This is quite a tough shrub, taking a low of –20°F.
APPEAL: It is valued for its early spring flowers which are often produced before the leaves. They are quite large, double and very deep red. The flowers are followed by aromatic greenish yellow quince-like fruits. This is a versatile shrub: it makes a good addition to the shrub or mixed border, or it could be trained flat against a wall. It also makes good and unusual groundcover for a bank.
CLIMATE: Zone 5 and above.
ASPECT: Full sun or partial shade, but it flowers best with plenty of sun.
PRUNING: Cut back flowered shoots after flowering to younger shoots or growth buds lower down.

FORSYTHIA IS magnificent, whether in the garden or as a cut flower.

FORSYTHIA

Forsythia suspensa

DECIDUOUS; TAKES PART-SHADE

ORIGIN: China.
SIZE: Forsythias grow to about 10 ft tall and 10 ft wide. They have an arching, spreading habit.
FROST TOLERANCE: Takes –4°F at least.
APPEAL: This is a spectacular plant in late winter, when the bare branches are covered with pendulous, golden yellow flowers. Cut branches make good indoor arrangements and if picked in bud, flowers bloom indoors.
CLIMATE: These shrubs are not at their best without a cold winter. They are ideally suited to zones 5 to 8. Very commonly planted for their late winter or early spring flowers.
ASPECT: A position in full sun gives the best results. However, forsythias are able to tolerate shade for part of the day.
PRUNING: Remove about a third of the oldest canes at ground level immediately after flowering. This will make way for the growth of young, vigorous new stems.

FUCHSIA

Fuchsia x hybrida

EVERGREEN; NEEDS PART OR FULL SHADE

ORIGIN: Hybrid from South American parents.
SIZE: Between 18 in and 3 ft high.
FROST TOLERANCE: Many kinds will take no frosts, while others take a low of 0°F to –9°F.
APPEAL: A long display of pendulous flowers which may be white, pink, red, mauve or purple. Smaller types make good pot or basket plants while the stronger growers are ideal shrubs for partly shaded areas of the garden.
CLIMATE: Fuchsias thrive in cool moist conditions. Many will grow outdoors in zone 6 and above, otherwise grow them in pots under glass and outside in summer.
ASPECT: Dappled or part-shade.
PRUNING: In frost-free areas, cut back to a main framework of branches in fall. In cooler parts, prune in early spring. Pinch tips to compact.

THERE ARE hundreds of types of fuchsia in many sizes, habits and colors.

THE FUCHSIA-FLOWERED gooseberry is not hardy but makes a fine wall shrub.

FUCHSIA-FLOWERED GOOSEBERRY

Ribes speciosum

EVERGREEN

ORIGIN: California.
SIZE: An erect-growing bushy shrub to at least 6 ft in height.
FROST TOLERANCE: It will take temperatures down to 0°F.
APPEAL: Valued for its clusters of dangling, deep red fuchsia-like flowers with protruding stamens in spring, followed by bristly red berries. The stems are bristly and spiny, reddish and quite attractive when young, carrying shiny lobed leaves. Grow in a shrub border or train it flat against a warm wall.
CLIMATE: Zone 7 and above.
ASPECT: Full sun and shelter from cold, drying winds.
PRUNING: After flowering, cut back the old flowered stems to young shoots or buds lower down and remove some of the oldest wood. If wall grown cut back the old flowered shoots to within two to four buds of a permanent framework of stems.

GREVILLEA

Grevillea "Moonlight"

EVERGREEN

ORIGIN: Hybrid.
SIZE: Reaches about 10 ft tall with a somewhat lesser spread. This is a fast-growing shrub.
FROST TOLERANCE: Takes 27°F.
APPEAL: There are well over 200 species of grevillea and many hybrids as well. Most are shrubs valued for their drought tolerance, screening or groundcovering capabilities and long season of bird attracting flowers, the season varying with species. Popular shrub types include "Robyn Gordon", "Honey Gem", "Misty Pink", "Ned Kelly" and "Moonlight". All have divided or lobed leaves and big, spidery flowers which come in colors of red, pink, cream, yellow, burnt orange or white.
CLIMATE: Grevilleas can be grown outside in mild regions—zones 9 and 10. Otherwise grow these shrubs as pot plants in a cool greenhouse or in a conservatory, in which case they could perhaps be summered outdoors.
ASPECT: Most grevilleas, including "Moonlight", need full sun.
PRUNING: Regular tip pruning compacts the plants. Do this from the start to encourage a bushy habit.

"MOONLIGHT" IS one of many hybrid grevilleas with a long blooming habit.

DIFFERENT TYPES of heaths together create a tapestry-like effect.

HEATH

Erica species

EVERGREEN

ORIGIN: Southern Africa, North Africa, Europe.
SIZE: From less than 3 ft to 10 ft tall. Moderate growth rate.
FROST TOLERANCE: The hardiest European species can take –9°F at least but some of the South African species accept light frosts only.
APPEAL: Ericas are popular both for their fine, often colorful foliage and the masses of winter or spring flowers. The color range includes white, pink, violet, coral, crimson and bicolors. Different types may be massed together for a tapestry-like effect and they are often grown with dwarf conifers. They grow well in pots or well-drained rock gardens.
CLIMATE: Zone 5 and above. However, species and their varieties vary, so check before you buy to ensure they are suitable for your zone.
ASPECT: Must have full sun and good air circulation.
PRUNING: Shear lightly straight after flowering. Never cut into the older wood—it won't reshoot.

HIBISCUS

Hibiscus rosa-sinensis

EVERGREEN

ORIGIN: China, Southeast Asia.
SIZE: Varies with type from about 3 ft to over 12 ft. Fast growing.
FROST TOLERANCE: Accepts 32°F, perhaps 30°F but it does better in frost-free climates.
APPEAL: Popular for their very long season of big, showy flowers in summer and fall, hibiscus are grown as hedges, screens, specimens, or in mixed plantings. Smaller types make good potted plants. Flowers are in every color but blue and green.
CLIMATE: A flamboyant-looking shrub for zones 9 and 10. In other zones it is best grown as a pot plant in a cool greenhouse or conservatory. The plants could then be stood outside on a patio or terrace for the summer.
ASPECT: Full sun is essential. Takes coastal exposure.
PRUNING: Wait until spring before pruning. Some varieties can be cut back by about a third of their growth while others are best tip pruned only. Be guided by the vigor and growth habit of your plant— if it grows strongly you may prune more heavily.

"APPLE BLOSSOM" is a big, dense hibiscus shrub growing to about 12 ft.

HIMALAYA HONEYSUCKLE

Leycesteria formosa

DECIDUOUS

ORIGIN: Himalayas and Western China.
SIZE: A suckering shrub up to 6 ft in height.
FROST TOLERANCE: Takes a minimum of 0°F.
APPEAL: Flowers in late summer and fall. Red-purple bracts surrounding the pendulous trusses of white flowers last for a long period. Red-purple berries follow. The attractive green stems are hollow and cane-like. Grow in a shrub border or on the edge of a woodland garden.
CLIMATE: Zone 7 and above. This shrub can be grown in protected places in the north.
ASPECT: Will grow and flower equally well in full sun or partial shade. Protect from cold drying winds. In areas prone to hard frosts protect roots by mulching with bulky organic matter in fall.
PRUNING: In early spring cut back old flowered stems to young shoots or buds lower down.

THE HIMALAYA honeysuckle has attractive stems as well as flowers.

HYDRANGEAS REPAY plenty of water with a remarkable display of huge flowers.

HYDRANGEA

Hydrangea macrophylla

DECIDUOUS; NEEDS SHADE

ORIGIN: Japan, China, Korea.
SIZE: Reaches 3 ft or more tall and at least as wide. Fast growing.
FROST TOLERANCE: If sheltered from freezing winds will take –4°F.
APPEAL: The big, rounded flowers make a great show through summer, and in cooler districts old flower heads will develop fall tones. Flowers may be pink, blue, white or red with many in-betweens. These good background plants are often used to disguise fences and are lovely in tubs.
CLIMATE: Zones 6, 7 and 8 suit this hydrangea. Needs humidity and a lot of water in summer.
ASPECT: Not suitable for full sun. Even in zone 6 some shade during the hottest times is desirable. Elsewhere grow in the shade cast by buildings or trees. They grow at the coast if sheltered from direct sea winds.
PRUNING: Cut back stems that have flowered straight after blooms fade. Leave unflowered shoots for next year's blooms. Cut back old, overgrown bushes hard in late winter or early spring and remove the oldest stems at ground level.

JAPANESE FATSIA

Fatsia japonica

EVERGREEN

ORIGIN: Japan and South Korea.
SIZE: A suckering shrub up to 14 ft in height.
FROST TOLERANCE: It accepts 21°F or slightly below.
APPEAL: Grown for its bold foliage effect. The large hand-shaped glossy deep green leaves are carried on thick stems. There are several varieties, some with variegated leaves. Heads of creamy white flowers are produced in the fall followed by black berries. Grow it in a shrub border, as a specimen plant, or as a tub plant on a patio or under glass.
CLIMATE: Zone 8 and above. It is grown as a pot plant under glass in the north but can be grown outside in mild regions. Good for coastal gardens. Also tolerates town and city atmospheric pollution.
ASPECT: Light shade or full sun with shelter from wind. Partial shade for variegated varieties.
PRUNING: None needed.

THE JAPANESE FATSIA has bold foliage and attractive flowers in fall.

JAPANESE ROSE is a loose, rambling shrub that flowers in spring.

JAPANESE ROSE

Kerria japonica

DECIDUOUS; NEEDS SHADE

ORIGIN: Japan and China.
SIZE: Grows to about 6 ft tall and almost as wide. The plant produces many arching canes from a central clump. Moderate growth rate.
FROST TOLERANCE: With shelter from freezing winds, accepts –20°F.
APPEAL: This is a good screening plant and can also be a feature of mixed shrub plantings. Flowers are bright yellow and the serrated leaves color yellow before falling in fall. The form with double flowers, "Plena", is commonly grown.
CLIMATE: This commonly grown shrub is hardy north and grows in zone 5 and above. This, though, is a plant for cool, moist climates.
ASPECT: Prefers full sun but tolerates shade for part of the day or a position in bright, dappled shade.
PRUNING: Remove some of the older canes at ground level after bloom to make space for new growth.

LAVENDER IS *one of the essential components of the cottage garden.*

LAVENDER

Lavandula species

EVERGREEN

ORIGIN: Mediterranean region.
SIZE: Varies from dwarf shrubs less than 20 in tall to big, rounded bushes more than 3 ft high and wide.
FROST TOLERANCE: Some such as *L. augustifolia* take a low of 0°F to –9°F. Check before you buy.
APPEAL: Has highly aromatic gray-green foliage topped by spikes of spring flowers ranging from very pale to deepest purple. Grow it with other shrubs or as a background to annuals, perennials or bulbs, or in containers. It is sometimes grown as a hedge.
CLIMATE: Depending on species, zones 6 to 10. A Mediterranean climate is ideal. Lavender dislikes wet humid summers and poorly drained soils.
ASPECT: Needs an open situation in full sun with very good air circulation. Do not crowd it with other plantings.
PRUNING: Tip prune young plants and shear older lavenders after bloom.

LILAC

Syringa vulgaris and
S. x *hyacinthiflora* cultivars
DECIDUOUS

ORIGIN: Southern Europe.
SIZE: Grows up to 10 ft tall. Slow to moderate growth rate.
FROST TOLERANCE: Very hardy, accepts –31°F at least.
APPEAL: A great favorite for cool climate gardens, lilac has large trusses of sweetly perfumed flowers that may be white, pink, mauve, violet, crimson or shades in between. Flowers may be single or double and there is a great range of lovely cultivars from which to choose. Grow it as a specimen, as a screening plant or in massed plantings if the garden is large enough. It makes a beautiful and incredibly fragrant informal hedge.
CLIMATE: Zone 4 and above. A long cold winter is essential for lilac to flower well. Many frosts are needed to produce a good display of flowers.
ASPECT: Needs full sun but protection from strong, drying winds.
PRUNING: Remove spent flower stems as soon as they fade. Suckering growth at the base of the plant can be cut out with a sharp spade.

LILAC IS one of the greatest joys of a cool climate spring.

SPINY MAHONIA is a good tall screening shrub but keep it away from paths.

MAHONIA

Mahonia lomariifolia
EVERGREEN; NEEDS PART-SHADE

ORIGIN: Mountains of west China.
SIZE: Reaches 6–14 ft tall with many erect stems growing upwards and outwards from the base. Moderate growth rate.
FROST TOLERANCE: Accepts 5°F at least.
APPEAL: Mahonias produce spikes of small, bright yellow flowers, mainly in winter or spring, and continue their decorative effect with berries in various shades of blue through to early winter. They have shiny, very spiny, holly-like leaves and are good for screening and as background plantings for smaller shrubs.
CLIMATE: Zone 7 and above. Best in cool moist areas. Mahonias are not suitable for the tropics or for hot, dry places.
ASPECT: Tolerates dappled shade or early sun but must be shaded from hot afternoon sun.
PRUNING: Cut out thin, weak growth at ground level. Otherwise no pruning is needed.

MEXICAN ORANGE BLOSSOM

Choisya ternata

EVERGREEN

ORIGIN: Mexico.
SIZE: Reaches around 5–6 ft tall and at least as wide. Fast growing.
FROST TOLERANCE: Takes extreme lows of 10°F if sheltered from freezing winds. It prefers a warmer climate with little or no frost.
APPEAL: This shrub has glossy leaves and, in spring, white flowers that look and smell like orange blossom. Grow a few together for a massed display or as an informal hedge, or use it in mixed shrub borders. It grows in pots.
CLIMATE: Suitable for growing in zone 7 and above. Prefers warmer climates and grows well in the south and in California. In colder regions can be grown in pots under glass. Worth trying against a warm wall in less-favorable climates. Dry summer heat may brown the leaves.
ASPECT: Needs warmth and shelter from cold wind. Does best where it gets sun for all or most of the day.
PRUNING: Little needed beyond removal of the spent flower stems.

CHOOSE Mexican orange blossom for its fragrance and masses of white blossom.

THIS MOCK ORANGE is considered one of the best colored foliage shrubs.

MOCK ORANGE

Philadelphus coronarius "Aureus"

DECIDUOUS

ORIGIN: This species is a native of Europe and south-west Asia. The variety is of garden origin.
SIZE: This is an erect-growing shrub reaching a height of about 8 ft.
FROST TOLERANCE: Takes a temperature down to –20°F.
APPEAL: This is essentially a foliage shrub, valued for its bright yellow leaves. During summer the color fades to yellow-green. Highly fragrant cream-white bowl shaped flowers are produced in early summer. Grow it in a shrub or mixed border.
CLIMATE: Zone 5 and above.
ASPECT: Full sun or partial shade. Bear in mind that in full sun the younger foliage may be scorched, especially in very hot sun.
PRUNING: Prune after flowering by cutting back the old flowered shoots to young shoots or growth buds lower down. Some of the old wood can be cut out completely.

OLEANDER

Nerium oleander

EVERGREEN

ORIGIN: Mediterranean region.
SIZE: Grows 6–12 ft tall, many erect stems growing upwards and outwards.
FROST TOLERANCE: Will take 10°F with some damage. Best where lows don't fall below 21°F.
APPEAL: Is very drought tolerant and useful for screening and windbreaks. It has a long flowering period over spring and summer and a good range of color—white, pink, cerise, crimson and apricot—in singles and doubles. There is also a form popular with flower arrangers that has variegated cream and green leaves. All parts of the plant are poisonous if eaten.
CLIMATE: Will grow outdoors in zones 9 and 10. In colder zones grow as a pot plant in a cool greenhouse and stand outdoors on a patio for the summer. Although drought tolerant, extra water will be needed where summers are hot and dry.
ASPECT: Full sun. Tolerates windy sites and extreme coastal exposure.
PRUNING: Tip prune after bloom each year. Overgrown bushes can be cut back severely in late winter to restore dense, bushy growth.

ABLE TO THRIVE on neglect, oleanders suit both the coast and inland gardens.

ORANGE BROWALLIA has masses of warm-colored spring flowers.

ORANGE BROWALLIA

Streptosolen jamesonii

EVERGREEN

ORIGIN: Northern South America.
SIZE: Up to 6 ft tall with an arching, spreading habit that makes the shrub almost as wide. Fast growing.
FROST TOLERANCE: Will take a little frost, down to 21°F.
APPEAL: A long display of yellow-orange-red flowers from around midwinter, through into spring. It has a graceful, arching habit that looks good against a sunny fence, in mixed shrubberies or as a background to annuals. There is a smaller growing form, "Ginger Meggs", which is sometimes available.
CLIMATE: It can be grown outdoors in zones 9 and 10. Otherwise grow it as a pot plant in a cool greenhouse, in which case it can be summered outdoors in a warm sheltered spot.
ASPECT: Must have full sun and protection from strong wind.
PRUNING: Cut back after the main flowering flush. Older canes can be cut out at ground level.

THIS PHOTINIA has colorful young foliage and white spring flowers.

PHOTINIA

Photinia x fraseri

EVERGREEN

ORIGIN: This hybrid is of garden origin.
SIZE: A large upright-growing shrub to 16 ft in height.
FROST TOLERANCE: It is not as hardy as the deciduous species but will take a low of 10°F.
APPEAL: Grown for its lance-shaped leathery dark green leaves which are bright red or bronze when young, making an attractive display in the spring. White flowers are produced in the spring. There are several varieties with "improved" coloring of the young foliage. Grow it in a shrub border. Photinia can also be used for formal hedging.
CLIMATE: Zone 8 and above.
ASPECT: Needs a sheltered aspect. Can be grown against a warm wall. It will be happy in either full sun or partial shade.
PRUNING: No regular pruning required if grown as a shrub. Formal hedges will need trimming annually in late summer.

PIERIS

Pieris japonica

EVERGREEN; NEEDS PART-SHADE

ORIGIN: Japan, in moist forests on mountainsides.
SIZE: Reaches 6–10 ft tall, forming a rounded bush about two-thirds as wide. Slow to moderate growth rate.
FROST TOLERANCE: Accepts –4°F at least.
APPEAL: It is a lovely glossy-leaved shrub with sprays of white or pinkish flowers in spring (late winter in mild climates). New growth is pink or red and is a real feature of some cultivars. Grow pieris in mixed shrub borders, beneath open foliaged trees or as a striking specimen shrub. It is also suitable for container growing.
CLIMATE: Zones 6, 7 and 8 suit pieris species and their varieties. They like a cool moist climate. Keep them well watered and grow them among trees and other shrubs, not out in the open.
ASPECT: Needs shelter from strong wind and hot afternoon sun. Best in dappled sunlight or where direct sun is restricted to mornings.
PRUNING: Tip prune to remove spent flowers as they fade. No other pruning is generally necessary.

THE BRILLIANT RED new growth is a striking feature of some types of pieris.

THE SKY-BLUE FLOWERS of plumbago look lovely with lasiandra or cassia.

PLUMBAGO

Plumbago auriculata

EVERGREEN

ORIGIN: Eastern South Africa.
SIZE: Reaches 6–10 ft tall with a greater spread. Fast growing.
FROST TOLERANCE: Takes 23°F.
APPEAL: Grown for its very long season of pale blue flowers set on a dense cover of mid-green foliage. It makes a good informal hedge or screen and it can also be induced to climb a short distance. Flowers begin to appear in late spring and continue until the end of fall, with the main flush occuring at the end of summer. There is also a white-flowered form that is not as vigorous.
CLIMATE: Very tough and adaptable, plumbago grows well in zones 9 and 10. If necessary, provide shelter from hot, dry winds, and do not let it go short of water in the summer. In colder zones grow it as a pot plant under glass.
ASPECT: Prefers full sun all day but is satisfactory with half a day's sun.
PRUNING: Needs hard cutting back in late winter or it will quickly become loose and untidy. It can also be tip pruned or shaped at any time during the growing season.

RHODODENDRON

Rhododendron varieties

EVERGREEN; TAKES PART-SHADE

ORIGIN: Forests of the Himalayan region and Southeast Asia.
SIZE: Height varies with type from small shrubs to 16 ft tall, tree-like specimens. Slow to moderate growth.
FROST TOLERANCE: This varies with type from an ability to withstand –39°F to no tolerance at all.
APPEAL: Broad-leaf rhododendrons, with their big trusses of spring flowers, are the key feature of many lovely cool climate gardens while the Vireya rhododendrons perform a similar function in warmer areas.
CLIMATE: Ranges from zones 2 to 10 depending on species. Check before you buy to ensure plants will grow in your climate. Broad-leaf rhododendrons are from cool, moist climates and many are suited to zones 5 to 8. Vireya rhododendrons will not take frost and do not like very hot dry conditions, so are generally grown as pot plants in a cool greenhouse.
ASPECT: Shelter from strong wind. Provide morning sun and shade in the afternoon or light shade of tall trees.
PRUNING: Little or no pruning is needed. If necessary, it should be done straight after flowering.

THE BEST KNOWN rhododendrons are the broad-leaved types. They like cool areas.

ROCK ROSE

Cistus salviifolius

EVERGREEN

ORIGIN: Mediterranean region.
SIZE: Grows about 32 in tall with a somewhat wider spread. Fast growing.
FROST TOLERANCE: Takes 14°F.
APPEAL: This plant is grown for its short but showy display of simple, single flowers. In the species shown these are white but others bloom in pink, crimson or lilac. Rock roses are attractive when mass planted or used as an informal hedge, or try them with other Mediterranean region shrubs such as lavender and pride of Madeira. They will grow in pots.
CLIMATE: Zone 8 and above. Specially useful in the southern states and California. The plants like a Mediterranean climate with rainy winters and hot dry summers.
ASPECT: Must have full sun all day but tolerates strong wind, including sea winds.
PRUNING: Tip prune young plants to form a dense, compact bush. More mature plants should be cut back lightly straight after flowering.

THERE ARE many types of rock rose, all with simple, crepe-textured spring flowers.

VARIETIES OF rose-of-Sharon have single or double flowers in summer and fall.

ROSE-OF-SHARON

Hibiscus syriacus

DECIDUOUS

ORIGIN: Eastern Asia.
SIZE: This is a compact upright shrub reaching 10 ft in height, ideal for the smaller garden.
FROST TOLERANCE: It will take 0°F or a slightly lower temperature.
APPEAL: Large saucer-shaped colorful flowers in late summer and into fall. There are numerous cultivars which are grown rather than the species, with single or, less usual, double flowers in shades of blue, red, pink, purple or white. Plant hibiscus in the mixed or shrub border, ideally with evergreen shrubs for contrast.
CLIMATE: Zone 6 and above. This hibiscus is widely planted in the north and needs a long hot summer to flower well.
ASPECT: Full sun. Neutral to slightly alkaline soil suits these shrubs. In cold regions the plants should be mulched with organic matter to protect the roots from severe frosts.
PRUNING: No regular pruning needed. Remove any dead or dying wood in early spring.

SACRED BAMBOO

Nandina domestica

EVERGREEN; TAKES PART-SHADE

ORIGIN: Japan, China.
SIZE: Grows up to 6 ft tall with a clumping, bamboo-like habit. Moderate growth rate.
FROST TOLERANCE: Takes lows of 5°F.
APPEAL: Sacred bamboo is a multi-stemmed shrub that slowly spreads by suckers to make a clump. The foliage is profuse but gives an impression of lightness. Use it in Japanese-style gardens or anywhere foliage contrast is wanted. Small white flowers are followed by red berries in fall and winter. In cool climates foliage reddens in fall. This is a good screening plant, especially in narrow spaces, or try it in a big container.
CLIMATE: Can be grown in zone 6 in protected places but better in zone 7 and above where it will make maximum growth.
ASPECT: Accepts full sun or semi-shade. In shade, leaves are pale green but in sun they turn reddish.
PRUNING: Take out a few of the old canes entirely in late winter.

SACRED BAMBOO is not a true bamboo and so is not an invasive shrub.

GROW MALE AND FEMALE plants of the sallow thorn to ensure berries.

SALLOW THORN

Hippophae rhamnoides

DECIDUOUS

ORIGIN: Europe and Asia.
SIZE: The sallow thorn makes a large bushy specimen up to 20 ft in height.
FROST TOLERANCE: It is very hardy taking a low of –38°F.
APPEAL: A very spiny shrub grown for its bright orange-yellow berries which persist for a long period in fall and winter. Grow a group of male and female plants to obtain berries. The gray-green leaves covered in silvery or bronze scales are also attractive. Grow it in the shrub or mixed border. It also makes a good windbreak for coastal gardens and can be grown as a formal or informal hedge. This shrub will also stabilize loose soil, such as found on banks.
CLIMATE: Zone 3 and above. A good shrub for coastal gardens, tolerating winds off the sea.
ASPECT: Full sun. Neutral to alkaline soil is best, particularly if sandy.
PRUNING: Not necessary.

SHRUBBY CINQUEFOIL

Potentilla fruticosa var. *arbuscula*

DECIDUOUS

ORIGIN: Himalayas and China.
SIZE: A bushy compact shrub up to 3 ft in height.
FROST TOLERANCE: Exceedingly hardy, taking a low of at least –38°F.
APPEAL: This shrub has an exceedingly long flowering season, from late spring until well into fall. The shallow cup-shaped flowers are golden-yellow and the silvery-gray leaves are a further attraction. Grow it in the shrub or mixed border, ideally in a bold group for best effect. It is also suitable for growing in an ornamental container on a patio or terrace. There are other varieties of shrubby cinquefoil worth growing.
CLIMATE: Zone 2 and above.
ASPECT: Full sun is needed for best flowering.
PRUNING: In early spring lightly trim over the flowered shoots to maintain compact shapely plants. It is best not to cut into the old wood.

THIS SHRUBBY CINQUEFOIL has a long flowering season and attractive foliage.

ESSENTIALLY A foliage shrub, the shrubby groundsel also has yellow daisy flowers.

SHRUBBY GROUNDSEL

Brachyglottis greyi

EVERGREEN

ORIGIN: From the north island of New Zealand.
SIZE: It forms a compact mound of growth up to 6 ft in height.
FROST TOLERANCE: This shrub is not very hardy, taking a low of only 23°F.
APPEAL: This is essentially a foliage shrub, grown for its whitish-gray young leaves which later turn green on top. The edges of the leaves are attractively scalloped or wavy. Heads of bright yellow daisy-like flowers are produced in summer and early fall. This plant makes a good companion for many other flowering shrubs and can also be grown as a hedge.
CLIMATE: Suitable only for zones 8, 9 and 10. Good for coastal gardens, tolerating sea winds well.
ASPECT: Must be grown in full sun.
PRUNING: Does not need much pruning. Just lightly trim after flowering if necessary to maintain a shapely plant.

THE SIBERIAN DOGWOOD is one of the staples of the winter garden.

SIBERIAN DOGWOOD

Cornus alba "Sibirica"

DECIDUOUS

ORIGIN: The species is native to Siberia, China and Korea.
SIZE: An upright shrub which grows to a height of 2–10 ft.
FROST TOLERANCE: An exceedingly tough shrub, taking a temperature down to –38°F.
APPEAL: It is generally grown as a pollarded shrub with a thicket of young stems as these have the best bark color. They are bright red and make a brilliant show in the winter, especially when the sun is shining on them. Use this dogwood in shrub borders, perhaps with winter-flowering shrubs; or for a really pleasing effect plant it beside a garden pond.
CLIMATE: This dogwood will survive in zone 3 and above.
ASPECT: The best stem color is achieved in full sun.
PRUNING: Grow as a pollarded shrub by cutting down the stems in early spring each year to within two or three buds of their base.

SMOKE BUSH

Cotinus coggygria

DECIDUOUS

ORIGIN: Southern Europe to Asia.
SIZE: A rounded, bushy shrub to about 16 ft in height.
FROST TOLERANCE: This is a very hardy shrub which will take a low of –20°F.
APPEAL: It is one of the best shrubs for fall leaf color. The foliage turns to brilliant flame shades before it falls. There are also varieties with purple foliage which are at their best in summer, but which also take on fall tints. Plume- or smoke-like heads of fruits are produced in summer and fall. A good choice for the shrub border or as a lawn specimen. Try planting it in a group with silver birches for a dramatic effect in fall.
CLIMATE: Zone 5 and above.
ASPECT: Full sun or partial shade. Full sun for purple-leaved varieties.
PRUNING: Very little pruning needed—only the removal of any dead or dying shoots or branches.

THE SMOKE BUSH produces smoke-like heads of fruits in summer and fall.

HEBES ARE good coastal plants but also do well in gardens a little further inland.

SPEEDWELL

Hebe species and cultivars

EVERGREEN

ORIGIN: New Zealand mostly.
SIZE: From 20 in to 6 ft tall and wide with a dense, rounded habit. Moderate to fast growth rate.
FROST TOLERANCE: Most will accept 10°F.
APPEAL: Hebes are hardy, evergreen shrubs useful for exposed coastal planting and many other situations. Spring flowers are generally blue, mauve, pink and burgundy, with some varieties ageing to white to give a bicolored effect. There are many species and cultivars and all can be grown in mixed shrub borders or as informal hedges. The smaller types make good container plants.
CLIMATE: Zone 7 and above. Hebes are widely grown outdoors in mild climates such as California. Not well suited to very hot or steamy tropical climates. Good for coastal gardens. They like regular rainfall.
ASPECT: Full sun is essential.
PRUNING: Shear after flowering to remove spent blooms and maintain dense growth.

SPINDLE TREE

Euonymus fortunei "Coloratus"

EVERGREEN

ORIGIN: This species is a native of central and western China.
SIZE: This is a vigorous plant which can be grown as a shrub, when it will grow about 24 in tall, or as a climber when it will reach to over 16 ft in height.
FROST TOLERANCE: It will accept a minimum of 5°F.
APPEAL: Essentially an easily grown and adaptable foliage shrub. The dark green leaves become flushed with reddish-purple in fall and winter when the weather turns cold. Grow it at the front of a shrub border, as groundcover, or as a climber up a tree or a wall.
CLIMATE: It is suited to zone 7 and above.
ASPECT: Full sun is best but it will accept light shade. Provide shelter from cold drying winds.
PRUNING: The spindle tree can be lightly trimmed back in spring to maintain a shapely plant.

THE LEAVES of the spindle tree color spectacularly in fall and winter.

THIS ST JOHN'S WORT is notable for its very long flowering period.

ST JOHN'S WORT

Hypericum "Hidcote"

EVERGREEN/SEMI-EVERGREEN

ORIGIN: This hybrid is of garden origin.
SIZE: A bushy shrub of dense growth up to 4 ft in height.
FROST TOLERANCE: Hardy down to –20°F.
APPEAL: The hypericums are a large group and "Hidcote" is one of the best. It has an exceedingly long flowering period, the shallow bowl-shaped golden-yellow flowers being produced continuously from mid-summer to early- or mid-fall. This shrub is generally grown in a shrub or mixed border with other summer and fall-flowering subjects.
CLIMATE: This is a very hardy shrub which can be grown successfully in zone 5 and above.
ASPECT: Will be happy in full sun or partial shade, but it appreciates shelter from cold drying winds.
PRUNING: Lightly trim after flowering to maintain a shapely plant. Remove dead flower heads if time permits, but not absolutely necessary.

STAGHORN SUMAC

Rhus typhina

DECIDUOUS

ORIGIN: Temperate parts of eastern North America.
SIZE: A vigorous erect branching shrub to at least 16 ft in height.
FROST TOLERANCE: Down to –38°F.
APPEAL: The twigs are densely hairy or velvety, like stags' antlers. The large compound or pinnate leaves color up in fall—bright red, orange or yellow. Cones of crimson fruits are produced by female plants in fall—grow male and female plants to obtain fruits. There are a number of varieties with attractively cut leaves. Grow in a shrub border or woodland garden.
CLIMATE: It will thrive in zone 3 and above.
ASPECT: Full sun will result in best fall leaf color.
PRUNING: None, or cut back stems in early spring to within two or three buds of their base or to a taller permanent framework of stems. Hard pruning causes suckering which can be a nuisance, especially in lawns.

STAGHORN SUMACH is grown for fall color but the stems look good in winter.

STAR MAGNOLIA is an arresting shrub that looks particularly good in a lawn.

STAR MAGNOLIA

Magnolia stellata

DECIDUOUS

ORIGIN: Japan.
SIZE: Grows up to 22 ft tall in its habitat but in gardens 6–12 ft is more likely. It has several trunks forming a rounded, upright shrub almost as wide as it is tall. Slow to moderate growth.
FROST TOLERANCE: Takes –13°F if sheltered from freezing winds.
APPEAL: Fragrant, white, star-like flowers borne in late winter and a compact habit make this an ideal magnolia for the smaller garden. Grow as a specimen or in a prominent spot in a mixed planting. The cultivar "Waterlily" has outstanding pink flowers. It can be grown in a big tub.
CLIMATE: Best in zones 5 to 9. A cool, moist, humid climate is ideal.
ASPECT: Needs shelter from strong wind (to prevent destruction of the flowers) and a fully sunny spot.
PRUNING: Tip prune as flowers fade or at other times for shaping only. Heavier pruning is not necessary for this magnolia.

SUN ROSE

Also known as rock rose

Helianthemum nummularium

EVERGREEN

ORIGIN: Europe.

SIZE: 4–12 in tall, 3 ft across.

FROST TOLERANCE: Accepts –1°F at least.

APPEAL: Grown for its masses of small, mainly single, rose-like flowers in shades of pink, red, orange, yellow, terracotta and white, produced over a long period from late spring to mid-summer. Use this groundcover shrub for the front of borders, on low retaining walls, on rock gardens or in containers. Short lived, it is easily replaced every few years from cuttings taken in late spring or early summer.

CLIMATE: Very hardy and commonly grown in the north, it may succeed in zone 5 with winter protection but it is better in zone 6 and above. It likes hot dry summers and does not enjoy summer humidity.

ASPECT: Full sun is essential. Takes coastal exposure or windy locations further inland.

PRUNING: After flowering shear back shoots that have flowered to within 1 in of the old stems. This may encourage a second crop of flowers.

SUN ROSE is related to the shrub rock rose and the two look and grow well together.

TEA TREE can be short lived but is worth trying for the magnificent floral display.

TEA TREE

Leptospermum scoparium

EVERGREEN

ORIGIN: Australia and New Zealand.

SIZE: Varies with type from 3 ft to 10 ft. Plants are generally narrower than they are tall. Fast growing.

FROST TOLERANCE: Takes 23°F.

APPEAL: These are grown for their generous spring display and contrasting dark foliage. The flowers may be single or double, usually in shades of pink but also white and crimson, with some cultivars showing pink, white and red at the same time. Use tea trees as single specimens or mass them for more impact.

CLIMATE: The tea tree can be grown in zones 9 and 10. In colder areas grow it as a pot plant in a cool greenhouse or conservatory. It does not like very hot dry summers or the tropics.

ASPECT: Needs full sun and good air circulation. Tolerates exposed windy sites well, including the coast.

PRUNING: Cut back plants after flowering but take care to cut only the lighter tip growth as cutting into old wood can be fatal.

THORNY ELAEAGNUS

Elaeagnus pungens "Maculata"

EVERGREEN

ORIGIN: China and Japan.
SIZE: A densely growing shrub to 14 ft in height.
FROST TOLERANCE: Takes a minimum temperature of 0°F.
APPEAL: The leaves have a large golden-yellow blotch in the middle. A somewhat spiny shrub whose shoots, when young, are covered in brown scales, which is quite an attractive feature. White flowers are produced in fall but they are not very showy. Grow this shrub in a mixed or shrub border or as a specimen in the lawn. It also makes a good formal hedge.
CLIMATE: Zone 7 and above. Good for coastal gardens, tolerating winds off the sea. Although it takes dry conditions, avoid thin limestone soils.
ASPECT: Ideally full sun but it will perform well in partial shade.
PRUNING: None required, unless grown as a formal hedge, when it is trimmed annually. Any over-long shoots can be cut back in the spring to maintain a shapely plant.

THIS THORNY ELAEAGNUS is one of the best variegated shrubs.

THE TOSA SPIRAEA is a very reliable and easily grown small shrub.

TOSA SPIRAEA

Spiraea nipponica "Snowmound"

DECIDUOUS

ORIGIN: Japan.
SIZE: A vigorous but small arching shrub to about 4 ft in height.
FROST TOLERANCE: It takes temperatures down to –20°F. If young growth is damaged by late spring frosts cut it back.
APPEAL: This is an easy and very reliable shrub which is grown for its masses of white flowers in early summer, when it looks as if it is covered by a blanket of snow. It is a good subject for a shrub or mixed border and a group would make quite good groundcover.
CLIMATE: Zone 5 and above.
ASPECT: Best grown in full sun for optimum flowering.
PRUNING: As soon as flowering is over, cut back the old flowered stems to young shoots or buds lower down. Also, with well-established shrubs you should remove completely any very old wood to leave plenty of young growth.

TREE MALLOWS are a good choice for a Mediterranean-style garden.

TREE MALLOW

Lavatera olbia

SEMI-EVERGREEN

ORIGIN: Western Mediterranean.
SIZE: Height up to 6 ft or more.
FROST TOLERANCE: Not too hardy, taking a low of 10°F at the most.
APPEAL: This is a very easily grown shrub with boldly lobed hairy leaves and bristly stems. The solitary flowers, produced during the summer, are carried on longish stalks and are reddish-purple in color. Very similar is the species *L. thuringiaca* from central and south-east Europe which is perhaps more widely grown. It has numerous varieties. The tree mallows are ideal subjects for Mediterranean-style gardens.
CLIMATE: These shrubs enjoy a Mediterranean climate and will be happy in zone 8 and above. A good choice for Californian gardens.
ASPECT: Must be grown in full sun and in a sheltered situation.
PRUNING: In early spring cut back previous year's growth to a permanent woody framework.

VIBURNUM

Viburnum x burkwoodii

DECIDUOUS

ORIGIN: Hybrid with Asian parents.
SIZE: Grows 6–10 ft tall and at least 2 m wide, forming a neat, rounded bush. Slow to moderate growth rate.
FROST TOLERANCE: Accepts –4°F at least.
APPEAL: Viburnum is grown for its masses of very sweetly fragrant white flowers. These appear any time from late winter to mid-spring. Out of bloom, it is a tidy, densely foliaged shrub and, where fall nights are chilly, the leaves color before falling. Use viburnum as a specimen shrub or as part of a fragrant planting.
CLIMATE: Should succeed in zone 5 but better in zone 6 and above. But bear in mind that this is a plant for cool moist climates.
ASPECT: Grows best with full sun. Shelter from strong winds prolongs the flowering season.
PRUNING: Trim lightly after flowering to remove spent blooms. Thinning out dense growth from the center of the bush may be needed, too.

CLUSTERS OF small, fragrant flowers dot the viburnum for a few weeks in spring.

THE WARMINSTER BROOM is ideal for limited space in mild areas.

WARMINSTER BROOM

Cytisus x *praecox* "Albus"

DECIDUOUS

ORIGIN: This broom is of garden origin.

SIZE: It is quite a compact shrub with arching shoots and is suited to smaller gardens. It grows to a height of only 4 ft.

FROST TOLERANCE: Not too hardy, this broom will tolerate a low of only 0°F.

APPEAL: This shrub is grown for its abundance of white flowers which are produced in late spring. *C.* x *praecox* itself is also worth growing and has pale yellow flowers. There are other varieties that come in various shades of yellow. A good choice for the shrub border or for planting on banks.

CLIMATE: Zone 6 and above suits the Warminster broom.

ASPECT: Full sun is needed and it appreciates shelter from cold drying winds. Grows well in poor lime-free soils.

PRUNING: Only cut off the seed pods. Do not cut into old wood as this can kill the plant.

WEDDING BELLS

Deutzia gracilis

DECIDUOUS

ORIGIN: Japan.

SIZE: Usually well under 6 ft tall with many stems rising from a crowded base. These stems arch outwards. Fast growing.

FROST TOLERANCE: Accepts –4°F but performs better where winter lows do not fall below 14°F.

APPEAL: This plant is easily grown and extremely lovely when dripping with white, bell-shaped blossom. It is often seen in mixed shrubberies or as background plants to displays of spring flowering annuals and bulbs. There are other species with pink and double white flowers.

CLIMATE: Can be grown in zone 5 but better in zone 6 and above. Likes a cool moist climate.

ASPECT: Prefers full sun and protection from very strong wind. In warmer areas plants prefer morning sun and afternoon shade.

PRUNING: Trim off spent flower heads immediately after bloom. Remove some of the older canes at ground level at the same time to make way for new, vigorous growth.

WEDDING BELLS bloom in spring, the branches bending under their weight.

FOUNTAIN-SHAPED weigela spreads its arching growth widely. Give it space.

WEIGELA

Weigela florida

DECIDUOUS

ORIGIN: China, Japan and Korea.
SIZE: Reaches around 10 ft tall with an arching habit. Fast growing.
FROST TOLERANCE: Accepts –4°F at least.
APPEAL: This is a popular shrub in temperate and cool climates with a graceful habit and plenty of white, red or pink flowers in spring. There are many named hybrids, some with variegated cream and green foliage. Weigela makes a charming background plant. Even when leafless it is dense enough to form a screen.
CLIMATE: Can be grown in zone 5 but better in zone 6 and above. Not suitable for arid areas or the tropics.
ASPECT: Needs full sun and shelter from strong wind which damages flowers and may also burn the margins of soft new leaf growth.
PRUNING: Some of the oldest canes should be cut out at ground level after flowering. Don't shorten the flowered shoots as this tends to spoil the natural arching habit.

WITCH HAZEL

Hamamelis x *intermedia* "Pallida"

DECIDUOUS

ORIGIN: This is a hybrid of garden origin.
SIZE: It is a shuttlecock-shaped shrub with upright branches up to 14 ft in height.
FROST TOLERANCE: At least -13°F.
APPEAL: Invaluable for its winter flowering, generally performing in early and midwinter. The spider-like fragrant light yellow flowers, carried on bare branches, are very frost resistant. The plants start flowering at a very early age. The leaves turn yellow in fall before they drop, which is an added attraction. An ideal woodland-garden shrub, or grow it in a shrub border with evergreen shrubs for contrast.
CLIMATE: Hardy in the north, zone 5 and above. Best results in acid to neutral soil.
ASPECT: Full sun or partial shade and shelter from wind.
PRUNING: No regular pruning needed, although misplaced branches can be removed in early spring.

THERE IS NO finer winter-flowering shrub than this witch hazel.

•CHAPTER SIXTEEN•

HEDGES & SCREENS

High walls cost a lot to build and they make homes look and feel like jails. But a living screen or hedge has neither of those faults. It's cheap and easy to grow, looks beautiful, provides privacy, shade and shelter and improves the look of your home.

HEDGES OR SCREENS, WHAT'S THE DIFFERENCE?

A hedge is usually thought of as a closely spaced row of examples of the same plant, clipped so as to form a continuous wall of foliage in a stiff, geometric shape. A formal or clipped hedge may also consist of different types of plants, all with similar heights and growth habits so that the foliage, when intermingled and clipped, has the appearance of a living tapestry. Formal hedges need quite a lot of maintenance in the form of regular clipping. If you can't or won't do this, an informal hedge is an alternative. This is a row of the same type of plants that are naturally dense and foliaged to the ground. Being rarely or never sheared, an informal hedge does not have the geometric precision of a clipped hedge and may consume more space, especially depth, but it is an easy way to achieve the privacy and shelter of a formal hedge without the need for frequent clipping.

A FORMAL, clipped hedge creates an enclosure and provides privacy and shelter, but it takes time and dedication to maintain, especially in warmer areas where regrowth can be rapid. It is most appropriate for a formal garden.

A SCREEN also creates an enclosure, providing privacy and shelter, but it needs little in the way of regular maintenance. It will usually consume more depth than a clipped hedge and is best used around a natural-style, rather bushy garden.

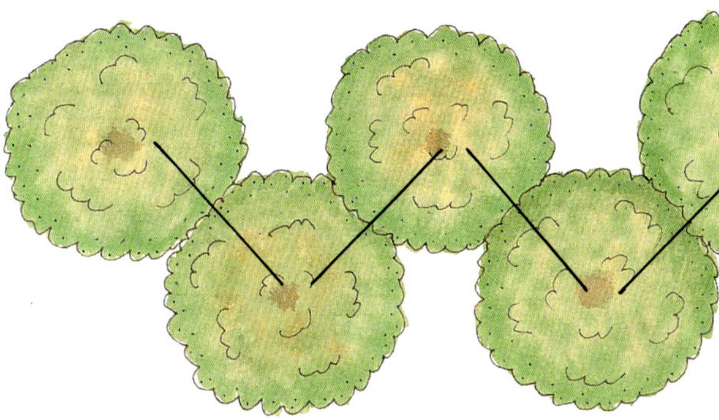

A STAGGERED double row of plants results in a denser and more effective hedge. The zigzag line shows the ideal layout.

TO KEEP animals in or out, erect a steel mesh fence between two rows of hedging plants. As the plants grow they will hide the fence from view.

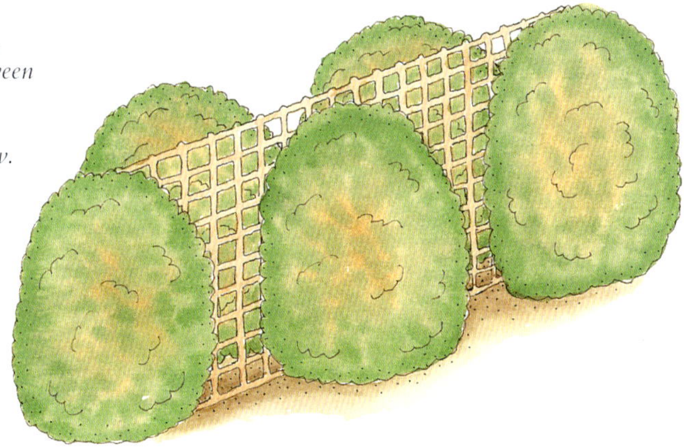

A screen is an even more informal type of hedge. It consists of a densely planted row of small trees or shrubs of various species. They are usually chosen with a maximum height in mind and because they have reasonably dense foliage. A screen is most successful when there is enough depth for at least two rows of plants, preferably three. The more depth you have, the less important it is that all the plants chosen have dense foliage as it is the combined mass of branches and foliage that creates the screen.

PLANT SELECTION

When selecting plants for screens and hedges, make sure that the chosen species suits the climate of your district, the aspect and the soil. Unsuitable plants may last a few years and then die, leaving a hard-to-fill gap in your hedge. Consider also the natural ultimate height and spread of the plant. If you want a 6 ft tall hedge, don't choose a shrub that grows to 15 to 16 ft or you'll spend a lot of time keeping it down. And as hedges and screens are long-term plantings, don't automatically opt for the fastest growing species.

If quick screening is essential, consider using fast-growing but expendable trees such as birch or alder behind your slower growing, long-term plants. They can be removed once the main hedge has developed some fullness. Just be careful that the expendables don't shade the hedge and don't plant them so close that they crowd the hedge or force it to grow away from them.

HEDGES ARE more than just green fences. Plants clipped to shape can be used within the garden as here. The bench is made more inviting by its hedge of clipped box.

THE SMALLER GROWING Japanese box is ideal for low, outline hedges around formal features, herb or vegetable gardens, rose beds or for lining and defining paths.

PHOTINIA GLABRA responds to clipping by producing a mass of new leaves which are bright red and very ornamental. Over time, the leaves turn green and the hedge can be clipped again. This plant will grow in mild frost-free areas but is best in cooler climates.

TOO BIG for its spot, this cotoneaster was saved from the axe by being shaped into a compact and novel awning.

PLANTS WITH dense, smallish leaves, such as this California privet, Ligustrum ovalifolium *are best for shaping.*

SOIL PREPARATION AND PLANTING

Before digging trenches or holes for planting, use a string line and pegs to mark the planting positions. This is essential for formal hedges to ensure that the planting line is straight and the spacing even. It is less important for informal hedges, but even so will give a better finished appearance. Most hedge plants are placed from 20 in to 3 ft apart, depending on growth habit and hedge style. Very close planting tends to make plants grow taller as they compete for sunlight but don't plant them too closely together or the plants may suffer from lack of root space.

Because hedges are close planted, root competition is intense and so you should dig in plenty of well-decayed manure or compost about a month before planting. You should also mix some blood and bone through the planting area or place some slow-release granular fertilizer at the bottom of the trench or planting holes. Cover the fertilizer with 1–2 in of soil so that the plant roots will not come into contact with it immediately.

Although it involves a lot more work, digging a wide trench along the entire length of the proposed hedge is almost always better than digging individual planting holes. With a trench, a much greater volume of soil can be enriched and the growing roots will more easily penetrate the turned soil.

Water the plants in their pots the night before planting, and when planting, loosen the root ball if roots seem tight. Plant so that the finished soil level will be the same as it was in the pots. Give a thorough watering to settle the plants in, and then mulch the area with old manure or compost. Regular watering and at least annual

GOOD CHOICES FOR HEDGES AND SCREENS

For clipped, formal hedges, evergreens with small leaves are best. For informal hedges, plants that are densely foliaged to the ground are ideal, while a screen may consist of any plants that will achieve the desired result. Evergreen shrubs are best for screening but even the mass of bare branches on deciduous shrubs has some screening effect and they let in winter sun.

The plants listed below make successful hedges and screens. You'll find entries for many of them in this book. Consult your local garden center to find the most suitable for your garden.

- **FORMAL HEDGE:** English and Japanese box, cherry laurel, photinia, spindle bush, dwarf honeysuckle, lavender, rosemary, cypress, juniper, sasanqua camellia
- **INFORMAL HEDGE:** orange jessamine, cotoneaster, firethorn, laurustinus, oleander, hibiscus, plumbago, rhododendron, grevillea
- **TEMPERATE MIXED SCREEN:** ceanothus, camellia, mahonia, rhododendron (tall species), deutzia, pittosporum, eucalyptus, *Quercus ilex*, *Cupressus macrocarpa*, *Cotoneaster* "Cornubia", elaeagnus, hibiscus, lavatera, ribes, oleander, Chinese lantern, escallonia
- **COOL MIXED SCREEN:** holly, osmanthus, Japanese oleaster, rhododendron, mock orange, weigela, euonymus osmanthus, Japanese oleaster, rhododendron, mock orange

mulching to keep the soil in good condition is essential for the best results with closely planted shrubs.

SHAPING AND PRUNING

Always prune any sort of hedge so that the top is slightly narrower than the bottom. This gives the lower growth enough light to live. This is especially important with conifers such as cypresses because once that lower growth dies, it does not generally regenerate. Conifers should be pruned little and often, and never into older wood, as many of them will not reshoot from bare wood.

With a formal hedge, pruning should begin early. Cut the vertical growth severely as soon as the plants are established. This encourages low branching and you should continue to trim the plants to shape as they grow. It will take several years for them to reach the desired height but if you let them grow to the height you want first and then start shaping, you may never achieve the density of foliage necessary for good privacy and you will almost certainly have bare branches at the base.

Even informal hedges and screens should be sheared lightly at least annually, and right from the start, so that they develop a thick, bushy habit.

In mild climates, maintenance pruning can be done at almost any time of year (but remember, quick regrowth is desirable). In frosty areas, don't prune after midsummer—this allows the existing growth to harden off which means that it will not be damaged by frost. Most hedges can be managed with pruners and hand hedging shears which are kept sharp. If, however, you have big hedges to maintain, a powered hedge clipper will make the job quicker and easier.

RIGHTS AND WRONGS OF HEDGING

ROUND TOPS are hard to maintain and straight sides can lead to die-back of the lower branches.

A FLAT TOP and flared sides: this is the ideal shape for any hedge, whatever its size may be.

A NARROW TOP sheds snow but the steep angle is hard to judge by eye when you are pruning.

A WIDE TOP and narrow base prevents sunlight reaching the lower branches, causing die-back.

SHEAR FORMAL hedges to shape whenever growth begins to look untidy. Remember, with conifers you cannot always cut into old, leafless parts of stem, and so don't let over-growth continue for too long

CHAPTER SEVENTEEN

CLIMBERS

Climbing plants can be used to cover fences or sheds, to decorate blank walls, to screen out unsightly views or cast shade from a pergola. They can also be a feature in themselves, if they are grown over an ornamental arch.

HOW CLIMBERS CLIMB

Climbing plants do not have self-supporting trunks or branches. They must use various modifications to lift themselves up towards the sunlight. Some "climbers" can be used as groundcovers, sprawling over the ground when no support is available. Climbers are classified according to the mechanism by which they climb and may be twiners, tendril producers, scramblers or self-clingers.

CLIMBERS IN POTS

While most climbers are planted directly into the ground, they can also be grown in containers. A large container, filled with good quality potting mix, can sometimes be ideal, for example when a climber is needed to cover a pergola over a paved area and it is impossible to plant into the ground. However, do consider the area you want the climber to cover in relation to the size of the pot, for the pot holds all the water and nutrients available. Will it be big enough to keep all those stems and leaves full of water? To provide cover for a pergola, you will need a very large container, and possibly several with a climber in each. All will need frequent watering and fertilizing.

CLIMBERS KILL TREES

Don't allow climbers to grow up into trees. Vigorous twining climbers such as wisteria can kill trees by strangling them, cutting off the flow of sap between the roots and the crown. They will also smother the foliage, depriving the tree of light. Self-clinging climbers may also cause tree damage by keeping the bark of the tree constantly shaded and moist, allowing an easy entry point for insects or fungi.

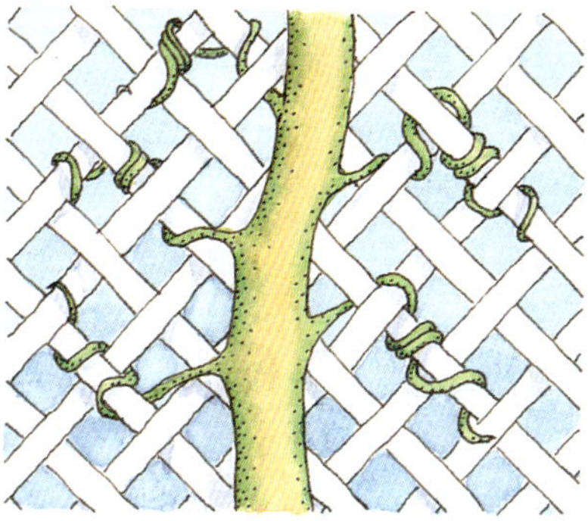

TENDRIL CLIMBERS have thin curling tendrils which coil around their support. Sweet pea and grape are good examples of this type of climber. The tendrils may be produced at the tips of leaves or from the point where the leaf joins the stem.

TWINERS ARE climbing plants that twine their new shoots entirely around a support. If that support is a plant and the twiner is vigorous, it can kill its host plant. Potato vine, clematis and wisteria are twining climbers.

SCRAMBLERS ARE climbing plants that climb by means of hooks or prickles that usually curve downwards. Rubus *(brambles) and climbing roses fall into this group. In the wild, they fall onto other plants and pull themselves upwards by scrambling over their hosts.*

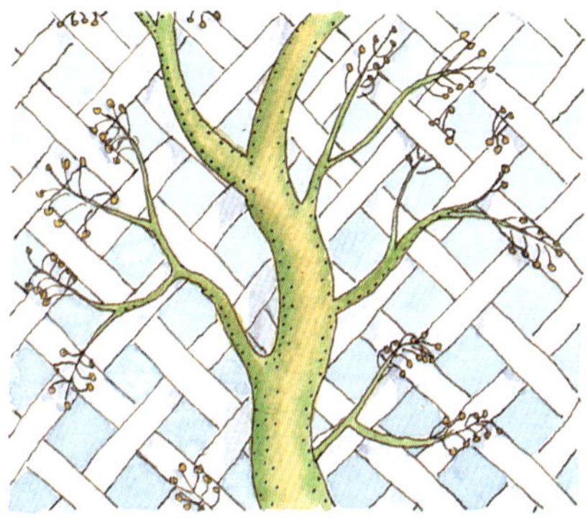

SELF-CLINGING CLIMBERS are not so numerous but these are the ones to use to cover blank masonry walls. Climbing hydrangea and ivy fall into this category. They cling to their support with adventitious roots that make their way into any crack in the surface.

Less vigorous climbers, such as some of the clematis hybrids, are better suited to cultivation in pots. Such climbers are too small to cover big areas but look lovely on wall-mounted trellises or twining up a stanchion. In tubs, very vigorous growers such as wisteria are best trained as standards or free-standing shrubs rather than as climbers. A very sturdy support is needed until they become self-supporting.

GROWING CONDITIONS

Aspect

Most climbers grow and flower best in full sun but there are some that tolerate degrees of shade. Ones such as clematis, which are described as needing a cool root run, like cool,

WITHOUT INTERVENTION from you, climbers will grow straight to the top of the support, leaving bareness below.

TRAIN THE growing stems horizontally from one side of the support to the other and you'll get an even cover of foliage.

shaded conditions at ground level but want their heads in the sun. Heavy mulching around the root area is one way of keeping the roots cool, but this can also be achieved by growing small groundcovering plants around the base of the vine. Some climbers, including climbing hydrangeas and ivy, will grow wholly in bright shade but this feature is not usual in the world of climbers. Almost all climbers flower in the sun. If you want a flowering climber over a pergola, choose one with pendulous blossoms, such as wisteria, or all the color will be on top. If you are growing the climber on a lattice panel or a steel mesh fence, the vast bulk of the flowers will be on the sunny side.

Soil

Many climbers are long-lived plants but even those that are not will respond to good soil preparation before planting. Check that the soil is adequately drained so that the roots will not be sitting in a waterlogged hole. You'll find information on soil improvement and drainage in Chapter Three on pages 24–7.

Water needs

All newly planted climbers, like any other plants, need regular watering until they are established. Check new plantings daily in summer, and water if the ground feels dry. Until the plant roots have made their way out into the surrounding soil, they are very vulnerable to water stress. Once established, they usually need a deep weekly watering during the warm months but check the entries for individual climbers as some are more drought tolerant than others. If you mulch the soil in which climbers are growing you will both improve its fertility and conserve soil moisture.

Pruning

Most climbers need pruning to restrict their size. Prune deciduous climbers in winter and evergreens straight after bloom unless they flower in fall, in which case prune in spring.

ACTINIDIA

Actinidia kolomikta

DECIDUOUS

ORIGIN: Temperate eastern Asia.
HABIT: This is a vigorous fast-growing twining climber which is capable of reaching a height of 16 ft or even more.
FROST TOLERANCE: It is very hardy and will take a minimum temperature of –20°F.
APPEAL: Grown for its unusual and highly decorative foliage. In the top half of the plant the large, rounded, deep green leaves are often variegated with white and pink. Fragrant white blooms appear in early summer, but these are not particularly showy, and they are followed, on female plants only, by yellow-green fruits.
CLIMATE: This climber is suitable for zone 5 and above.
ASPECT: Full sun or semi-shade are acceptable but provide shelter from strong and cold drying winds.
SUPPORT: Grow it on trellises and arbors or against a wall provided with strong wires.
PRUNING: In late winter prune to keep the plant within the space that is available.

THIS ACTINIDIA, one of the more unusual climbers, has variegated foliage.

THIS VERY ATTRACTIVE bramble has the advantage of being evergreen.

BRAMBLE

Rubus henryi var. *bambusarum*

EVERGREEN

ORIGIN: Western and central China.
HABIT: This is a tall vigorous climber which has a rather scrambling habit of growth.
FROST TOLERANCE: It will take a temperature down to 0°F.
APPEAL: This is a very easily grown bramble, as are most species. It is grown for its overall attraction and has the advantage of being evergreen. The stems are densely covered in white hairs when young and the deeply cut shiny dark green leaves have woolly white undersides. Saucer-shaped pink flowers appear in summer followed by shiny black berries. Grow it over an arbor, or train it to a wall or fence.
CLIMATE: Zone 7 and above.
ASPECT: Full sun or partial shade.
SUPPORT: It will need to be provided with a system of wires which are used for tying in the stems.
PRUNING: This is not often needed, but if required cut back the plant after flowering to keep it within bounds.

CLEMATIS

Many species and cultivars

DECIDUOUS AND EVERGREEN; TAKES PART-SHADE

ORIGIN: Temperate parts of both hemispheres and highland tropical areas (depending on species).
HABIT: These are light to medium twining climbers that are not usually overly vigorous. The growth rate is slow to moderate.
FROST TOLERANCE: Depends on the origin of the species. Some can take and need very cold winters while others accept light frosts only.
APPEAL: There are many species and hybrids of clematis. Some, such as the Jackmanii hybrids, have truly spectacular spring flowers. They are deciduous and can only be grown where winters are cold. In warmer areas, the little Australian native evergreen *C. aristata,* or "traveller's joy", makes a charming spring show with its starry, white flowers. Deciduous *C. montana* and its cultivars are also for cooler areas. In spring they produce masses of small flowers in white or pink.

TRAVELLER'S JOY is a dainty Australian clematis ideal for warmer climates.

CLIMATE: Jackmanii hybrids can be grown in zone 5 and above, while *C. montana* will be better in zone 6 and above. The slightly less-hardy *C. aristata* and closely allied species can be grown in zone 7 and above.
ASPECT: *C. aristata* prefers dappled sunlight while most other clematis plants prefer full sun but will tolerate semi-shade in their preferred cool climate. For best results keep the roots shaded, cool and moist but grow the upper parts of the plant in full sun.
SUPPORT: Needs lattice, trellis or a post on which to twine.
PRUNING: The timing and method of pruning depends on the species or cultivar grown. Some pruning may be needed to train these climbers to their supports. Many of the Jackmanii hybrids are pruned in late winter just before new growth commences. *C. montana* flowers on the previous season's growth and should be pruned after bloom. Some very old, established vines may need the removal of old canes at ground level.

C. MONTANA is a lovely vine with small flowers. It needs a cool climate to do well.

CLIMBING HYDRANGEA

Hydrangea anomala subsp. *petiolaris*

DECIDUOUS

ORIGIN: The species is a native of Japan, Sakhalin, Korea and Taiwan.
HABIT: It is very vigorous, clinging by means of aerial roots produced along its stems.
FROST TOLERANCE: This climber is quite tough and will take a minimum temperature of –9°F to 20°F.
APPEAL: It is one of comparatively few climbers that can be grown on a shady wall or fence. The heart-shaped deep green leaves turn yellow in fall before they drop and in summer heads of white fertile and sterile flowers are produced.
CLIMATE: Zone 5 and above.
ASPECT: Shade, partial shade or full sun. It dislikes cold drying winds so if necessary make sure it is protected.
SUPPORT: Will cling to flat surfaces so no additional support necessary.
PRUNING: Not much required. In early spring trim if necessary to keep the plant in its allotted space.

SHADY WALLS or fences are ideal for the climbing hydrangea.

COLCHIS IVY

Hedera colchica "Dentata Variegata"

EVERGREEN

ORIGIN: The species comes from the Caucasus to northern Iran but the variety is of garden origin.
HABIT: A vigorous self-clinging climber producing aerial roots on its stems.
FROST TOLERANCE: Not too hardy, it takes a minimum temperature of 0°F. Can be damaged by severe frost but often recovers in the spring.
APPEAL: The large thick leathery heart-shaped leaves are light green, blotched with gray-green and widely edged with cream. An excellent plant for a large wall. Makes good groundcover, especially in light shade with dry soil. Lightens up dark areas. There are several other excellent varieties of this ivy available.
CLIMATE: Zone 7 and above.
ASPECT: Ideal plant for light shade or partial shade, but provide shelter from cold drying winds.
SUPPORT: Will cling to flat surfaces.
PRUNING: In early spring trim to keep the plant within allotted space. Can also shear off some of the foliage if the plant becomes too heavy.

THE COLCHIS IVY can be a climber or groundcover, lightening up gloomy areas.

DUTCH WOODBINE

Lonerica periclymenum "Belgica"

DECIDUOUS

ORIGIN: The species comes from Europe, North Africa and Western Asia. This variety is of garden origin.
HABIT: The Dutch woodbine is a vigorous twining climber.
FROST TOLERANCE: A very hardy climber taking a minimum temperature of –20°F.
APPEAL: An extremely popular climber producing whorls of tubular, two-lipped, highly fragrant flowers in the summer. They are white, heavily flushed with red on the outside, and age to yellow. This climber is suitable for pergolas, walls, fences or free-standing trellis.
CLIMATE: Hardy in the north. Zone 5 and above.
ASPECT: Full sun or partial shade.
SUPPORT: Needs something to twine in and out of such as trellis panels or horizontal wires fixed to walls and fences.
PRUNING: As soon as flowering is over, cut back the flowered stems to young shoots lower down. This helps to avoid a tangled mess of stems building up.

THE DUTCH WOODBINE is valued for its highly fragrant flowers in the summer.

GOLDEN HOP, a herbaceous perennial, is one of the brightest-leaved climbers.

GOLDEN HOP

Humulus lupulus "Aureus"

DECIDUOUS

ORIGIN: Widely naturalized in north temperate regions.
HABIT: This is a fast growing twining herbaceous perennial.
FROST TOLERANCE: It is quite a tough plant and will take a minimum temperature of –9°F to 20°F.
APPEAL: This hop is grown only for its foliage. The large lobed leaves are bright golden yellow.
CLIMATE: Suitable for growing in zone 5 and above.
ASPECT: Grow in full sun for the brightest leaf color. Hops like moist soil which is rich in humus.
SUPPORT: Provide wires on a fence or wall for additional support. The stems will then twine around and through them.
PRUNING: In the early spring before growth appears, cut down all stems to ground level. Then a crop of new shoots will be produced and they will quickly grow up and cover their supports.

JAPANESE HYDRANGEA VINE

Schizophragma hydrangeoides

DECIDUOUS

ORIGIN: Japan and Korea.

HABIT: This tall vigorous climber clings to surfaces by means of aerial roots produced on the stems. It looks rather like a climbing hydrangea, with which it is sometimes confused.

FROST TOLERANCE: It is quite a tough plant, taking a temperature down to –20°F.

APPEAL: This climber is grown mainly for its large heads of white flowers which have conspicuous sterile outer flowers. These are produced in summer, against a background of large oval dark green leaves. Grow it against a wall or fence.

CLIMATE: It is suitable for zone 5 and above.

ASPECT: It will grow equally well in full sun or partial shade.

SUPPORT: As it is self-clinging, it needs no additional means of support, apart from its wall or fence.

PRUNING: No regular pruning needed. In spring if necessary cut back the plant to keep it within its allotted space.

THE JAPANESE hydrangea vine is sometimes confused with the climbing hydrangea.

ORNAMENTAL GRAPE produces fiery red fall foliage and the changing colors are remarkably vibrant with the sun on them.

ORNAMENTAL GRAPE

Vitis coignetiae

DECIDUOUS

ORIGIN: Japan, Korea.

HABIT: This heavy, vigorous, tendril climber is a moderate to fast grower.

FROST TOLERANCE: Accepts –13°F at least.

APPEAL: This ornamental grape is grown for its brilliant fall foliage and the wonderful shade it casts in summer. It is a very large, long-lived climber, which is extremely vigorous and able to cover quite a large area in one season. It is ideal for covering pergolas, losing its leaves by mid-fall and regaining them by mid-spring. It does produce small grapes but these are only good for the birds. Edible grapes can be messy over decks or patios when the grapes drop.

CLIMATE: This climber is very hardy and will succeed in zone 5 and above.

ASPECT: Full sun all day.

SUPPORT: Needs the support of a sturdy pergola.

PRUNING: Needs pruning for shaping and training and to control the size of the vine. The main pruning should be done in the dormant winter period but rampant growth can be cut back at any time during the growing season.

POTATO VINE

Solanum jasminoides

EVERGREEN OR DECIDUOUS;
TAKES PART-SHADE

ORIGIN: Brazil.
HABIT: The potato vine is a vigorous, fast-growing, medium to large, twining climber.
FROST TOLERANCE: It accepts 23°F but is deciduous in frosty areas.
APPEAL: Popular for its deceptively light looks and sprays of dainty white flowers, the potato vine is much more vigorous than it looks and in warm, humid conditions can get out of control unless frequently cut back.
It is evergreen in warm climates.
CLIMATE: It is not a very hardy climber, but will succeed in zone 9 and above.
ASPECT: The potato vine prefers a sheltered position in full sun but will tolerate partial shade.
SUPPORT: This vine needs wire mesh, netting or lattice for support.
PRUNING: Frequent pruning can be necessary in warmer climates. Trim off faded flowers and cut back older vines hard in spring to renew them.

IN WARM CLIMATES the potato vine flowers all year round, except in winter.

THE LITTLE white flowers of star jasmine appear in spring and summer.

STAR JASMINE

Trachelospermum jasminoides

EVERGREEN; ACCEPTS PART-SHADE

ORIGIN: China and south-east Asia.
HABIT: A small to medium twiner, it has a slow to moderate growth rate.
FROST TOLERANCE: Takes 22°F.
APPEAL: A handsome climber with glossy, dark green leaves and clusters of strongly perfumed, white flowers. There is also a less vigorous form with variegated foliage. Star jasmine can be grown over a fence, trellis or archway, or it can be trimmed as a low hedge or groundcover. It is long lived and very trouble-free.
CLIMATE: This is not a very hardy climber but will be happy in zone 9 and above.
ASPECT: Grows well in full sun or semi-shade. Heavy shade tends to make it thin out.
SUPPORT: Needs trellis, wire or netting to carry the twining stems.
PRUNING: You may wish to prune it back after flowers have finished. This vine has thick, milky sap which may be caustic or irritating to some skins and so wear gloves and long sleeves when pruning.

TRUMPET CREEPER

Campsis radicans

DECIDUOUS

ORIGIN: Native to south-east America.
HABIT: A very vigorous species climbing by aerial or stem roots.
FROST TOLERANCE: Quite a hardy climber despite its appearance. It will take a minimum temperature of –20°F.
APPEAL: A very showy climber with 3 in long tubular or trumpet-shaped orange to orange-red flowers, in late summer. Several varieties have flowers in different shades of orange or red as well as one with yellow flowers.
CLIMATE: It grows well in the southern states and is fairly hardy north, zone 5 and above.
ASPECT: Provide a sunny spot sheltered from cold winds, especially in colder regions. In warmer areas it will tolerate a more exposed site and partial shade.
SUPPORT: As it clings well to flat surfaces it can be grown on a tall wall or fence without additional support.
PRUNING: Allow a permanent framework of woody stems to build up. Then in early spring prune back the side shoots to within three or four buds of this framework.

THE TRUMPET CREEPER is quite hardy despite its exotic appearance.

VIRGINIA CREEPER

Parthenocissus quinquefolia

DECIDUOUS

ORIGIN: Eastern North America.
HABIT: This is an extremely tall vigorous climber that clings firmly to flat surfaces by means of adhesive discs on the ends of tendrils.
FROST TOLERANCE: It is exceedingly hardy, taking a temperature down to –31°F.
APPEAL: The Virginia creeper is grown for its large lobed leaves which take on brilliant red shades in fall before they drop. Grow this climber on high walls, fences and arbors but do not attempt it if there is insufficient space. There are several varieties available.
CLIMATE: Zone 4 and above.
ASPECT: Grows equally well in sun or shade.
SUPPORT: It will cling firmly to flat surfaces and needs no additional means of support.
PRUNING: If necessary in early winter trim the plant to keep it within its allotted space. It can be trimmed again in summer if necessary.

ONLY CONSIDER Virginia creeper if there is sufficient space available to grow it.

THE YELLOW flowers of winter jasmine are welcoming in winter or early spring.

WINTER JASMINE

Jasminum nudiflorum

DECIDUOUS

ORIGIN: A native of western China.
HABIT: This is not a true climber but produces long green stems that can be trained to supports.
FROST TOLERANCE: It will take a minimum temperature of –9°F.
APPEAL: This is an easily grown shrub which is highly valued for its welcoming bright yellow winter and early spring flowers. If shoots are cut during winter and placed in a vase indoors the flowers will quickly open. It is generally trained flat against a wall or fence.
CLIMATE: Suitable for zone 6 and above.
ASPECT: Full sun or partial shade.
SUPPORT: Tie in the stems to a system of horizontal wires or to a trellis panel fixed to the wall or fence.
PRUNING: This is carried out after flowering by cutting back old flowered shoots to young shoots or buds lower down. Also if necessary remove completely some of the oldest wood.

POSSIBLY THE best loved climber of all, wisteria grows and flowers in cold and warm climates. It is a very vigorous, long-lived vine that needs a strong and durable support.

WISTERIA

Wisteria floribunda, W. sinensis

DECIDUOUS

ORIGIN: China, Japan.
HABIT: This very vigorous, heavy twining climber has a moderate to fast growth rate.
FROST TOLERANCE: Accepts –13°F at least.
APPEAL: Wisteria is grown for its short but spectacular display of pervasively fragrant flowers. They appear in early spring in long pendulous clusters and are usually mauve-blue but may also be pink or white. Wisteria is a very vigorous climber, ideal for covering pergolas or archways or for training along verandah railings or fences. It may also be trained as a standard, either in the ground or in a large tub. In cold climates, the leaves turn bright yellow before falling.
CLIMATE: Unsuitable for the tropics, wisteria is extremely hardy, growing well in zone 5 and above.
ASPECT: Full sun is essential and shelter from wind will preserve the flower display.
SUPPORT: Needs a very strong, durable support. Do not allow a wisteria to grow up into a tree as its weight may break branches and its bulk may eventually smother and so kill the tree.
PRUNING: Vigorous growth may need cutting back more than once during the growing season. Wisteria blooms on spurs on lateral growths off the main canes. These laterals should be cut back to within five compound leaves in midsummer and shortened again during the dormant winter period. Winter pruning should also thin out surplus stems and shorten long shoots.

• CHAPTER EIGHTEEN •

ANNUALS

No other plants give your garden the seasonal color and interest that annuals do. They're easy to grow, quick to bloom and some keep on going for months. You'll enjoy growing annuals—they're fun and you see the results within weeks.

Annuals are plants that grow to full size, flower, seed and die within one year or one season. Generally, annuals are planted twice a year: in fall to give a floral display through late winter and spring, and then in spring to give garden color in summer and fall. But if you really like change, you could plant different annuals at the start of every season.

There are annuals for almost every situation. Most grow best in sunny spots but there are some that prefer the shade. Do, however, be careful to plant at the correct time as some annuals are "short-day" plants and will not flower if the hours of daylight are too long. The correct planting times are included with all the other important growing details in the entries for individual flowers on the following pages.

SOIL PREPARATION

Good soil preparation will go a long way toward preventing problems with annuals. All annuals prefer well-drained soil, and so if you know that your soil is heavy and stays wet for long periods after rain, take steps to improve it before the planting season (see pages 24–5 for details on how to improve soil drainage). If drainage is not a problem, and it won't be for most gardeners, simply dig over the planting site, breaking up clods as you go. Incorporate compost or well-rotted cow manure and a handful of complete plant food per square yard as you dig. The finished bed should be light and crumbly and easy to dig with a trowel.

SEED OR SEEDLINGS?

You can grow your own annuals from seed or by buying seedlings. Starting from seed is cheaper and some annuals, such as sweet pea, nasturtium and sunflower, are best grown this way. They should be sown where they are to grow, and this is not difficult as the seed is large and easy to handle. Other plants, such as primula and poppy, have seed as fine as dust, which is not easy to sow well. If you mix a little fine sand with it you will find it easier to sow it evenly. Seed can be sown directly into the ground and thinned out later or started off in seed trays and planted out later.

Despite their much higher cost per plant, many gardeners prefer to buy seedlings because, frankly, they are easier. They also have the advantage of putting you several weeks ahead and if you want a colorful display for

FLOWERS HAVE a special charm and attraction. People are drawn to them and can't help but smile when they see a bed of colorful blooms. And there's just as much pleasure for the grower. You see results quickly and can have fun playing with color combinations.

a special occasion it is easier to gauge the time from planting to flowering. It is also possible to buy seedlings at the flowering stage for an almost instant effect. Plant seedlings as soon as you get them home, directly where they are to grow. They are easy to separate and should be planted at the same depth in the soil as they were in their punnets. Do pay attention to the spacing details given on the label—overcrowding leads to less than perfect results, while too wide a spacing creates unwanted gaps.

SOWING SEED

When growing flowers from seeds, it is very important to follow the specific directions: seed can fail if overwatered or underwatered, or when the seed has been planted too deeply or at the wrong time of year.

If you are not sowing the seeds directly where the flowers are to grow (and this is not always possible, especially with very fine seeds) you should sow them into seedling trays or punnets of seed-raising mix. This is a special, very fine potting mix available from garden centers. Sow seed according to the packet directions and place pots or trays in a warm, sheltered spot. Keep the mix just moist at all times, taking care that it is not too wet or the seedlings will rot. Conversely, it must never dry out. Water with a fine mist or sink the trays into shallow water as this avoids any chance of dislodging seeds. Don't fertilize the seeds: that comes later when the little plants have the roots to absorb it.

Seedlings take anything from a few days to three weeks to appear, depending on the plant, and this information should be given on the packet. Seeds will always germinate fastest in warm, moist conditions. Once seedlings are 1–2 in tall, gently lift them out of their seed trays with the handle of a teaspoon and place them in their permanent positions. This is called "pricking out". If the seeds have been sown in their permanent positions, they won't need pricking out but you should thin out seedlings that are growing too close to each other. If you are gentle, you can transplant these excess seedlings to other positions in the garden.

WATERING

All annuals need frequent watering until they are established, but once they are, reduce watering to a good soak once or twice a week.

FERTILIZING

When soil has been well prepared with compost or manure and a ration of complete plant food, plants usually perform quite well without additional fertilizer. However, if you like to feed, apply soluble or liquid plant food once a month. There's no value in overfeeding as this can force many annuals into sappy leaf growth at the expense of flowers. Never apply fertilizer to bone-dry soil. Water first, apply fertilizer, and then water again.

FLOWERING

Don't allow tiny plants to flower. As buds appear, pinch them out with your fingertips. If you allow annuals to flower when they are tiny they will never develop into good-sized plants and their life will be very short. Pinching also produces a bushier plant with more potential flowering stems.

To get the most flowers, dead-head often—cut off the spent flowers about once a week. If you don't remove the spent blooms, the plant will divert its resources into setting seed and stop producing a fresh crop of flowers.

MOST ANNUALS grow so well in pots, you can have a colorful display anywhere you want it. Here, a group of containers creates a cheerful welcome on the front porch.

WHAT CAN GO WRONG?

Yellow leaves

■ Plants may have been overwatered or may be too dry.

■ Plants may need feeding—try feeding with a half-strength solution of one of the soluble plant foods. If this is the problem you should see an improvement within a week or two. Give another dose of fertiliser to complete the re-greening process.

Curled or distorted leaves

■ Look for aphids, small sticky insects clustering on the stems or leaves. Wash them off with the hose, spray with soapy water or use an insecticidal soap or pyrethrum spray to get rid of them.

■ Check that herbicide has not been used nearby: even a small amount of spray drift can cause this problem.

■ Some virus diseases of plants manifest themselves this way. These are not common in annuals but there is no cure for virus disease in plants.

Black spots on leaves

■ Black spots may be fungal leaf spots. Avoid watering late in the day, try to avoid wetting leaves and spray with a copper-based fungicide if the problem becomes serious.

Meandering trails in leaf tissue

■ These trails may indicate leaf miner, especially on some kinds of daisies. It won't affect flowering but can be unsightly. However, control can only be achieved by spraying with a systemic insecticide. It may be better to ignore the problem unless you are showing your garden in a competition.

Grey/white powder on leaves

■ White or grey powder could be powdery mildew, which is a problem on sweet peas and many other plants. A spray with sulphur can halt the progress of the disease. Avoid watering late in the day. If the problem persists, your climate may be too humid for that plant.

Yellowish mottle on the upper side of the leaf, rusty brown spots on the underside

■ This mottling is probably evidence of rust, a fungal disease that can be serious on snapdragons, calendulas and chrysanthemums, in particular. Remove the worst affected leaves, avoid watering late in the day and try not to wet the foliage. Spray with a copper-based or other suitable fungicide.

Holes chewed in leaves or edges

■ Holes may be snail or slug damage. Search for snails and if you do not have dogs use one of the proprietary snail baits. Snails and slugs leave silvery trails behind.

■ Caterpillars, crickets and grasshoppers can chew leaves too. Try dusting your plants with derris dust on several consecutive nights to catch the culprits. Caterpillars leave clusters of spherical droppings.

Seedlings cut off at ground level

■ This is probably cutworm damage. These insects hide in the soil during the day and come out at night to feed. Dust plants liberally with derris dust, a very safe insecticide, several nights in a row.

ONE OF the easiest annuals to grow, alyssum will resow itself although the quality of bloom eventually declines.

ALYSSUM

Also known as sweet Alice

Lobularia maritima

TAKES PART-SHADE

SIZE: About 6 in tall with a low, spreading habit.
CLIMATE: Can be grown outdoors all year round in zone 7 and above.
ASPECT: Grows best in full sun but will accept a few hours light shade.
PLANTING: In zones 7 and above alyssum can be sown where it is to flower in spring or summer. This is the easiest method. In colder zones sow in trays under glass in spring.
FLOWERING SEASON: The main flowering season is from late spring to late summer. The plants are quick growing and flowering generally starts eight weeks after sowing.
CUT FLOWERS: Not suitable.
COLOR RANGE: White, pink, purple and apricot shades are sold.
USES: Good edging plant or use in the center of driveways or between the cracks in paving or walls. Useful in pots, baskets and windowboxes.

AMARANTHUS

Amaranthus

SIZE: Over 3 ft tall.
CLIMATE: It will not tolerate frost. Can be grown outdoors all year round in zone 10 and possibly in zone 9. In other areas grow this as a summer bedding plant.
ASPECT: Full sun all day.
PLANTING: Grow from seed planted in middle to late spring or from purchased seedlings.
FLOWERING SEASON: In warm to hot areas plants should provide brilliant color from early summer to at least the middle of fall.
CUT FLOWERS: Yes. For a dramatic display, cut the whole stem.
COLOR RANGE: Foliage color is brilliant and different in all varieties. Usual shades are red, pink, yellow and green.
USES: When subtle just won't do, say it with amaranthus. These are big, dramatically different plants ideal for a tropical-look planting or for the back of a deep flower border. They are as striking as sunflowers and look good with them, or other yellow, red or orange flowers. Best used boldly.

THE BRIGHTLY colored foliage is the chief attraction of amaranthus.

ONE OF the finest cut flowers, asters are also good value in the garden.

ASTER

Callistephus chinensis

EVERGREEN; TAKES SHADE

SIZE: 16–24 in tall.
CLIMATE: It will not stand frost and is hardy in zone 10 and possibly in zone 9. Aster does not like very wet summers.
ASPECT: Needs full sun and shelter from strong wind.
PLANTING: Sow seed in early to middle spring. The fine seed should be covered very lightly. In warmer areas, seedlings are worth planting until the middle of summer. In cold areas where frosts are possible in spring, sow seeds indoors and plant out when frosts are finished.
FLOWERING SEASON: Early summer to early fall in most areas. Midsummer plantings bloom through most of fall.
CUT FLOWERS: Excellent cut flower, popular in the floral trade.
COLOR RANGE: Pink, blue, mauve, white, red and purple.
USES: Beautiful when massed in a bold garden display, or use asters as part of a mixed flower border.

AURORA DAISY

Arctotis

SIZE: Up to 12 in tall but spreading to nearly 3 ft across.
CLIMATE: Can be grown outside all year round in zone 9 and above. In other areas grow this as a summer bedding plant.
ASPECT: Needs full sun all day—flowers close in shade or on dull days. Sloping ground is ideal.
PLANTING: Sow seeds in early spring for summer bedding plants. In frost-free areas seeds can also be sown in the fall for early flowering the following year. Not ideal for tropical areas as it is not well suited to growing in humid conditions.
FLOWERING SEASON: Spring to late summer.
CUT FLOWERS: Not suitable.
COLOR RANGE: White and pink, red, yellow and orange.
USES: Attractive large-scale groundcover and ideal for hot, sunny beds. Aurora daisies can also be used in baskets and wide pots.

VERY STRIKING in bloom, aurora daisies are effective as a large-scale groundcover.

BABY BLUE EYES

Nemophila menziesii

TAKES PART-SHADE

SIZE: Up to 8 in tall.
CLIMATE: It is hardy down to 5°F. A native of California.
ASPECT: Full sun to half shade.
PLANTING: Sow seed from late summer to late fall and, in cold areas, in very early spring. Sow seed directly where plants are to grow. If you live in the tropics or hot inland areas, sow in early fall, as soon as the weather cools.
FLOWERING SEASON: Late winter, spring and summer. The floral display lasts longer in cooler areas.
CUT FLOWERS: Not suitable.
COLOR RANGE: Usually china blue with a white eye but there is also a mainly white variety.
USES: A pretty plant at the front of a flower border or for lining paths. It is also a fine partner for early spring bulbs and an excellent basket, pot or window-box flower.

BABY BLUE EYES is charming on its own, or contrasts well with pretty meadowfoam.

LIGHT AND LACY baby's breath creates an airy, cloud-like effect.

BABY'S BREATH

Gypsophila elegans

SIZE: 18–24 in tall with fine stems bearing dainty flowers.
CLIMATE: Grows best in cooler areas such as zones 6–8 but worth trying in warmer zones.
ASPECT: Must have shelter from strong wind and prefers full sun.
PLANTING: Seeds of baby's breath are normally sown where the plants are to flower in the early spring. Space plants 4–6 in apart so that they support each other.
FLOWERING SEASON: Plants take 8–10 weeks to flower from seed. As the display is short-lived, successional sowings every three weeks are needed for continuous flowering.
CUT FLOWERS: Ideal cut flower. Can be used alone or to complement other flowers.
COLOR RANGE: Usually white but there are also varieties available with pink or purplish pink flowers.
USES: Delightful in big drifts or scattered through a border of other annuals or perennials. Try it in the cracks of retaining walls or as part of a meadow-style planting.

BALSAM IS the lesser known cousin of the popular busy lizzie or Impatiens.

BALSAM

Impatiens balsamina

TAKES PART-SHADE

SIZE: Standard form grows to 24 in tall. There are half-size dwarf forms.
CLIMATE: Grows best where summers are not cool and wet. Likes warm but not excessively dry weather.
ASPECT: Unlike the more common *Impatiens* (busy lizzie), balsam likes full sun, especially in cooler climates. In the tropics or hot inland areas it enjoys afternoon shade.
PLANTING: Sow seeds or plant seedlings in early spring. In cool areas, if frosts are still possible then, plant indoors until frost has passed. In the tropics, seed can be sown virtually year-round. Everywhere, barely cover the very fine seed.
FLOWERING SEASON: During warm weather (spring through summer). In tropical and frost-free places, flowering is continuous.
CUT FLOWERS: Not suitable as a cut flower, but potted plants can be used as temporary indoor decoration.
COLOR RANGE: Red, magenta, pink, white and yellow.
USES: A pretty and unusual garden plant or try it in pots or troughs.

BEGONIA

Begonia semperflorens

TAKES SHADE

SIZE: 6–12 in tall; rounded habit.
CLIMATE: Grows year-round in humid, frost-free gardens but is a summer annual in cooler climates. Hot, dry conditions are unsuitable.
ASPECT: Prefers morning sun, afternoon shade and protection from strong, drying wind. Bright, dappled sunlight is also suitable.
PLANTING: Seed is extremely fine and hard to handle and seedlings are the preferred way to start this plant. In frosty areas do not plant until very late spring; elsewhere plant after the weather has warmed up in spring. Plant out 6–8 in apart.
FLOWERING SEASON: In tropical and frost-free areas, plants are rarely without flowers. In cooler places, blooms appear right through summer.
CUT FLOWERS: Not suitable as a cut flower. Potted plants make good temporary indoor plants.
COLOR RANGE: Pink, white and red. Leaves may be green or reddish.
USES: Ideal edging plant. Attractive in pots, baskets and windowboxes and one of the few flowers that will bloom well in some shade.

BOTH THE waxy flowers and the glossy leaves are attractive in bedding begonias.

BLUE DAISY

Felicia amelloides

SIZE: This is a straggling sub-shrub which will grow to about 24 in tall.
CLIMATE: It can be grown outdoors all year round in zones 9 and 10. In colder areas grow it as an annual bedding plant.
ASPECT: Grow in full sun for optimum flowering. Does well in poor to moderately fertile soil. Hates damp conditions.
PLANTING: Sow seeds in spring and plant out when danger of frost is over.
FLOWERING SEASON: Flowers for a long period in summer and into fall.
CUT FLOWERS: Suitable for cutting but not generally thought of as a cut flower.
COLOR RANGE: The daisy-like flowers come in shades of blue, or sometimes white. There are numerous varieties of this plant.
USES: Summer bedding mainly and also suitable for summer display in patio containers. Plant blue daisy permanently in front of shrub border in frost-free areas.

THE SHRUBBY blue daisy can be grown in beds and containers for summer display.

CALENDULA GIVES cheery color, in mild areas in winter but in zone 6 in summer.

CALENDULA

Also known as pot marigold or English marigold

Calendula officinalis

SIZE: 12–20 in tall and bushy.
CLIMATE: Suitable for zones 6 and above, but it is not happy in very warm regions.
ASPECT: Needs full sun.
PLANTING: Generally calendulas are sown in the spring but they can also be sown in fall for earlier flowering the following year. In frost-prone areas protect fall sowings with cloches. Sow where they are to flower and thin out to 10–12 in apart each way.
FLOWERING SEASON: From late winter to spring or, where winters are very cold, in summer. The flowering season is longer in cooler areas.
CUT FLOWERS: Good cut flower, used widely in the floral trade. Cutting flowers helps to lengthen the flowering period. Cut when flowers are well formed but before the petals open out too far.
COLOR RANGE: Yellow, orange and honey.
USES: Striking when massed or use clumps here and there among other flowers. Good in pots.

CALIFORNIA POPPY

Eschscholzia californica

SIZE: 10–18 in tall; mounding shape.
CLIMATE: Although a native of California, it will thrive in zone 6 in a minimum temperature of 0°F to –9°F.
ASPECT: Full sun is essential.
PLANTING: Sow where plants are to grow as they are not easy to transplant. Sow in fall or, in cold places, in late winter or early spring.
FLOWERING SEASON: Long flowering period through spring and summer at least.
CUT FLOWERS: May be used as cut flowers. Cut long stems and place them in water immediately.
COLOR RANGE: Orange, red, pink, yellow and cream in single or double flowers.
USES: Very beautiful in big drifts, wildflower-style, or use as part of a flower border. A very good choice for hot, dry banks.

ONCE YOU plant the brilliant California poppies, you'll always have them.

CANDYTUFT PEPPERED with heartsease makes a delightful color combination.

CANDYTUFT

Iberis umbellata

EVERGREEN; TAKES SHADE

SIZE: 12–16 in tall and bushy. There are also several popular dwarf varieties.
CLIMATE: It is suitable for growing in zone 7 and above.
ASPECT: Best in full sun but will tolerate a few hours shade a day.
PLANTING: Best planted where they are to grow as they are not easy to transplant. If sowing in pots, use small pots to minimize disturbance when transplanting. Space seed 6–8 in apart to give the best display. Sow in fall and, in cold areas, in early spring as well.
FLOWERING SEASON: Flowers in spring and summer.
CUT FLOWERS: Good cut flower. Flowers that are well formed but not overmature should last well if picked early in the day and immediately plunged into water before arranging.
COLOR RANGE: White, pink, mauve and purple.
USES: Use for edgings, mass plantings or with other flowers for a multi-colored display. Attractive in pots.

AS WELL AS this feathery type, look for the strange "cockscomb" varieties.

COCKSCOMB

Also known as Prince of Wales feathers or feathery amaranth

Celosia cristata

SIZE: Tall forms grow to 30 in, dwarf forms to just 12 in.
CLIMATE: Best in warm areas but possible in cold climates if not planted out too early.
ASPECT: Must have full sun all day for best results. In cooler areas it must be given a warm sheltered spot.
PLANTING: In warm areas sow seed during spring; in cool zones sow after frosts have finished or sow indoors. Sow seed in pots or trays, lightly covered with seed-raising mix. Plant out tall forms 12–16 in apart and dwarf forms 6–8 in apart. Seedlings are sold from about mid-spring.
FLOWERING SEASON: Long display through summer and fall.
CUT FLOWERS: May be used fresh or hung upside down to dry.
COLOR RANGE: Red, orange and yellow.
USES: Mass for bright, unusual display, use for edging or in pots.

COLEUS

Also known as flame nettle or painted leaves

Solenostemon scutellarioides, syn. *Coleus* x *hybridus*

NEEDS SHADE

SIZE: About 20 in tall.
CLIMATE: Not ideal where summers are hot and dry such as zones 4, 7 and 8. Good elsewhere.
ASPECT: Can be grown outside all year round in zone 10 and above and in other areas use as summer bedding.
PLANTING: Easily grown from soft-tip cuttings taken in spring, but can also be raised from seed sown in spring. Do not cover but keep just moist until seedlings appear. In the garden, space 12 in apart.
FLOWERING SEASON: Grown for its leaves, not its insignificant flowers which are pinched out as soon as seen—once plants have flowered, leaf growth stops.
CUT FLOWERS: Not suitable. Use potted coleus indoors instead.
COLOR RANGE: Leaves are colored and patterned in many shades of red, yellow, green and pink.
USES: Mass together with *Impatiens* for a bright display in shade or use them as a groundcover. Ideal for a tropical-look planting.

EASILY GROWN in moist, humid gardens, coleus gives good color in shade.

CORNFLOWER

Centaurea cyanus

SIZE: Tall forms grow to 36 in, dwarf varieties will reach 12 in.
CLIMATE: Fairly hardy, suitable for zone 7 and above.
ASPECT: Best in full sun but in warmer climates will manage with half a day's sun. Easily blown over.
PLANTING: Sow in pots or directly where plants are to grow in fall to early winter. Space them 6–8 in apart. Where winters are very cold, early spring sowings are advisable.
FLOWERING SEASON: Late spring in most areas but into summer in cool zones. Dead-head regularly or flowering may be over quickly.
CUT FLOWERS: Excellent cut flower. Popular in posies or alone. Pick early in the day and scald stems before arranging them in cool water.
COLOR RANGE: Intense "cornflower" blue is the most popular but mixtures including white, pink, and paler blue are also available.
USES: Mass or use as part of a flower border, especially in combination with white and yellow flowers. Looks well in meadow plantings.

USE CORNFLOWERS to add splashes of blue to your late spring flower garden.

COSMOS SEEDS germinate fast and once you have plants, they reseed themselves.

COSMOS

Cosmos bipinnatus

TAKES PART-SHADE

SIZE: Up to 5 ft tall with an open, airy habit.
CLIMATE: Will not stand frost and is generally grown as a summer display plant in cold areas.
ASPECT: Best in full sun but in warmer areas at least will tolerate shade for a few hours. Everywhere needs some shelter from strong winds.
PLANTING: Sow in spring directly where plants are to grow. They are frost tender, and so don't sow before late spring in cool zones or sow earlier under cover and transplant when frosts have passed. Space plants 12–16 in apart. In the tropics sow any time from fall to the end of winter.
FLOWERING SEASON: Early summer to fall in zone 6 and above if spent flowers are nipped off.
CUT FLOWERS: Ideal cut flower. Even a few are very decorative.
COLOR RANGE: White, pink, mauve, magenta, yellow and orange.
USES: Best planted in drifts or as background plants in mixed borders. Suitable for meadow plantings.

THE INDIAN or annual pink has delicately scented flowers.

DIANTHUS

Also known as Indian pink or annual pink

Dianthus chinensis

SIZE: 8–12 in tall, forming rounded, grassy-leaved plants.

CLIMATE: Hardy in zone 7 and above.

ASPECT: Needs full sun.

PLANTING: This dianthus is generally grown as an annual and sown in early spring, under glass in frost-prone areas. Cover seed with no more than 1/4 in of compost or soil. Plant out seedlings 6 in apart in their flowering positions.

FLOWERING SEASON: The main flowering period is in the summer from spring-sown seed. The flowers are delicately scented.

CUT FLOWERS: Not as long lasting as carnations but can be useful in posies and small arrangements.

COLOR RANGE: Single flowers come in pink, red and white or combinations of these.

USES: Lovely when massed as a groundcover or use clumps in the front of a flower border or for edgings. Grows well in pots, troughs, windowboxes or baskets.

ENGLISH DAISY

Also known as lawn daisy

Bellis perennis

TAKES PART-SHADE

SIZE: Just 4–6 in tall.

CLIMATE: This is very hardy, thriving in zone 4 and above. It likes a cool winter, but not too wet.

ASPECT: Performs best in full sun but will accept some light shade.

PLANTING: Sow seeds outdoors in late spring for flowering the following year. Plant out young plants in fall, 6 in apart each way. It is easier to buy in young plants in the fall.

FLOWERING SEASON: Flowers appear in late winter and early spring or, in cooler places, in early summer.

CUT FLOWERS: Flowers make a lovely posy either alone or mixed.

COLOR RANGE: Flowers may be single or double and come in white pink or red.

USES: Use in a low border or in rockeries, tubs and troughs. The white, single-flowered variety can become a "weed" in lawns although many gardeners enjoy the effect.

DEAD-HEAD English daisies to prolong bloom and prevent unwanted spread.

CREATE YOUR own wildflower meadow by planting a big area of everlastings. Good companions include cream California poppies and lupins.

EVERLASTING DAISY

Acroclinium roseum,
syn. *Helipterum roseum*

SIZE: 15–18 in tall with flowers on thin, wiry stems.
CLIMATE: The everlasting daisy will not tolerate frost and is only hardy in zone 10 and above. Elsewhere grow as a summer-flowering annual. It likes a dry rather than a humid climate.
ASPECT: Full sun is essential. Takes coastal exposure.
PLANTING: Where frosts are light or unknown, sow seed in fall. Where winters are very cold, sow as soon as frosts have finished in spring. Sow directly into the garden; cover seeds lightly. Thin to 6 in apart.
FLOWERING SEASON: Usually flowers 8–10 weeks after sowing. The display is long lasting.
CUT FLOWERS: Ideal cut flower. Best cut and dried by hanging bunches upside down in a dry, airy place. Pick when flower petals are still rounded in towards the center.
COLOR RANGE: Flowers may be soft pink or white.
USES: Grown for garden display and for the papery flowers which are used in dried arrangements. It is very attractive when massed over a broad area, wildflower style.

GARDENER'S TIP

Germination of paper daisies can be erratic and it is a good idea to sow the seed more thickly than you may need. You can improve the rate of germination by sowing into a thin mulch of fine gravel laid over the planting site. A depth of a 1/4–1/2 in of gravel is all that is needed. Keep it moist until the seeds have sprouted.

FLOSS FLOWER

Ageratum houstonianum

TAKES PART-SHADE

SIZE: Tall forms grow to 20 in while dwarf types may reach 8 in.
CLIMATE: It will not take frost. Hardy in zone 10 and maybe in zone 9.
ASPECT: Part-shade in warm and tropical areas, full sun elsewhere.
PLANTING: Seeds are generally sown in early spring and the young plants set out when danger of frost is over. Seeds can also be sown in fall, under glass in frost-prone areas, for flowering in the following year. Sow in pots or trays and lightly cover the seed. Space tall varieties 10–12 in apart, dwarf types 4–6 in.
FLOWERING SEASON: Plants produced from early spring sowings will start flowering in early summer and continue into the fall. Fall sowings will result in spring-flowering floss flowers.
CUT FLOWERS: Scald stems after picking. Soak them before arranging.
COLOR RANGE: Flowers may be blue-mauve, pink-mauve or white.
USES: Good edging plants or use in mixed flower borders.

USE FLOSS FLOWERS to complement blue, white, purple or yellow flowers.

A PRETTY PARTNER for spring bulbs, forget-me-not reseeds once established.

FORGET-ME-NOT

Myosotis sylvatica

TAKES DAPPLED OR PART-SHADE

SIZE: 10–15 in tall with a loose, open habit.
CLIMATE: A flower for cool, moist climates, forget-me-not does particularly well in zones 6–8.
ASPECT: Grows in sun or shade, the latter being better in warmer areas. Suits dappled sunlight under deciduous or open evergreen trees.
PLANTING: Seed is sown in an open-ground seed bed in late spring and the young plants are planted in their flowering positions in the fall. Set the young plants about 6 in apart each way.
FLOWERING SEASON: Late winter and spring.
CUT FLOWERS: Good for cutting. Lovely in small posies and as a filler in larger arrangements.
COLOR RANGE: Sky blue, pink and white.
USES: Grown under trees, forget-me-not creates a woodland atmosphere. Often naturalized in gardens, the plants can be used in massed plantings, as fillers between shrubs or as groundcover under trees.

FOXGLOVE

Digitalis purpurea

NEEDS PART-SHADE

SIZE: Standard types grow to about 5 ft tall. The smaller "Foxy" will reach about 3 ft in height.
CLIMATE: Most suitable for cooler climates, from zone 6 up to zone 8.
ASPECT: Grows in part or dappled shade. Must have plenty of water.
PLANTING: Sow the very small seed in trays or pots, barely covered. Sow in early summer or as soon as the seed is ripe and plant out in flowering positions when large enough to handle. Space 16 in apart. Seeds can also be sown direct in the ground where the plants are to flower. Foxgloves also generally self-sow freely.
FLOWERING SEASON: Spring and summer. In cool to cold zones they may flower from summer to fall.
CUT FLOWERS: Not suitable.
COLOR RANGE: Flowers may be white, cream, pink, magenta or purple with a spotted lip on each flower.
USES: An essential part of the cottage garden that may be grown in groups, as background plants, in borders or under tall, open trees. All parts of the plant are poisonous if eaten.

BEST IN big groups, foxgloves also look good with delphiniums and larkspurs.

SOME HYBRID gazanias have big, strikingly colored or patterned flowers.

GAZANIA

Gazania species and hybrids

NEEDS FULL SUN

SIZE: About 8 in tall but spreading to about 20 in across.
CLIMATE: Gazanias can be grown outdoors all year round in zones 9 and 10. Accepts 21°F. Where temperatures fall below that, grow as annuals.
ASPECT: Full sun is essential as flowers close in shade. Plants take extreme coastal exposure and also hot, inland conditions.
PLANTING: Raise plants by sowing seeds in early spring. In frost-prone areas do not plant outside until danger of frost is over.
FLOWERING SEASON: The main flowering period is early summer to early fall, but in frost-free areas will have a longer flowering period.
CUT FLOWERS: Not suitable for cutting. The flowers close indoors.
COLOR RANGE: All the warm colors, mostly with contrasting centers. Some varieties have striped petals and although most gazanias have dark olive-green leaves, there are also types with velvety gray foliage.
USES: Gazanias are easy-care plants that tolerate poor, dry soil, even beach sand and exposure to salt wind. Used extensively for summer bedding in beds and containers.

ZONAL GERANIUMS or pelargoniums are popular in frost-prone areas.

GERANIUM

Also known as pelargonium or zonal pelargonium

Pelargonium x hortorum

SIZE: Many varieties grow around 18–24 in tall when they are used as annuals.
CLIMATE: Likes a hot, dry climate as in zone 10 where they can be grown outdoors all the year round. They will not take frost and in frost-prone areas are generally grown as summer bedding plants. Geraniums do not like cold, wet conditions.
ASPECT: Full sun with shelter from cold winds. Seed-raised varieties are sown in late winter. Plant out when danger of frost is over.
FLOWERING SEASON: The main flowering is from early summer to early fall, but there may be flushes of flowers at other times.
CUT FLOWERS: Suitable for cutting but not generally thought of as a cut flower.
COLOR RANGE: All shades of red, pink, orange, purple and white.
USES: Mainly used for summer bedding in beds and containers.

GLOBE AMARANTH

Also known as bachelor's buttons

Gomphrena globosa

SIZE: 12 in tall with a shrubby habit.
CLIMATE: Hardy in zone 9 and above. Otherwise treat this plant as a half-hardy annual.
ASPECT: Must have a sunny spot.
PLANTING: Sow in spring under cover in pots or seed trays. Plant out seedlings 8–12 in apart. In frost-free climates fall sowings can be made.
FLOWERING SEASON: From spring sowings, flowers appear during summer and fall. Fall sowings will bloom in the following spring.
CUT FLOWERS: Good cut flower. May also be dried by hanging them upside down in a dry, airy place.
COLOR RANGE: Magenta-purple is the usual color but strains with white, pink or red flowers are sometimes sold. There are also dwarf forms with orange flowers.
USES: Usually seen lining paths or edging flower borders, it is also good in pots or window-boxes.

GLOBE AMARANTH is ideal for edges and a good source of fresh or dried flowers.

LATE BLOOMING godetia is useful in the garden. It bridges the gap between spring and summer displays.

GODETIA

Also known as farewell to spring or rocky mountain garland

Clarkia amoena

TAKES PART-SHADE

SIZE: 12–30 in tall.
CLIMATE: Suitable for zone 6 and above. It likes a cool, rainy climate.
ASPECT: The best results are in full sun but the plant will perform well enough in dappled or part-shade.
PLANTING: Sow where plants are to flower or in pots during spring. Also sow in the fall for earlier flowering the following year. Barely cover seed with soil. Transplant seedlings 8–12 in apart.
FLOWERING SEASON: Spring-sown plants will flower during the summer, fall sown will create their display from the following spring.
CUT FLOWERS: Lovely cut flower.
COLOR RANGE: The satiny, cup-shaped flowers come in white and shades of red, pink and lavender, usually with a contrasting color.
USES: Godetia is most attractive when mass planted.

HOLLYHOCK

Alcea rosea

SIZE: The standard type will reach 8 ft but there are shorter forms ranging down to about 3 ft.
CLIMATE: Suitable for zone 6 and above. Grows best in areas of low humidity as then it will be less prone to humidity-induced diseases.
ASPECT: Needs sun and shelter from strong wind. Stake the tall forms.
PLANTING: To grow as an annual sow in flowering positions in early spring—as a biennial, for flowering the following year, sow in mid-summer.
FLOWERING SEASON: Early spring sowings will flower in the following summer, while fall sowings will not flower until the spring of the following year.
CUT FLOWERS: Hollyhocks are not suitable for cutting and are best left in the garden.
COLOR RANGE: Hollyhocks produce single or double flowers in most colors except blue.
USES: An essential element of cottage gardens, hollyhocks are most effective when planted in groups at the back of a border, or behind or between smaller shrubs.

HOLLYHOCK is a charming old-fashioned flower raised from seed or seedlings.

HONESTY

Also known as money plant

Lunaria annua

NEEDS PART-SHADE AT LEAST

SIZE: 18–28 in tall and bushy habit.
CLIMATE: Grows best in cooler areas such as zones 6–8. In warmer areas provide shelter from hot winds.
ASPECT: Takes full sun only in zone 6. Elsewhere, it needs shade during the hottest hours and will even perform well in full shade.
PLANTING: Sow seeds of honesty in the spring as soon as ripe. Sow in pots or directly into open ground. Space plants 12 in apart each way.
FLOWERING SEASON: From the middle of spring and lasting into summer, especially in cooler areas.
CUT FLOWERS: Can use as a cut flower but mostly flowers are left to mature on the plant. Use the silvery seed pods in dried arrangements.
COLOR RANGE: Flowers may be white or rosy-purple.
USES: Honesty is grown for its circular, smooth, silvery seed pods as much as its flowers. It gives a good display when massed in shade or scattered about under groups of trees.

THE FLAT SEED PODS of honesty are usually dried for indoor arrangements.

A CABBAGE in fancy dress, kale makes a striking addition to the winter garden.

KALE

Also known as ornamental or flowering kale

Brassica oleracea acephala

SIZE: Usually less than 12 in tall and in the shape of a rosette.
CLIMATE: Suitable for cooler zones, from zone 6.
ASPECT: Full sun is essential.
PLANTING: Sow seeds in pots under glass in early spring or in growing positions in mid-spring. Space plants about 12 in apart each way.
FLOWERING SEASON: Kale is grown for its colored and frilled foliage, not for the unremarkable flowers which should be pinched out as soon as they are seen. Normally at its best in winter and early spring.
CUT FLOWERS: The whole plant would have to be cut but kale makes a striking, unusual decoration, or grow a few in pots for indoor display.
COLOR RANGE: Leaves may be red, purple, pink, white or any combination of these.
USES: A good edging plant for flower or vegetable gardens and especially impressive when massed.

DAINTY LINARIA usually seeds itself and reappears in the garden year after year.

LINARIA

Also known as toad flax or eggs and bacon

Linaria maroccana

TAKES PART-SHADE

SIZE: 12–18 in tall with an erect, multi-stemmed habit.
CLIMATE: Hardy in zone 6 and above.
ASPECT: Best in sun but in warmer areas will tolerate a few hours shade.
PLANTING: Seeds are best sown where they are to grow. In warm zones sow in fall; in cool zones, early spring sowing is advisable. Thin seedlings to about 4 in apart.
FLOWERING SEASON: Winter and spring in warm areas, early summer in cool zones.
CUT FLOWERS: Linaria can be used as a cut flower if picked when flowers are fully out but not faded.
COLOR RANGE: A wide color range is available, including white, cream, yellow, pink and red, usually with a contrasting tone.
USES: Linaria has dainty little flowers like tiny snapdragons and looks lovely in big drifts, wildflower-style.

LIVINGSTONE DAISY

Dorotheanthus bellidiformis

SIZE: 4–6 in tall but spreading to about 8 in across.
CLIMATE: This will not take frost and is hardy only in zone 10 and above. In other areas grow as a half-hardy annual.
ASPECT: Needs full sun all day.
PLANTING: The tiny seeds are sown in pots or trays in the spring or summer and planted out when large enough. Can also be sown direct into the open ground. Do not plant out or sow outdoors until the risk of frost is over. Space plants about 6 in apart.
FLOWERING SEASON: The main flowering period is summer.
CUT FLOWERS: Not suitable.
COLOR RANGE: The sparkling, daisy flowers come in a big range of bright colors, usually with white.
USES: Livingstone daisy is a good plant for seaside gardens and is ideal for mass planting on banks, in rockeries, in pots and hanging baskets. It has a prostrate habit and rather fleshy leaves.

COLORFUL AND long-blooming, livingstone daisies are ideal groundcover.

LOW-GROWING lobelia brings useful purple and blue shades to a spring garden.

LOBELIA

Lobelia erinus

TAKES PART-SHADE

SIZE: 4–6 in tall with a mounding, spreading habit.
CLIMATE: It will not take frost and is hardy only in zone 10 and above. Grow as a half-hardy annual in other areas.
ASPECT: Accepts part or dappled shade in warm and tropical areas. In cooler places, full sun is advisable.
PLANTING: Normal sowing time is late winter. Sow in pots or trays under cover and plant out when there is no danger of frost. Do not cover the fine dust-like seed. When planting, space plants 4–6 in apart each way. Close-plant pots and baskets for full effect.
FLOWERING SEASON: Summer and into fall.
CUT FLOWERS: Not suitable.
COLOR RANGE: Deep and sky blues are most usual but some mixes also contain magenta, white and mauve flowers. Some varieties have a contrasting white center.
USES: With its neat, mounded growth and masses of small flowers, lobelia is the ideal edging plant, filler, pot, basket or windowbox subject.

LOVE-IN-A-MIST

Also known as devil-in-a-bush

Nigella damascena

TAKES PART-SHADE

SIZE: 16–24 in tall with an open, airy habit.
CLIMATE: Hardy in zone 6 and above.
ASPECT: Both full sun and light shade are suitable.
PLANTING: Sow in fall and, in cool climates, early spring directly where it is to grow. Thin plants to about 8 in apart. Love-in-a-mist does not always transplant well and so if you are sowing in pots, use peat pots that can be planted when the seedlings appear.
FLOWERING SEASON: Fall sowings will flower in the following spring. Spring sowings bloom in the summer.
CUT FLOWERS: This is a delightful cut flower. Remove foliage from the lower part of the stalk to prolong flower life.
COLOR RANGE: Sky blue but also white, purple and shades of pink.
USES: Fine, feathery foliage, which slightly veils the flowers, gives love-in-a-mist its name. It is good for mass planting or as a filler between shrubs.

NOT OFTEN seen now, love-in-a-mist has the look of a wildflower and is a good choice for a meadow-style planting.

LUPIN
Lupinus hartwegii

SIZE: 12–18 in tall.
CLIMATE: Hardy in zone 9 and above. In cooler areas grow as a half-hardy annual.
ASPECT: Full sun is essential.
PLANTING: In frost-free climates it is best to sow seeds where they are to grow. Otherwise they can be sown in late winter or early spring in pots under cover and planted out when danger of frost is over.
FLOWERING SEASON: The main flowering period is summer, but flowering will start in spring in warmer climates.
CUT FLOWERS: A good cut flower if picked when buds are coloring. Scald stems to prolong vase life.
COLOR RANGE: Blue, white or pink are most common but there are varieties in shades of yellow, too.
USES: Lupins are beautiful when massed or in clumps throughout the flower garden. Try them as a broad-scale planting.

ANNUAL LUPINS are lower and have shorter flowers than the perennial types.

FRENCH MARIGOLDS are not as common as the bigger-flowered African variety.

MARIGOLD
Tagetes species

SIZE: The big, globular flowers of the African marigold (*T. erecta*) are produced on plants 20–30 in tall while the smaller, single flowers of the French marigold (*T. patula*, shown) appear on 8–16 in tall plants.
CLIMATE: This will not take frost and is hardy only in zone 10 and above. In other areas grow as a half-hardy annual.
ASPECT: Must have a well-drained, sunny position. African marigolds need wind protection.
PLANTING: Marigolds are mostly sown in pots or trays under cover in early to mid-spring and planted out when danger of frost is over. In warm areas seed can be sown directly in open ground in late spring. Space plants 8–16 in apart depending on size.
FLOWERING SEASON: Mostly through summer and fall. May flower into winter in warm areas.
CUT FLOWERS: Suitable for cutting and long lasting with frequent water changes. Some people find their smell unpleasant.
COLOR RANGE: Yellow, orange and mahogany tones.
USES: Easy to grow and long flowering, marigolds are suitable for massed plantings and for pots.

ALLOW MEADOWFOAM to spill over walls or use it for edgings or groundcover.

MEADOWFOAM

Also known as poached egg flower or fried eggs

Limnanthes douglasii

SIZE: 8–12 in tall.
CLIMATE: Native of the west coast of the USA; hardy down to zone 6.
ASPECT: Full sun is essential.
PLANTING: Sow in fall or, in cooler areas, in very early spring where they are to grow. Cover lightly and keep just moist. Thin to 6–8 in apart. For a formal bed of these flowers, sow seed in trays, under cover in late winter, and plant out in rows in spring.
FLOWERING SEASON: Spring into early summer. In the coolest climates, flowering occurs in summer.
CUT FLOWERS: Meadowfoam is unsuitable for cutting.
COLOR RANGE: Meadowfoam has white tipped, yellow petals.
USES: Plants are good for edgings, damp rockeries and for planting between pavers. They enjoy cool, moist soil around their roots.

MEALY CUP SAGE

Salvia farinacea

SIZE: This perennial, generally grown as an annual, attains a height of 24–35 in.
CLIMATE: It will grow outdoors all year round in zones 9 and 10. In colder regions, subject to frost, grow it as an annual.
ASPECT: This plant needs to be grown in a position in full sun. Suitable for dryish and poorish soils.
PLANTING: Can be sown in mid-spring for summer bedding. Plant out when danger of frost is over.
FLOWERING SEASON: Through summer and into fall.
CUT FLOWERS: The flowers are suitable for cutting.
COLOR RANGE: The spikes of flowers come in shades of blue and also white, depending on the variety grown. White mealy stems are a further attraction.
USES: Generally grown as a summer bedding plant, and also suitable for patio containers. In frost-free areas plant it in a shrub or mixed border.

THE MEALY CUP SAGE, shown here in its variety "Strata", is an unusual summer bedding plant.

BIG, BUSHY and vibrant, the Mexican sunflower is ideal for hot, sunny climates.

MEXICAN SUNFLOWER
Tithonia rotundifolia

SIZE: Grows at least 3 ft tall, sometimes nearly twice that, with a bushy, spreading habit.
CLIMATE: It will not tolerate frost and is hardy only in zone 10 and above. In other areas grow as a half-hardy annual.
ASPECT: Must have full sun, with some wind protection.
PLANTING: Sow directly into the ground or into pots in spring. Space at least 20 in apart. In cold climates, start plants indoors in earliest spring, potting them up if necessary. Set them out after frosts have finished.
FLOWERING SEASON: Flowers appear throughout summer and early fall, especially if spent blooms are removed regularly.
CUT FLOWERS: Suitable for use as a cut flower.
COLOR RANGE: Flowers are usually orange but there is also a rare yellow-flowered form.
USES: A reliable, easy-care annual, Mexican sunflower is best planted at the back of borders or in massed plantings. This plant is extremely drought tolerant.

MONKEY FLOWER

Mimulus species

NEEDS PART-SHADE AT LEAST

SIZE: Varies from 8 in to nearly 3 ft in height. Plants tend to have a sprawling habit.
CLIMATE: Best in humid, rainy climates. Grows well in zone 10. In cooler zones grow as a half-hardy annual.
ASPECT: Likes a bright spot but not burning midday or afternoon sun. Must have constantly moist, even boggy soil.
PLANTING: As seed is extremely fine and hard to handle, most gardeners plant bought seedlings in spring. They are spaced 8 in apart.
FLOWERING SEASON: From late spring through summer.
CUT FLOWERS: Not suitable.
COLOR RANGE: Red, orange and yellow, usually with contrasting spots and stripes.
USES: Good for cool, damp places in gardens, monkey flowers also do well in pots. They are beautiful beside ponds and will trail into the water. Some species are perennial but in cooler areas they are annuals.

MONKEY FLOWER is a pretty flower but do bait for snails, which love the leaves.

JEWEL-LIKE NEMESIAS offer a wide range of shades for any garden color scheme.

NEMESIA

Nemesia strumosa

TAKES PART-SHADE

SIZE: Standard forms grow 12–16 in tall, dwarf strains reach 8 in.
CLIMATE: This will not take frost and is hardy only in zone 10 and above. In other areas grow as a half-hardy annual.
ASPECT: Best in full sun but will accept some light shade.
PLANTING: In warm zones sow in late summer to early fall, in cool zones in spring. Sow directly into the ground or into pots, lightly covering the fine seed. Space or thin to 6–8 in. In very cold areas, start indoors in earliest spring and plant out when frosts have passed. Pinch prune when plants are 3-4 in tall.
FLOWERING SEASON: In warm zones flowers appear in winter and early spring. In cool zones, summer is the flowering season.
CUT FLOWERS: Possible but better kept for garden display.
COLOR RANGE: A very wide range of colors is available, usually with two colors per flower.
USES: Mass plant for best effect.

NEVER OUT of fashion, pansies are one of the most charming flowers you can grow.

PANSY

Viola x wittrockiana

TAKES PART-SHADE

SIZE: 6–10 in tall but spreading to 10–12 in across.
CLIMATE: Grows best in zones 7 and 8.
ASPECT: Accepts full sun or dappled or part-shade. In hot climates, pansies like afternoon shade.
PLANTING: Sowing is generally in mid- to late summer for flowering the following spring. May not need winter protection in cold zones. Can also be sown under cover in late winter. The fine seed is best sown lightly covered in pots and planted out at about 6 in intervals.
FLOWERING SEASON: Summer sowings will start flowering from the following spring. Spring sowings will start flowering in summer. Pansies have a long flowering period, which can be encouraged further by regularly removing dead flowers.
CUT FLOWERS: Good cut flower. Use in float bowls or add to posies.
COLOR RANGE: Virtually every color but green is available. Lightly scented, the flowers have darker centers resembling little "faces".
USES: Lovely in pots and troughs, as edging plants or massed.

PAPER DAISY

Also known as strawflower

Bracteantha species

SIZE: 8–20 in tall.
CLIMATE: It will not take frost and is hardy only in zone 10 and above. In other areas grow as a half-hardy annual. Hard to grow in very humid areas as it likes a warm dry climate.
ASPECT: Full sun is essential.
PLANTING: Sow seed in late summer and fall or, in cold climates, in early spring. Seed can be sown directly where it is to grow except in cold areas where it should be started under cover early in pots. Space or thin seedlings to 6–8 in.
FLOWERING SEASON: Spring, summer and early fall. Dead-head often to prolong flowering.
CUT FLOWERS: Ideal cut flower that dries and lasts for years. Pick flowers when petals are well formed but still incurved. Hang bunches upside down in a dry, airy place.
COLOR RANGE: Cream through yellow, orange and red.
USES: Makes a credible addition to a wildflower or meadow planting but also looks good when massed or as part of a mixed flower border.

THE SHINY, stiff flowers of paper daisies make long-lasting dried arrangements.

CUT PETUNIAS back when they grow lanky to get another flush of flowers.

PETUNIA

Petunia hybrida

SIZE: The standard form grows to 10–16 in; dwarf types reach 6 in.
CLIMATE: This will not take frost and is hardy only in zone 10 and above. In other areas grow as a half-hardy annual.
ASPECT: Full sun is essential.
PLANTING: Seed is fine and hard to handle. Sow it in pots or trays when the weather warms in spring, or earlier indoors with bottom heat. Petunias are not the easiest annuals to raise well. Most gardeners are content to buy seedlings; they are a lot easier. Plant them at 6–10 in spacings and pinch out growing tips when 8–4 in high to encourage bushiness.
FLOWERING SEASON: In most regions summer is the main flowering period and the display carries on into fall until the arrival of frosts. Regular dead-heading prolongs flowering and therefore it is well worth doing.
CUT FLOWERS: Can be used as a cut flower but its main worth is in the long garden display.
COLOR RANGE: Available in many colors and bicolors.
USES: Probably the best summer flowering annual for massed displays, petunia is also good in pots and hanging baskets.

PHLOX

Phlox drummondii

SIZE: 6–12 in tall, mounding habit.
CLIMATE: This is frost hardy and will take a minimum temperature of 21°F. Therefore it is hardy in zone 9 and above.
ASPECT: Full sun is essential.
PLANTING: In cooler regions it is normal to sow seeds in early spring in pots or trays under cover. Plant out in late spring or early summer when danger of frost is over. In frost-free areas seeds can be sown direct in the ground where they are to flower. Seeds should only be lightly covered. Space plants 4 in apart each way. Pinch out when plants are 3–4 in high.
FLOWERING SEASON: Spring sowings will flower during the summer and maybe into fall.
CUT FLOWERS: Not generally used but they last reasonably well if cut when flowers have just opened.
COLOR RANGE: White, cream, yellow, pink, red and lavender shades, often with a contrasting eye.
USES: Lovely when massed or mixed with other low-growing flowers. A good edging plant and very attractive in pots, baskets and windowboxes.

YOU'LL BE delighted with phlox whether you use it alone or with other flowers.

POLYANTHUS ARE useful for cool season color in moist, partly shaded spots, but many gardeners seem to prefer them in wide, shallow pots that can be brought indoors.

POLYANTHUS

Also known as primrose

Primula x polyantha

NEEDS PART-SHADE

SIZE: Flowers are 6–8 in tall above a rosette of basal leaves.

CLIMATE: Hardy in zone 6 and above. Cool, moist areas are most suitable for growing polyanthus.

ASPECT: Needs semi-shade to shade in most areas but tolerates full sun in cool zones.

PLANTING: The very fine seed is difficult to sow and raise successfully. Sow on the surface of pots or trays and barely cover. Water from below. Sow in early summer as polyanthus are slow to grow and flower. Plant out at 6–8 in intervals when large enough to handle. Consider buying seedlings instead. It is a lot easier.

FLOWERING SEASON: Late winter to spring—it flowers over a long period if spent flowers are pinched off regularly.

CUT FLOWERS: Not suitable for cutting but potted plants may be brought indoors in bloom. The flowers are lightly but sweetly fragrant and this feature is most noticeable indoors.

COLOR RANGE: A big range of colors, usually with a contrasting eye.

USES: A cheerful little plant to brighten the dullest spot, polyanthus is perfect in pots, mass planted in the garden or used around ponds.

GARDENER'S TIP

When sowing any sort of very fine seed, mix it with fine, dry sand first. The sand lets you see where you've sown and it helps to distribute the fine seed evenly.

POPPY

Also known as Iceland poppy

Papaver nudicaule

SIZE: Grows about 20 in tall with a basal rosette of leaves.
CLIMATE: An extremely hardy poppy thriving in zone 2 and above.
ASPECT: Full sun and shelter from strong wind is essential.
PLANTING: It is best to sow seeds of Iceland poppies direct in the open ground where they are to flower, as they do not transplant well. The normal sowing time is spring. The seed is very fine so only lightly cover it with soil. Thin out seedlings to 8–12 in apart each way as soon as they are large enough to handle easily.
FLOWERING SEASON: The main flowering period is summer. Don't allow tiny plants to flower. Remove any buds that form until the plant is quite big and well developed.
CUT FLOWERS: Excellent cut flower. Pick when buds are just opening for long vase life. Burn the cut ends before arranging.
COLOR RANGE: Cream, yellow, pink, orange and rose.
USES: The best effect is achieved when plants are massed over as big an area as possible.

ONE OF the simplest but loveliest cut flowers, poppies also make a delightful show in the garden.

PORTULACAS THRIVE in heat and don't need much water. They flower for months.

PORTULACA

Also known as sun plant

Portulaca grandiflora

SIZE: 6 in tall; spreading shape.
CLIMATE: This will not take frost and is hardy only in zone 10 and above. In other areas grow as a half-hardy annual.
ASPECT: Full sun is essential.
PLANTING: The normal sowing period in frost-prone regions is early to mid-spring under cover. The young plants are then set out when danger of frost is over. In frost-free areas the seeds can be sown in spring or fall direct in their flowering positions. Space plants about 4 in apart each way.
FLOWERING SEASON: Long flowering period through summer into fall. In the tropics, portulacas flower in winter and spring.
CUT FLOWERS: Not suitable.
COLOR RANGE: Single or double flowers may be white, yellow, pink or red.
USES: Portulaca is ideal for hot, dry spots in the garden, for pots and hanging baskets.

USE SALVIA alone or soften the red by planting it with gray-leaved plants.

SALVIA

Also known as scarlet sage

Salvia splendens

SIZE: Mostly 10–12 in high but there are cultivars growing to 20 in.
CLIMATE: This will not take frost and is hardy only in zone 10 and above. In other areas grow as a half-hardy annual.
ASPECT: Full sun is essential. Salvia loves a hot, sunny spot.
PLANTING: In most regions, especially those subject to frosts, seeds are sown in pots or trays under cover in mid-spring. The young plants are then set out when danger of frost is over, spacing them about 8 in apart each way.
FLOWERING SEASON: When sown as above, the main flowering period is in the summer and through into fall. Frosts will put a stop to the display. In warm regions the flowering period is extended.
CUT FLOWERS: Not suitable.
COLOR RANGE: Usually bright red but there are also forms with white, purple or striped flowers.
USES: Plants have upright growth which displays the colorful flowers well. Salvia is used in massed garden displays but is useful in pots, too.

SNAPDRAGON

Antirrhinum majus

SIZE: Standard form grows to 24 in or more; dwarf types reach 10 in.
CLIMATE: Hardy only in zones 9 and 10. In other regions treat as a half-hardy annual.
ASPECT: Needs full sun with protection from the strongest wind.
PLANTING: The main sowing period is early spring, but can also be sown in late summer and early fall. Sow under cover in frost-prone regions. Bottom heat encourages good germination. Barely cover the fine seed and plant out when seedlings are big enough to handle. Space dwarf forms at 6 in intervals, tall forms 12–16 in apart. They are not easy to raise from seed and most gardeners are content to buy seedlings.
FLOWERING SEASON: The main flowering period based on the above sowings is spring through summer. Antirrhinums take 16–20 weeks from seed to flowering stage.
CUT FLOWERS: Good cut flower. Scald stems before arranging.
COLOR RANGE: All the warm shades from cream through yellow, orange, pink, red and purple.
USES: Snapdragons are best in massed garden displays but dwarf forms are suitable for pots and troughs.

SNAPDRAGON IS a favorite with children, who love the snapping flowers.

EASILY BLOWN OVER, grow spider flowers in big, self-supporting groups.

SPIDER FLOWER

Cleome hassleriana, syn. C. spinosa

TAKES LIGHT SHADE

SIZE: To 5 ft tall on a single stem.
CLIMATE: This tender plant will suffer in temperatures below 41°F.
ASPECT: Prefers full sun with shelter from strong wind. Will tolerate a few hours light shade.
PLANTING: In frost-prone zones seeds are sown under cover in spring and germinated with bottom heat. Seedlings will need acclimatizing to outdoor conditions before they are planted out, when danger of frost is over. Space plants 12 in apart each way at least.
FLOWERING SEASON: Has a long display in summer and fall. In the tropics, seed sown in late summer will flower in late winter and spring.
CUT FLOWERS: Unusual cut flower that makes big and impressive arrangements. Lightly scented.
COLOR RANGE: Flowers are either pink, white or rose.
USES: These tall plants are used at the back of borders or grouped as accent plants through the garden. They look good along front fences, as a sort of annual flowering hedge.

STATICE

Also known as sea lavender

Limonium sinuatum

SIZE: Flowers grow about 16 in high over a clump of basal leaves.
CLIMATE: A fairly hardy plant, it will thrive in zone 9 and above all year round. In other regions it is treated as a half-hardy annual.
ASPECT: Full sun is essential. Accepts coastal exposure.
PLANTING: In frost-prone regions seeds are sown under cover in early spring, in pots or trays. Young plants are then planted out in late spring or early summer, setting them 12–16 in apart each way. Sow seeds in-situ in warm regions.
FLOWERING SEASON: The main period based on the above sowing is summer. In warm areas this will be extended.
CUT FLOWERS: Ideal cut flower. Can be used for the vase or bunches can be cut and dried by hanging them upside down in an airy place.
COLOR RANGE: White or purple, pink, apricot, yellow and blue, always with a splash of white.
USES: Statice tolerates hot, dry conditions but can also be used for general garden display.

WHERE STATICE likes the conditions, it will live and flower for a number of years.

STOCKS ARE a good choice for the cutting garden but take five months to bloom.

STOCK
Matthiola incana var. *annua*

SIZE: Varies from 12 to 30 in tall, depending on variety.
CLIMATE: It can be grown outside all year round in zone 7 and above.
ASPECT: Needs full sun and shelter.
PLANTING: Sowing is generally undertaken in early spring to produce plants for summer bedding. When growing as biennials for flowering the following year, seed is sown in mid-summer. Plants may need winter protection in cold regions. Sow in pots or trays under cover. Plant 6–8 in apart. Lay snail bait around seedlings.
FLOWERING SEASON: Spring and summer, depending on sowing time.
CUT FLOWERS: Good cut flower. Scald stems and change vase water every couple of days. Flowers are strongly and sweetly scented.
COLOR RANGE: There is a full range of pastel colors with some stronger purples, red and magenta.
USES: Stocks are lovely in massed plantings and the taller ones are used as background plants in mixed borders. Good drainage is vital.

STURT'S DESERT PEA
Clianthus formosus

SIZE: Prostrate, running annual with flowers on erect, 12 in stems.
CLIMATE: This is a desert plant which can be grown outside all year round in zone 10 and above. It likes dry sunny conditions. Ideal for southern California.
ASPECT: Full sun is essential.
PLANTING: Hard to transplant and best sown where it is to grow. Before sowing, soak seed overnight in warm water. Sow in winter or early spring into deep, sandy or gravelly soil. Water deeply but not again until seedlings emerge. Thereafter, water deeply but infrequently.
FLOWERING SEASON: Spring and summer.
CUT FLOWERS: Not suitable.
COLOR RANGE: Flowers are bright red with a glossy black spot.
USES: A highly unusual groundcover but hard to grow out of its desert homeland. Some people use vertically placed terracotta pipes filled with sandy gravel or grow them in very well-drained, raised garden beds.

YOU'LL HAVE a great talking point if you are successful with Sturt's desert pea.

QUICK TO GROW, sunflowers are a great way to get children interested in gardening. They're fascinated by the size of the flowers and in many communities there are sunflower-growing contests that kids love to enter.

SUNFLOWER

Helianthus annuus

SIZE: The tallest of annuals, sunflowers can reach a height of 10 ft. Shorter varieties, ranging down to 3 ft, are also available and these are better for garden use.
CLIMATE: Hardy throughout the USA to southern Canada.
ASPECT: Must have full sun and shelter from strong wind.
PLANTING: Sow in spring where they are to grow. Space seeds at least 20 in apart—very tall varieties need wider spacings. Seeds are large and easy to handle. In colder regions, if earlier blooms are wanted, start seeds under cover in early spring using bottom heat. Plant out when large enough to handle.
FLOWERING SEASON: Based on the above sowing times, flowering takes place throughout summer and into fall.
CUT FLOWERS: This is a very good cut flower but use a heavy-based vase or add some weight to the bottom of the vase to prevent it toppling over. Flame or scald stems before arranging.
COLOR RANGE: Flowers are usually bright yellow but varieties that flower in russet shades are also available. They are usually smaller.
USES: Sunflowers are eye-catching when planted at the back of a flower border and are very attractive to seed-eating birds. They are very impressive when massed or when used as a flowering hedge.

GARDENER'S TIP

Sunflowers have rough, slightly sharp stems and sandpapery leaves. Don't plant them among shrubs or other tall flowers as these plants will be damaged as the sunflowers rub against them in the wind.

SWEET PEA
Lathyrus odoratus

SIZE: Climbers grow 6–10 ft tall while bush types will reach 20 in.
CLIMATE: Hardy in zone 6 and above. Sweet peas like mild climates.
ASPECT: Full sun is essential.
PLANTING: Sow seed where it is to grow, 1–2 in deep and 3–4 in apart. In frost-free or near frost-free areas, sow in early fall. In cool to cold areas, sow early to mid-spring. Only low bush types do not need a supporting trellis.
FLOWERING SEASON: Fall-sown sweet peas flower in winter and early spring. In cool to cold areas they flower in late spring and summer.
CUT FLOWERS: Superb cut flower and cutting prolongs the flowering period. Sweet peas are richly fragrant.
COLOR RANGE: Mixtures contain a wide range of colors.
USES: They are usually planted against walls, fences or garden arches. Use dwarf forms in baskets or tubs.

SWEET PEAS are good for soil but don't grow them in the same spot every year.

SWEET WILLIAM covers itself in spicily fragrant, very colorful flowers.

SWEET WILLIAM
Dianthus barbatus

SIZE: Standard forms grow to 15 in, while dwarf forms reach only 8 in.
CLIMATE: Best in cool areas. Hardy in zone 4. Possible in warm zones.
ASPECT: Full sun is essential.
PLANTING: The sweet William is often grown as a biennial, sowing outdoors in late spring or early summer to flower in the spring and summer of the following year. Sow in a nursery bed and plant out the young plants in fall. Can also be grown as an annual to flower in summer of the same year, by sowing suitable varieties in early spring under cover. Space plants 4–6 in apart.
FLOWERING SEASON: Spring and summer.
CUT FLOWERS: This is a good cut flower with a spicy fragrance.
COLOR RANGE: White, pink, red or a combination of these.
USES: This is an excellent bedding plant and its compact habit makes it ideal for pots or windowboxes.

TORENIA

Also known as wishbone flower

Torenia fournieri

TAKES PART-SHADE

SIZE: Grows 8–12 in tall with an erect, many branched habit.
CLIMATE: Dislikes cold conditions. Does well in zones 9 and above. Elsewhere grow as a half-hardy annual, or under glass as a pot plant.
ASPECT: Takes full sun or part-shade. In hot areas, the latter is best.
PLANTING: Sow the very small seeds in pots or trays in spring. Barely cover the seed and take care with watering. Space seedlings at 6–8 in intervals. In the tropics, sow any time.
FLOWERING SEASON: Flowers appear in summer and fall. In the tropics, blooms appear about three months after sowing.
CUT FLOWERS: Not commonly cut but it could be added to posies.
COLOR RANGE: Flowers are mauve and purple with a yellow splash. There is also a form with flowers in pinkish tones.
USES: Torenia's compact growth makes it ideal for massed plantings, or for use as a filler or in pots.

TORENIA FLOWERS look a little like a cross between snapdragons and pansies.

VERBENA IS a successful groundcover in hot, sunny spots, even in arid areas.

VERBENA

Verbena x *hybrida*

SIZE: About 10 in tall with a wide-spreading habit.
CLIMATE: This will not take frost and is hardy only in zone 10 and above. In other areas grow as a half-hardy annual.
ASPECT: Full sun is essential.
PLANTING: In frost-prone regions seeds are sown in trays or pots under glass in early spring to provide plants for bedding out in late spring or early summer, when frosts are over. Use bottom heat for germination. Space young plants 12 in apart each way for good groundcover.
FLOWERING SEASON: Flowers over a very long period—through summer and into fall until frosts begin.
CUT FLOWERS: Not usually cut but could be added to mixed posies.
COLOR RANGE: Flowers may be white or pink, red, mauve, purple or apricot, often with a white eye.
USES: Good for general garden display, groundcover or edging. It does well in pots and baskets.

WARM-TONED wallflowers seem just the right shade on winter's dull days.

WALLFLOWER

Erysimum cheiri

TAKES PART-SHADE

SIZE: 12–20 in tall; bushy habit.
CLIMATE: Takes a minimum temperature of 7°F so is suitable for zone 7 and above. In colder regions overwintering plants will have need of frame protection.
ASPECT: Prefers full sun but tolerates some shade for part of the day.
PLANTING: Sowings are generally made in an outdoor seed bed in late spring or early summer and young plants transplanted to their flowering positions in fall, or overwintered in a frame. Ideal spacing is 8–10 in apart each way. Pinch out growing tips of seedlings to encourage branching.
FLOWERING SEASON: Spring, but in mild areas flowering may start in late winter.
CUT FLOWERS: A lovely cut flower that lasts with frequent water changes. It is very sweetly fragrant.
COLOR RANGE: Very wide range of colors including yellow, brown, cream, red, orange and purple.
USES: Beautiful when massed and good partners for spring bulbs, they may also be used in pots.

ZINNIA

Also known as youth and old age

Zinnia elegans

SIZE: Standard forms grow to 28 in or more, dwarf types reach 8 in.
CLIMATE: Being a native of Mexico, this zinnia loves hot dry weather. It is grown as a half-hardy annual in the USA. Summer humidity can lead to mildew on the leaves.
ASPECT: Full sun is essential with shelter from strong wind.
PLANTING: Sow seeds in early spring in pots or trays under glass. Or sow in late spring out of doors where the plants are to flower. Successional sowings several weeks apart result in a longer display of flowers. Space tall varieties 15 in apart, dwarf forms 8 in apart. Pinch out growing tips when plants are 4–6 in high.
FLOWERING SEASON: From late spring throughout the summer.
CUT FLOWERS: Good and long-lasting cut flower. Scald stems and change the water frequently.
COLOR RANGE: Cream through yellow, orange, pink, red and purple. "Envy" has greenish flowers.
USES: With their upright growing habit, zinnias are best used in massed garden displays. Smaller forms look good in pots.

A MASS OF zinnias provides garden color for months, and cut flowers, too.

• CHAPTER NINETEEN •

PERENNIALS

Unlike annuals, which are short lived, perennials are flowers that live from year to year. Choose those that are suited to your climate and these easy-care flowers will return for a bigger and better display, year after year.

There are two types of perennial flowers—herbaceous and evergreen. Herbaceous perennials die back to the ground for a period each year, reshooting a few months later to grow and bloom again. Most herbaceous perennials come from climates with very cold winters. In order to survive them, they close down their above-ground parts in fall but the roots remain alive. In spring, they reshoot. If you grow these winter-dormant perennials where winters are mild, they won't go completely dormant and soon exhaust themselves to death with continuous growth.

In warmer areas (frost-free or nearly so) you'll have more success with evergreen perennials, which come from a climate like yours. They may slow their growth in winter but they keep all their leaves. Of course, you can still grow herbaceous perennials in frost-free climates, but those from the coldest places will probably behave more like annuals, and the warmer your climate, the more this will be so.

PERENNIAL BORDERS

Perennials can be planted among shrubs, as a complement to a display of bulbs or annuals, or in separate beds—the perennial border. A border is a planted area designed to be seen mostly from one side. You can also grow shrubs or annuals there if you like (a mixed border). Most perennials need full sun, although there are some that take shade.

The great attraction of a perennial border or bed is the wonderful massed display of color that is produced. Of course, you have to choose the colors and their placement within the border and that is where the artistry comes in. Your job is to know when each

A MIXED BED contains annuals, shrubs and perennials for months of color.

PERENNIALS GIVE long and colorful displays. They have the advantage of being long lived so that, unlike annuals, they do not need seasonal replacement.

species flowers and in what color, and to place those that bloom at the same time in pleasing color combinations. This can be done on paper. Draw the bed to scale on graph paper and allot a space to each type you want to grow. They don't all have to flower at the same time, but those that do should look good together. By choosing species that bloom at different times you can have a succession of flowers in a succession of color schemes.

ASPECT AND SOIL PREPARATION

Perennials usually need full sun and shelter from strong wind. The bed itself can be any size but the smaller it is the fewer types of perennials you should try to grow. Remember, many will become big and will not be suitable for narrow spaces. The marvellous perennial borders seen in many English gardens are all quite long and 10–14 ft deep at least.

Because perennials are long lived, good soil preparation is essential. Start by clearing the area of weeds and grasses. This must be done thoroughly as it is hard to remove weeds once the flowers are growing. Spraying the site with glyphosate (a herbicide) is an easy and effective way to weed, and when the first lot is dead, dig over the site, water well and wait for the next crop of weeds to emerge. Spray again, but don't be in a hurry to plant for you may have to spray once or twice more, especially if the area is infested with persistent weeds that arise from bulbs or perennial roots. When the area is clear, follow the instructions on soil and drainage on pages 23–7 and you will have created the ideal home for perennials.

ROUTINE MAINTENANCE

Always water deeply but infrequently. In hot weather on sandy soils this may need to be twice weekly but generally once a week is ample.

Perennials should not need a lot of fertilizing either. Apply complete plant food as growth begins, and if the soil has been well prepared this should be enough for the whole growing season. A mulch of decayed manure or compost around the plants will improve growing conditions too.

Keep the area weeded until the plants cover the ground or grow annuals as in-fill plants around them. Once the perennials are in bloom, dead-head regularly to prolong the display, and in fall, when herbaceous perennials begin to die back, they can be cut to ground level. Evergreens are not cut back.

DIVISION

You divide and replant perennials whenever the clump becomes overcrowded and congested, usually after three or four years growth but it can be longer. Evergreens are divided after flowering, while herbaceous perennials are divided when they are dormant. Division rejuvenates them.

To divide plants, lift (dig up) the whole clump, shake off the excess soil and pull the clump apart or cut it into sections. With very large, heavy clumps, you may have to use an axe, cleaver or sharp spade. Replant the sections straight away, trimming off any very long roots. Remember the outer growths are the youngest and most vigorous, and in some cases the center of the plant may have died out and can be discarded. If you are unable to replant at once or have pieces to give away, wrap them in damp newspaper or hessian and keep them in a shaded, sheltered spot.

A TYPICAL English herbaceous border. This can be copied in the USA in regions that have cold winters. For best effect make sure it is long and at least 10–14 ft across.

VERY TOUGH, agapanthus is one of the easiest of all perennials to grow.

AGAPANTHUS

Agapanthus praecox subsp. *orientalis*

EVERGREEN; TAKES PART-SHADE

ORIGIN: South-eastern South Africa.
SIZE: Flowers rise 4 ft above the leaves. There are dwarf forms, too.
CLIMATE: Suitable for zone 9 and above. Drought tolerant, but to flower well it needs regular water year round, especially during spring. In colder climates grow in the warmest, most sheltered spot or choose a more hardy, deciduous species and variety.
FROST TOLERANCE: Will take very little frost, no more than –21°F. Any more will damage the leaves.
ASPECT: Full sun is best. The more shade plants get, the fewer the flowers. In inland areas, shelter from afternoon summer sun and hot winds is advisable.
FLOWERING SEASON: Late spring and summer.
CUT FLOWERS: Good cut flower. Scald stem ends in boiling water for 15 seconds. Use a heavy vase.
COLOR RANGE: White and shades of blue.
USES: Stabilizes soil on slopes or use to line a drive. It is very attractive in big drifts or clumped together in tubs.

ASTILBE

Astilbe hybrids

HERBACEOUS; NEEDS PART-SHADE

ORIGIN: Hybrids of several different species from eastern Asia, North America and Europe.
SIZE: Typically around 20 in tall but there are shorter and taller types.
CLIMATE: Not for hot arid or hot humid places. Best in zones 6 to 8.
FROST TOLERANCE: Takes –4°F.
ASPECT: Takes full sun if the soil remains moist but prefers dappled or partial shade. Needs constantly moist, even boggy soil.
FLOWERING SEASON: Flowering is from late spring through summer.
CUT FLOWERS: Flowers can be cut for indoor decoration.
COLOR RANGE: White, pink, red and mauve.
USES: Astilbe looks best when mass planted and is ideal by ponds or watercourses, in bog gardens or for naturalizing under trees.

GROUP ASTILBES together in light shade for a charming woodland effect.

BALLOON FLOWER

Also known as Chinese bellflower

Platycodon grandiflorus

HERBACEOUS; TAKES PART-SHADE

ORIGIN: China, Japan.
SIZE: Reaches 8–12 in tall with a clumping, multi-stemmed habit.
CLIMATE: Prefers a cool to cold climate, growing best in zones 4 to 8. Short lived in frost-free climates.
FROST TOLERANCE: Accepts –31°F if mulched in late fall.
ASPECT: Grows in sun or dappled or partial shade. Protect from sun at the hottest time of the day in summer.
FLOWERING SEASON: The big, starry flowers are produced from early to late summer.
CUT FLOWERS: Good cut flower.
COLOR RANGE: Mauve blue is the most usual color but there are also white and pale pink forms.
USES: This is a lovely plant for the summer border. Clumps are compact and spread slowly. They are best planted where they can remain undisturbed for some years.

RELATED TO campanulas, the balloon flower continues the mauve-blue theme right through the summer months.

BEARD TONGUE is extremely hardy to barely frost tolerant, depending on type.

BEARD TONGUE

Penstemon species and hybrids

HERBACEOUS

ORIGIN: United States.
SIZE: Varies from 4 in to 3 ft in height. Some are erect, others sprawl.
CLIMATE: Hardy species will survive in the north—some even in zone 3. Others are more tender and only suit the south. Not suited to hot dry locations. Check hardiness before you buy.
FROST TOLERANCE: Varies with type from –31°F to light frosts only.
ASPECT: Best in full sun with protection from strong wind. Must have very well-drained, sandy or gravelly soil. Mulch with gravel, not organic matter.
FLOWERING SEASON: Long flowering season from late spring through summer.
CUT FLOWERS: It does not last well as a cut flower.
COLOR RANGE: White and shades of pink, red, purple, lavender and blue.
USES: Plant in massed borders or among shrubs or annuals. Grows well in poor, well-drained soil and is usually short lived.

BEAR'S BREECHES

Acanthus mollis

HERBACEOUS; NEEDS PART-SHADE

ORIGIN: Mediterranean region.
SIZE: Reaches 28 in to 3 ft tall with a spread of 3 ft or more.
CLIMATE: This is not one of the hardiest perennials as it originates from a warm climate but it will succeed in zone 6 and above.
FROST TOLERANCE: Accepts at least 0°F.
ASPECT: Can be grown in full sun or partial shade. Best results are obtained in a fertile, moisture retentive yet well-drained soil. These plants do not like wetness around them in winter.
FLOWERING SEASON: Late spring and summer. Although pleasant enough in bloom, this plant is grown more for its glossy, lobed leaves.
CUT FLOWERS: Tall flower spikes may be cut for indoor arrangements.
COLOR RANGE: Flowers are liver red and white.
USES: Ideal under trees and very attractive by water. Mass plant for best effect.

ACANTHUS *is a good choice for shady areas that are always kept moist.*

C. PERSICIFOLIA *is an erect bellflower that is particularly generous in bloom.*

BELLFLOWER

Campanula species

HERBACEOUS AND EVERGREEN; TAKES PART-SHADE

ORIGIN: Occurs widely in the northern hemisphere, mostly Europe and Central Asia.
SIZE: Varies with species from ground-huggers to spires 3 ft high.
CLIMATE: Depending on type, some will thrive in zones 3 and 4. The majority are suited to zones 5 to 8. Do check hardiness before you buy.
FROST TOLERANCE: Most take 5°F, many accept much lower temperatures. A handful will tolerate only light frosts.
ASPECT: Grows in part shade or in full sun in cooler areas.
FLOWERING SEASON: Mid-spring to early summer, often profuse.
CUT FLOWERS: Some of these plants make good cut flowers.
COLOR RANGE: Shades of light and dark blue but also white and pink.
USES: Ideal for a mixed border and should be positioned according to size. They are easy to grow in the right climate and are long lived there.

BERGAMOT

Also known as bee balm or Oswego tea

Monarda didyma

HERBACEOUS; TAKES DAPPLED OR PART-SHADE

ORIGIN: Eastern United States and eastern Canada.
SIZE: Reaches 24–36 in tall with a dense, bushy habit.
CLIMATE: Likes cool, moist conditions such as those found in zones 4 to 8. Does not do well where summers are hot and dry.
FROST TOLERANCE: Accepts –22°F and needs a cold winter.
ASPECT: Grows well in full sun, or in dappled or partial shade. Needs rich, moisture-retentive soil.
FLOWERING SEASON: Long flowering period in summer.
CUT FLOWERS: Good cut flower.
COLOR RANGE: Flowers may be red, pink, white or purple. Cultivars such as "Cambridge Scarlet" and "Croftway Pink" are outstanding.
USES: Bergamot is easy to grow but invasive and needs regular reduction. Use it in a mixed border or massed.

BERGAMOT IS a pretty plant with aromatic leaves useful in potpourris.

THE LIGHTLY fragrant flowers of bergenia appear over a very long period.

BERGENIA

Bergenia species and cultivars

EVERGREEN; NEEDS PART-SHADE

ORIGIN: Siberia, Central Asia and northern China.
SIZE: Grows to about 10 in tall with flowering stems rising to 16 in.
CLIMATE: Some are very hardy and thrive in zones 3 to 5. Others need zone 6 and above. It pays to check hardiness before you buy.
FROST TOLERANCE: Some will take a low of –31°F or lower.
ASPECT: Prefers dappled shade or part-shade. Takes winter sun but the leaves burn if exposed to hours of hot summer sun.
FLOWERING SEASON: Flowers appear in midwinter in mild areas, spring in cooler climates.
CUT FLOWERS: They make a good cut flower but give better value if left on the plant.
COLOR RANGE: Usually pink or mauve-pink but there are hybrids with rosy pink to red blooms.
USES: Bergenias make ideal plants for bordering garden beds or for growing in large clumps in a shady rockery or under trees. They are easy-care, long-lived plants. Suitable for pots.

DESPITE ITS name, big blue lilyturf is a dwarf perennial, ideal for groundcover.

BIG BLUE LILYTURF

Liriope muscari

EVERGREEN; NEEDS PART- OR FULL SHADE

ORIGIN: China, Taiwan and Japan.
SIZE: This is a dwarf perennial reaching a height of only 12 in when in flower.
CLIMATE: This perennial is hardy in parts of zone 6. Better suited to milder climates.
FROST TOLERANCE: It is not one of the hardiest perennials and will take a minimum temperature of 0°F.
ASPECT: This is a shade-loving plant which needs to be sheltered from cold drying winds. Ideally grow it in an acid or lime-free soil. It likes a moist soil although conversely will tolerate drought, but will not make such good growth in dry conditions.
FLOWERING SEASON: The flowers are produced throughout fall.
CUT FLOWERS: Not generally thought of as a cut flower, but can be arranged indoors.
COLOR RANGE: The flowers are bright deep violet.
USES: Makes excellent groundcover for shade or part-shade, say in a woodland garden or shrub border.

BLACK COHOSH

Cimicifuga racemosa

HERBACEOUS; NEEDS PART-SHADE

ORIGIN: It grows wild in eastern North America.
SIZE: Up to 7 ft in height, but usually a little less under cultivation, around 5 ft.
CLIMATE: It is a very hardy perennial succeeding in zone 4 and above. But not suited to warm zones.
FROST TOLERANCE: Will take a low of between –20°F and –31°F.
ASPECT: It needs to be grown in part-shade and thrives in moist soil which is rich in humus. Ensure protection from wind which can whip plants around.
FLOWERING SEASON: This perennial flowers in midsummer.
CUT FLOWERS: The flowers can be cut and are useful when something a bit different is wanted for arranging.
COLOR RANGE: The white flowers are scented, however they are not pleasantly so.
USES: This is a handsome and very distinctive plant for woodland gardens, wild gardens and for mixed borders with moist soil.

BLACK COHOSH, one of the more distinctive perennials, is extremely hardy.

THE DAINTY FLOWERS of bleeding heart dangle from slender, arching stems.

BLEEDING HEART

Dicentra spectabilis

HERBACEOUS; NEEDS PART-SHADE

ORIGIN: Japan and eastern Asia.
SIZE: Usually about 3 ft tall with a similar spread.
CLIMATE: As this is a woodland plant in the wild it likes a cool, moist climate as in zones 6 to 8. It does not enjoy hot, humid conditions in which it will quickly die out.
FROST TOLERANCE: Accepts –4°F at least.
ASPECT: Best in filtered sunlight or morning sun. Strong, hot sun makes them shrivel up. Must have rich, constantly moist soil.
FLOWERING SEASON: It should be in bloom for several weeks from middle to late spring.
CUT FLOWERS: Not suitable.
COLOR RANGE: Flowers are white and pink in the shape of a heart. There is an all-white form, too.
USES: With fern-like foliage and curving stems bearing pretty flowers, this is an all-time favorite perennial. It can be grown in a mixed border or in the filtered shade of trees. It is herbaceous, dying right back to the ground in fall or early winter.

BLUE POPPY

Meconopsis betonicifolia

HERBACEOUS; TAKES PART-SHADE

ORIGIN: Himalayan region, in very high altitude alpine meadows in China and Tibet.
SIZE: Reaches 20–28 in tall.
CLIMATE: A cool moist climate is essential. It can only be grown in zones 7 and 8 and possibly in zone 6.
FROST TOLERANCE: Accepts 1°F at least.
ASPECT: Needs partial shade with shelter from strong wind. It tolerates full sun where summers are mild.
FLOWERING SEASON: Blooms appear any time from late spring to early summer.
CUT FLOWERS: These are exquisite cut flowers if you can bear to remove them from the garden.
COLOR RANGE: Flowers are an astonishing clear, sky blue.
USES: This beautiful blue poppy is not easy to grow, demanding a cool to cold climate and woodland conditions. In gardens, naturalize it near trees or beside water.

SUCCEED WITH the blue poppy and you can give yourself a gold star for gardening.

CAMPION

Lychnis coronaria

HERBACEOUS; TAKES PART-SHADE

ORIGIN: South-eastern Europe.
SIZE: Flower stems 16–20 in tall rise from basal rosettes of soft, gray leaves.
CLIMATE: Campion does not like continuous high humidity or frequent summer rain. It is very hardy and can be grown in zone 4 and above, up to zone 8.
FROST TOLERANCE: Accepts –31°F at least.
ASPECT: Grows best in full sun but will tolerate a little shade.
FLOWERING SEASON: Flowering is from late spring through summer, depending on climate. Blooming will be later and last longer in colder areas.
CUT FLOWERS: Not suitable for cutting. The flowers don't last.
COLOR RANGE: Pinkish white or deep magenta.
USES: Easily grown in a sunny, well-drained spot, campion tends to be short lived but it seeds itself so that you always have a fresh supply. It can be grown as a border plant or as part of a mixed perennial display. This is an easy-care plant that establishes fast.

CAMPION'S iridescent flowers are well contrasted with the gray leaves.

CARDINAL FLOWER produces stems of burgundy leaves topped with red flowers.

CARDINAL FLOWER

Lobelia cardinalis

HERBACEOUS; TAKES PART-SHADE

ORIGIN: Eastern North America.
SIZE: Grows to 36 in tall with a narrow, erect habit.
CLIMATE: The cardinal flower is very adaptable. Plants are successful in zone 3 and above and in the wild it is found as far south as Florida.
FROST TOLERANCE: Takes lows of –39°F.
ASPECT: Full sun or partial shade.
FLOWERING SEASON: Long flowering period through summer.
CUT FLOWERS: Not suitable.
COLOR RANGE: Flowers are bright scarlet.
USES: This plant can be used in a mixed border or mass planted among shrubs as long as the ground retains plenty of moisture. In its natural habitat it is a plant of wet meadows and river banks, and in gardens it can be grown in boggy, poolside soil or standing in water.

CARNATION

Dianthus caryophyllus

EVERGREEN

ORIGIN: Europe and western Asia.
SIZE: Reaches 12–18 in tall.
CLIMATE: It is thought to be a native of the Mediterranean region and consequently is not very hardy. Best in zone 8 and above.
FROST TOLERANCE: Takes –14°F.
ASPECT: Full sun, shelter from wind and free-draining, fertile soil are all essential. Carnations need plenty of water in summer, much less in winter, but not constant wetness at any time. Don't water the foliage.
FLOWERING SEASON: Most flowers appear in spring and fall.
CUT FLOWERS: Pick early in the day by snapping off at a shoot. Flowers should be at least partly opened when picked. Change water every two days.
COLOR RANGE: Virtually every color but blue, often with two or more colors in each flower.
USES: Grows well in hot, sunny well-drained spots and may also be grown in containers.

THEIR SWEET spicy fragrance has made carnations a favorite world-wide.

THERE ARE both annual and perennial chrysanthemums in a big range of sizes.

CHRYSANTHEMUM

Argyranthemum, Leucanthemum and *Dendranthema* species

HERBACEOUS OR SEMI-EVERGREEN

ORIGIN: Northern temperate zone.
SIZE: These plants grow from 12 in to over 3 ft high.
CLIMATE: Depends on type: dendranthema zones 4 to 6 and above, leucanthemum zones 5 or 6 and argyranthemum zone 9.
FROST TOLERANCE: This varies with type from –31°F to 21°F.
ASPECT: A sheltered spot in full sun is essential. Soil must be well drained and rich in rotted organic matter.
FLOWERING SEASON: Spring, summer and fall depending on the type grown.
CUT FLOWERS: They are popular and long lasting cut flowers. Change water every two days and nip off about 1/4 in of stem at each change.
COLOR RANGE: White or yellow is the typical color of many chrysanthemums but there are also hybrids in a range of reds, pinks, oranges and mauves.
USES: Low types make good edges while the taller varieties are impressive in mixed flower borders.

YOU CAN GROW cinquefoils from seed or by dividing the roots in winter.

CINQUEFOIL

Potentilla species

HERBACEOUS; TAKES PART-SHADE

ORIGIN: North America, Europe and Asia.
SIZE: Varies with species from 2 in to 20 in and more.
CLIMATE: The hardiest of the perennial cinquefoils are suitable for zone 5 and above.
FROST TOLERANCE: Accepts lows of –13°F.
ASPECT: Needs full sun in cool regions but tolerates part-shade in warmer districts.
FLOWERING SEASON: May begin flowering in late spring in warm districts, but the main blooming time is summer and early fall. Flowers may be single or double.
CUT FLOWERS: Flowers do not last well when cut.
COLOR RANGE: White or shades of yellow, red or pink.
USES: This charming perennial is a member of the rose family, and plants are often grouped as part of a bed of mixed flowers. They are also suitable for growing in pots.

COLUMBINE

Also known as granny's bonnets

Aquilegia hybrids

HERBACEOUS; TAKES PART-SHADE

ORIGIN: North temperate zone. The hybrids are of garden origin.
SIZE: 18–28 in tall with a basal mound of blue-green leaves.
CLIMATE: Cooler climates are the most suitable. They are mostly extremely hardy and will thrive in zone 4 and above. They are definitely not suitable for hot or arid areas.
FROST TOLERANCE: Takes a low of between –20°F and –31°F.
ASPECT: Needs full sun in cool areas, part-shade in warmer places.
FLOWERING SEASON: The middle of spring to early summer in warm areas but it may continue most of summer in cool zones.
CUT FLOWERS: Good cut flower with lovely, grayish leaves.
COLOR RANGE: White, pink, crimson, yellow, blue and various pastel combinations.
USES: The charming, informal flowers are ideal scattered under trees or near water and are good in pots.

COLUMBINES BRING the look of a woodland dell to the garden.

THE LONG STEMS of small flowers on coral bells produce a light, airy effect that's pleasing without being imposing.

CORAL BELLS

Heuchera sanguinea

EVERGREEN; TAKES PART-SHADE

ORIGIN: South-western United States, Mexico.
SIZE: Has a low rosette of leaves with flower stems up to 24 in tall.
CLIMATE: Needs a cool or temperate climate but will thrive in the south. It is hardy north and can be grown in zone 3.
FROST TOLERANCE: Accepts lows down to 20°F.
ASPECT: Best in full sun but tolerates light shade. In warmer districts it will benefit from shade on hot afternoons.
FLOWERING SEASON: It has a long flowering period throughout spring into early summer.
CUT FLOWERS: Flowers do not last well when cut.
COLOR RANGE: Usually red but there are hybrids with white, pink or dark red flowers.
USES: Coral bells is a neat plant suitable for edging or mass planting at the front of the border. Mass plantings produce a striking floral display.

COREOPSIS

Also known as tickseed

Coreopsis species

HERBACEOUS

ORIGIN: North America.
SIZE: Reaches 24–36 in tall and about half as wide.
CLIMATE: Some species can be grown in zone 4 and above but many will thrive only in zone 8 and above. Do check hardiness before you buy.
FROST TOLERANCE: The hardiest species will take a low of between –9°F and –20°F.
ASPECT: Full sun gives the best results but it will accept a little shade.
FLOWERING SEASON: It has a long flowering period through summer and fall with some species blooming in spring.
CUT FLOWERS: Flowers can be cut for indoor decoration.
COLOR RANGE: Mostly yellow but there are also russet shades.
USES: These plants are very easy to grow and will give a great show with little care. Plant them in bold clumps in a mixed border or mass them wildflower style.

GOOD IN warm or cold climates, coreopsis now grows in many parts of the world.

PRETTY CORYDALIS makes an attractive groundcover for moist shade.

CORYDALIS

Corydalis species

HERBACEOUS; NEEDS SHADE

ORIGIN: Northern temperate zone.
SIZE: About 16 in tall.
CLIMATE: Many species thrive in zone 6 and above. Some are suited to zone 5 and above.
FROST TOLERANCE: Many will take a low of –9°F and some even –20°F.
ASPECT: Enjoy dappled shade or a spot that receives morning sun.
FLOWERING SEASON: Middle to late spring with a few flowers during early summer.
CUT FLOWERS: Good additions to mixed posies but are not long lived.
COLOR RANGE: Yellow, blue, cream, white or pinkish flowers, depending on species.
USES: Lovely groundcover under trees and can also be used in big containers with other shade lovers. These plants may self-seed freely and, in warmer areas especially, can get out of hand. Minimize spread by collecting unwanted seed heads.

CRANESBILL

Geranium species

HERBACEOUS AND EVERGREEN

ORIGIN: Southern Africa and northern temperate countries.
SIZE: Grows from 16 to 36 in or more, usually as a rounded or wide-spreading clump.
CLIMATE: Some are extremely tough, being suited to zone 3, while others cannot take much frost and will not thrive below zone 9. Many come in between, being suitable for zones 6 to 8.
FROST TOLERANCE: Varies greatly with the species grown. Herbaceous types take more frost than do evergreens.
ASPECT: A mostly sunny spot usually gives the best results but dappled or afternoon shade helps in hot areas.
FLOWERING SEASON: Spring and early summer.
CUT FLOWERS: Not suitable.
COLOR RANGE: Mostly in the mauve, purple and pink range.
USES: Grows well among rocks or beside trees or big shrubs. Can self-seed into the cracks between paving stones or be grown in drystone walls.

TRUE GERANIUMS produce simple flowers on neat plants and can self-seed freely.

INDIVIDUAL DAYLILY flowers last only a day but there is a long succession of them.

DAYLILY

Hemerocallis species and hybrids

HERBACEOUS OR EVERGREEN; TAKES PART-SHADE

ORIGIN: East Asia and Japan.
SIZE: From 16 in to over 3 ft.
CLIMATE: Herbaceous types are best for frosty areas, zone 5 and above, and evergreens for frost-free climates.
FROST TOLERANCE: Deciduous types are hardy to at least −13°F. Evergreens prefer no frost.
ASPECT: Best in full sun but in warm climates tolerates partial shade.
FLOWERING SEASON: Different varieties bloom from spring to fall. Flowers may be single, semi-double or double.
CUT FLOWERS: Whole stems can be cut.
COLOR RANGE: Huge range of colors available.
USES: All daylilies are suitable for massing, for lining paths or drives or for clumping here and there around the garden. They are very easy and rewarding to grow.

DELPHINIUM

Delphinium elatum hybrids

HERBACEOUS; TAKES PART-SHADE

ORIGIN: The species is native to Europe and Siberia. The hybrids are of garden origin.
SIZE: Stately perennials that can grow up to 7 ft in height, depending on variety.
CLIMATE: Very hardy, suitable for zone 3 and upwards.
FROST TOLERANCE: They accept lows of between −31°F and −38°F.
ASPECT: Best in sun but takes half a day's shade. Wind shelter is essential.
FLOWERING SEASON: Spring and early summer in warm zones, middle to late summer elsewhere.
CUT FLOWERS: Good cut flower. Cut when the lowest flowers are fully open and the top buds are colored.
COLOR RANGE: Shades of blue, purple, lavender, pink or white.
USES: Good massed or as background plants in mixed borders.

AMONG THE tallest of perennials, stately delphiniums bring grandeur to the garden.

EPIMEDIUM IS an excellent groundcover plant for part-shaded areas.

EPIMEDIUM

Epimedium grandiflorum

HERBACEOUS; NEEDS PART-SHADE

ORIGIN: Japan, southern Manchuria (China) and north Korea.
SIZE: A dwarf perennial growing to a height of only 8–12 in.
CLIMATE: It is not one of the hardiest perennials, but succeeds in zone 7 and above.
FROST TOLERANCE: Takes a low of 0°F. In regions prone to frosts, give the plants a deep mulch of organic matter for the winter. This will protect the roots and crowns of the plants.
ASPECT: Grow in part-shade and ensure the plants are sheltered from cold drying winds. A fertile humus rich soil gives best results.
FLOWERING SEASON: Mid- to late spring and maybe even into early summer.
CUT FLOWERS: Can be cut but not generally thought of as a cut flower. Good for mini arrangements.
COLOR RANGE: White, yellow, pink or purple.
USES: Excellent groundcover under trees or large shrubs. Good choice for a woodland garden or partially shaded rock garden.

GAURA

Gaura lindheimeri

HERBACEOUS

ORIGIN: Southern United States.
SIZE: Flowering stems may reach 3 ft or more in height.
CLIMATE: Suitable for growing in zone 6 and above. A good plant for mild and warm climates. Tolerates heat, dryness and high humidity but heavy rains will flatten plants if they are unsupported.
FROST TOLERANCE: Accepts –4°F at least.
ASPECT: Full sun is essential. Needs very well-drained soil.
FLOWERING SEASON: It has a very long flowering period from spring throughout summer, sometimes into fall.
CUT FLOWERS: Gaura is not suitable for cutting.
COLOR RANGE: Flowers are white. Buds are pink.
USES: Easy to grow and long lived, gaura can be grown in a mixed border and suits the cottage garden style well. In a large garden it can be massed or repeated as an accent plant throughout the garden.

GROW GAURA in dry, well-drained soil and don't feed it, or stems will be lax.

GEUM

Geum chiloense

EVERGREEN OR HERBACEOUS; TAKES PART-SHADE

ORIGIN: Chile.
SIZE: Flower stems 12–20 in tall rise from dense rosettes of hairy leaves.
CLIMATE: Geums are not too hardy and are suited to zone 6 and above. They may remain evergreen in warm climates.
FROST TOLERANCE: Takes lows of at least 0°F.
ASPECT: Prefers full sun but can also be grown in semi-shade, especially in warmer areas. Likes moist soil.
FLOWERING SEASON: Gives a long flowering display through late spring and summer. Regular dead-heading is essential to prolong the display. Long-stemmed flowers may be single or double.
CUT FLOWERS: Not long lasting when cut.
COLOR RANGE: Scarlet, yellow, orange and apricot shades.
USES: Geum is attractive when used singly, in groups in mixed borders or in large drifts. It is good in pots.

GEUM HAS an airy looseness that suits wild, informal gardens.

GOATSBEARD IS an easily grown perennial provided it is given moist soil.

GOATSBEARD

Aruncus dioicus

HERBACEOUS; TAKES PART-SHADE

ORIGIN: Europe, Asia and North America.
SIZE: A tall-growing perennial attaining 4–6 ft in height.
CLIMATE: It is very tough and can be grown in zone 4 and above, but bear in mind it prefers cool climates.
FROST TOLERANCE: It will take a low of between –20°F and –31°F.
ASPECT: This is a plant for moist soil that is not prone to drying out in the summer. It grows best in partial shade but it will take full sun provided the soil is moist.
FLOWERING SEASON: From early to midsummer.
CUT FLOWERS: The spikes of flowers are good for cutting, especially for unusual flower arrangements.
COLOR RANGE: Creamy-white.
USES: Grow it in a woodland garden or in a mixed border with moist soil. Most effective when planted in a large group with a dark-leaved shrub forming a background.

HOSTAS HAVE remarkable leaves, and if you grow them be sure to bait for snails.

HOSTA

Also known as plantain lily

Hosta species and hybrids

HERBACEOUS; NEEDS DAPPLED OR PART-SHADE

ORIGIN: China, Korea and Japan.
SIZE: Grows 24 in tall and as wide.
CLIMATE: Suitable for cool and temperate areas only. They are well suited to zones 5 to 8 but do not like hot, dry or hot, humid places.
FROST TOLERANCE: They take lows of down to –9°F at least.
ASPECT: Needs shade or dappled sunlight. Grows in sunny spots in very cool zones. Yellow or gold leaf forms need some direct sun, preferably a few hours in the morning. Constantly moist, humus-rich soil is essential.
FLOWERING SEASON: Flowers are produced in late spring or summer but hosta is grown for its leaves.
CUT FLOWERS: They can be used as a cut flower but are not especially long lasting.
COLOR RANGE: Most species bloom in shades of mauve. Leaves come in hundreds of patterns but only a few may be sold in particular areas.
USES: Hostas look best mass planted near water features or in shady areas under trees. As clumps grow larger they create a weed-free groundcover.

JAPANESE ANEMONE

Also known as windflower

Anemone x hybrida

HERBACEOUS OR SEMI-EVERGREEN; NEEDS PART-SHADE

ORIGIN: Garden origin.
SIZE: Plants form rounded mounds about 30 in tall with flower stems rising another 30 in above.
CLIMATE: Likes a cool, moist climate and does best in zones 6 to 8. Does not enjoy hot, dry or steamy summers. They are among the most widely planted anemones for fall color.
FROST TOLERANCE: Accepts –4°F quite easily.
ASPECT: Prefers bright shade or partial shade with shelter from strong wind. Needs moist, rich soil.
FLOWERING SEASON: Single or double flowers appear from late summer through fall depending on the weather and district.
CUT FLOWERS: Suitable for cutting but not long lasting.
COLOR RANGE: White or pink.
USES: Massed under trees they give a moist, woodland effect or grow them at the back of a shady border.

IN FROST-FREE GARDENS, Japanese anemone is not completely herbaceous.

THE BILLOWING masses of small flowers of lady's mantle look light and lacy.

LADY'S MANTLE

Alchemilla mollis

HERBACEOUS; TAKES PART-SHADE

ORIGIN: Anatolia, Caucasus.
SIZE: Grows 8–16 in tall and wide.
CLIMATE: This is a very easily grown and adaptable plant that likes a cold or at least a cool climate. It grows well in zone 4 and above, up to zone 8. This plant does not like summer humidity.
FROST TOLERANCE: Accepts –31°F at least.
ASPECT: Full sun is best except where summers are hot. There it prefers partial shade.
FLOWERING SEASON: Late spring through early summer.
CUT FLOWERS: Not suitable.
COLOR RANGE: The masses of small flowers are greenish-yellow.
USES: This is a quick-growing herbaceous perennial mostly used along the edges of paths or borders. It is good for suppressing weeds and sows itself freely, often popping up in cracks in paths or paving. It provides a lovely contrast to stronger colors.

LENTEN ROSE

Also known as Christmas rose

Helleborus orientalis

EVERGREEN; NEEDS PART-SHADE

ORIGIN: Greece, Turkey and the Caucasus.

SIZE: The species and its hybrids grow to about 18 in high.

CLIMATE: The Lenten rose will be happy in zone 6 and above.

FROST TOLERANCE: It will take a low of –9°F.

ASPECT: Dappled sunlight under trees or other partially shaded spots.

FLOWERING SEASON: Winter and early spring.

CUT FLOWERS: Good cut flower.

COLOR RANGE: The wide range of hybrids, which are grown in preference to the species, come in shades of pink, red, purple, cream and white. Many hybrids have attractively spotted flowers.

USES: Best planted under deciduous trees and left undisturbed. May be short lived in areas that are too warm for them, but they tend to self-seed and so you do not lose them.

THE LENTEN ROSE is one of the few winter-flowering perennials.

SPRING-FLOWERING lungwort makes good groundcover in shade or part-shade.

LUNGWORT

Pulmonaria angustifolia

HERBACEOUS; NEEDS FULL OR PART-SHADE

ORIGIN: Found in the wild over much of Europe.

SIZE: A dwarf spreading perennial reaching only 12 in in height when in flower.

CLIMATE: It is extremely hardy, succeeding in zone 3 and above. Not a plant for very mild or warm regions.

FROST TOLERANCE: It will take a low of between –31°F and –38°F.

ASPECT: This is very much a shade-loving plant. It thrives in moist soil which is rich in humus.

FLOWERING SEASON: It has a long flowering period, creating a display throughout spring.

CUT FLOWERS: The flowers can be cut and arranged indoors and are ideal for mini arrangements.

COLOR RANGE: Bright blue.

USES: A superb and easily grown groundcover perennial for the woodland garden, wild garden or shrub border. Also grow it in bold groups at the front of a mixed border.

IF STARTING hybrid lupins from seed, sow into well-moistened soil but don't water again until seedlings emerge. A ration of high phosphorus fertilizer develops big flowers.

LUPIN

Lupinus polyphyllus hybrids

HERBACEOUS; TAKES PART SHADE

ORIGIN: The species is found from California to British Columbia. The hybrids are of garden origin.
SIZE: Grows to around 5 ft tall.
CLIMATE: The species is exceedingly hardy and thrives in zone 3. Lupins are not at all suitable for frost-free areas as they need a cold winter to allow them to become dormant.
FROST TOLERANCE: Accepts at least –35°F but will need a thick, protective mulch where such low temperatures are possible.
ASPECT: May be grown in full sun or semi-shade but needs shelter from strong winds.
FLOWERING SEASON: A short but spectacular flowering period from late spring to early summer.
CUT FLOWERS: Flowers may be cut for the vase but their display gives more value in the garden.
COLOR RANGE: Mixes include every shade but green, always with a hint of white.
USES: This herbaceous perennial produces tall, densely packed spires of flowers and the foliage is attractive too. Lupin is best seen when massed or it can be used at the back of a perennial border. It is not a long lived plant.

GARDENER'S TIPS

- Don't plant lupins in heavily manured soil and don't apply fertilizer that is high in nitrogen as this leads to leaves, not flowers.
- Lupins do like lime and you should add a handful for every square yard of soil and dig it in prior to planting.

MEADOW RUE

Thalictrum aquilegifolium

HERBACEOUS; NEEDS DAPPLED OR PART-SHADE

ORIGIN: Europe and Asia.
SIZE: About 3 ft tall, half as wide.
CLIMATE: Zone 6 and above.
FROST TOLERANCE: Takes at least –4°F.
ASPECT: Prefers light shade or morning sun only. In cool districts, where summers are mild, such as zone 6, it can be grown in full sun or partial or dappled shade.
FLOWERING SEASON: Flowers appear some time during late spring and summer, depending on climate.
CUT FLOWERS: Flowers do not cut well.
COLOR RANGE: Flowers are mauve-pink in the species but there is a white form and one with deeper violet blooms.
USES: Easy and quick to grow, with attractive blue-green foliage and pretty flowers, meadow rue can be planted in mixed borders or in clumps in light shade under trees. Other meadow rues worth seeking out are *T. delavayi* and *T. dipterocarpum*. All look good in wooded gardens.

GARDENER'S TIP

Woodland flowers won't bloom in deep, dark shade. They should be grown under deciduous trees, under high branching or open foliaged evergreens or on the edges of clearings in the garden. In nature, they would receive sun in early spring.

MEADOW RUE is a dainty perennial with fern-like, grayish leaves that are attractive in themselves. The tall stems of airy mauve flowers are a spring or summer bonus.

WHEN WELL GROWN Michaelmas daisies literally cover themselves with bloom.

MICHAELMAS DAISY

Aster species

HERBACEOUS; TAKES LIGHT SHADE

ORIGIN: North America.
SIZE: From about 10 to 36 in tall.
CLIMATE: Suitable for cold or temperate regions only. The plants need a cold winter to ensure they become dormant. Many are extremely hardy, being suited to zone 2 and above. But do check hardiness before you buy.
FROST TOLERANCE: Some will accept at least –40°F.
ASPECT: Best in full sun. Tolerates light shade but the blooming there may not be so prolific.
FLOWERING SEASON: It has a long flowering display from late summer well into fall.
CUT FLOWERS: As cut flowers these last very well if water is changed every day or two.
COLOR RANGE: Flowers may be white, blue, violet, pink or red.
USES: There is a large variety of these easily grown daisies, including *A. novi-belgii*, *A. ericoides* and *A.* x *frikartii*. All make lovely additions to the late summer border or can be grouped on their own.

MILFOIL

Also known as yarrow

Achillea millefolium hybrids

HERBACEOUS

ORIGIN: Europe and western Asia.
SIZE: Grows up to 3 ft tall with a very vigorous, spreading habit.
CLIMATE: Extremely hardy, thriving in zone 3 and above. Not suitable for subtropical climates.
FROST TOLERANCE: Takes at least –31°F.
ASPECT: Full sun is essential.
FLOWERING SEASON: Summer and early fall. Regular removal of spent flower stems or cutting for the vase will prolong blooming.
CUT FLOWERS: Good cut flower.
COLOR RANGE: The species has flattish heads of white flowers and feathery foliage but cultivars have flowers in shades of pink, apricot and crimson. The related *A. filipendulina* has bright yellow flowers.
USES: Impressive in large drifts, or use it at the back of borders or as a permanent planting among annuals.

'MOONSHINE" is a hybrid milfoil. The hybrids are less invasive than the species.

MOUNTAIN FLAX is striking in the garden with its dramatic evergreen leaves.

MOUNTAIN FLAX

Phormium cookianum

EVERGREEN

ORIGIN: New Zealand.
SIZE: When in flower it reaches 7 ft in height. The leaves grow up to 5 ft in length.
CLIMATE: This is one of the more tender perennials, succeeding in zone 8 and above.
FROST TOLERANCE: It will take a minimum temperature of 10°F. In regions prone to frosts, give the plants a deep winter mulch of organic matter to help protect the roots and crown.
ASPECT: Phormiums need full sun and are especially good plants for coastal gardens.
FLOWERING SEASON: The flowers are produced in the summer but phormiums are grown mainly for their dramatic foliage.
CUT FLOWERS: Not really suitable for cutting.
COLOR RANGE: Grown mainly for its light green sword-like leaves. There are numerous varieties in various foliage colors. The flowers are green, tinged yellow or orange.
USES: Mountain flax makes a striking focal point in the garden, perhaps near a patio, terrace or building.

OBEDIENT PLANT

Physostegia virginiana

HERBACEOUS; TAKES PART-SHADE

ORIGIN: Canada, United States.
SIZE: Grows up to 36 in tall, with an erect, multi-stemmed habit.
CLIMATE: This is a very hardy plant and is suitable for zone 4 and above.
FROST TOLERANCE: Accepts –22°F at least.
ASPECT: Grows in full sun or part shade. Shelter it from strong wind.
FLOWERING SEASON: From middle to late summer until well into fall. Frequent cutting of blooms produces a second flush of flowers.
CUT FLOWERS: Good cut flower. Scald cut stems before arranging.
COLOR RANGE: Pinky mauve but also pink, red and white.
USES: Lovely in large drifts, in a border or among other garden shrubs. This plant spreads by stolons (runners) and also by seed so that large clumps can develop in one season. Obedient plant will need fairly frequent reduction in most gardens.

OBEDIENT PLANT is so called because the stems can be bent to shape.

ORIENTAL POPPY

Papaver orientale

HERBACEOUS

ORIGIN: Anatolia, western Asia.
SIZE: Over 3 ft tall.
CLIMATE: This is an extremely hardy and easily grown poppy that will succeed in zone 3 and above. A long, cold winter is essential for success with these plants as it allows them to become completely dormant.
FROST TOLERANCE: Needs at least 28°F and accepts –40°F.
ASPECT: Full sun with some protection from strong winds.
FLOWERING SEASON: Flowering is from late spring to summer.
CUT FLOWERS: Spectacular cut flowers. Pick them as the buds are opening and scald the stems for 10–15 seconds before arranging.
COLOR RANGE: White, apricot, orange, mauve, pink, red, maroon, or combinations of these.
USES: Magnificent in a perennial border or mass together for an eye-catching display. Foliage can be untidy towards the end of the season and the plants are usually grown behind something else that is slightly lower. Oriental poppies are long lived where the climate suits them.

ORIENTAL POPPIES produce big, crinkled flowers, often with central black blotches.

PASQUE FLOWERS have silky hairs that give them a delicate, silvery appearance.

PASQUE FLOWER

Pulsatilla vulgaris

HERBACEOUS; TAKES PART-SHADE

ORIGIN: Northern Europe.
SIZE: 12 in tall with a similar spread.
CLIMATE: The pasque flower is very hardy as it originates from high alpine meadows and therefore prefers a cool climate. It will succeed in zone 5 up to zone 8.
FROST TOLERANCE: Accepts –12°F at least.
ASPECT: Grows best in full sun but tolerates partial shade, especially in the warmer parts of its range.
FLOWERING SEASON: Early spring, sometimes before the leaves in cold places. Flowers last well on the plant and the show is prolonged by the pretty, silky seed heads.
CUT FLOWERS: Not usually cut but they should last well.
COLOR RANGE: Flowers of the species are a soft purple but pink, white and red forms are also sold.
USES: One of the earliest flowers to bloom in spring, pasque flower should be planted in groups or drifts to get the best effect. If you have sensitive skin, wear gloves when handling them.

PEONY

Paeonia species and cultivars

HERBACEOUS; TAKES PART-SHADE

ORIGIN: Western China and Siberia.
SIZE: About 3 ft tall with a similar or greater spread.
CLIMATE: A cool to cold climate is essential. Plants must go completely dormant for at least two months of the year. The most popular herbaceous peonies, varieties of *P. lactiflora* and *P. officinalis*, are suited to zones 6, 7 and 8.
FROST TOLERANCE: The hardiest take a low of –9°F.
ASPECT: Needs full sun or partial shade with protection from wind.
FLOWERING SEASON: Mid-spring to early summer. Flowers may be single or double.
CUT FLOWERS: Cut flowers just as the blooms are opening.
COLOR RANGE: Flowers are available in white and cream and every shade of pink, red and purple.
USES: Beautiful to look at and fragrant too, peonies are among the aristocrats of the plant world. They make dramatic feature plants and a large group in full bloom is an unforgettable sight. Peonies can also be grown in containers for patio or deck display.

THERE ARE both shrubby and perennial forms of peony. None is for warm areas.

EASY-TO-GROW perennial phlox has a place in any cool climate flower garden.

PHLOX

Phlox paniculata

HERBACEOUS

ORIGIN: Eastern United States.
SIZE: Grows 24 in to 3 ft tall and about half as wide.
CLIMATE: Suitable for zone 4 and above. Basically a cool-climate plant, it may be short-lived in warm regions.
FROST TOLERANCE: Accepts –22°F at least.
ASPECT: Full sun with shelter from strong wind gives the best results.
FLOWERING SEASON: Long display in summer and early fall.
CUT FLOWERS: Not suitable.
COLOR RANGE: Flowers may be white or shades of pink, red, orange, mauve or purple, often with a contrasting center.
USES: Perennial phlox looks best mass planted, either in solid blocks of one color or mixed. With mixed plantings make sure that the taller forms do not obscure the shorter ones. Phlox can be a major feature of a perennial border or it can be used as a background to summer annuals.

PINKS TOLERATE dry conditions well as long as the soil is not shallow.

PINK

Dianthus cultivars

EVERGREEN

ORIGIN: Pinks are of hybrid origin.
SIZE: The height varies with type from 4 to 12 in. Plants form tufted mats of grayish leaves.
CLIMATE: Modern pinks are very hardy as cold-tolerant species have been used in their breeding. Most can be grown in zone 5 and above.
FROST TOLERANCE: All pinks will accept at least –12°F.
ASPECT: Needs full sun all day.
FLOWERING SEASON: Some pinks flower during spring only, others have a long flowering period from spring to early fall. Most varieties are strongly clove scented.
CUT FLOWERS: Long lasting and fragrant cut flowers.
COLOR RANGE: Flowers may be white or shades of pink, red, crimson or salmon.
USES: Pinks look well in containers or at the front of mixed flower borders. Low-growing varieties can be massed for a small-scale groundcover or used to line paths.

PRIMROSE

Primula denticulata

HERBACEOUS; PREFERS PARTIAL SHADE

ORIGIN: Himalayas, China.
SIZE: This is a dwarf perennial at only 12–18 in high when in flower.
CLIMATE: It is a tough plant and will succeed in zone 5. This primula is not really suited to very mild or warm climates.
FROST TOLERANCE: Takes a low of between –9°F and –20°F.
ASPECT: Prefers partial shade but full sun is tolerated if the soil remains steadily moist.
FLOWERING SEASON: It has quite a long flowering period, starting in early spring and often carrying on through to early summer.
CUT FLOWERS: The blooms can be cut and used for indoor flower arrangements.
COLOR RANGE: The globular heads of flowers come in shades of purple or pink-purple, plus white, all with a yellow eye.
USES: Superb for moist woodland gardens and shrub borders. Looks best when mass planted in drifts between shrubs and trees.

A DISTINCTIVE primrose for the moist and partially shaded woodland garden or shrub border.

EVERGREEN WHERE winters are mild, red hot pokers are herbaceous in frosty areas.

RED HOT POKER

Also known as torch lily

***Kniphofia* species and cultivars**

HERBACEOUS OR EVERGREEN; TAKES PART-SHADE

ORIGIN: South Africa.
SIZE: Varies with type from 2 ft to 7 ft. Clumps spread at least as wide.
CLIMATE: Red hot pokers may be hardy in the north if they are given a thick mulch to protect the roots and crowns. Most will thrive in zone 8 and above. Some will thrive in zones 5 to 7. Do check hardiness before you buy.
FROST TOLERANCE: The hardiest will take a low of at least –13°F.
ASPECT: Needs full sun except in hot, inland areas where shade on summer afternoons helps. Accepts coastal exposure but strong winds tend to make the leaves look untidy.
FLOWERING SEASON: Varies with species or cultivar. Many flower in late spring and summer or summer into fall, but *K. praecox* blooms from midwinter to spring.
CUT FLOWERS: Pick when the lower flowers have opened. Scald the cut stem ends before arranging.
COLOR RANGE: Usually orange and yellow together but also plain cream, yellow or coral shades.
USES: Eye-catching feature or tub plants. Use the smaller forms in flower borders. Don't disturb for years.

RED VALERIAN

Centranthus ruber

EVERGREEN

ORIGIN: Mediterranean region.
SIZE: Grows 20–36 in tall; bushy.
CLIMATE: Coming from a mild climate, the red valerian is suitable for zone 7 and above.
FROST TOLERANCE: Takes a low of 0°F.
ASPECT: Full sun is essential. Grows best in very well-drained, poor soil.
FLOWERING SEASON: Long display from spring until early fall. Cut plant back after the first flush for more flowers.
CUT FLOWERS: Not suitable.
COLOR RANGE: Flowers may be deep pink, red or white.
USES: This evergreen perennial is very easy to grow but will often exceed its boundaries by self-sowing where it is not wanted. It is ideal for a low-maintenance garden and is often planted in mixed borders, in large rockeries or on dry, fast-draining banks where it is useful for erosion control. Makes a good partner for lavender.

FRAGRANT RED *valerian self-seeds but unwanted plants are easily removed.*

SALVIA X SUPERBA *is an easy perennial that should be in every mixed border.*

SAGE

Salvia species and cultivars

HERBACEOUS; TAKES PART-SHADE

ORIGIN: Southern United States, Mexico and South America.
SIZE: Size varies with species, from about 24 in to around 6 ft. Most are spreading, sprawling plants.
CLIMATE: Sage is unsuitable for the tropics and humid subtropics. They are variable in their hardiness, the toughest being suitable for zone 5, while the most tender will take little or no frost. It is best to check hardiness before you buy.
FROST TOLERANCE: The hardiest sages will take a low of between –9°F and –20°F.
ASPECT: Full sun. In warm areas, sages accept a few hours shade.
FLOWERING SEASON: Most have a very long flowering period in the summer, and often continue into fall.
CUT FLOWERS: Not suitable.
COLOR RANGE: Shades of blue or purple, often with white.
USES: The taller sages are ideal for the back of the border or for fillers between shrubs but the bog sage, *S. uliginosa*, can be rather invasive. All sages are easy-care plants.

SEA HOLLY

Eryngium bourgatii

HERBACEOUS

ORIGIN: Mountains of Spain.
SIZE: Reaches 16–24 in tall, sometimes taller.
CLIMATE: Despite its origins this is a very hardy perennial and is well suited to zone 5 and above.
FROST TOLERANCE: Takes –13°F.
ASPECT: Grows in any open, airy position in full sun. Enjoys extreme coastal exposure.
FLOWERING SEASON: The long-lasting flowers appear during summer.
CUT FLOWERS: Can be cut and dried for permanent arrangements.
COLOR RANGE: Flowers are a curious metallic silvery-blue.
USES: An unusual looking plant with stiff, spiny leaves and flowers. The cultivar "Oxford Blue" has especially good color. Other species widely grown include *E. amethystinum*, *E. giganteum*, *E. maritimum* and *E. planum*. All are curious feature plants but not comfortable to handle.

SEA HOLLY requires extra sharp drainage and not overly rich soil.

THIS VARIEGATED sedge makes excellent groundcover among shrubs.

SEDGE

Carex morrowii "Variegata"

EVERGREEN; TAKES PART-SHADE

ORIGIN: The species is native to Japan, where it is found in mountain woodland, but the variety is of garden origin.
SIZE: This is variable but it grows up to 16 in in height.
CLIMATE: It is not one of the hardiest plants but is suitable for zone 8 and above.
FROST TOLERANCE: Takes a low of 10°F.
ASPECT: Suitable for sun or for partial shade.
FLOWERING SEASON: Flowers are produced in the summer.
CUT FLOWERS: The flowers are not especially attractive and therefore are not suitable for cutting.
COLOR RANGE: This tufted plant is grown for its grassy foliage which is narrowly striped with white near the margins.
USES: This variegated sedge gives best effect when it is mass planted. It is an excellent groundcover among shrubs. It is also suitable to grow in containers on a patio or terrace, with other suitable plants.

SHASTA DAISY

Leucanthemum x superbum, syn. Chrysanthemum maximum

HERBACEOUS OR SEMI-EVERGREEN; TAKES PART-SHADE

ORIGIN: Shastas arose in gardens.
SIZE: Flowers stand 20 in tall.
CLIMATE: A very hardy daisy, suitable for zone 5 and above.
FROST TOLERANCE: Takes –13°F.
ASPECT: Where summers are mild, grow in full sun all day, but in hotter areas, provide dappled shade
FLOWERING SEASON: Late spring and summer. There is a double form.
CUT FLOWERS: Cutting flowers prolongs the display.
COLOR RANGE: Flowers are white with bright yellow centers.
USES: It is ideal in mixed beds, its big white flowers providing the perfect accompaniment to other brightly colored blooms.

HERBACEOUS IN *cold climates, shastas don't die back completely in mild areas.*

THE SMALL *globe thistle is ideal for creating dramatic effects in borders.*

SMALL GLOBE THISTLE

Echinops ritro

HERBACEOUS; TAKES PART-SHADE

ORIGIN: South-east Europe to central Asia.
SIZE: It grows to a height of only 24 in.
CLIMATE: This has proved to be an extremely hardy perennial. It is hardy north, in zone 3.
FROST TOLERANCE: Will take a low of between –31°F and –38°F.
ASPECT: Best grown in a position that receives full sun but it will be successful in part-shade. Best results are achieved in poor soil rather than in highly fertile conditions.
FLOWERING SEASON: It has a long flowering period and starts in late summer.
CUT FLOWERS: The flowers are good for cutting and drying for use in winter arrangements. Or they can be used fresh.
COLOR RANGE: Bright blue flowers, the heads being metallic blue before the flowers open.
USES: This is a bold plant ideal for creating a dramatic effect in herbaceous or mixed borders, where it contrasts with many other plants. It is also a good choice for a wild garden.

SPIDERWORT

Also known as trinity flower or widow's tears

Tradescantia virginiana

HERBACEOUS; LIKES AFTERNOON SHADE

ORIGIN: Eastern United States.
SIZE: Reaches 12–24 in tall with many soft stems.
CLIMATE: Zone 7 and above. Likes a rainy, humid climate and in drier regions this plant will need plenty of summer water.
FROST TOLERANCE: Accepts –1°F if its roots are mulched with straw in fall.
ASPECT: Grows best with morning sun or in bright, dappled shade all day. Takes full sun in mild climates.
FLOWERING SEASON: The long succession of flowers appears from late spring through to fall.
CUT FLOWERS: Not suitable.
COLOR RANGE: White, pink, mauve or violet.
USES: Spiderwort is a spreading plant with tapering strappy leaves and showy triangular flowers, which each lasts only one day. Grow them at the front of mixed flower borders or in bright, dappled shade.

INTENSE VIOLET is just one of the colors available in spiderworts. It self-seeds.

STOKES ASTER is easy to grow and gives good decorative value in the garden.

STOKES ASTER

Stokesia laevis

HERBACEOUS OR EVERGREEN; TAKES DAPPLED SHADE

ORIGIN: South-east United States.
SIZE: Flower stems rise 12–20 in from a low clump of leaves.
CLIMATE: This native perennial is easily grown in zone 6 and above. In dry areas give it plenty of summer water. Some leaves remain year round where winters are not very cold.
FROST TOLERANCE: Accepts –4°F at least but if that is possible, mulch roots with straw in fall.
ASPECT: Prefers full sun but will grow in dappled sunlight, especially where summers are very hot.
FLOWERING SEASON: Long display in summer and fall.
CUT FLOWERS: Good cut flower and cutting prolongs blooming.
COLOR RANGE: Blue-mauve, white and pink.
USES: Good in mass plantings but fits in well with mixed border plants. It can be grown in containers, too. In warm regions it can be quite vigorous.

SUNFLOWER

Helianthus decapetalus

HERBACEOUS

ORIGIN: Central and south-east USA.
SIZE: Grows to over 3 ft tall with a similar spread. Fast growing.
CLIMATE: A hardy perennial suitable for growing in zone 5 and above. In dry regions it will appreciate being given plenty of water in summer.
FROST TOLERANCE: Takes –13°F.
ASPECT: Needs full sun all day and shelter from strong winds.
FLOWERING SEASON: Flowering begins in late summer and can continue until the middle of fall.
CUT FLOWERS: Impressive cut flower. Pick as soon as it is fully open.
COLOR RANGE: Bright yellow with a rusty brown central disc.
USES: Perennial sunflower is vigorous and can spread rapidly. Flowers are prolific and usually single, but some varieties have fully double flowers. This is an undemanding plant that will grow even if neglected. It should be planted at the back of the border or in bold clumps among shrubs. Planted in rows three or four deep, sunflower makes a striking flowering hedge over summer.

PERENNIAL SUNFLOWERS are not at all fussy about soil so long as it drains freely.

THRIFT IS a good choice in cottage gardens where it is often used to line paths.

THRIFT

Also known as sea pink

Armeria maritima

EVERGREEN

ORIGIN: Europe and the areas around the Mediterranean.
SIZE: Grassy leaves are about 6 in tall with flower stems rising to 10 in.
CLIMATE: This is a very adaptable plant, being widely distributed in the wild, and it thrives in various climates. Extremely hardy, it will be happy in zone 4 and above.
FROST TOLERANCE: Accepts –22°F at least.
ASPECT: Must have full sun all day. Thrift tolerates dry, windy conditions and salt spray.
FLOWERING SEASON: There is a long flowering period through spring and summer as long as plants are dead-headed regularly.
CUT FLOWERS: Makes a good cut flower or you can dry flowers for permanent arrangements.
COLOR RANGE: Flowers may be white, pink or almost red.
USES: Thrift can be used as a groundcover, as an edging plant, in rockeries or on dry walls and even in containers. It sometimes will grow between paving stones.

VIOLET

Viola odorata

EVERGREEN

ORIGIN: Europe.
SIZE: About 8 in tall but spreads widely by creeping stems.
CLIMATE: As it comes from climates that are not too severe, it is not as hardy as some perennials, but will thrive in zone 8 and above.
FROST TOLERANCE: Accepts 14°F at least.
ASPECT: Prefers a position where it gets midday shade in summer but full sun in winter is ideal. Too much shade will result in few or no flowers. If in doubt, choose more sun.
FLOWERING SEASON: Winter and early spring.
CUT FLOWERS: Is superb in posies, either alone or with other small blooms. It is highly fragrant.
COLOR RANGE: Violet, white or shades of pink.
USES: Plant beside paths or at the front of flower borders. Grows well under lightly leafed, deciduous trees.

VIOLETS ARE easy to grow but won't bloom if you give them too much shade.

YELLOW ALYSSUM blooms at the same time as spring bulbs such as tulips.

YELLOW ALYSSUM

Also known as gold dust or mad wort

Aurinia saxatilis

EVERGREEN

ORIGIN: Europe and Anatolia.
SIZE: Makes a mound of gray-green leaves 12–18 in tall and wide.
CLIMATE: A plant for cooler climates, it is extremely hardy and will thrive in zone 3 and above. Does not enjoy hot, humid summers.
FROST TOLERANCE: It takes a low of at least –31°F but in such conditions would benefit from a thick mulch of straw placed over the root area in fall.
ASPECT: Must have full sun all day. Grow in very well-drained but rather poor sandy or gravelly soil. In over-rich or well-fertilized soil the plants grow lanky and are inclined to sprawl.
FLOWERING SEASON: Early spring. On a well-grown specimen they can completely cover the plant.
CUT FLOWERS: Not suitable.
COLOR RANGE: Flowers are bright, golden yellow.
USES: Spectacular when massed. Use as groundcover or in hanging baskets.

• CHAPTER TWENTY •

BULBS

Few plant groups offer as much variety and pleasure for so little effort as do bulbs. Even people without gardens can enjoy them in pots and while most people think of bulbs as spring flowers, there are bulbs that bloom in all other seasons, too.

WHICH BULBS ARE RIGHT FOR YOU?

The whole point of growing bulbs is that they are easy. You plant them once and they return to grow and flower every year after that. They multiply too, so that you end up with many more flowers than you started with. That's how it should be, but for many gardeners bulbs don't behave like that. They may flower well enough in the year that they are planted but after that, nothing. If this happens to you, there's a simple reason for it; your climate is unsuitable. Not for all bulbs, just the ones that don't come back bigger and better than before.

Many bulbs come from areas where summers are hot and dry but winters are extremely cold. They start to grow in late winter, flower in early spring and die back by summer. The bulb itself allows the plant to remain alive underground. But if you don't experience a freezing winter followed by a hot, dry summer, the bulb isn't grateful for your pleasant climate, it's confused by it and just doesn't grow properly. Your strange climate turns what should be a long-lived perennial into an expensive annual that has to be replaced every year.

Happily there are also bulbs that come from areas with mild winters and these are the ones to grow if you, too, have frost-free or almost frost-free winters. They appear in fall, grow through winter, flower in early spring and quickly die back. They die back because they're expecting the hot, dry summer of their homelands. If you have a wet summer, you could have trouble with these bulbs, too. They will rot unless the soil you have them in drains fast. Alternatively, you could lift them after they've died back and store them in a dry, dark place until the following fall.

HOW TO PLANT BULBS

Choose an open planting site where the bulbs will receive sun for at least half a day, preferably longer. There are a few that will grow well in shade but most like sun. All bulbs must have good drainage or they will rot.

Don't plant bulbs in rows as it looks unnatural. Plant them in clumps or groups instead. The depth of planting depends on the size of the bulb but it is usually two or three times the diameter of the bulb. Plant with the pointy end up except for ranunculus and anemone, which have the claws or points facing down. Leave enough space between the bulbs for offspring bulbs to develop and water in well after planting. Don't water again without checking to see if the soil has dried out. Often it is not necessary to water again until leaf shoots have started to appear.

POTTING UP BULBS

Hardy bulbs are not indoor plants and must be grown outside. They can, however, be brought indoors when about to bloom. To grow bulbs in a pot, place some potting mix in the base of the container and then plant the bulbs a little more shallowly than you would in the soil. You may mix in a little blood and bone or complete plant food if you wish. Crowd the bulbs in so that they are close but not actually touching each other and then fill the pots to within about 1 in of the rim—water well and drain. Water only when the potting mix is starting to dry out but increase watering once the leaf shoots appear. Feed monthly with liquid or soluble plant food and you can bring the pots indoors when the flower buds are starting to bloom.

ROUTINE CARE OF BULBS

Once leaf shoots have emerged, plants should be given regular deep watering but the ground should not be kept wet. After the flowers have finished, cut them off but leave the stems and don't cut back the foliage. If you cut off the leaves before they have died down naturally, the bulb will not have the reserves to grow and flower the following season. After flowering, fertilize the plants with blood and bone or complete plant food and continue to water regularly until the leaves begin to die off naturally. This may take two or three months.

If your climate suits them, bulbs do not need lifting every season. Most are

COMBINING BULBS into a pleasing color scheme can yield breathtaking results. Here white tulips and pink and blue anemones bloom on a ground of white violas.

YOU DON'T HAVE to have this much space to grow bulbs in a natural style. You can clump daffodils under a single deciduous tree or plant them in drifts under your lawn.

left in the ground and lifted only every two or three years when growth becomes congested and flowering declines. Lift when the plants are dormant, using a garden fork to raise the whole clump. Discard any damaged, soft or rotted bulbs and any that are surplus to your needs and allow the rest to dry in a cool, airy spot. When they are dry, brush off excess soil and store the bulbs in net bags or old stockings until the usual planting time for that species. Most bulbs can be treated this way but lilies are an exception. Because they have no protective outer sheath on their bulbs, they must be lifted, divided if necessary and replanted at once.

Some bulbous plants such as freesias produce quite a lot of seed if the spent flower stems are not cut off. You can collect these seeds when they are ripe or allow them to self-sow. Seedlings may take three years or more to flower and may not be true to type, but the results can be interesting.

WHERE TO BUY BULBS

Most good garden centers display bulbs in mesh packets with attached pictures and growing instructions. Some garden centers also sell bulbs in bulk. Another option is to send away for catalogues from bulb growing nurseries and order bulbs by mail—these growers advertise in popular gardening magazines. This can be a good option if you want a lot of bulbs as it can be somewhat cheaper.

When choosing at the garden center, handle bulbs carefully: don't bruise them. Select firm, well-rounded bulbs and make sure there are no soft spots. Try to make your selection early in the season so that you have a choice of the best on offer. If you are not planting them for a while, store the bulbs in paper or net bags and keep them in a cool, dry, airy place. Store cool climate bulbs such as tulip, hyacinth or daffodil in the crisper drawer of the refrigerator if the weather is still warm.

ANEMONE

Anemone coronaria

ORIGIN: Southern Europe, Anatolia, western Asia.
SIZE: 16–24 in tall, 10 in wide.
CLIMATE: It is not too hardy and can only be grown out of doors all year round in zone 8 and above. Can be grown in pots under glass in very cold areas.
FROST TOLERANCE: Accepts 10°F but prefers to live where winters are milder.
ASPECT: Grows best in full sun with some wind protection.
PLANTING: Plant in fall, pointed end down. In zone 8 and above bulbs can also be planted in early spring.
FLOWERING SEASON: Fall plantings flower in early spring; early spring plantings bloom in summer. There are singles and doubles.
CUT FLOWERS: Cut the flowers rather than pull them from the plant.
COLOR RANGE: White or shades of red, pink, cerise, blue, mauve and violet. Single colors are available.
USES: Plant in solid blocks for the best effect or use them in wide containers. The "De Caen" strain has single poppy-like flowers. "St Bridgid" has semi-double to double flowers.

DON'T BOTHER saving anemone tubers. They're short lived and very cheap.

BABOON FLOWERS grow well in quite poor soil so long as drainage is good.

BABOON FLOWER

Babiana stricta

TAKES PART-SHADE

ORIGIN: South-west South Africa.
SIZE: Reaches about 12 in tall.
CLIMATE: Grow outdoors all year round only in zone 9 and above. Suits mild and temperate regions of the southern USA. In colder climates, grow in pots under glass.
FROST TOLERANCE: Accepts –21°F if sheltered overhead and planted against a sunny wall.
ASPECT: Full sun in humid areas, but inland, afternoon shade helps.
PLANTING: Plant corms in fall, 6–8 in deep.
FLOWERING SEASON: Late winter or spring (the cooler the climate, the later the flowering).
CUT FLOWERS: Flowers cut well.
COLOR RANGE: Deep, royal blue but also other shades of blue, mauve, magenta, pink and white.
USES: Forms a neat fan-shaped clump of ribbed or pleated leaves. They look best planted in groups at the front of a border, in rockeries or in containers.

BELLADONNA FLOWERS are sweetly fragrant and appear before the leaves.

BELLADONNA LILY

Amaryllis belladonna

TAKES PART-SHADE

ORIGIN: South-west South Africa.
SIZE: Grows to 20–28 in tall with a clump of strappy leaves.
CLIMATE: Grow out of doors all year round in zone 8 and above. Do not allow to dry out in winter.
FROST TOLERANCE: Takes 10°F but prefers warmer winters.
ASPECT: Likes full sun but tolerates shade for part of the day, especially in hot inland climates.
PLANTING: Plant in summer. In frost-free climates, allow the neck of the bulb to protrude above ground. In colder areas, plant more deeply.
FLOWERING SEASON: Late summer or early fall.
CUT FLOWERS: Good cut flower. Cut cleanly from above the bulb.
COLOR RANGE: Pink or white.
USES: Good in bold clumps and can also be grown in pots. Best flowering comes from bulbs that have been left undisturbed for several years.

BLUEBELL

Hyacinthoides non-scripta ("English" bluebell), *H. hispanica* ("Spanish" bluebell)

NEEDS PART-SHADE

ORIGIN: Western and southern Europe and North Africa.
SIZE: Flower stems rise 16–20 in above a clump of strappy leaves.
CLIMATE: The bluebells prefer cooler climates and are suitable for zone 5 and above.
FROST TOLERANCE: Accepts –22°F at least.
ASPECT: Prefers morning sun or bright dappled shade all day.
PLANTING: Plant in fall, 4 in deep in rich soil. Leaves appear in late winter or early spring.
FLOWERING SEASON: Bluebells flower in spring, generally late in that season.
CUT FLOWERS: Flowers can be cut but do not last long in the vase.
COLOR RANGE: Usually blue but also pink or white.
USES: They are ideal for naturalizing under deciduous or lightly foliaged evergreen trees. The blue flowers are a great foil for spring-flowering shrubs with pink or white flowers. Bluebells are trouble-free and multiply fast.

IN FALL and winter, keep the soil moist where bluebells are planted.

CHECKERED LILY

Fritillaria meleagris

TAKES LIGHT SHADE

ORIGIN: From northern Europe to the Caucasus.
SIZE: It attains a height of up to 12 in when in flower.
CLIMATE: It is hardy in zone 4 and above.
FROST TOLERANCE: Takes a temperature down to –31°F.
ASPECT: Grow this bulb in full sun or light shade and in fertile, well drained yet moisture-retentive soil.
PLANTING: Plant any time in fall.
FLOWERING SEASON: Spring.
CUT FLOWERS: Not recommended for cutting.
COLOR RANGE: The pink or purple flowers are checkered with shades of red-purple and white. There are numerous varieties including one with white flowers.
USES: The checkered lily is an excellent subject for naturalizing in grass areas. Being a dwarf bulb it also looks at home on rock gardens. Try it also in raised alpine beds or even in alpine troughs on the patio or terrace.

THE CHECKERED LILY can be naturalized in grass or grown on a rock garden.

VALUED FOR its winter flowers, the common snowdrop is very versatile.

COMMON SNOWDROP

Galanthus nivalis

NEEDS PART-SHADE

ORIGIN: Europe.
SIZE: A miniature bulb at only 4 in in height when in flower.
CLIMATE: Very hardy, it will be happy in zone 4 and above, but is not suited to mild or warm climates.
FROST TOLERANCE: Will take a temperature down to –31°F.
ASPECT: Needs to be grown in partial shade. Best results in a moist, humus-rich soil.
PLANTING: The bulbs can be planted any time in fall. The best time to lift and divide congested clumps is immediately after flowering.
FLOWERING SEASON: One of the few winter-flowering bulbs.
CUT FLOWERS: Yes—ideal for miniature arrangements.
COLOR RANGE: The flowers are white with green markings. The many varieties include double-flowered and yellow-marked.
USES: A superb choice for the woodland garden or shrub border. Excellent for naturalizing in grass. The best effect is obtained when bulbs are mass planted in large groups or drifts. Plant small groups on rock gardens.

CROCUS
Crocus species

ORIGIN: Mediterranean region, Middle East and Central Asia.
SIZE: Grows 8 in or less high. The goblet-shaped flowers rise above a few strappy, grass-like leaves.
CLIMATE: This varies with the species. The hardiest are suitable for zones 4 or 5, while many are suitable for zones 6, 7 or 8. Check hardiness before you buy.
FROST TOLERANCE: All will take 14°F; some tolerate –22°F at least.
ASPECT: Full sun is ideal but the plants will accept a few hours shade.
PLANTING: Plant in late summer or fall about 3 in below the surface. Soil must drain well.
FLOWERING SEASON: Different species flower in fall, winter or in early spring.
CUT FLOWERS: Not suitable.
COLOR RANGE: White, pink, mauve and yellow, sometimes striped.
USES: Naturalize under grass or plant beneath deciduous trees. It is lovely in pots brought indoors in bloom.

CROCUS *is one of the first bulbs to bloom in spring, often appearing through snow.*

CYCLAMEN HEDERIFOLIUM *flowers in late summer and fall before foliage appears.*

CYCLAMEN
Cyclamen hederifolium
NEEDS DAPPLED OR PART-SHADE

ORIGIN: Southern Europe to Turkey.
SIZE: This is a miniature cyclamen, no more than 6 in in height when in flower.
CLIMATE: Suitable for zone 6 and above. Enjoys a Mediterranean climate. It is a good subject for dry soils in shade or part-shade.
FROST TOLERANCE: Accepts a low of –9°F.
ASPECT: Needs dappled or part-shade. It will accept a few hours of direct sun.
PLANTING: Plant 1–2 in deep in summer.
FLOWERING SEASON: The flowers are produced in mid- to late fall before the foliage appears.
CUT FLOWERS: Not suitable.
COLOR RANGE: Shades of pink, also white.
USES: Ideal for mass planting in a woodland garden under or around shrubs and trees. Plant bold drifts in a shrub border. Also suitable for growing on the rock garden.

WITHOUT FREQUENT FROSTS, daffodils will not reflower in subsequent years.

DAFFODIL

Narcissus species

ORIGIN: Europe, especially the south-west, North Africa, western and central Asia.
SIZE: Grows about 20 in tall.
CLIMATE: Best suited to cool climates, not suitable for the tropics. Hardiness varies—some are suitable for zone 4 and above, others for zone 6 and above. Check before you buy.
FROST TOLERANCE: The hardiest will take a low of –31°F.
ASPECT: Full sun with shelter from strong winds.
PLANTING: Best planted early to late summer or early fall.
FLOWERING SEASON: Late winter to mid-spring.
CUT FLOWERS: An exceptional cut flower but don't mix daffodils with other flowers until they have spent a day in a vase on their own.
COLOR RANGE: Plain yellow is most usual but hybrids are available with white, yellow and white, and pink flowers.
USES: Daffodils look wonderful mass-planted or in groups of five or more. They make great pot plants, too.

DAHLIA

Dahlia species and cultivars
TAKES PART-SHADE

ORIGIN: Mexico, in elevated areas.
SIZE: Height varies with type from 24 in to 6 ft.
CLIMATE: Take little or no frost. Can only be grown outdoors all year round in zone 9 and above.
FROST TOLERANCE: Accepts 30°F, possibly 28°F. Where lower temperatures are expected, lift the tubers after the first frost and store them in a frost-free place until spring.
ASPECT: Full sun for best flowering although the plants will perform well in shade for part of the day. All dahlias, especially tall varieties, need shelter from wind.
PLANTING: Plant from middle to late spring with the neck, containing the sprouting eye, pointing up.
FLOWERING SEASON: Early summer to late fall. Cut flowers or dead-head to prolong blooming.
CUT FLOWERS: Good cut flower. Scald stems before arranging.
COLOR RANGE: Huge range including bicolors and tricolors.
USES: Ideal additions to a summer flower border or can be massed together. Some are good in pots.

THERE ARE many different flower shapes and sizes in dahlias. All are magnificent.

THE VERSATILE dog-tooth violet can be grown in borders or grass areas.

DOG-TOOTH VIOLET

Erythronium dens-canis

FOR SHADE OR PART-SHADE

ORIGIN: Europe and Asia.
SIZE: 4–6 in in height.
CLIMATE: Zone 3 and above.
FROST TOLERANCE: Takes a low of –38°F. Mulch in winter with leafmould to protect the bulbs from severe frost.
ASPECT: Needs to be grown in shade or part-shade. Dappled shade is good. Best results in well-drained yet moist soil containing plenty of leafmould.
PLANTING: Any time during fall.
FLOWERING SEASON: This is a spring-flowering bulb.
CUT FLOWERS: Not recommended for cutting.
COLOR RANGE: The flowers are rose-pink to purple. There is also a white-flowered variety. The leaves have attractive red-brown mottling.
USES: Grow in the woodland garden, on the rock garden or under shrubs and trees, ideally deciduous kinds. Best planted in bold groups and drifts for maximum impact. It will also grow well in long-grass areas.

DUTCH IRIS

Iris xiphium hybrids

ORIGIN: Dutch iris are hybrids from Mediterranean region parents.
SIZE: Grows to about 28 in tall.
CLIMATE: Likes a cool to cold winter and does best in zones 6 to 8.
FROST TOLERANCE: Takes –10°F.
ASPECT: Needs full sun with some protection from strong wind.
PLANTING: Plant bulbs in fall. Mulch soil surface after planting.
FLOWERING SEASON: From late winter to late spring, depending on climate. Flowers are not long lasting.
CUT FLOWERS: A lovely cut flower. Pick them when the colored bud resembles a sharpened pencil.
COLOR RANGE: White and shades of yellow and blue, all with a yellow or orange blotch on the petals.
USES: Dutch iris is a lovely garden subject, especially when mass planted in solid blocks of color. It can also make a good container plant.

IN ZONE 2, don't plant Dutch iris until late fall. Store bulbs in the fridge.

SWEETLY FRAGRANT freesia can be left for years without attention.

FREESIA

Freesia species and hybrids

TAKES PART-SHADE

ORIGIN: South Africa.
SIZE: Grows to 10–12 in tall.
CLIMATE: Can be grown outdoors all year round in zone 9 and above. Elsewhere, freesias make good pot plants under glass.
FROST TOLERANCE: Accepts –28°F, possibly a little lower.
ASPECT: Full sun is best but this plant accepts light shade where winters are warm.
PLANTING: Plant from early to late fall, depending on the district. Plant early in cooler districts.
FLOWERING SEASON: Flowers from middle or late winter through to mid-spring. It is highly fragrant.
CUT FLOWERS: A lovely cut flower. Pick it when the lowest flower is fully open.
COLOR RANGE: White and shades of cream, yellow, pink, red, mauve and purple.
USES: Freesias multiply fast and naturalize easily. Let them spread throughout the garden or try them, deeply planted, in pots.

GLADIOLUS

Gladiolus species and hybrids

ORIGIN: Southern Africa and the Mediterranean region.
SIZE: Varies from 20 in to over 3 ft.
CLIMATE: Zone 9 and above. Most are frost tender and in the north are grown outdoors between spring and fall frosts. Some, such as the species shown, are hardy in zone 6.
FROST TOLERANCE: Mostly none. In cold areas, lift corms after the first frost and replant in spring.
ASPECT: Prefers full sun with shelter from strong wind.
PLANTING: In frost-free areas plant the corms from late fall to late winter; in cool areas plant in spring.
FLOWERING SEASON: Spring or summer. Modern garden hybrids (the typical gladiolus) flower about 100 days after planting.
CUT FLOWERS: Cut as the second flower is opening. Change the water daily and remove faded blooms.
COLOR RANGE: White and shades of pink, red, yellow, orange, apricot and mauve. Many bicolors.
USES: Gladiolus is often used as part of a mixed flower border but is also attractive when massed.

GLADIOLUS COMMUNIS *SUBSP.* BYZANTINUS *is hardy and spreads freely.*

GLORY-OF-THE-SNOW

Chionodoxa luciliae

ORIGIN: Western Turkey.
SIZE: Height 3–6 in when in flower.
CLIMATE: A very hardy bulb which will thrive in zone 4 and above.
FROST TOLERANCE: Takes temperatures down to –31°F.
ASPECT: As glory-of-the-snow likes plenty of light, grow it in full sun. Best performance in moist soil.
PLANTING: The bulbs can be planted from early to late fall.
FLOWERING SEASON: This is one of the first of the spring bulbs to appear. It flowers in early spring.
CUT FLOWERS: The flowers are not really suitable for cutting, although you could try them in miniature arrangements.
COLOR RANGE: Bright blue flowers with a white center. There is also a white variety and one with pink flowers. "Gigantea" has larger blooms than the species.
USES: Use in rock gardens, raised beds, or containers. It looks terrific mass planted among shrubs, where it can be allowed to self-seed freely.

GLORY-OF-THE-SNOW is one of the first spring bulbs to appear.

SPREAD BULBINELLA around the garden for winter drama and bright color.

GOLDEN WAND LILY

Bulbinella floribunda

TAKES PART-SHADE

ORIGIN: South-western South Africa.
SIZE: Grows 24–32 in tall.
CLIMATE: This is not a very hardy bulb but will thrive in zone 8 and above.
FROST TOLERANCE: Takes the odd 18°F, possibly 14°F but not for extended periods.
ASPECT: Prefers full sun or a few hours shade. Where summers are hot, some shade is advisable.
PLANTING: Plant in late summer or earliest fall with the tops of the fibrous roots at ground level.
FLOWERING SEASON: Middle to late winter or early spring.
CUT FLOWERS: Makes a striking and unusual cut flower. Don't pick until the lower buds have opened.
COLOR RANGE: Typically bright yellow but there is an orange form.
USES: Plant as background for lower flowers or naturalize in informal groups. Plants need a lot of water in winter, hardly any in summer.

GRAPE HYACINTHS appear with daffodils, contrasting well with their yellow shades.

GRAPE HYACINTH

Muscari armeniacum

TAKES PART-SHADE

ORIGIN: Mediterranean region.
SIZE: Grows about 8 in tall.
CLIMATE: This is a very hardy and easily cultivated bulb which can be grown in zone 4 and above.
FROST TOLERANCE: Takes –22°F.
ASPECT: Where winters are cold and gray, full sun is best. In sunnier, warmer places, some midday, dappled shade helps.
PLANTING: Plant in fall 2–3 in deep into fertile, well-drained soil.
FLOWERING SEASON: Late winter or early spring.
CUT FLOWERS: Not long lasting.
COLOR RANGE: Violet or white.
USES: Mass under deciduous trees or use to line paths. It is good at the front of mixed flower beds and is an excellent potted bulb. Water well whenever leaves are present but keep as dry as possible during summer.

HARLEQUIN FLOWER

Sparaxis tricolor

TAKES PART-SHADE

ORIGIN: Cape Town region of South Africa.
SIZE: Reaches about 16 in tall.
CLIMATE: Zone 9 and above. In frost-prone areas grow outdoors between spring and fall frosts. Lift and store for winter, or grow under glass.
FROST TOLERANCE: Accepts 19°F, possibly lower, but is better where frosts are rare or unknown.
ASPECT: Needs full sun all day except in zones 3 and 8 where shade until late morning is better.
PLANTING: Plant in fall or spring, depending on climate.
FLOWERING SEASON: Spring and summer.
CUT FLOWERS: This is a good cut flower if picked when fully open.
COLOR RANGE: It is available in a big range of colors, including red, pink, orange and purple, with a contrasting throat.
USES: Best when mass planted but can also be grown in containers where they should be crowded for best effect. The bulbs increase rapidly.

SHOWY, EASY-CARE harlequin flowers thrive in dry areas.

INSTEAD OF cutting the fragrant flowers, bring potted hyacinths indoors to bloom.

HYACINTH

Hyacinthus orientalis cultivars

TAKES PART-SHADE

ORIGIN: Turkey, the Middle East.
SIZE: Grows to about 16 in tall.
CLIMATE: Needs a cool or cold winter. Very hardy bulbs, succeeding in the north in zone 3 and above.
FROST TOLERANCE: Takes a low of at least –38°F, especially if thickly mulched over winter.
ASPECT: Does well in sun or partial shade but not heavy shade.
PLANTING: Plant in late summer or early fall in cool areas, late fall or early winter in warmer districts. Mulch after planting.
FLOWERING SEASON: From late winter to mid-spring.
CUT FLOWERS: Good cut flower. Change the water daily.
COLOR RANGE: White and shades of pink, red, blue, mauve as well as purple.
USES: Good in rows or other formal settings or grow them in pots. Once in bud, they can be brought indoors to bloom. Handling hyacinth bulbs can irritate sensitive skins.

JONQUIL

Narcissus jonquilla

TAKES PART-SHADE

ORIGIN: Spain and Portugal.
SIZE: Grows about 16 in tall.
CLIMATE: Hardy in zone 4 and above.
FROST TOLERANCE: Takes a low of at least –20°F.
ASPECT: Grows best in full sun but tolerates shade for part of the day.
PLANTING: Plant in late summer or fall, about 4 in deep.
FLOWERING SEASON: Varies with climate. In warm areas it may flower in the winter while in cooler regions it may wait until late spring. They are sweetly fragrant.
CUT FLOWERS: Lovely cut flowers, but like daffodils they should be kept in a vase on their own for a day before adding other blooms.
COLOR RANGE: White, yellow or bicolors.
USES: Jonquils are the popular alternative in areas where daffodils don't flower reliably. They have a number of flowers on each stem and look lovely planted in groups in the garden or in pots. They are very hardy and they will often survive in old, abandoned gardens long after everything else has perished.

MOST JONQUILS look like small daffodils but this variety, "Erlicheer", is a double.

THE KAFFIR LILY is one of the best bulbs for cut flowers.

KAFFIR LILY

Also known as crimson flag

Schizostylis coccinea

ORIGIN: South Africa.
SIZE: When in flower it is about 24 in high.
CLIMATE: Suitable for zone 7 and above, it grows particularly well in the open along the Pacific Coast and in Hawaii. It is often grown under glass in colder zones.
FROST TOLERANCE: Takes a low of 0°F. Provide a thick mulch of organic matter for winter to protect bulbs from frost.
ASPECT: Full sun. Shelter from cold drying winds if necessary. Moisture-retentive soil ensures best results.
PLANTING: Spring. This is also the time to lift and divide congested clumps of lilies.
FLOWERING SEASON: Late summer to early winter.
CUT FLOWERS: Flowers are excellent for cutting—plants are often grown specifically for this purpose.
COLOR RANGE: Crimson-red, or clear pink in the variety "Mrs Hegarty".
USES: Grow in containers under glass for cut flowers or display. Grow in a mixed or herbaceous border.

LILY

Lilium species and cultivars

TAKES PART-SHADE

ORIGIN: Lilies are widely distributed throughout the northern hemisphere.
SIZE: The size varies with species but they are commonly over 3 ft tall.
CLIMATE: They do not often enjoy hot, dry, humid climates. Many species are hardy, being suitable for zone 4, while others need a less severe climate such as zone 6 and above. Check hardiness before you buy.
FROST TOLERANCE: Varies but the hardiest will accept –20°F at least.
ASPECT: Full sun or partial shade. All need shelter from strong wind.
PLANTING: Plant as soon as possible after purchase, in fall, winter or early spring—bulbs must not be allowed to dry out. Mulch after planting.
FLOWERING SEASON: Varies with species and climate between late spring and fall. Many flower from middle to late summer.
CUT FLOWERS: All make good cut flowers if picked when flowers are just open or when all buds are colored. Leave a third of the stem behind.
COLOR RANGE: White and many shades of yellow, pink, red and orange, often spotted or streaked.
USES: Best if planted in groups and they also make excellent potted plants.

THERE ARE lilies suitable for all climates, from harsh to warm.

NOT A TRUE bulb but often classed as one, lily-of-the-valley is grown from pips.

LILY-OF-THE-VALLEY

Convallaria majalis

ORIGIN: Widespread in the northern hemisphere temperate zone.
SIZE: Grows up to 10 in tall.
CLIMATE: An extremely hardy rhizomatous perennial that has become naturalized in eastern North America. Suitable for zone 3 and above.
FROST TOLERANCE: Takes –38°F.
ASPECT: Prefers very bright dappled shade or part-sun in the coolest areas.
PLANTING: Plant in fall 2 in deep and 2–3 in apart, or divide clumps in fall or winter.
FLOWERING SEASON: Early to late spring, later in cooler areas.
CUT FLOWERS: This is one of the most highly prized cut flowers of all with a sweet, pervasive perfume.
COLOR RANGE: Typically white but there is also a pink form. Several varieties have patterned leaves.
USES: This is an ideal groundcover for informal woodland effect under deciduous trees or grow it in pots brought indoors when in bloom.

NERINE

Also known as Guernsey lily

Nerine bowdenii

TAKES PART-SHADE

ORIGIN: South Africa.
SIZE: Flower stems rise 12–18 in tall.
CLIMATE: Suitable for zone 8 and above. Elsewhere grow it in pots under glass. It does not like hot humid regions.
FROST TOLERANCE: It will take a low of at least 10°F, especially if grown against a sunny wall and sheltered from freezing winds.
ASPECT: Prefers full sun or, in hot areas, afternoon shade.
PLANTING: Plant outdoors in early spring. Plant in fall or spring when growing under glass. Make sure the neck of the bulb is just above soil level. Once planted, leave undisturbed for years.
FLOWERING SEASON: Heads of pink blooms appear during fall.
CUT FLOWERS: Good cut flower.
COLOR RANGE: Flowers of *N. bowdenii* are pink. Others bloom in white, pink, red, scarlet or apricot.
USES: Grow them in groups, as part of a mixed flower border or crammed into containers.

NERINES PRODUCE their spidery flowers on long stems before the leaves appear.

ORNAMENTAL ONION

Allium caeruleum

ORIGIN: Siberia, Turkestan.
SIZE: This ornamental onion attains at least 24 in in height when in flower.
CLIMATE: It will thrive in zone 7 and above.
FROST TOLERANCE: It will take a low of 0°F.
ASPECT: Like most of the alliums this species needs to be grown in a position in full sun. A well-drained soil is also recommended.
PLANTING: The bulbs can be planted any time during fall.
FLOWERING SEASON: This plant flowers over quite a long period in early summer.
CUT FLOWERS: The flowers are suitable for cutting and arranging as indoors decoration.
COLOR RANGE: The small star-shaped flowers, which are carried in rounded heads, are bright blue.
USES: Grow this allium in the herbaceous or mixed border. It looks particularly good with ornamental grasses and also makes an attractive companion for bush roses. Try it also in the wild garden.

SOME ONIONS are highly ornamental and this one looks at home in flower borders.

CHEAP TO BUY, easy to grow, ranunculus can be bought in mixed or single colors.

RANUNCULUS

Ranunculus asiaticus

ORIGIN: South-east Europe and south-west Asia.
SIZE: Grows to about 20 in tall.
CLIMATE: Zone 9 and above. Elsewhere grow outdoors between the spring and fall frosts.
FROST TOLERANCE: Accepts 23°F if planted against a sunny wall or with some overhead shelter.
ASPECT: Prefers full sun all day, with shelter from very strong wind.
PLANTING: Where there are light or no frosts, plant in middle to late fall. Where colder, plant in late winter or spring when frosts are almost over.
FLOWERING SEASON: Fall-planted bulbs bloom from late winter; bulbs planted in late winter bloom late spring and early summer.
CUT FLOWERS: Cut flowers early in the day. Change the water often.
COLOR RANGE: The many-petalled flowers come in white, cream, yellow, red and pink.
USES: These bright and colorful spring-flowering bulbs can be massed in mixed colors or blocks of a single color, in gardens or containers.

FAST TO multiply, spring starflower can be left alone for many years.

SPRING STARFLOWER

Ipheion uniflorum

TAKES PART-SHADE

ORIGIN: Uruguay, Argentina.
SIZE: Spring starflower grows about 8 in tall.
CLIMATE: The spring starflower is a reasonably hardy bulb and is suitable for cultivation in zone 6 and above.
FROST TOLERANCE: These bulbs accept a low of between 0°F and –9°F, but where such temperatures are frequent, mulch over bulbs with straw in fall.
ASPECT: The spring starflower requires full sun or partial shade.
PLANTING: Plant in late summer or early fall, on their sides.
FLOWERING SEASON: Any time from midwinter in frost-free areas; spring in cooler places. The display can continue for many weeks.
CUT FLOWERS: Not suitable.
COLOR RANGE: The colors of the flowers range from shades of sky to darker blues and white.
USES: Spring starflower makes an ideal edging but should be planted in large drifts wherever it is grown to produce its best effect. Fast to multiply, the spring starflower can be left alone for many years. It is a charming pot plant, best in wide, shallow dishes.

TULIP

Tulipa species and hybrids

TAKES PART-SHADE

ORIGIN: Central Asia, southern Russia and Anatolia.
SIZE: Reaches heights of 16–28 in.
CLIMATE: Many species and hybrids are very hardy and suit zone 5 and above. Others need a less severe climate, so check hardiness before you buy. A cold winter is necessary and they like a summer baking.
FROST TOLERANCE: Many tulips will accept a low of at least −31°F.
ASPECT: Needs full sun or sun for at least half a day. Always provide some protection from strong winds.
PLANTING: In warmer zones place bulbs in the refrigerator for 6–8 weeks before planting. This is unnecessary in areas with long, cold winters. Plant bulbs in early fall in cold areas, late fall or early winter in warmer areas.
FLOWERING SEASON: Early to late spring, depending on variety.
CUT FLOWERS: Choose blooms that are not fully open and cut early in the morning. Change vase water frequently for longest life.
COLOR RANGE: All colors except green and true blue. Many varieties have stripes or streaks.
USES: Best in mass plantings of one color but can be mixed. Very good container plants.

PLANT TULIPS into soil colder than 52°F or roots will not form. Roots take nine weeks to form at 52°F.

NEAT, DARK GREEN leaves and lovely flowers make zephyr lily an all-year bulb.

ZEPHYR LILY

Also known as storm lily or rain lily

Zephyranthes candida

TAKES PART-SHADE

ORIGIN: South America.
SIZE: Grows about 8 in tall.
CLIMATE: Zone 9 and above. However, the zephyr lily can be hardy just into the north given winter protection. Bulbs of zephy lily can be lifted and stored for the winter in frosty regions.
FROST TOLERANCE: Will take a low of 21°F.
ASPECT: Prefers morning sun or dappled shade all day. Takes full sun in cooler areas.
PLANTING: Plant any time from spring until middle to late summer.
FLOWERING SEASON: Flowers appear from late summer into fall, especially after rain.
CUT FLOWERS: Not suitable.
COLOR RANGE: Flowers are white. Other species have yellow or pink flowers.
USES: Good for planting under trees and shrubs or in pockets of a rockery. It is an excellent path liner and can also be grown in containers.

• CHAPTER TWENTY-ONE •

ROSES

Undeniably the best loved flowers of all, roses are set to become even more popular. Gardeners world-wide are rediscovering the huge range of old-fashioned roses that were once as popular as the big-flowered, hybrid tea rose is today.

In nature, roses are exclusively plants of the northern hemisphere. They are found on all three continents there, but more than three-quarters of the 125 wild species come from China and Central Asia. They are not tropical plants and most are not found in extremely cold climates either. Rather, they are native to temperate areas where winter lows are usually warmer than 40°F and summers warm to hot but not excessively humid.

SOFT AND FRAGRANT, roses are the mainstay of the romantic garden.

SOME ROSES including "Albertine", flower only once, in early summer.

ONCE FLOWERING Rosa glauca *(syn.* R. rubrifolia*) has attractive foliage and hips.*

IDEAL CLIMATES

Today's roses, all bred from wild parents, grow and flower best in cool to mild climates without extremes of cold, excessive heat and humidity. The most popular types, the hybrid teas and floribundas, are grown in America but these and other hybrid groups require winter protection in the colder climates. In the central states the bushes need to be mounded with soil for the winter, from 6–12 in above the stem bases, to prevent the roots and stem bases from being killed by frost. Top the soil mound with a mulch of straw or other bulky organic matter to provide further protection—the further north, the more protection required, especially increasing the depth of insulating organic matter. This protection is given only when growth is stopped in fall by frosts.

Roses grow well in the middle states. However, in some zones the plants may suffer from debilitating humidity-induced diseases such as rose black spot and mildew. Roses are fine in zones with very hot dry summers, provided they are kept well watered. Plants weakened by unsuitable climates will attract pests—so roses grown in the subtropics and tropics will require pesticides that are neither good for you nor the environment.

Very wet summers are not good for roses because the blooms will be ruined by gray-mould disease or botrytis, causing flowers to rot before they fully open. Heavy rain also causes further damage to the flowers.

Seek out varieties that are most resistant to mildew and black spot if you live in a climate that is conducive to these diseases. If summer rain ruins flowers, consider growing the older varieties that flower only in early summer.

ONCE FLOWERING OR REPEAT BLOOMING

Some roses, usually older varieties or species, flower only once in early

DIFFERENT SHAPES FOR DIFFERENT PURPOSES

Patio or groundcover roses
These are small, low-growing roses. They are wider than they are tall, with many twiggy branches arising from a short stem. The patio roses can be less than 12 in tall while the groundcover roses may grow to 3 ft tall but are usually kept lower by pruning.

Upright bush roses
These include the hybrid tea (the most widely grown rose) but also some of the more old-fashioned roses. Growth is upright and the plants are taller than they are wide. They range in height from about 5 ft to perhaps 10 ft. Although the flowers are gorgeous, the plants themselves can look stiff and be quite hard to use in anything but a formal setting.

Rounded shrub roses
Medium to large growers, shrub roses have a rounded, more natural look than bush roses. They are fast growing and can be used at the back of a shrub border, as a screen or as a feature on their own. They are usually densely foliaged to the ground and can make good windbreaks.

Climbing roses
Climbers develop very long canes which grow from the base and need the support of a trellis, structure, strong shrub or tree. They don't twine but climb by means of their backward facing thorns. Climbers vary in size, the biggest being truly huge, so be sure you have space for your choice.

Rambling roses
Ramblers are similar to climbers but are allowed to sprawl. The canes flower at their ends but only once and are removed after bloom. On the whole, ramblers are very large plants and can be extremely charming in bloom.

Suckering roses
Suckering roses spread into dense thickets via underground stems which send up short branches at intervals. These unusual roses make good barrier plantings or groundcover. The natural species, *Rosa gallica*, has this habit.

summer. The show lasts 4–6 weeks and can be truly spectacular. Today's popular hybrid tea roses and many others have a repeat blooming or "remontant" habit: flowers come in flushes throughout summer and fall. Often there is an abundant display in early summer followed by further but less spectacular flushes throughout summer and into fall.

Repeat blooming may seem the better, but don't automatically choose a remontant variety over a once-bloomer. In hot climates, summer flowers are often burned and not very attractive, and in rainy or humid climates they are also destroyed by weather and diseases. A variety that gives a single, spectacular display in early summer will avoid problems caused by unsuitable summer weather, and many of the loveliest roses of all are once blooming.

WHAT ROSES NEED

Full sun

Roses are not shade lovers and must have a position where they receive at least five hours of direct sun every day, more if possible. Where summers are very hot, give them the sun in the morning and early afternoon as late shade helps preserve the flowers.

Air movement

The more humid your climate, the more open, sunny and breezy the site should be. Humidity and a sheltered, still position are an invitation to fungus diseases. Conversely, frequent strong or gusty winds will destroy the flowers and damage the stems and foliage. Neighboring plants will also suffer as the thorny rose branches thrash about. The perfect spot for growing roses is breezy but not constantly windy.

FALL FOR its simple, single flowers, but make sure you have the room before you choose Rosa multiflora *var.* cathayensis. *It needs about 19 ft of lateral space.*

Rich, well-drained soil

Roses do best in very fertile soil that is moisture retentive but never sodden for long periods. They will grow well in both clay-based, fairly heavy loams and lighter, more sandy soils so long as the former drains freely and the latter contains plenty of rotted organic matter. If you have any doubts about the drainage of your soil, don't plant roses there—they will quickly rot in soil that stays wet (see pages 26–7 for details on how to improve soil drainage). Roses have big appetites but you can satisfy them by mulching at least annually with rotted manure and a ration of rose food.

TYPES OF ROSES

Although there are only 125 natural species, over the centuries these have been crossed and re-crossed to create thousands of hybrids and many different classes or types of roses. The most commonly grown roses today belong to the "hybrid tea" class but there are also "floribundas", "grandifloras", "hybrid perpetuals", "noisettes", "polyanthas" and many, many more. Gardeners who just want a few roses don't really have to unravel all that. They just need to know what the rose will grow into.

Many roses, especially the natural species and some of the old-fashioned types, grow very large and have a mounding, spreading or suckering habit not at all like the upright and fairly compact tea roses we are all familiar with. They can make wonderful screens or hedges, big and impressive additions to a border of shrubs or large-scale groundcovers. The climbing forms are often magnificent but they can cover the house if you let them. If you fall in love with a picture of an old-fashioned, heritage or species rose (or any other unfamiliar variety), be sure to find out what it will do before buying it. There's nothing wrong with a big and vigorous plant except when it is grown in a space that is too small for it.

HOW TO PLANT ROSES

Potted roses can be bought and planted year round, but the main rose buying and planting season is late fall, winter and early spring. However, winter planting is not possible in cold zones due to frozen ground. The plants are dormant then and they are sold with their bare roots wrapped rather than in pots of soil. The main disadvantage of buying roses then is that they aren't in flower, and so unless you know what you want, you have to rely on colored labels, which may or may not be an accurate representation of the plant in bloom.

As roses are very long-lived plants and can be big and important features in the garden, it's worth taking the time to do some research. Visit rose gardens and garden centers in spring when the roses are in full bloom. Note the ones you like and do try to see a mature example so that you can get an idea of its ultimate size. You may be able to buy a potted specimen there and then but if you can't, you'll know what to order next winter and meantime you can be improving the soil where you plan to plant the roses.

Potted roses

Potted roses can be planted like any other container-grown plant.

- Dig a hole two or three times wider than the pot but about the same depth. Loosen the soil in the bottom.
- Crumble some of the excavated soil into the hole to form a high mound in the middle.
- Take the rose from its pot, untangle and tease out the roots, place them over the mound and spread them downwards and outwards.
- Refill the hole with the crumbled excavated soil, ensuring that the rose is no deeper in the ground than it was in the pot. Tamp down gently to firm the soil around the roots and water in well. Top up if there is subsidence.

CORRECT SPACING gives roses room to spread and will give fine results in a few years.

- Mulch around the plant with compost or some other rotted organic matter and water again.
- After a few weeks, new growth will begin and you can sprinkle a ration of complete plant food or slow-release fertilizer around the rose.

Bare-rooted roses

In winter, dormant roses are sold with their roots wrapped but with little soil around them. When you get them home, unwrap and soak the roots in a bucket of water while you prepare the planting holes.

- Make the holes wide and about 12 in deep, and make a mound as described above.
- Spread the roots downwards and outwards over the mound and refill the hole with the excavated soil. If any of the roots are damaged or too long, trim them back with very sharp, disinfected pruners—the roots can be shortened to about 8 in without harming the plant.
- Be sure not to bury the rose too deeply as the graft union (the bend or lump on the stem between the roots and branches) must be above soil level when planting is complete.
- Don't add fertilizer at this stage but you can mulch around the plant after you have watered it in. Use well rotted cow or poultry manure, compost, straw or any combination of these materials.
- Water once a week if necessary (feel the soil under the mulch first and if it is moist, don't water).
- When you see new growth, sprinkle a ration of complete plant food, rose food or slow-release fertilizer around the plant and water it in.

If you are not able to plant bare-rooted roses immediately, open the packaging to allow ventilation of the stems and keep the plants cold but not frozen or exposed to frost. Don't allow the roots to dry out but don't sit them in water. Plant them as soon as possible.

IN THE LONG RUN, you'll get better results from your roses if you improve the entire area in which they are to grow rather than the planting holes themselves.

Enriching the planting hole

It is *not* a good idea to enrich the soil in the planting hole with compost or rotted manures. By doing so, you will create a well of fertility, which will encourage the roots to stay within that area and not to spread into the surrounding soil as they must if the rose is to flourish. If your soil is not fertile enough, improve all of it, not just isolated pockets.

If you are planning to plant several roses together, dig over the entire area they will cover, incorporating rotted organic matter and fertilizer as you go. Mulch the area, water well and let it lie for a month or so before you buy and plant the roses. Once planted, the roses will establish quickly, their roots easily able to penetrate the loosened, aerated, moist soil.

ROUTINE CARE OF ROSES

Once established in well-drained, fertile soil, roses are remarkably tough plants. They have a good, deep root system and mature plants will usually cope with dry spells. Of course, all roses do better where soils stay moist but this can be achieved with a deep soaking once a week at most, less during cooler weather or in soils that are deep and fertile.

If you keep the plants mulched with rotted organic matter or straw you will not only conserve soil moisture but also improve its structure and fertility as the mulch is worked into the soil by the worms it encourages. Add more mulch at least annually, usually in winter or spring when the plants are pruned, but you can also mulch in summer.

Each year in spring, when new growth begins, an application of complete plant food, rose food or slow-release fertilizer designed specifically for roses will supply them with all the nutrients they need for the year.

Pests and diseases

Roses have quite a few enemies but, like all plants, if they are growing in conditions that suit them, they will generally remain healthy and vigorous enough to fight off diseases and outgrow pest attacks. If you do not use a lot of toxic sprays and your garden and neighborhood is fairly densely planted, you will find that birds, lizards and predatory insects will clean up many of the pests that attack roses. Others you will be able to see and squash by hand, and there are several non-toxic remedies for specific rose pests. Aphids (greenfly), for example, can be controlled with garlic based sprays, which you can make at home, and treatments containing *Bacillus thuringiensis* kill caterpillars but nothing else. You will find pictures of many common pests and measures to control them in Chapter Eight, beginning on page 43.

As already mentioned, diseases such as black spot and powdery mildew can be made worse by humidity and summer rain. If you live in a humid area then it is important to seek out roses that are resistant to mildew and black spot and replace varieties that are constantly infected. Fungicides are toxic chemicals and a rose that needs frequent spraying forever is not worth having. See Chapter Eight for more information on diseases.

Pruning roses

Roses are really quite easy to prune once you know how and you'll find full details on how to go about this essential task on pages 70–1, in the chapter on pruning.

THE RICHNESS OF ROSES: FLOWERS IN SO MANY COLORS, SO MANY FORMS

Mention roses and most people think of the modern, hybrid tea variety, one of which, "Princess Grace de Monaco", is shown in the photograph at right. Their buds are plump and pointed and open into big, many petalled flowers. Hybrid tea roses are so popular you could be forgiven for thinking that all roses have that sort of bloom, but they don't. Rose breeders have been busy for a long time and there are now centuries worth of shapes, sizes and colors for you to choose from.

THE HYBRID TEA is well known but it isn't the only type of rose.

Many roses have just one row of petals surrounding a central boss of stamens. They are charming in their simplicity and can make a lovely contrast when planted with other, more full-flowered types. Some roses have flowers described as "muddled"—their petals appear to be crammed together in an irregular fashion. In others, the flowers are quartered, the petals being folded together in four distinct sections and these are just some of the rose forms that are available to you.

AT THEIR SIMPLEST, roses have a single row of petals surrounding a boss of stamens. This is "Geranium", a compact selection from a vigorous wild rose.

"ENGLISH" ROSES produced by David Austin are modern versions of old roses. Many, such as "Graham Thomas", have similar, flattish but very full flowers.

THESE BIG FLAT FLOWERS with many crumpled petals were popular last century. This one, released early last century and still sold, is "Charles de Mills".

INSTEAD OF a few big flowers, some roses produce enormous trusses of little flowers. This is "Ballerina", a long-flowering shrub that grows to about 10 ft tall.

"ALBERTINE", first seen in the early 1920s, is a strong climber that produces masses of loose-petaled, ruffled flowers described as muddled or informal.

MORE THAN a single but not quite a double, David Austin's "Shropshire Lass" has cupped flowers with a central ring of smaller, curled petals.

THE FLOWERS of "Snow Carpet" are typical of many miniature roses. They are small, flattish and tightly packed with row upon row of petals.

ROSA RUGOSA *is a wild rose that makes an impressive large-scale hedge or windbreak. It grows to 6 ft tall with a similar spread, and if you have plenty of space it does not need pruning or any special care. Flowers may be rose-pink or white and appear in early summer, followed by attractive hips. It is very spiny and exceedingly hardy (zone 2).*

WAYS TO USE ROSES

Hybrid tea roses—the typical rose—certainly produce some of the world's loveliest flowers, but as garden plants they are not always easy to use. They are stiff, often sparse, upright shrubs that seem most successful when grown rather formally in beds of their own. But a formal rose garden won't suit every landscaping style and that's where the many other types of roses come in.

There are low, spreading types and suckering shrubs that are ideal for groundcovers, miniatures for growing in low borders or in pots and baskets, bushes big and small that you can use in a planting of mixed shrubs or for screening, and wonderful climbers and ramblers that are ideal for covering pergolas or fences.

Roses are truly remarkable plants with a diversity of size and form that is worth getting to know. You'll find there are many varieties for the purpose you have in mind but be sure to know the ultimate size of any rose before buying it. Some can grow quite large.

COMBINATIONS OF *shrubby roses produce wonderful floral effects as the plants grow over and through each other. Here, dark red "Elmshorn", pink "Ballerina" and "Penelope" make a spectacular background and give good shelter for a planting of annual and perennial flowers in front.*

GROUNDCOVER ROSES *are small plants 24–28 in tall but with an ability to spread 3 ft in all directions. Some give one big burst of bloom, others flower almost continuously during the warmer months. They look best when massed over a big area and can easily be kept low by shearing off any upward-growing shoots.*

ONE OF *the best ways to use roses is as a background to other, lower plants: for this climbers and big shrub roses are ideal. Here they give height to the whole planting, shade and shelter the house behind and when the roses are out of bloom their dark green leaves remain a good background to the flowers in front.*

DISPLAY CLIMBING ROSES *to advantage and create an interesting feature by running a free-standing pergola through the garden. Climbing roses can also be grown against walls or fences but will need the support of a strong trellis. Some climbing roses are much more vigorous than others, and so seek one that will suit the space you have available.*

•CHAPTER TWENTY-TWO•

LAWNS

A lawn means different things to different people. It may be the garden's showpiece, a foil for shrubs and flowers, a playground, a picnic spot or just groundcover. Whatever your lawn means to you, however, you will need to spend time maintaining it.

All lawns are a long-term investment in terms of both time and money. Even if you are content to have your lawn grow reasonably well and not be too overrun with weeds, you will need to spend some time on maintenance. To achieve the perfection of a velvety smooth, immaculate lawn you will need to spend a great deal of time on it.

PLANNING A LAWN

Don't rush into establishing your lawn: taking time to plan it carefully will pay off in the long run. Ensure the soil is well prepared and consider the climate, the amount of direct sun the area receives and the primary use the lawn will have. There are grasses that withstand heavy wear and grasses that cope with shade, but none do both, and no turf withstands constant rough wear without looking the worse for it.

Plan your lawn area so that it will be easy to mow and maintain. Avoid sharp corners, wiggly edges and don't

AN IMMACULATE LAWN is a lovely sight to see and wonderful to walk on, too. But it's not an easy look to achieve and you may be better off with more shrubs and trees.

WIGGLY EDGES look too busy and distracting and make mowing hard, too.

have lots of small garden beds—they not only make mowing hard but spoil the effect of a sweeping lawn.

Concrete mower strips make edging easier but shouldn't be put in until after turf has been established. If they are installed before the turf and the soil subsides even slightly, they will be more of a hindrance than a help.

Choosing your grass

Lawn grasses fall into two main categories: warm season grasses and cool season grasses. The warm season grasses are perennial, running grasses best suited to frost-free areas. Many lose color in winter but they do not die off unless winters are severe (in which case they are inappropriate). Cool season grasses are mostly tufty and tussock forming, although a few run. They grow well in cool climates and during the cooler months in a warm climate but are very difficult to maintain during hot, humid summers when they are prone to attack by fungal diseases.

Preparing the soil

Friable, sandy loam is the best soil on which to establish turf. Soil needs to be loose and workable to a depth of 6–10 in. The incorporation of large quantities of organic matter into the soil well ahead of turf laying or sowing will improve aeration and drainage and in sandy soils will aid moisture retention.

If you have a clay subsoil you may need to bring in soil and cover the area to be turfed to a depth of at least 4 in. Try to get a guarantee from the soil supplier that the soil is weed-free and check that the soil is not full of silty clay that will set like cement after watering. Added soil must be well mixed with the existing soil so that water, air and roots can penetrate easily. Heavy clay soils are best treated with an application of gypsum at a rate of about 11 oz per square yard, or if the soil is known to be very acid, garden or agricultural lime can be applied at a rate of 4 oz per square yard. Clay soils should never be cultivated when they are very wet or very dry—they need to be just moist.

Removing weeds

The area to be turfed should be free of stones, roots and any other debris. Be sure to remove all weeds, paying particular attention to those with bulbs such as oxalis, onion weed and nut grass, as they are very hard to control once grass is established.

REMOVE WEEDS before you lay grass and you'll have few weeds in future.

Adding fertilizer

The surface should be raked level and be fine and crumbly. Apply a "new-lawn" fertilizer or blood and bone to the area according to label directions and lightly rake or water it in. Water the area lightly for a few days before sowing the seed or laying turf so as to firm the soil and provide a moist layer on which grass can establish.

Drainage

Check the drainage of the area where the lawn is to go. Dig a hole, fill it with water and see how long it takes for the water to drain away. If water remains in the hole for more than twenty-four hours, you will have to consider laying subsoil drains (see page 27) or creating a slight slope on the area. A slope of 1 in 70 will prevent the formation of wet spots.

ESTABLISHING A LAWN

Lawns can be established by laying turf, which gives an instant lawn, or sowing seed. The latter option is much less expensive but you will need to keep the sown area free of any traffic for several weeks.

Laying turf

Turf grass is living grass that is available in machine-cut rolls. It has been severed from most of its root system so it needs to be laid as soon as possible after cutting. Try to ensure that the turf is delivered only when you are ready to lay it. If there is any delay in laying, keep the rolls in a shaded place and keep them damp (covering them with wet hessian helps). To lay the rolls, place them on the prepared ground with their edges pushed firmly together. If the ground slopes, lay the rolls across the slope, not down it, to avoid erosion.

It is a good idea to roll the newly laid turf to ensure good contact with the soil. Thoroughly water the turf and keep it moist for the first ten to fourteen days. This may mean watering more than once a day in hot or windy weather. After this cut back watering to every second day. In three weeks the grass should be established and watering can be reduced to a heavy soaking once a week. Mow lightly after about three weeks.

Sowing seed

For even coverage, mix the seed with some dry sand or dry sawdust. Divide the area to be sown into sections, and divide the seed into the same number of lots so that sowing can be fairly uniform. After sowing, lightly rake the seed into the surface soil and water gently, being careful not to allow pools to form that may wash the seed into patches. You may need to water several times a day if the

LAYING TURF

USE A PLANK to press turves down.

LAY THE TURVES as if they were bricks.

FIRST SOW east-west, then north-south, then west-east and then south-north.

weather is windy or hot. The surface must be kept just moist at all times after seeding or results will be poor.

Germination time varies with grass types and may be anywhere from five days to three weeks. Warm season grasses are usually sown in spring or early fall. Cool season grasses may be sown in mid-spring or late summer. Don't mow until the grass has reached 1$^1/_2$–2 in high.

GENERAL MAINTENANCE

Mowing

As a general rule all lawns should be high cut rather than shaved. A handy hint is never to remove more than one-third of the leaf blade at any one cutting. If grass has been allowed to grow very long it is better to reduce the height gradually rather than to cut it low with one mowing and risk scorching what is left. As winter approaches, raise the mower height to help maintain the grass through the colder months. Grass growing under trees should be cut very high, to 3–4 in, if it is not to die out.

Topdressing

Topdressing has no intrinsic benefits for the lawn and is only necessary to fill in hollows and to maintain levels. It is best done in spring or early fall.

TOPDRESSING TO FILL HOLLOWS

If there is a large hollow, apply only $^1/_4$–$^1/_2$ in of topdressing at a time and wait until the grass grows through it before applying more. Washed river sand or good quality sandy loam is best for topdressing.

Fertilizing

The average home lawn is probably fertilized only once or twice a year, in spring as new growth starts and again in late summer or early fall. However, very high quality lawns are fertilized every four to six weeks during the growing season.

Use a complete lawn food, pulverized poultry manure or blood and bone. Don't use sulfate of ammonia as it makes the soil acid and kills earthworms.

Watering

It is better to water heavily and less often. Heavy, infrequent watering encourages deep rooting of grasses that are better able to withstand drought. Grass watered heavily every week or ten days is much stronger and healthier than if given a daily sprinkle.

Sparse lawns

Lawns can become thin and sparse for a number of reasons:

- The grass has been mown too low. Constant low mowing weakens lawns severely. Warm season grasses such as couch should be mown at 1–1$^1/_2$ in, while buffalo and kikuyu grasses should not be cut at less than 1$^1/_2$ in.

Cool season grasses are generally cut at 1 1/2–2 in, except the bent grasses which can be cut much lower.

- The wrong grass has been chosen for the site or conditions have changed. You may have started off with an open, sunny lawn, but with tree growth it has become shady. Areas under trees are also dry and there is great root competition. Soil dryness and root competition may also lead to poor water penetration. Use a commercial wetting agent on this area to ensure deep moisture penetration. If that doesn't work, put down another kind of grass in the problem area or grow groundcovers instead.
- The area has been subjected to heavy wear so that the soil has become compacted. To remedy this see "Aeration" below.
- The lawn has been killed with kindness. Lawns are sometimes made sparse by over-enthusiastic watering. A well-established home lawn should not need watering more often than once a week if it is done deeply. In very hot, windy weather it may be necessary to water twice.
- Grass growth may also become poor and thin if soils become too acid. This is most often caused by regular use of sulfate of ammonia and some other high nitrogen fertilizers. Switch to organic fertilizers and give the lawn a dressing of lime or dolomite during the winter.

Aeration

In compacted or poorly aerated soils root growth, and therefore grass growth, will be poor. To improve conditions, you need to get air and water into the soil. This may be done by using a coring machine, but only if you have sandy soils. In clay, it is better to use a garden fork pushed into the ground and worked back and forth in rows about 4 in apart. Then apply sand mixed with lime or dolomite and brush it into the holes. The lime, used at the rate of about 4 oz per square yard, helps to open the clay and thus improve aeration. Clay soils are best worked when they are just slightly damp. If the soil is too wet you will create more problems and if it is too dry it will be too hard to work.

AERATING THE LAWN

Thatch

Thatch is a mat or layer of old runners that builds up under the top of the turf. It makes the lawn spongy and can inhibit the penetration of water, air and fertilizer, but it can be ignored unless you are after the perfect lawn. Buffalo, kikuyu, Queensland blue couch and bent grass are especially prone to thatching. Some may need to be dethatched each year with a scarifier or vertical mower. After dethatching, rake off the excess grass, then water and fertilize the lawn.

Buffalo lawn cannot be dethatched or scalped to get rid of the thatch—you will probably kill it. To get rid of the sponginess, sweep or hose topdressing mixed with poultry manure, or blood and bone and hydrated or slaked lime into the thatched areas of the lawn.

WHAT CAN GO WRONG?

Weeds

Most serious weed problems result from low mowing or occur in grass that has never established well because of shade or a poor choice of grass type. Remove individual weeds by hand. For heavy weed infestation, selective herbicides can be used, but before you buy one read the label to check it is suitable for your grass and weeds.

Pests

■ GRASS-EATING CATERPILLARS. Various kinds of caterpillars and grubs may feed on the leaves and defoliate or partially defoliate the lawn. In late summer and fall they appear, feeding mostly at night and hiding during the day. Control by spraying with a proprietary caterpillar killer or lawn grub killer.

■ CURL GRUBS. These fat, creamy white grubs are most destructive during summer and fall. Lawns growing under stress and lawns that are mown too often and too severely are most affected. Spray the lawn with a lawn grub killer as directed on the pack.

■ EARTHWORMS. Earthworms do a great job aerating the soil, leaving little mounds on the surface. They are harmless, beneficial creatures but if you are a perfectionist and want to eradicate them, fertilize the area with sulfate of ammonia.

■ ANTS. Ants make nests in dry areas. If the lawn is badly disrupted by ant nests, treat it with a commercial wetting agent, followed by a deep watering. Ants are not a threat to turf, just their nests.

Diseases

■ FUNGAL LEAF SPOTS. These mostly occur in warm, humid summers. Whole areas of turf may appear yellowish, but close examination of the leaf blades shows brownish or reddish spots. Spray with a lawn fungicide and don't water for forty-eight hours after.

■ DOLLAR SPOT. This problem can occur in spring or in fall when there is a combination of warm temperatures and high humidity. Individual spots are small, round and well defined, turning brown and then yellowing. A fine cobweb can be seen on the spots early in the morning. Control by spraying with a suitable lawn fungicide.

■ KIKUYU YELLOWS. This is a problem restricted to kikuyu that can eventually kill large areas of grass. It usually occurs in periods of rainy, abnormally warm, humid weather in spring and summer. Runners are yellow with brown flecking and the infection can usually be traced back to one stand of turf. Affected plants are easily removed from the soil. There is no real cure for the problem and the best advice is to use a herbicide to kill off the affected grass and then to replant or resow the area.

Other problems

There are many other problems of lawn grasses. If you are an average gardener you may never have any of them if you have a reasonably well-drained site, if the grass suits the aspect and the climate and if you don't cut the grass too low.

■ *Some warm season grasses*

BERMUDA GRASS

Also known as couch or scutch grass
Cynodon dactylon
HERBACEOUS

APPEAL: Especially in the USA, Bermuda grass is possibly the most widely grown lawn grass. It is a soft, comfortable grass to sit or lie on. There are many hybrids and natural selections available, and the varieties differ in growth habit and leaf type. None tolerates shade.
CLIMATE: It is adapted to both coastal and semi-arid conditions but becomes dormant in cold, frosty winters. It is an important lawn grass in the southern states, zones 7 through to 10. Browning off in winter doesn't harm the grass, it soon recovers when the warmer weather returns.
WEAR: Bermuda grass is a hard-wearing, tough grass.
MOWING: Mow to no less than 1/2 in high. An even higher cut improves its drought tolerance.
PROBLEMS: This grass can develop thatch, a spongy layer of old runners beneath the surface. It is highly invasive of garden beds but can be kept out with an effective mower strip placed around the lawn.

THE FINE LEAVES of Bermuda grass will produce a smooth, high quality lawn.

IMPROVED QUALITY BERMUDA GRASS VARIETIES

These improved quality Bermuda grass varieties will give an excellent looking lawn.

■ ***"Greenlees Park".*** A high density grass suitable for home gardens and general landscape use, it is also used on bowling greens and cricket grounds. It has natural low, flat growth, wears well and requires little maintenance. It quickly browns off where winters are cool but soon recovers its dark green color when the weather warms up in spring.

■ ***"Wintergreen".*** This variety is a light to medium green, fine-leaf grass with good winter color if it is fertilized well during summer and fall. It has high wear tolerance. Its growth is very dense and it is a low maintenance turf. It is used on high wear areas such as tennis courts and football fields as well as in home gardens.

■ ***"Windsor Green".*** This is a superior selection of Bermuda grass. It has fine, bright green leaves, is very dense, hard wearing and grows more slowly than other couches, thus requiring less mowing. Winter color is good if it is well fertilized. It is used on sports fields as well as in home gardens and parks.

■ ***"Santa Ana".*** A Californian hybrid that has been widely used in the past for sports fields and home gardens, this is a good choice for very warm areas but loses its color rapidly at the first sign of frost or even temperatures under 45°F.

BUFFALO GRASS makes a hard-wearing lawn ideal for families with young children.

BUFFALO GRASS

Also known as St Augustine grass

Stenotaphrum secundatum

APPEAL: Known in the USA as St Augustine grass, this grass should not be confused with what Americans know as buffalo grass (*Buchloe* species). *Stenotaphrum secundatum* was named buffalo grass after the ship *Buffalo*, which carried it to Australia last century. Originally from the West Indies, it is a perennial, running grass that makes a good, dense lawn, not prone to weed invasion if always cut high. A selected variety, "soft" buffalo, is now available.

CLIMATE: It has become naturalized in southern California to Florida and Texas, and in tropical America. Best suited to warm (frost-free) and warm humid areas such as zones 9 and 10 and above. It is grown as a lawn grass along the southern coast and also throughout California. In warm climates it will accept quite a lot of shade but not full shade for all or even most of the day.

WEAR: Tolerates average domestic wear and recovers quickly if rested.

MOWING: Buffalo must never be shaved closely. Cut it to a height of 1½–2½ in.

PROBLEMS: Can become spongy and may need topdressing if a perfect lawn is required. Standard buffalo is scratchy and can cause itching and irritation but the new strain of soft buffalo does away with this problem.

GREENKEEPER'S TIP

If you already have a buffalo lawn and want to establish it elsewhere, it is a simple matter to do so. In spring, remove some runners with a few roots attached and plant them in prepared soil in the new site. The runners soon start to spread—the more you plant, the quicker you'll have a new lawn.

DURBAN GRASS

Dactyloctenium australe

APPEAL: Durban grass is the most shade tolerant of all the warm season grasses but it grows well in sun too. It is dark green and rather coarse but makes an excellent lawn in some problem areas. It spreads quickly in spring and that is the best time to get it established. Though tolerant of shade, it is not for full, deep shade.
CLIMATE: It originates from South Africa and needs a warm, frost-free climate. In the USA, zones 9 and 10 and above are best.
WEAR: Durban grass will quickly have a track worn through it if used as a path but will stand up to normal home garden use.
MOWING: Durban grass must never be cut lower than 2 in and should be higher if it is in very shaded areas. Mowing should, however, be quite regular as the lawn looks untidy if it is allowed to grow long.
PROBLEMS: No particular pest or disease problems are known for this grass. Problems usually arise with Durban grass only when it has been cut too low or if its need for regular water is neglected.

THICK AND LUSH, Durban grass can look weedy if not kept mown.

WITH ITS very vigorous runners, kikuyu becomes a rich, thick lawn quickly.

KIKUYU

Pennisetum clandestinum

APPEAL: Kikuyu is a very soft, broad-leaf grass originally from East Africa. It is a very pleasant grass to sit on. While it is very vigorous and needs frequent mowing in warm weather, it can make a good lawn, especially on large areas. It can be highly invasive of surrounding garden beds if there is not an effective barrier.
CLIMATE: Grows best in warm, humid districts, including the tropics. It is widely used in several countries, including Australia and South Africa, as lawn grass. It is not too well known in the USA but could be used in zone 10 and above.
WEAR: Kikuyu has reasonable wear tolerance. When worn by heavy traffic, it recovers quickly once rested.
MOWING: The minimum cutting height is $1^1/2$ in and it can be cut even higher. You will, however, have to cut it often.
PROBLEMS: It is generally free of problems if well maintained. There is, however, a fatal disease known as "kikuyu yellows" which is described on page 273. There is no cure other than to replace the grass.

QUEENSLAND BLUE COUCH makes a soft, luxurious looking lawn that is popular for its attractive blue-green color.

QUEENSLAND BLUE COUCH

Digitaria didactyla

APPEAL: This grass, which originates in East Africa and Madagascar, is known simply as blue couch in the USA. It can make a very dense, soft lawn if well maintained and it is used on golf courses and bowling greens in some areas. It can invade garden beds if it is not cut regularly.
CLIMATE: Needs a warm, frost-free climate—zone 10 and above. It is used in Florida for golf courses and for fine lawns.
WEAR: It is a reasonably hard-wearing grass if subjected to normal domestic use.
MOWING: Needs regular mowing to maintain density but it should never be cut less than 3/4 in high.
PROBLEMS: No particular pest or disease problems are known. This grass is, however, very sensitive to herbicides and so it is important to keep the sward dense to avoid weed invasion. When weeds do appear, they are best removed by hand.

■ *Some cool season grasses*

BENT GRASS

Agrostis tenuis, A. palustris

APPEAL: Browntop bent (*A. tenuis*) and creeping bent (*A. palustris*) make very fine lawns but they are high maintenance grasses. Browntop bent is better for home lawns than creeping bent, which needs lots of water and fertilizer. Both are used on bowling and golf greens.
CLIMATE: These grasses grow best in cool, wet climates. Browntop bent has very poor tolerance of heat, while creeping bent is more tolerant but requires copious watering to maintain its quality. The bent grasses are suitable for the north, through to zone 8.
WEAR: Bents do not withstand heavy wear well. Creeping bent recovers faster after wear.
MOWING: Bent can tolerate close mowing down to about 1/2 in in very high maintenance turf but home lawns will be better if cut about 3/4 in high.
PROBLEMS: Bent is prone to fungal disease if grown in warm, humid areas. Thatch can be a problem.

BENT GRASS lawns look luxurious but are best left to the enthusiasts.

THE BEAUTY of chewings fescue is its long, lush leaves. Never scalp it.

CHEWINGS FESCUE

Festuca rubra var. *commutata*

APPEAL: This is a fine, dark green, tufted grass that forms a dense lawn. It is often used in mixes with Kentucky blue grass to make a very good quality lawn blend. It can also be mixed with bent grass. Chewings fescue can be grown under trees as long as it is cut high. It is a good all-purpose lawn.
CLIMATE: A very hardy grass for the north through to zone 8. It prefers cool wet climates.
WEAR: Chewings fescue has a moderate wear tolerance only. In high traffic areas, such as paths, it quickly looks rather threadbare.
MOWING: This grass is one that is best cut high, to no less than 1 1/2 in, with 2 in preferred.
PROBLEMS: Thatch tends to build up in very acid soils. Apply lime to the lawn area, 4 oz per square yard if the soil is known to be very acid. This grass is likely to suffer from fungal disease if grown in warm, humid districts.

KENTUCKY BLUE GRASS

Poa pratensis

APPEAL: Kentucky blue grass is a creeping grass, which is unusual among cool season grasses. It grows well year round, and when used alone or in combination with other grasses it makes a very pleasant lawn. It is widely used in parks and sports fields because of its good recovery rate and fine, luxurious appearance.
CLIMATE: This is a very widely grown lawn grass in the USA, being highly suitable for the humid northern regions through to zone 8. It grows best in cool, humid climates and also does well in areas where winters are very cold but summers are dry. It dislikes warm, humid climates, especially those with summer rain.
WEAR: It has medium wear tolerance and recovers well after wear.
MOWING: The minimum height should be 1 in but 2 in is better for the grass.
PROBLEMS: No particular pest or disease problems unless it is grown in an unsuitably humid climate where fungal disease could cause trouble.

WHEN WELL GROWN, few lawns look better than one of Kentucky blue grass.

IF YOU LIKE the look of longer lawns, the soft rye grasses are a good choice.

RYE GRASS

Lolium multiflorum, L. perenne

APPEAL: Annual (*L. multiflorum*) and perennial (*L. perenne*) rye grasses are often included in seed mixtures that give quick cover. Ryes, which are tufted grasses, are usually not suitable for lawns where a "bowling green" finish is required as they do not mow very evenly. They are, however, soft to sit on and good for children's play.
CLIMATE: Grows best in cool areas. Suitable for the north through to zone 8. This grass has poor tolerance of high temperatures.
WEAR: It has fairly good wear tolerance. Of the cool season grasses only some of the fescues have better wear tolerance.
MOWING: Rye grass is not tolerant of close mowing. The minimum height of the cut should be around 1 1/2 in or patchiness will develop.
PROBLEMS: No particular pest or disease problems affect these grasses if they are grown in a suitable climate.

TALL FESCUE

Festuca elatior, syn F. arundinacea

APPEAL: Tall fescue is a tufted grass that tolerates a wide range of conditions. It is probably the most drought and wear resistant cool season grass and is often combined with other grasses for a higher quality lawn. Its rapid establishment and deep roots make it ideal for stabilizing slopes or banks. It grows best on well-prepared soil that is not shallow.
CLIMATE: Tall fescue is best in cool areas, either humid or arid. It is more heat tolerant than most other cool season grasses. Suitable for the north through to zone 8 or 9.
WEAR: It has good wear tolerance and an ability to recover quickly from wear damage.
MOWING: It should not be mown less than 1 1/2 in high.
PROBLEMS: Tall fescue is not susceptible to many problems unless it is grown in warm areas with wet or very humid summers (such as zones 1 and 2). In these climates it is likely to be attacked by various fungal diseases.

TALL FESCUE will withstand heat and dryness without frequent watering.

•CHAPTER TWENTY-THREE•

GROUNDCOVERS

Groundcovers are living carpets. They create a soft, natural look, suppress weeds and help maintain an even temperature and moisture level in the soil. Groundcovers are often easy-care plants and can be good substitutes for grass.

In nature there is always something growing on the ground under trees and shrubs except where there is very deep leaf litter or the light levels are very low (as on the floors of rainforests, which are clear of growth). In the garden, groundcovers can perform this function too as there are many that will tolerate bright shade, while even in sun groundcovers can be much more attractive than grass. They're especially useful on sloping ground where mowing would be difficult or dangerous, or where erosion is likely.

As with any other type of plant, it is important to choose the right groundcover for the aspect, climate, soil and space available. Some groundcovers, such as the dead nettle (*Lamium galeobdolon*), can be very vigorous, even invasive, especially in moist, shady spots, while other mat-forming plants, such as thrift (*Armeria maritima*), are more sedate and easy to confine.

Groundcovers come in a number of different forms, including running, trailing or mat-forming plants, or those with simple horizontal growth. Some climbing plants, such as ivy, are used as groundcovers and, in fact, any low plant can serve this purpose.

CLEAR WEEDS FIRST

Most groundcovers are long-term plantings and so it is worth putting some effort into good soil preparation and weeding. As there may be root competition for the new plantings it is a good idea to dig in some well-decayed manure or compost a few weeks before planting, but be careful not to build up the soil level under the canopies of existing trees more than an inch and don't pile soil or mulch up around their trunks. Raising the soil level under trees can suffocate the surface roots and lead to the eventual death of the tree.

Weed eradication is most important as it is very frustrating to find weeds coming up through the groundcover. Most weeds will not be entirely eliminated in one go. Dig out or spot spray with glyphosate the weeds you can see. Once they are dead, fork over the soil again, water it and wait for the next crop of weeds to emerge. If you do this two or three times before you plant the groundcover you have a good chance of reducing the bank of weed seeds lying dormant in the ground. Perennial weeds, such as onion weed and oxalis, which arise from bulbs, will need a determined effort to eradicate them.

GROUNDCOVERS ARE especially useful under trees and bishop's hat, or epimedium, is a good choice beneath deciduous trees. Do remember that the deeper the shade, the harder it will be for anything to grow, but plants with dark green leaves will be most successful.

EARLY CARE

The ultimate spread of a groundcover will depend on the type of plant, soil conditions and the degree of care received. The spacing of individual plants at planting time will depend on how fast you need the cover and how large you expect each plant to grow. Most spreading groundcovers grow quite quickly and it is not a good idea to overplant an area simply to get an instant effect—the plants will have nowhere to grow.

It is important to mulch areas of bare soil between plants while they are growing as this helps prevent further weed growth and also helps feed the plants and condition the soil. Most groundcovering plants will need regular feeding during the growing season because of the intense root competition that exists if they are planted under mature trees and shrubs. Regular, deep watering is needed too, especially in the early stages when the roots will be concentated at the surface and likely to dry out.

LATER MAINTENANCE

Once established, most groundcovers need little maintenance beyond shearing off spent flower stems or trimming to confine them to a specific area. If they grow too tall, shear them at the start of the growing season or after bloom to reduce their height. When weeds appear through the groundcover, pull them out promptly or paint them with herbicide, being careful not to get any of the chemical on the groundcover. Don't let weeds flower and set seeds.

ALPINE PHLOX

Also known as moss phlox or mountain phlox

Phlox subulata

ORIGIN: North-eastern areas of Canada and the United States.
APPEAL: Alpine phlox grows about 6 in high and spreads into a mat about 20 in across. In bloom it is a mass of small, flattish flowers. It grows well in rockeries, trailing over walls or on slightly sloping ground where excellent drainage is assured.
CLIMATE: Grows best in cool or cold climates. It is well suited to zone 3 and above, but is not recommended for warm coastal areas or the subtropics or tropics.
FROST TOLERANCE: Accepts lows of –39°F.
GROWING CONDITIONS: Must be grown in full sun. Likes gritty, well-drained soil.
FLOWERING SEASON: Masses of small, starry flowers are produced from mid-spring to early summer. The abundant flowers completely cover the plant.
COLOR RANGE: Usually pink but also white and many shades of lilac, blue and red.

OVER TIME alpine phlox loses vigor. Take cuttings to start new plants.

BABY'S TEARS makes a cool, soft, lush-looking groundcover in bright shade.

BABY'S TEARS

Also known as cuddle bug

Soleirolia soleirolii

NEEDS SHADE

ORIGIN: Western Mediterranean, naturalized in western Europe.
APPEAL: This is a flat, mat-forming, creeping groundcover with tiny leaves. It flourishes in shady, damp conditions and is often used around the base of potted plants or under shrubs in shady, moist areas.
CLIMATE: Suitable for zone 9 and above but in hot, dry areas it must be kept moist and sheltered from drying winds. Plants may die back if winters are frosty but usually return in spring.
FROST TOLERANCE: This plant can be damaged or killed by frost settling directly on it but it is able to withstand 21°F if planted at the base of a wall, in the cracks of a wall or if sheltered by foliage overhead.
GROWING CONDITIONS: Needs bright full shade or dappled shade in warm areas. Where summers are mild, it will tolerate a little morning sun.
FLOWERING SEASON: Flowers are insignificant. The plant is grown for its lush, little leaves.
COLOR RANGE: Leaves are a bright mid-green.

GROW BELLFLOWERS in fertile, well-drained soil that may be slightly alkaline.

BELLFLOWER

Campanula portenschlagiana, C. poscharskyana

TAKES PART-SHADE

ORIGIN: Southern Europe, Balkans.
APPEAL: Evergreen and easy to grow, they are vigorous without being troublesome, good weed suppressors and delightful in flower. They are about 6 in high but can spread a good distance. Can be grown as a groundcover, in walls, pots and troughs. They sometimes self-seed.
CLIMATE: Prefers cool and Mediterranean climates and is not suitable for the subtropics or tropics. *C. poscharskyana* is the hardier of the two and is suitable for zone 3 and above. *C. portenschlagiana* can be grown in zone 4 and above. Shelter them from hot winds.
FROST TOLERANCE: *C. poscharskyana* will take a low of –38°F and the other will accept –31°F.
GROWING CONDITIONS: Best in semi-shade but in zone 6 plants will take more sun.
FLOWERING SEASON: Mid-spring to early summer.
COLOR RANGE: Flowers are mauve-blue or white.

BLUE BUGLE FLOWER

Ajuga reptans

NEEDS SHADE

ORIGIN: Europe, Anatolia.
APPEAL: A lovely groundcover, blue bugle grows as a neat rosette of leaves but spreads by running stems. It rarely grows more than 6 in high although the flower spikes may be taller. It is an ideal groundcover under trees and is a good soil binder. It is also used as a border plant and can be grown in troughs or pots.
CLIMATE: This perennial is suitable for zone 6 and above. In warm regions shelter from hot dry winds and ensure the soil remains moist.
FROST TOLERANCE: Takes –9°F.
GROWING CONDITIONS: Best in shade or dappled sunlight. In cool climates it will tolerate a few hours morning sun. It likes rich, moisture-retentive soil.
FLOWERING SEASON: Small, tubular flowers on a spike appear in spring, or early summer in cool areas.
COLOR RANGE: Flowers are bright blue. Leaves are dark green, bronzed green or mottled cream, pink or burgundy as in the cultivars "Burgundy Glow" and "Multicolor".

A DENSE, weed-suppressing groundcover, blue bugle is ideal beneath trees or shrubs.

CATMINT HAS aromatic leaves and small but pleasant blue flowers.

CATMINT

Nepeta x faassenii

HERBACEOUS; TAKES PART-SHADE

ORIGIN: Catmint is of garden origin.
APPEAL: The gray-green leaves are a lovely foil for brighter blooms and its small flowers are produced over a long period, too. It is quick to establish and rarely grows taller than 8 in, with a spread of about 20 in. Grow in a hanging basket or container or use as an edging plant in the garden. There is a cultivar known as "Six Hills Giant" which is taller, with bigger flowers.
CLIMATE: A very hardy perennial, suitable for zone 3 and above. Suitable also for regions with a Mediterranean climate. It likes a cool, rainy winter and hot, dry summer.
FROST TOLERANCE: Accepts a low of –38°F.
GROWING CONDITIONS: Full sun but will tolerate shade for a few hours daily. Needs good drainage. Takes coastal exposure.
FLOWERING SEASON: From late spring throughout summer, sometimes into early fall.
COLOR RANGE: Flowers are light mauve-blue.

CRANESBILL

Geranium macrorrhizum

NEEDS SHADE

ORIGIN: Southern Europe.
APPEAL: This semi-evergreen perennial has very aromatic foliage which takes on attractive red tints in the fall, and it flowers freely early on in the summer. When in flower it is about 20 in high. Of very easy culture, this geranium is recommended for groundcover in the wild or woodland garden or in the shrub border.
CLIMATE: A very hardy plant, despite its origins, being suitable for the north in zone 5 and above. It will also be happy growing in a Mediterranean climate.
FROST TOLERANCE: It will take a low of –20°F.
GROWING CONDITIONS: Good in the dappled shade of woodland, it will also take sun for part of the day, especially if the soil is moist.
FLOWERING SEASON: Flowers are produced in early summer.
COLOR RANGE: The flowers may be pink, purple-pink or white. There are several varieties available in different colors.

THIS CRANESBILL has very aromatic foliage which takes on red tints in the fall.

CREEPING JENNY

Lysimachia nummularia

TAKES PART-SHADE

ORIGIN: Europe.
APPEAL: This groundcover has small, rounded leaves on stems that root as they grow. The bright lime-green leaves seem to light up an area and it is lovely in hanging baskets. Growth is flat, rarely more than 1 1/2 in above the ground, but it spreads rapidly.
CLIMATE: Prefers a cool, moist climate and is suitable for zone 4 and above. Where summers are hot and dry, keep the soil steadily moist and ensure shelter from hot drying winds.. It is not drought tolerant at all.
FROST TOLERANCE: Takes –31°F if sheltered from freezing winds.
GROWING CONDITIONS: Grow it in dappled or semi-shade. The golden form will lose its bright color unless it gets enough sun or bright light. In cooler climates it will take shade or sun.
FLOWERING SEASON: Small flowers are produced in late spring and early summer but it is the lush foliage that is the main attraction.
COLOR RANGE: Flowers are yellow and there is a golden-leaved form called "Aurea".

CREEPING JENNY likes moisture and can even be grown in boggy ground.

YELLOW ARCHANGEL is one type of dead nettle. Others have mauve or white blooms.

DEAD NETTLE

Also known as yellow archangel

Lamium galeobdolon*, syn. *Lamiastrum galeobdolon

NEEDS PART-SHADE

ORIGIN: Europe and Anatolia.
APPEAL: A pretty, soft-leaved groundcover that spreads by running stems. It is very vigorous and can be invasive, and although individual plants are generally only 8–10 in high they can spread to cover 6 ft in one season. A variegated form with silver splashes on the leaves is usually grown. A good basket plant.
CLIMATE: Zone 6 and above is the most suitable.
FROST TOLERANCE: Takes –9°F.
GROWING CONDITIONS: Best in shade or semi-shade when sheltered from strong wind. Likes rich, well-drained soil.
FLOWERING SEASON: Flowers appear in spring and early summer but plants are grown for their foliage.
COLOR RANGE: The flowers are yellow; the leaves are variously marked with silver.

ENGLISH IVY

Hedera helix

TAKES SHADE

ORIGIN: Europe.
APPEAL: A climber that also makes a dense, low-maintenance groundcover. It is especially good in shady areas under trees but don't allow it to climb up into the trees or it may strangle and kill them. Ivy may also be used in place of a lawn in formal areas where it is kept well clipped. It is most suitable, too, for planting where it can spill over a wall or bank.
CLIMATE: A very hardy plant that is suitable for zone 5 and above. Not for the tropics or subtropics.
FROST TOLERANCE: This ivy accepts –20°F.
GROWING CONDITIONS: Full sun or part, dappled or full shade. In hot areas, shade is advisable.
FLOWERING SEASON: Flowers are tiny and inconspicuous and are followed by blue-black berries. They are only produced on very mature, adult foliage and so are not often seen on plants that are kept clipped.
COLOR RANGE: Leaves may be plain dark green or any of dozens of other colors and patterns. Dark-leaved forms are best for shade.

IVY MAKES a dense groundcover either in sun or full shade. It is drought resistant.

WHEN MASS planted the Japanese spurge creates a wonderfully textured effect.

JAPANESE SPURGE

Pachysandra terminalis

NEEDS SHADE

ORIGIN: Northern China and Japan.
APPEAL: This widely grown spreading evergreen groundcover perennial is of easy culture and produces an 8 in high carpet of dark green foliage. When mass planted, as for groundcover, it creates a wonderfully textured effect. Use it for groundcover in the shrub border, woodland garden or wild garden.
CLIMATE: It is a very hardy plant, suitable for zone 5 and above.
FROST TOLERANCE: It will take a low of –20°F.
GROWING CONDITIONS: This is very much a plant for shade. It is suitable for full or partial shade and gives best results in steadily moist soil.
FLOWERING SEASON: The flowers are produced in spring or early summer.
COLOR RANGE: The whitish flowers are not particularly showy and the plant is grown more for its foliage. There is a variety with white and green variegated foliage.

KUMA BAMBOO GRASS provides an unusual groundcover with winter interest.

KUMA BAMBOO GRASS

Sasa veitchii

TAKES SHADE

ORIGIN: A true bamboo that is found growing wild in Japan.
APPEAL: This dwarf bamboo spreads moderately vigorously and has shiny deep green lance-shaped leaves. The edges of these die back and turn straw-colored in fall, which is a striking feature throughout fall and winter. The slender canes are gray-green or purple. It makes excellent groundcover in the woodland garden, wild garden or shrub border. Height is variable but usually in the region of 24–36 in. In some conditions, for instance in full sun, it may reach a height of 6 ft.
CLIMATE: Suitable for zone 8 and above.
FROST TOLERANCE: It will take a low of 10°F.
GROWING CONDITIONS: This bamboo will take deep shade, but also takes full sun, and it performs best if the soil remains steadily moist.
FLOWERING SEASON: Not applicable.
COLOR RANGE: Not applicable.

LUNGWORT

Pulmonaria rubra

NEEDS SHADE

ORIGIN: France and Spain.
APPEAL: This dwarf evergreen perennial has bright green leaves and is valued for its early flowers which are produced over a long period. Height is 16 in when in flower. Very easily grown, it can be used as groundcover in the woodland garden, wild garden or shrub border.
CLIMATE: Not one of the most hardy groundcovers, it is suitable for zone 6 and above.
FROST TOLERANCE: This lungwort will take a low of –9°F.
GROWING CONDITIONS: Grow it in full or partial shade and in steadily moist soil rich in humus. After flowering cut off the old leaves to encourage a flush of fresh new foliage.
FLOWERING SEASON: It has a long flowering period, from late winter through spring and often into early summer.
COLOR RANGE: Brownish red, deep red-purple, or blackish red, sometimes deep violet. There are several varieties in different colors.

LUNGWORT COMES into flower early in the year and continues for a long period.

ESTABLISH MONDO GRASS by separating clumps into sprigs planted 5 in apart.

MONDO GRASS

Ophiopogon japonicus

NEEDS PART-SHADE

ORIGIN: Japan.
APPEAL: This dense-growing, grass-like plant has dark green, strap-like leaves growing about 10 in high. It grows in clumps and spreads slowly by running stems. A good groundcover for shade, it also makes a fine border plant. There is a dwarf form that rarely grows more than 3 in high.
CLIMATE: Suitable for zone 7 and above. In warm climates, if necessary, keep it well watered during summer and sheltered from hot, drying winds. It is fairly drought resistant.
FROST TOLERANCE: Takes 1°F if sheltered from freezing winds.
GROWING CONDITIONS: In warm to hot areas, full or partial shade is best. Plants will grow in full sun but will need plenty of water. Where summers are mild and often cloudy, grow it in full sun.
FLOWERING SEASON: Spring flowers are insignificant and hidden by the foliage.
COLOR RANGE: Flowers are white or mauve and are followed by shiny, blue berries, usually hidden.

OX-EYE CHAMOMILE

Also known as dyer's chamomile

Anthemis tinctoria

ORIGIN: Europe and Anatolia.
APPEAL: A striking and easy-care groundcover that is vigorous but never gets out of hand. Plants need renewing every two or three years but they are easy to propagate by cuttings.
CLIMATE: Suitable for zone 6 and above. It especially enjoys a Mediterranean climate. In wet climates it must be grown in soil that drains freely. This plant can rot where summers are wet and humid. In hot dry regions make sure plants are well supplied with water.
FROST TOLERANCE: Takes –9°F.
GROWING CONDITIONS: Full sun is essential. The soil should be well drained but need not be rich. It takes coastal exposure.
FLOWERING SEASON: From late spring through summer, sometimes into fall. Flowers can be picked.
COLOR RANGE: The species has rich, bright yellow flowers but there is also a lemon-yellow form.

EASILY ESTABLISHED from rooted stems, ox-eye chamomile blooms for months.

ROSE-OF-SHARON will brighten up shady areas with its showy flowers.

ROSE-OF-SHARON

Hypericum calycinum

TAKES PARTIAL TO DEEP SHADE

ORIGIN: Turkey and Bulgaria.
APPEAL: This evergreen shrub is easily grown and indeed has a vigorous spreading habit of growth. It creates a carpet of foliage up to 24 in high and is noted for its large showy bowl-shaped flowers which are carried singly in summer. Makes excellent groundcover in the shrub border, wild garden or on shady banks.
CLIMATE: This is a very hardy plant, flourishing in the north in zone 5 and above. Not suitable for warm climates.
FROST TOLERANCE: It will take a low of –20°F.
GROWING CONDITIONS: Grows best in partial to deep shade but will take sun for part of the day. Cut all the stems down to soil level in the spring to encourage a crop of new shoots.
FLOWERING SEASON: It has a long flowering season, from mid-summer to mid-fall.
COLOR RANGE: The flowers come only in yellow.

SHORE JUNIPER

Juniperus conferta

TAKES PART-SHADE

ORIGIN: Japan.
APPEAL: A spreading shrub with horizontal branches, shore juniper may ultimately spread 10 or 14 ft. It can be grown on flat ground but looks attractive on banks or spilling over walls. It is fast growing and long lived. There are a number of other horizontal junipers worth considering, especially if you are in a cold climate.
CLIMATE: This is not one of the hardiest junipers but is suitable for zone 6 and above. It is especially good in coastal gardens and indeed can be grown very close to the sea, even on the seashore, but it will also succeed in inland areas.
FROST TOLERANCE: Takes –9°F.
GROWING CONDITIONS: Likes full sun but will accept partial shade. It readily tolerates exposed windy sites, including full coastal exposure. Soil must be well drained.
FLOWERING SEASON: The plant is grown for its dense foliage.
COLOR RANGE: The species has bright green leaves: in "Emerald Sea" they are emerald green while in "Blue Pacific" they are blue-green.

SHORE JUNIPER is a tough conifer that takes sea winds, hard frosts and heat.

USE SNOW-IN-SUMMER as a spillover plant or small- or large-scale groundcover.

SNOW-IN-SUMMER

Cerastium tomentosum

ORIGIN: Europe and Anatolia.
APPEAL: The silvery foliage provides a good color contrast in the garden. It has a low, creeping habit with stems rooting as they travel. Ideal for sunny banks and dry areas, it is quite quick growing and long lived. It suppresses weeds well but may also invade areas where it is not wanted. It is easy to dig out any offending sections.
CLIMATE: Often rots in areas of high summer rain and humidity. The best climate is zone 4 and through to zones 8 or 9. In wet areas make sure the plant is grown in very well-drained soil. In hot dry areas ensure the plants receive a plentiful supply of water as necessary. This plant likes most of its water in late fall and in winter.
FROST TOLERANCE: Takes –31°F.
GROWING CONDITIONS: Full sun is essential.
FLOWERING SEASON: Masses of small flowers appear in mid-spring or, in cooler areas, in early summer.
COLOR RANGE: The simple flowers are white.

VINCA

Also known as periwinkle

Vinca minor

NEEDS PART-SHADE

ORIGIN: South and eastern Europe.
APPEAL: The plant has a creeping growth, rooting at intervals, and one plant will eventually cover 6 or 10 ft. It is good for shaded areas under trees, on banks or in large rockeries. Its growth can be rather vigorous, even invasive in warm climates although it is not as invasive as its close relative *V. major*. This is a very easy-care plant that will withstand poor conditions.
CLIMATE: This is a very tough and adaptable plant that is suitable for zone 4 and above.
FROST TOLERANCE: Accepts a low of –31°F.
GROWING CONDITIONS: Vinca grows best in bright shade, filtered sunlight or with morning sun only. In hot, inland areas grow it in shade, sheltered from hot winds and in moisture retentive soil.
FLOWERING SEASON: The small flowers appear in spring.
COLOR RANGE: Flowers are blue, white or purple and there are several variegated leaf forms as well.

VINCA IS not spectacular but is very easy to grow and largely trouble-free.

WOOLLY WILLOW

Salix lanata

ORIGIN: Found in Arctic and sub-arctic Europe and Asia.

APPEAL: This dwarf bushy deciduous willow, which grows to a height of 3–5 ft, has white woolly young shoots and rounded gray-green leaves that are densely covered in light gray wool. It makes good groundcover in a shrub border or wild garden.

CLIMATE: This is one of the hardiest shrubs available, being suitable for zone 1 and above. Not suitable for warm climates.

FROST TOLERANCE: Incredibly, it will tolerate conditions below –45°F.

GROWING CONDITIONS: This willow needs to be grown in a position in full sun. It performs best in moist soil and is not suitable for shallow limestone soils.

FLOWERING SEASON: Catkins are produced in late spring as the leaves are unfurling.

COLOR RANGE: The male catkins are deep yellow, the females grayish yellow in color.

THE WOOLLY WILLOW is one of the toughest groundcover shrubs.

THE YELLOW-LEAVED spotted dead nettle makes striking groundcover in shade.

YELLOW SPOTTED DEAD NETTLE

Lamium maculatum "Aureum"

NEEDS SHADE

ORIGIN: Europe, North Africa and western Asia. The variety is of garden origin.

APPEAL: This mat-forming perennial is grown for its highly attractive and unusual foliage. It makes stunning groundcover among shrubs in a border, or in a woodland garden. When in flower during the summer it will be no more than 8 in high.

CLIMATE: Despite its delicate appearance, it is hardy in zone 4 and above, but is not recommended for very warm climates.

FROST TOLERANCE: It will take a low of –31°F.

GROWING CONDITIONS: Yellow spotted dead nettle is best grown in light shade, not in very dark conditions. The dappled shade cast by deciduous trees is especially good.

FLOWERING SEASON: Summer.

COLOR RANGE: Yellow leaves with white centers. The flowers are pink. Some people consider that the flowers detract from the foliage and cut them off before they open.

•CHAPTER TWENTY-FOUR•

FERNS

Ferns were among the earliest plants to evolve on earth and many still grown today were around when the dinosaurs ruled. There are over 10,000 species known: most are from the tropics but there are many native to quite cold areas.

Ferns like bright light but not direct sun. They need humidity and shelter from strong wind, although some species grow in fairly exposed places.

SOIL FOR FERNS

The ideal soil for ferns is a well-drained loam with high organic matter content. Although ferns like moist conditions they will not tolerate heavy, waterlogged clays and effort put into soil improvement will always pay off. Mulching around ferns with old manure, compost or decaying leaf litter improves growing conditions.

When growing ferns in pots, use a top quality potting mix that has good moisture-retentive properties. Suitable potting mixes should be available from garden centers. If you want to you can use a standard grade mix and add about one-third by volume of peat or peat substitute, or you can even add sieved cow manure.

WATERING

Ferns will always need watering during prolonged periods of dry weather, and thorough soaking of the area is better than frequent light sprinklings. On hot, windy days, when humidity is low, it may be necessary to spray ferns frequently to cool and humidify the atmosphere. In winter, when days are short and cold, watering should be less frequent.

Potted ferns should be kept just moist but never allow water to remain in the saucer permanently. Twenty minutes or so after watering, empty excess water from the plant saucer. Don't keep potted ferns in heated rooms as the atmosphere will be much too dry for them.

FERTILIZING

Ferns like to be fertilized during their growing season from spring through to early fall. A little, often is better than applying large, strong doses all at once. Ferns seem to thrive on regular weak doses of organic fertilizers such as seaweed extract, fish emulsion or liquid blood and bone. Slow-release granules are also convenient to use and are available in blends suitable for ferns.

PRUNING FERNS

Ferns generally need little or no pruning other than the removal of dead or dying fronds. If a fern with creeping stems exceeds its allotted space it is a simple matter to sever that stem (rhizome), and discard it or pot it up to regrow.

HARDY FERNS are essential subjects for a woodland or wild garden and they also create a charming effect in a moist shady shrub border.

WAYS TO PROPAGATE FERNS

Division

Division may be as simple as cutting off a section of a creeping stem that has some roots attached to it and planting it separately. This is easily done with the hare's foot fern. Clumping ferns such as maidenhair can be divided by cutting through the clump with a sharp knife and pulling the sections apart. Although some of the outer sections may die, the bulk of the fern will survive and prosper.

Bulbils

Some ferns, such as the tender hen and chickens fern (*Asplenium bulbiferum*)—not included in this chapter— produce tiny plantlets on the fronds. You can pin the old frond to the ground to allow the plantlets to develop roots or you can carefully remove them when they are well developed and plant them carefully. If removed before they are mature enough, the young ferns will not survive.

Growing from spores

Fern spores are found on the undersides of mature fronds. They may be massed as a velvety covering or arranged as yellow or brown spots or lines. Raising ferns from spores is not easy, takes a lot of time and is not usually undertaken by gardeners who just want another fern or two. One relatively easy way to do it is to place a seedling tray full of seed-raising mix under the leaves of the fern you want to propagate. When the spores (which are dust fine) are ripe, some will fall onto the tray. If this tray is kept moist always, tiny ferns will eventually develop. When big enough to handle, they can be pricked out and potted up individually to grow on. The whole process can take a year or two and only a few ferns will survive.

THE FLESHY LEAVES of the button fern will tolerate extended dry periods.

BUTTON FERN

Pellaea rotundifolia

ORIGIN: New Zealand.
APPEAL: A small, neat fern with dark, shiny, round leaflets growing along its central wiry stem. More compact than most ferns, it can be grown outdoors in warmer areas but must be grown indoors in cool zones. In its native range it grows in a variety of habitats from open forest to more exposed dry areas.
CLIMATE: Grown outdoors in California, zone 10, but in other, colder areas it is sometimes treated as a pot plant in greenhouses and conservatories, where it needs to be provided with a humid atmosphere.
FROST TOLERANCE: It will take a low of 30°F.
ASPECT: Enjoys bright light and likes a few hours of morning sun. Dappled sunlight most of the day would be ideal.
CARE: Keep moist in spring and summer but fairly dry in winter. Tolerates dryness and even some shrivelling between waterings is not fatal. Lightly mulch with decayed manure in spring and apply a small amount of slow-release fertilizer.

DEER FERN

Blechnum spicant

ORIGIN: The deer fern is found in the wild from Alaska to California, and throughout Europe and Asia.
APPEAL: It is a small evergreen terrestrial fern with pinnate fronds up to 24 in long. Try planting it in a bold group in a woodland or wild garden. Plant it also in a shrub border, provided there is a suitable shady position.
CLIMATE: It is suitable for zone 5 and above. The deer fern takes a drier atmosphere than most other ferns.
FROST TOLERANCE: It will accept a low of – 20°F.
ASPECT: Suitable for part or deep shade, this fern is best grown in moist, acid (lime free) soil which is rich in humus such as provided by leafmould, shredded tree bark or garden compost.
CARE: Plenty of moisture is needed at the roots. Only light feeding should be given in summer—a very dilute liquid organic fertilizer applied about once a month.

A DWARF PLANT, the deer fern makes the most impact when it is planted in bold groups.

THE EUROPEAN POLYPODY is an epiphyte that will grow on trees or rocks.

EUROPEAN POLYPODY

Polypodium vulgare

ORIGIN: Widely distributed in Europe and Asia.
APPEAL: An evergreen epiphytic fern with pinnate dark green fronds up to 16 in in length. As it is an epiphyte, it can be grown on rocks or trees. Also suitable for growing on banks. Ideal for the woodland or wild garden, it makes good groundcover for the winter if mass planted. A number of garden-worthy varieties is available.
CLIMATE: A very hardy fern suited to zone 3 and above.
FROST TOLERANCE: It will take a low of –40°F.
ASPECT: Grow it in moderately fertile soil that is rich in humus. Well-drained stony soil is also acceptable. It takes full sun or dappled shade but make sure that plants are sheltered from cold drying winds.
CARE: Keep this fern moist in summer. Only light feeding is needed in summer—a very dilute liquid organic fertilizer should be applied about once a month.

HART'S TONGUE FERN

Asplenium scolopendrium

ORIGIN: This well-known fern is widely distributed in North America and Europe.
APPEAL: A dwarf terrestrial evergreen fern for the woodland garden or for planting among shrubs in a shady border. The bright green upright strap-like fronds grow to 6 in or more in length. There are numerous varieties including some with wavy-edged and crested fronds.
CLIMATE: It is suitable for zone 5 and above.
FROST TOLERANCE: A moderately hardy fern taking a low of –20°F.
ASPECT: Grow this fern in partial shade. It likes humus-rich moist soil but with good drainage. If necessary drainage can be improved by adding grit to the soil before planting. Prefers alkaline soil.
CARE: Water well in summer but far less or not at all in winter. Only light feeding needed in summer—apply a very dilute liquid fertilizer about once a month.

THE DWARF hart's tongue fern is distinctive with its upright uncut fronds.

ALTHOUGH THE hedge fern likes moist conditions, it won't tolerate excessive winter wet.

HEDGE FERN

Polystichum setiferum

ORIGIN: Widely distributed in Europe.
APPEAL: This is a terrestrial evergreen fern with soft, deep green pinnate fronds up to 48 in long. Best grown in a woodland or wild garden and also suitable for the shady shrub border. There is available a number of varieties with very divided fronds which creates a feathery appearance.
CLIMATE: Suitable for zone 7 and above.
FROST TOLERANCE: It will take a low of 0°F.
ASPECT: Will take partial to deep shade. Best grown in moist yet well-drained, fertile, humus-rich soil.
CARE: Before the new fronds unfurl in spring, remove the dead ones. This fern dislikes excessive winter wet so if necessary protect the crown of the plant from rain in winter. Keep moist in summer. Only light feeding is needed in summer—a very dilute liquid organic fertilizer should be applied monthly.

LADY FERN

Athyrium filix-femina

ORIGIN: Widely distributed in the temperate northern hemisphere.
APPEAL: A deciduous terrestrial fern with bright green pinnate fronds up to 3 ft long. This is a fern for the shrub border or woodland garden where it associates well with many other shade-loving perennials such as primulas and hostas. There are many varieties available, all of which are well worth growing. Some have attractively crested or finely divided fronds.
CLIMATE: A very hardy fern suitable for zone 3 and above.
FROST TOLERANCE: The lady fern will tolerate a low of –40°F.
ASPECT: This fern needs a shaded site sheltered from the wind. Tolerant of all but very dry conditions, it is best in moist, fertile, neutral to acid soil to which plenty of leafmould or well-rotted garden compost has been added before planting.
CARE: Keep moist in summer. Only light feeding is needed in summer—apply a very dilute liquid organic fertilizer about once a month.

THE DELICATE appearance of the well-known lady fern belies its hardiness.

MAIDENHAIR FERNS

Adiantum species

ORIGIN: Widespread in the warm and tropical parts of the world.
APPEAL: Maidenhair ferns are the lightest, most delicate-looking ferns of all and may be the most widely grown. They are used in pots or baskets, or as groundcover in moist shady or partly sunny places.
CLIMATE: The native species will grow well outside if the garden environment resembles their natural habitat, provided they are sheltered from wind. Hardy species such as *A. pedatum* are suited to zone 5 and above. Tender species should be grown under glass.
FROST TOLERANCE: The hardy species will take a low of −20°F.
ASPECT: Bright light but not too much direct sun. Filtered sunlight or early morning sun is ideal. Protect from strong, drying wind.
CARE: Keep moist in warm weather but allow plants to dry out almost completely between waterings in winter. Feed with weak solutions of liquid organic fertilizer once or twice a month during summer.

SOFT AND delicate looking, maidenhairs are really quite tough in moist soil.

THE LARGE upright fronds of the male fern may remain green throughout winter in mild areas.

MALE FERN

Dryopteris filix-mas

ORIGIN: North America and Europe.
APPEAL: A deciduous or almost evergreen terrestrial fern which is an excellent subject for the woodland garden or shrub border. The fronds grow up to 4 ft in length and are about 1 ft wide. Several varieties with crested fronds are available and are well worth obtaining.
CLIMATE: Suitable for zone 2 and above.
FROST TOLERANCE: Extremely hardy, it will take a low of −50°F.
ASPECT: Best grown in moisture-retentive soil which is rich in humus. This can be provided by working leafmould, garden compost or shredded pine bark into the soil before planting. Provide part shade and shelter from winds.
CARE: Keep the plants steadily moist in summer. They only need to be slightly moist in winter when they are resting. Only light feeding is needed in summer—apply a very dilute liquid organic fertilizer about once a month.

OSTRICH FERN

Matteuccia struthiopteris

ORIGIN: This distinctive fern comes from cool temperate regions of Europe and Asia.
APPEAL: A large bold deciduous terrestrial fern with erect pinnate fronds from 3 to 5 ft in length. It is an ideal fern for the woodland garden and looks lovely mixed with candelabra primulas. If there is a pool or stream in the woodland garden, grow this fern at the water's edge.
CLIMATE: A very suitable fern for the north, growing in zone 2 and above.
FROST TOLERANCE: It is very hardy and will take a low of –50°F.
ASPECT: Best grown in part or light dappled shade and moderately moist, but not too dry, neutral to slightly acid soil. It also likes a fertile loamy humus-rich soil.
CARE: Keep moist in summer. Only light feeding is needed in summer—a very dilute liquid organic fertilizer applied about once a month.

THE OSTRICH FERN has a distinctive shape and looks good with shade-loving primulas.

AN EXCELLENT waterside plant, the royal fern will take sun or shade.

ROYAL FERN

Osmunda regalis

ORIGIN: Europe and Africa.
APPEAL: A deciduous terrestrial fern for woodland or wild garden or moist border. It is also an ideal choice for planting on the edge of a garden pool or stream. The bright green pinnate fronds grow up to 6 ft in length. In fall they turn golden brown, an additional attraction.
CLIMATE: Hardy in zone 3 and above.
FROST TOLERANCE: It will take a temperature down to –40°F.
ASPECT: Thrives in shade and very moist soil. Fertile soil rich in humus, preferably acid, is relished. Light dappled shade is ideal but this fern is also suitable for full sun if the soil remains moist.
CARE: It is essential to keep the soil moist at all times. Only light feeding is needed in summer—apply a very dilute liquid organic fertilizer about once a month.

SENSITIVE FERN

Onoclea sensibilis

ORIGIN: Widely spread in northern temperate regions of both hemispheres.
APPEAL: This deciduous terrestrial fern has pinnate fronds 4 ft or more in length. It is very easily grown, so much so that in the right conditions it can become weedy. However, it is also a very attractive fern which deserves a place in a shady moist border. Ideal also for planting on the edge of a pool or stream.
CLIMATE: Suitable for the north, it is hardy in zone 4 and above.
FROST TOLERANCE: It will take a low of –30°F.
ASPECT: This fern is sensitive to early frosts, hence the common name. Best in a sheltered position with moist, fertile soil rich in humus. It prefers slightly acid soil. Grow it in light dappled shade as sun will scorch the fronds.
CARE: Keep moist in summer. Only light feeding is needed in summer—a very dilute liquid organic fertilizer can be applied about once a month.

THE SENSITIVE FERN is so named because it is sensitive to early frosts.

THE TASMANIAN tree fern is a woodlander needing a spot sheltered from wind.

TASMANIAN TREE FERN

Dicksonia antarctica

ORIGIN: Mainland of Australia and Tasmania.
APPEAL: In mild regions this dramatic fern is evergreen. It produces pinnate fronds up to 10 ft long on top of a thick fibrous trunk. Grow as a specimen plant in a woodland garden. Also suited to growing in pots in conservatories and greenhouses, the best method for cold regions.
CLIMATE: This tree fern is grown outside in mild temperate regions and in California, zones 8–10.
FROST TOLERANCE: It will take a low of 20°F.
ASPECT: Outside, grow this fern in moist acid soil which is rich in humus, and in part or full shade. Protect from wind. Under glass, bright but filtered light and moderate humidity are needed. Provide maximum light in winter. The plant can be moved out of doors for the summer.
CARE: Water well when in growth. Once a month liquid feed with a high-nitrogen fertilizer. Keep only slightly moist in winter. Outdoors, during hot dry weather, spray or hose down the plant daily.

• CHAPTER TWENTY-FIVE •

ORCHIDS

There are more orchids in the world than any other type of plant, and they are found on six continents in almost every habitat between the Arctic and the tropics. The flowers they produce include many of the most exquisite and desirable of all.

ORCHIDS INDOORS

Most orchids, with their gorgeous and long-lasting flowers, are bought for indoor use and you can get the longest possible display from them by giving them a good position. Place in the brightest light short of full sun, in a well-ventilated room. In winter, group orchids closely with other indoor plants (this raises the humidity around them) and keep them well away from heaters. Keep the soil lightly, evenly moist, don't feed in winter and, if the weather is warm enough, place them outside occasionally in a humid, shaded spot. With careful care, orchids can live for long periods or indefinitely indoors. However, the best way to grow them out of doors is in a greenhouse or conservatory, provided the minimum temperature can be maintained.

THE GROWING MEDIUM

Even outdoors, orchids are usually grown in pots, although some can be mounted on slabs, fixed among rocks or even attached to trees. In pots, all the epiphytic (tree-dwelling) and some terrestrial (ground-dwelling) orchids should be grown in a special, soil-less orchid potting mix, which can be bought at garden centers.

WATERING AND FEEDING

Most need plenty of water during summer but they should be allowed to dry out between waterings during their dormant phase (right after flowering or in winter). However, remember that very coarse orchid potting mixes don't hold much water and may "dry out" in a day or two.

Fertilizer, too, should only be applied to plants in active growth. Use a special orchid fertilizer or a very weak solution of a liquid or soluble plant food. Water the plants first and then apply the fertilizer.

POTTING ON

Pot on orchids only if the plant has filled its container and do it straight after bloom. A number of orchids, including dendrobiums, produce offsets on the older canes and these can be detached once you see that the offset has a well-developed root system. Other orchids, including cymbidiums, grow from bulbous bases (called pseudobulbs) which soon become congested and need dividing. Division is done in spring but as methods vary with species you should consult an orchid reference book, which will give details of the simplest way to divide your plants.

CATTLEYA ORCHIDS
Cattleya species and hybrids

ORIGIN: South America.
APPEAL: Known as the "Queen of Orchids", cattleyas produce showy flowers with daffodil-like trumpets. They are exquisite houseplants.
CLIMATE: Cattleyas cannot be grown out of doors in North America. Instead grow them indoors or, even better, in a greenhouse with a minimum night temperature of 41°F and a maximum day temperature of 86°F. This temperature regime suits a wide range of species and hybrids.
ASPECT: Filtered sunlight with high humidity always.
FLOWERING SEASON: Various types of cattleya flower somewhere between fall and spring. Very few bloom in summer.
COLOR RANGE: White and many shades of cream, yellow, pink, cerise, purple and magenta, mostly bicolors and tricolors.
ROUTINE CARE: Water freely during the warmer months. In winter water only often enough to prevent the canes from shrivelling—keep them dry most of the time. Feed during the growing season.

NEVER EXPOSE cattleyas to full sun at midday. Filtered light is ideal.

EASY TO GROW and spectacular in bloom, cymbidiums are the world's favorite orchid.

CYMBIDIUM ORCHIDS
Cymbidium species and hybrids

ORIGIN: Southeast Asia, China, the lower Himalayas and Australia but most cymbidiums grown are hybrids.
APPEAL: The gorgeous flowers last 6–8 weeks on the plant or can be cut for the vase.
CLIMATE: These orchids are excellent houseplants and are suitable for a greenhouse or conservatory with a minimum night temperature of 50°F and a maximum day temperature of 75°F. They are sometimes planted out of doors in southern California.
ASPECT: Don't grow in heavy shade. Plants need half a day's sun. Air movement keeps leaves healthy.
FLOWERING SEASON: From fall through winter and spring, depending on the variety chosen and the climate.
COLOR RANGE: White and many shades of cream, yellow, pink, red, brown and green, or they can be in combinations of these.
ROUTINE CARE: Water and lightly feed plants often from late spring to late summer, easing off as the cooler weather arrives. Divide clumps, straight after bloom, every 2–3 years or when the pots are completely filled.

DENDROBIUM ORCHIDS

Also known as bamboo orchids

Dendrobium species

ORIGIN: Tropical Asia, Australia and the Pacific Islands.

APPEAL: These versatile orchids are charming on trees, rocks or in pots. Varieties suit several climate zones.

CLIMATE: Easily grown orchids but not out of doors in North America. Excellent windowsill plants indoors and suitable for the greenhouse or conservatory with a minimum night temperature of 50°F and a maximum day temperature of 86°F.

ASPECT: Depends on species. Some tolerate full sun but others prefer dappled sunlight or partial shade.

FLOWERING SEASON: Varies with the species from spring to late summer or fall.

COLOR RANGE: Dendrobiums bloom in a huge range of colors and are often spotted or streaked with a contrasting shade.

ROUTINE CARE: Water freely in warm weather but only occasionally in winter. Feed lightly but often during spring and summer.

DENDROBIUM SPECIOSUM, *the rock lily, blooms very well every second spring.*

PLEIONE DIES DOWN *completely in winter but pops up again in spring.*

PLEIONE

Pleione species

ORIGIN: Northern India, Southeast Asia and China.

APPEAL: Only about 8 in tall, this is an extremely pretty little orchid that is easy to grow in wide, shallow pots. It can be grown in the ground if drainage is good.

CLIMATE: These are half-hardy orchids taking a temperature down to 32°F. They are often grown in a frost-free but cool greenhouse, but can be grown outdoors in frost-free areas—zone 9 and above would be suitable.

ASPECT: It needs filtered sun.

FLOWERING SEASON: Spring and early summer. Individual flowers are not long lived but a mass of the plants gives a good show. Flowers appear before the leaves and each pseudobulb flowers only once.

COLOR RANGE: White, pink, cerise, mauve or purple.

ROUTINE CARE: Keep the mix moist once growth has started but reduce watering as fall nears. Keep dry over winter. Feed a weak solution often during late spring and summer. Repot annually at the end of winter, when plants can be divided.

THE SLIPPER ORCHID is a delightful small orchid best raised in pots.

SLIPPER ORCHID

Also known as lady slipper orchids

Paphiopedilum **species and cultivars**

ORIGIN: Southeast Asia, some Pacific islands and the Himalayas.
APPEAL: These small plants have fleshy leaves, and very attractive and unusual pouched flowers which make an impressive indoor display.
CLIMATE: Cannot be grown out of doors in North America. A warm greenhouse with a minimum night temperature of 55°F and a maximum day temperature of 86°F will suit a wide range of species and hybrids.
ASPECT: Bright, filtered light is ideal.
FLOWERING SEASON: Varies with type from early summer through to fall.
COLOR RANGE: Flowers are green, white, yellow, red or purple, mostly with at least two colors on each bloom.
ROUTINE CARE: Give plenty of water and frequent light feedings from late spring to early fall. Reduce water and fertilizer as winter nears and move the plant to a warm and sheltered, but not fully sunny spot.

STANHOPEA ORCHIDS

Also known as leopard orchids

Stanhopea **species**

ORIGIN: Central America.
APPEAL: Stanhopeas produce big, rather strange looking flowers which have a strong, chocolatey fragrance. They must be grown in a wire or slatted hanging basket so that the pendulous flowers can poke through the bottom. They are easy to grow.
CLIMATE: Cannot be grown out of doors in North America, but ideal for a greenhouse with a minimum night temperature of 55°F and a maximum day temperature of 86°F. Provide high humidity in summer.
ASPECT: They like dappled sunlight. Use 50–60 per cent shadecloth if grown in a shadehouse or glasshouse.
FLOWERING SEASON: There are summer and fall flowering species.
COLOR RANGE: Usually shades of cream heavily splashed or spotted with maroon.
ROUTINE CARE: Water often over the summer, less often in winter. Feed the plants with occasional doses of liquid or soluble plant food.

BIZARRE LOOKING and strongly fragrant, stanhopeas appeal to the curious.

• CHAPTER TWENTY-SIX •

CACTI & SUCCULENTS

There are no better plants for hot, dry spots but there's more to them than just drought tolerance. They have a stark beauty that adds drama and contrast to the garden, greenhouse or conservatory and you won't see more spectacular flowers.

"Succulent" describes any plant with fleshy leaves or stems that store water. Cacti are specific types of plants, almost always without leaves and with spines in clusters. All cacti come from the Americas but succulents are found in many dry places.

ADVANTAGES

There are thousands of different types of cacti and succulents ranging in size from little "buttons" to trees, but they all have one thing in common: drought tolerance. In gardens, they are useful for hot, sunny areas and look best and most believable if grouped together in a dry landscape.

Individual plants, especially the tree or shrub-sized ones, often make striking specimen plants that look stark against the sky and contrast well with softer, more pendulous plants. In pots, cacti and succulents are in a class of their own. They thrive in places where more traditional flowers would quickly wither.

Despite their prickly nature, these plants can be fascinating for children, some of whom develop a lifelong interest in gardening after early success with these underrated little plants.

USING DRY CLIMATE PLANTS

Cacti and succulents aren't all from deserts. Many are from seasonally dry climates such as the monsoonal tropics or places with a Mediterranean climate. In the former, frequent, heavy downpours occur in summer followed by seven to nine months of rainless or near rainless weather. In a

CACTI AND SUCCULENTS can be grown in pots in a greenhouse if the climate is unsuitable for outdoor cultivation.

POT-GROWN CACTI and succulents can be placed out of doors for the summer and returned to the greenhouse in fall.

Mediterranean climate, most rain falls in winter with summers being hot and dry. Mediterranean climates are cooler, too, and there are many cacti and succulents that will tolerate quite severe frosts.

Knowing the origins of these plants allows you to choose cacti and succulents that come from a climate like yours or, if that is not possible, allows you to know when you should and shouldn't water. Maintaining them will be made easier, too, if you don't interplant varieties from different climates, since their water needs will be different.

Almost all types need sun and very well-drained soil but there are some that tolerate partial shade and you should check on the needs of unfamiliar types before placing them.

A landscape of dry climate plants can be very unusual and impressive. Don't overplant it as dry places are sparsely vegetated and use rocks, gravel, sand, weathered logs or other suitable props to create an effect that's strange yet striking.

IMPRESSIVE INDIVIDUALS

If you don't want to devote a large area of the garden to cacti and succulents, consider using one of the larger types as a specimen tree. There are several big cacti, of types seen in American westerns. Some of the euphorbias will develop tree-like dimensions over time but don't plant water-loving species around them.

ROUTINE CARE

Where most people live, rain falls more regularly than in the places where most cacti and succulents originate. These are, therefore, truly plants that can live on rain. Even wrong-season rain need not hurt them if the soil drains freely. You don't even need to feed them; the soil you have is almost certainly rich enough.

In pots, they will need more frequent watering because of the restricted root room and you should keep them lightly moist during their growing season. Unlike other plants, they won't die if you forget—they'll just do better if you remember.

APPLE CACTUS

Cereus peruvianus, syn. C. uruguayanus

ORIGIN: Brazil to Argentina.
SIZE: Usually 16–20 ft tall but can be taller with a short trunk that soon branches into many upright arms. The plant can spread to over 10 ft across.
APPEAL: Ease of growth, dramatic appearance and beautiful blooms make this a good choice for a specimen cactus tree. It makes an authentic centerpiece to a planting of smaller dry climate plants. It can be grown in a pot but needs regular repotting and eventual planting out as the roots do not enjoy constriction. Its skin is a pleasing blue-gray.
CLIMATE: The apple cactus can be grown out of doors in zones 9 and 10 and above. In other regions it can be grown in a pot in a greenhouse or conservatory and moved outside for the summer, perhaps onto a sheltered patio. Alternatively, the pot could be plunged to its rim in the soil in a bed or border.
FROST TOLERANCE: Accepts 28°F, possibly 27°F.
ASPECT: Full sun is essential.
FLOWERS: Big, white flowers are produced on summer nights but not until the plant is relatively mature. They are worth waiting for, however, as they can be very striking on moonlit nights.

GARDENER'S TIP

In rainy areas, ensure good soil drainage by growing cacti on big mounds of gravelly soil bought from a landscape supply company.

CEREUS HAS the classical cactus look and grows faster than other "tree" types.

IN ARID AREAS collect the fruits before they fall to prevent the plant spreading.

GOLDEN BARREL CACTUS

Also known as mother-in-law's cushion

Echinocactus grusonii

ORIGIN: Mexico.
SIZE: Grows into a sphere three feet across but may become more cylindrical with age.
APPEAL: An impressive plant covered with golden spines that glow in the sun. It looks good in pots but better in groups in a dry landscape.
CLIMATE: It can be grown out of doors all the year round in regions resembling its natural habitat, being suitable for zones 9 and 10 and above. This is also a favorite plant for pot culture and can be placed out of doors for the summer. The pots could be plunged in soil to stop them drying out.
FROST TOLERANCE: Accepts 23°F at least.
ASPECT: Full sun is essential. It does not like high humidity.
FLOWERS: Bright yellow flowers appear in summer but only when plants are relatively big and mature.

SLOW GROWING but worth the wait, golden barrels can be a garden highlight.

JADE PLANT is easy to strike from cuttings and an ideal deck or patio plant.

JADE PLANT

Also known as silver dollar plant

Crassula arborescens

ORIGIN: Cape area of South Africa.
SIZE: Grows up to 10 ft tall but is usually under three feet with a short trunk and many short branches.
APPEAL: The neat, rounded habit, glossy, red-edged leaves and heads of dainty flowers make this a charming succulent shrub with a tree-like habit. It makes a good container plant and can also be used formally to line paths or define entrances.
CLIMATE: Suitable for growing out of doors in zone 9 and above. In other regions grow it in a pot or tub under glass and place out of doors for the summer.
FROST TOLERANCE: Prefers frost-free gardens but accepts 28°F, possibly lower if given overhead shelter.
ASPECT: Full sun is best but jade plant will tolerate a few hours shade.
FLOWERS: Heads of small, pink flowers appear in spring. They are generously produced and quite pretty.

JELLY BEANS

Sedum rubrotinctum

ORIGIN: Central America.
SIZE: This is low-growing to about 10 in but with a greater spread. Over time, the plant forms mounds.
APPEAL: Grown for its colorful, jelly-bean-like leaves and heads of brilliant yellow flowers, this plant makes a good groundcover for dry banks and also looks good in wide, shallow pots. In full sun and cooler weather the leaves turn red.
CLIMATE: Suitable for growing out of doors in zone 9 and above. In other regions grow it in pots under glass. It could be placed out of doors for the summer, perhaps including it in summer bedding schemes, plunging the pots in the soil to prevent them drying out.
FROST TOLERANCE: Accepts the odd light frost but is better in frost-free locations.
ASPECT: Full sun gives the best foliage color but plants will grow in partial shade.
FLOWERS: Heads of small, brilliant yellow flowers appear in spring.

JELLY BEANS grow well near rocks or as a groundcover on dry banks of deep soil.

KALANCHOES, with a spectacular display, bring spring early to frost-free gardens.

KALANCHOE

Kalanchoe blossfeldiana

ORIGIN: Madagascar.
SIZE: About 12 in tall and wide with thick leaves and a bushy habit.
APPEAL: This popular houseplant will flower for months in a sunny room. Kalanchoe also makes a good outdoor container plant and can be grown in the garden as well. It looks particularly striking when massed and by grouping several in complementary colors you can create a tapestry-like effect over the winter and spring months.
CLIMATE: It can be grown out of doors in the south, in zone 9 and above, otherwise grow it as a pot plant in the home or greenhouse.
FROST TOLERANCE: May accept the odd 32°F but should be grown outdoors only in frost-free areas.
ASPECT: Full sun gives good results but shade on hot afternoons won't hurt kalanchoes.
FLOWERS: Heads of yellow, red, pink or orange flowers appear in winter and spring. They are very bright and cheery and stand out well against the olive-green leaves.

MAMMILLARIA

Mammillaria species

ORIGIN: Mainly Mexico but also south-western United States and Central America.
SIZE: Generally small although they come in a wide range of shapes.
APPEAL: Easy to grow in pots or in the ground, mammillarias produce plenty of pretty flowers and many also have decorative spines or hair.
CLIMATE: These cacti can be grown out of doors in zones 9 and 10 and above. In other regions they are ideally suited to pot culture, either in the home or in the greenhouse or conservatory. Being small plants, a large collection of different kinds can be accommodated in a small space.
FROST TOLERANCE: Those from elevated areas will tolerate frosts of 23°F at least but lowland species prefer frost-free gardens.
ASPECT: Full sun except in very hot areas where light afternoon shade is appreciated. Those with a dense covering of hairs need full sun.
FLOWERS: Produced in spring or summer, the flowers are small but pretty and may be white, cream, yellow, pink, red or mauve.

MAMMILLARIAS ARE popular pot plants but seen at their best in dry landscapes.

ORCHID CACTUS

Epiphyllum species

ORIGIN: Central America.
SIZE: The lobed, leaf-like stems may reach three feet in length, especially in the tropics, but are usually shorter than this. The plants have an arching, pendulous habit.
APPEAL: Spectacular in hanging baskets or, in frost-free areas, in trees, orchid cacti have a short season of magnificent flowers that are best seen from below.
CLIMATE: The orchid cactus is suitable for growing out of doors in zones 9 and 10 and above. In other regions it makes a superb pot plant and is often seen on windowsills indoors. Also suitable for a warm conservatory or greenhouse where it enjoys high humidity in summer. Can be placed outside for the summer.
FROST TOLERANCE: May accept the odd 30°F but prefer frost-free gardens. Give most water in summer.
ASPECT: Must be sheltered from hot summer sun but can be given increasing sun as winter nears.
FLOWERS: The big flowers may be white, cream, pink, red or scarlet and appear in spring.

MAGNIFICENT IN BLOOM, some orchid cacti emit a delicate, sweet perfume.

• CHAPTER TWENTY-SEVEN •

PLANTS FOR PONDS

Water has long been considered desirable in gardens, both for its appearance and the opportunity it offers to grow a whole new class of plants—the aquatics. Water plants can bring a pond to life and include some of the loveliest flowers of all.

CHOOSING WATER PLANTS

The size of your pond and its depth will determine the type of aquatic plants and the numbers of each that you can grow. It's a mistake to overplant a pond so that the water itself disappears beneath foliage, for the pond then becomes virtually invisible, blending in with the surrounding garden beds.

- As a general rule, plants should occupy no more than a third of the surface area. This means that big aquatics, such as full-size waterlilies and lotus, should not be grown unless your pond has a surface area of at least 33 square feet, as each plant of these species takes up about 10 square feet of space.
- Many aquatics, including full-size waterlilies and lotus, need relatively deep water and only grow well when there is at least 18 in of water above them (some need up to 36 in).
- There are plenty of lovely aquatics that will grow in shallow water, including the beautiful water iris, and there are small, floating water plants that are ideal for very small ponds.
- There are also dwarf waterlilies, which can be grown in small, shallow ponds or even tubs and sinks, and in zones 6 to 8 lotus will grow in much shallower water than in warm or tropical gardens.
- If at all possible, you should aim to have a fairly deep pond because deep water has a more stable temperature which suits both plants and fish. It also evaporates less quickly.

PLANTING THE POND

Apart from floating plants, which are simply thrown in, aquatics are usually planted in pots of good soil and then submerged. That way they are easier to lift and divide when growth becomes congested and they are easy to remove if you find they are taking over the pond.

If the plants are to be grown in deep water, it's a good idea to submerge the pots in stages, gradually setting them deeper and deeper as the plants grow. If you lay 1 in of gravel on top of the soil in the pots you will minimize discoloration of the water by the soil and also prevent fish from stirring up mud.

Use pots without drain holes or line them with plastic to prevent soil washing into the water. Remember, full-size waterlilies and lotus need at least 18 in of water above them and this should be measured from the top of the pot.

THE WATERLILY: THE QUEEN OF AQUATICS

Gorgeous, sweetly scented waterlilies are one of the loveliest and most popular of all aquatics and there are species suitable for all climates. They all like plenty of plant food in the form of rotted manure or other organic matter, and don't plant any type of waterlily where it can be splashed by a fountain or falls as the droplets will ruin the flowers.

Tropical waterlilies

Those from tropical regions come in a range of rich, dark blues and purples as well as white and pastel shades, and the flowers are more richly fragrant than those from cooler climates. They can be left outdoors year round in frost-free climates, but if grown in cool areas they must be lifted in early fall and stored in moist soil, above freezing point until late the following spring. Even then, these plants sometimes die.

Cool climate waterlilies

Cool climate waterlilies are less fragrant but no less beautiful. They come in white and pastel shades and some extraordinary deep, rich reds. Their flowers are usually held closer to the surface than tropicals that bloom above the water. Cool climate waterlilies can be left in the pond over winter but you should lift and repot them into fresh soil each spring. As they grow it may be necessary to pot the plants on into bigger containers.

PLANTING WATERLILIES

1. Fill a large pot with good soil enriched with well-rotted cow manure. Hollow out a planting hole for the roots.

2. Set the roots into the hole with the crown just above the soil level. Work quickly to avoid drying out the roots.

3. Hold the plant in position and bury the roots with soil. If the soil isn't fertile, add slow-release fertilizer.

4. Sprinkle 1 in of sand or fine gravel on top to keep the soil in place and stop the water from discoloring.

5. Sink the lily into the water a little at a time, lowering it at weekly intervals over about six weeks to 18 in.

6. Blooms appear in less than six weeks as a rule and should continue to appear right throughout the summer.

LOTUS

Nelumbo nucifera

ORIGIN: Tropical Asia and far northern Australia.
CLIMATE: It is possible to grow lotus in any climate zone except where the water freezes. The plant is dormant in winter.
ASPECT: Full sun is essential. Choose a very warm spot in cooler areas, perhaps backed by a wall.
DEPTH OF WATER: Lotus cannot grow in water deeper than about 8 ft and the warmer the climate the deeper the water should be. Normally it should be at least 18 in deep. However, in cool temperate and Mediterranean climates the plants are best grown in shallow water, under 8 in in depth. Shallow water warms up faster and warmth during the spring, summer and early fall is important to success with lotus.
FLOWERING SEASON: Late spring and summer. The seed pod that forms after the flowers have fallen is also highly decorative and can be dried for permanent arrangements. The flowers have a delicate scent.
COLOR RANGE: White and various shades of pink.

THE MAGNIFICENT LOTUS can be grown in many places but it is a very big plant.

MARSHWORT IS the right scale of aquatic for use in small ponds.

MARSHWORT

Also known as floating heart

Nymphoides species

ORIGIN: Australia, Asia, America, Europe. There are several species.
CLIMATE: There are species suitable for all climates.
ASPECT: Best in full sun but tolerates a few hours shade where summers are hot.
DEPTH OF WATER: Needs 4–18 in of water above it.
FLOWERING SEASON: The flowers appear late spring to early fall. They are small but freely produced and each petal is fringed. The leaves are also quite decorative, some being heart-shaped, others more roundish. They form a dense mat over the surface.
COLOR RANGE: White or bright yellow. The leaves of some species are attractively streaked in purple.

WATER IRIS

Iris species

ORIGIN: Water iris is widespread in the northern hemisphere.
CLIMATE: Those sold as Louisiana iris are particularly suitable for zones 8 to 10 but they will also grow in zones 6 and 7. Japanese water iris (*I. laevigata*) and the yellow flag (*I. pseudacorus*) are not recommended for tropical, dry subtropical and hot arid regions.
ASPECT: Full sun is usually best but where summers are hot, Louisiana irises especially enjoy afternoon shade.
DEPTH OF WATER: Needs 2–15 in of water over the rhizomes.
FLOWERING SEASON: Flowers in late spring and early summer.
COLOR RANGE: Yellow and shades of blue/violet are the natural colors but there is a huge number of hybrids available in a much wider range of colors and bicolors.

YELLOW FLAG grows in boggy soil, at the edges of ponds or in water.

IN SMALL PONDS, waterlilies in a single color usually look best.

WATERLILY

Nymphaea species

ORIGIN: Widespread throughout the world. Almost all are hybrids.
CLIMATE: Tropical varieties can be grown outdoors permanently in zones 9 and 10 and above. Water temperature must remain above 50°F in winter. Elsewhere, grow cool climate varieties, which are suitable for zone 4 and above (these will also grow in the tropics).
ASPECT: Plant tropicals in full sun. Cool climate types enjoy shade from early afternoon in summer except in cool temperate climates such as zone 6 where full sun is needed.
DEPTH OF WATER: Varies from 4 in to 39 in depending on the ultimate size of the types chosen.
FLOWERING SEASON: Cool climate waterlilies bloom from spring until fall. Tropical waterlilies flower into early winter.
COLOR RANGE: The color range covers white, cream, yellow, orange, pink, red, blue and purple. The tropicals have the blue colors, the cool climate types the reds. Both share the other colors.

• CHAPTER TWENTY-EIGHT •

Fruits

There's nothing sweeter than home-grown fruit, but fruiting species are generally not easy-care plants. Most need spraying, many need pruning and there are other periodic jobs. If you know you won't do these chores, stick to flowers and shrubs.

The biggest problem with growing your own fruit is getting the quality of produce you've come to expect from your fruiterer. You wouldn't buy small, spotted or deformed fruit but that's precisely what you'll get if you don't take the same care of your trees as commercial growers do. That means a regular program of spraying, feeding, watering and pruning. If you don't like the idea of spraying, you must be prepared to accept damaged produce. Moreover, if you don't spray, your trees could become so infested that the fruit won't be worth harvesting and the neglected trees and rotting fruit will be unsightly as well as being a source of infestation for other fruit trees in the district.

WHICH FRUIT?

Your climate will dictate which fruit you can grow. Many of the most popular fruits, such as apples, pears, peaches, cherries and raspberries, need to be grown in or do best in places with frosty or at least cool winters, while mangoes, guavas, citrus and others like winters that are frost-free or warmer. If you try to grow fruit well outside its preferred climate, the number and quality of the fruit you pick will be low and the plant, stressed by the conditions, will be more likely to suffer attacks by pests.

CROSS-POLLINATION

Another consideration is cross-pollination. Most fruit trees will pollinate themselves but some stone and pome fruits, notably apples, pears, plums and cherries, need another, related tree nearby or the fruit set will be very poor. If you haven't the room for more than one tree, check that your choice is self-fertile.

TREE SIZE

Some fruit trees grow quite big and it is always a good idea to check on the ultimate height and spread of any that you buy. If space is restricted, consider planting dwarf varieties only, or perhaps espalier a plant or two against a sunny wall. Even if you have plenty of space, smaller plants can be a good idea as the yield is smaller and less likely to create a sudden glut.

WHERE TO PLANT

Fruit-bearing plants generally need very rich, well-drained soil and a position in full sun. They are often quite ornamental and can be used instead of non-fruiting species—they do not need a place on their own.

ON-GOING CARE

To produce good-quality fruit, plants need plenty of water, regular feeding and removal of pests and competing weeds. Some will also need pruning, usually annually but sometimes less often. Pruning not only helps to produce the best quality fruit, it also controls the plant's size, making harvesting and spraying easier.

Watering

Watering is most important during spring, summer and early fall and is best applied weekly or fortnightly (depending on temperature and windiness). Water slowly (to avoid run-off) and water deeply. Light sprinklings are not helpful at all.

IMAGINE WALKING into the garden and plucking ripe, sun-warmed fruits like these, straight from the trees.

Feeding

Feed fruiting plants two or three times a year. Use complete plant food and spread it beneath and beyond the foliage canopy but well away from the trunk (there are no feeding roots there). You'll need at least 4 lb per mature tree, less for youngsters, but this will depend on the tree. Alternatively, you can feed with composted manure as this acts as a soil-improving mulch, but as it is relatively weak you will need 13–22 lb per mature tree. Timing of feeding is given in the individual entries.

Problems

Weeds compete with the fruiting plant for water, food and space, and they can harbor pests and diseases. Remove them promptly, and don't grow grass or other plants under fruit trees—keep the area clear and well mulched instead. Pests are most prevalent during the warmer months and will soon build up into a plague if left unchecked. Inspect plants often and take prompt action when insects are seen. Identify them (some may be harmless or beneficial), but if they are pests, dispose of those you can see by hand. If the numbers are too great, use an appropriate chemical spray (see pages 43–56 for more information).

CHILLING REQUIREMENT

Some plants need a period of low temperatures or they won't fruit. This period is known as their chilling requirement and is expressed in the number of hours they must be exposed to temperatures below 50°F. The figure is cumulative and does not have to occur in one stretch—days can be warmer than 50°F so long as nights are cooler. The chilling requirement, if applicable, is included in the entry.

■ *Citrus fruits*

KUMQUAT

Fortunella species

SIZE: Usually grows to around 6 ft tall but can be twice that size or more.
CLIMATE: Grown in the USA as novelty or decorative fruits in the "citrus belt", zones 9 and 10. They do not enjoy temperatures above 100°F.
FROST TOLERANCE: Takes 22°F, possibly lower for short periods.
FLOWERING SEASON: Any time from late spring to midsummer. Flowers are very small.
FRUITING SEASON: Fruit ripens in fall but hangs on until mid-spring. It is very decorative.
CROSS-POLLINATION: Not necessary; kumquats are self-fertile.
WATERING: Pay particular attention to watering from spring to the middle of fall. Water less in winter.
FEEDING: Feed citrus trees in late winter and again at midsummer. Use packaged citrus food as directed on the pack or rotted poultry manure.
PROBLEMS: Scale insects and sap-sucking bugs and aphids are the most serious pests of kumquats.

KUMQUATS MAKE a delicious marmalade and the plants are decorative in pots.

LEMON TREES are decorative and are among the most useful fruit trees to grow.

LEMON

Citrus limon

SIZE: Reaches 15–20 ft tall with a similar or wider spread.
CLIMATE: In the USA the lemon is grown in California and Florida, zones 9 and 10. Protection from frosts below 28°F is essential to prevent damage. The variety "Meyer" is the hardiest lemon.
FROST TOLERANCE: Lemons will accept 28°F. "Meyer" lemons will accept 22°F at least.
FLOWERING SEASON: Spring; smaller flushes in summer and fall.
FRUITING SEASON: Fruit ripens from fall to spring but because of the flushes of flowers there is usually some ripe fruit on the trees.
CROSS-POLLINATION: Not necessary; lemons are self-fertile.
WATERING: Pay particular attention to watering from spring to the middle of fall. Water less in winter.
FEEDING: Feed in late winter and again at midsummer. Use packaged citrus food or rotted poultry manure.
PROBLEMS: Scale insects, bugs, aphids and fruit fly will all attack lemon trees. Collar rot can occur when mulch is built up around the trunks of lemon trees.

"VALENCIA" ORANGES also cross-pollinate "Ellendale" or "Imperial" mandarins.

MANDARIN

Citrus reticulata

SIZE: Reaches 6–12 ft tall or more.
CLIMATE: California and Florida, zones 9 and 10, are suitable for the mandarin. It is grown commercially and in the home garden.
FROST TOLERANCE: Depends on variety. The most hardy will accept 22°F at least and all take light frosts.
FLOWERING SEASON: Spring.
FRUITING SEASON: Varies with type from early fall until spring.
CROSS-POLLINATION: Not needed, but fruit set and size are better if "Ellendale" and "Imperial" have each other nearby.
WATERING: Keep it well watered from spring to mid-fall. Water less in winter but do not neglect watering entirely.
FEEDING: Feed mandarin trees in late winter and again at midsummer. Use packaged citrus food as directed on the pack or rotted poultry manure.
PROBLEMS: Sap-sucking bugs, scale insects, aphids and fruit fly may all attack mandarins. Trees will often bear heavily one year with little the next. Minimize this by removing 25–50 per cent of fruit as it forms.

ORANGE

Citrus sinensis

SIZE: Reaches 6–20 ft tall or more.
CLIMATE: Widely grown in the tropics and subtropics but in the former the flavor is usually insipid. In the USA it is grown outside in zone 10, Florida and parts of California. Must be protected from heavy frosts.
FROST TOLERANCE: Trees will accept 28°F, possibly a little lower.
FLOWERING SEASON: Spring.
FRUITING SEASON: Depends on variety. Navel oranges ripen in fall and early winter, "Valencia" oranges ripen in spring and summer.
CROSS-POLLINATION: Not necessary; oranges are self-fertile.
WATERING: Water most heavily during the warmer months but do not let the soil go dry in winter.
FEEDING: Feed in late winter and again at midsummer. Use packaged citrus food or rotted poultry manure.
PROBLEMS: Sap-sucking bugs, scale insects, aphids and fruit fly may all attack oranges. Navels, which ripen in the cooler months, are less susceptible to fruit fly. Valencias will often bear heavily one year with little the next. Minimize this by removing 25–50 per cent of fruit as it forms.

ORANGES ARE decorative, sweetly fragrant and make good shade trees.

Berry fruits

BLUEBERRY

Vaccinium species

SIZE: Lowbush types are under 18 in tall, highbush and rabbit-eye types reach 5 ft or more.
CLIMATE: Lowbush blueberries are very hardy and can be grown in zone 2 and above. Highbush blueberries are not quite so hardy and are suitable for zone 4 and above.
FROST TOLERANCE: Lowbush blueberries will take a low of –50°F and highbush a low of –30°F.
FLOWERING SEASON: Spring.
FRUITING SEASON: Varies with type from late spring to early fall.
CHILLING REQUIREMENT: Both of these blueberries need at least 850 hours below 50°F.
CROSS-POLLINATION: Best crops are achieved if planted in groups.
WATERING: Although not aquatic plants, blueberries do come from very moist areas. Never allow the plants to go dry but don't waterlog them.
FEEDING: Apply rotted poultry manure as a thick mulch in fall.
PROBLEMS: Birds are the main pest and plants must be netted.

PICK BLUEBERRIES as soon as they ripen. Handle carefully as they bruise easily.

GOOSEBERRIES MAKE a delicious jam or they can be eaten fresh when ripe.

GOOSEBERRY

Ribes uva-crispa

SIZE: About 3 ft tall and wide.
CLIMATE: The gooseberry is a relatively hardy fruit and will be happy in zone 5 and above. They enjoy cool to mild summers and shade from mid-afternoon.
FROST TOLERANCE: Takes –20°F.
FLOWERING SEASON: Flowers appear in early spring.
FRUITING SEASON: Late spring and early summer.
CHILLING REQUIREMENT: At least 800 hours below 50°F.
CROSS-POLLINATION: Not necessary; gooseberries are self-fertile.
WATERING: Water as necessary. Keep moist in spring and summer and especially while fruits are developing.
FEEDING: Grow gooseberries in soil enriched with rotted manure and mulch with the same in late fall. Give a ration of complete plant food in late winter.
PROBLEMS: Birds may take the fruit, and if so netting will solve the problem. Gooseberries are susceptible to mildews, rusts and moulds and should not be allowed to grow too thickly. Treat with a suitable fungicide at the first sign of fungus diseases.

RASPBERRY

Rubus idaeus

SIZE: Plants form long, scrambling canes that can reach 6–10 ft in length.
CLIMATE: The raspberry is a very hardy fruit and can be grown successfully in zone 4 and above.
FROST TOLERANCE: Accepts at least –30°F.
FLOWERING SEASON: Spring.
FRUITING SEASON: Early summer to midsummer.
CHILLING REQUIREMENT: At least 1,000 hours below 50°F.
CROSS-POLLINATION: Not necessary; raspberries are self-fertile.
WATERING: Keep soil consistently moist from early spring to fall. Rain is sufficient moisture in winter. Soil must drain freely.
FEEDING: Apply a mulch of rotted manure in winter and give a ration of complete plant food in early spring.
PROBLEMS: Birds are the major animal pest but raspberries are also attacked by thrips, caterpillars and mites. Mildews and other fungus diseases are common and should be treated with a suitable fungicide.

RASPBERRY IS one of summer's most eagerly awaited berries.

YOU'LL NEED at least a dozen plants to get worthwhile crops of strawberries.

STRAWBERRY

Fragaria species

SIZE: Grows about 8 in tall, spreading by runners.
CLIMATE: Strawberries can be grown in zone 6 and above but bear in mind that the flowers are susceptible to spring frosts.
FROST TOLERANCE: Accepts a low of –10°F.
FLOWERING SEASON: Flowers in spring and summer.
FRUITING SEASON: Spring, summer and fall are the fruiting seasons. In subtropical areas, fruit ripens in winter, too.
CROSS-POLLINATION: Not necessary; strawberries are self-fertile.
WATERING: Keep evenly moist.
FEEDING: Plant into well-drained soil enriched with plenty of rotted manure and compost. Apply a ration of controlled-release fertilizer in spring or use liquid or soluble fertilizer.
PROBLEMS: Fruit will be taken by birds and damaged by snails and slugs. Aphids, mites, thrips and bugs may all attack the plants. All strawberries will eventually be infected with a virus disease and plants should be periodically replaced with certified virus-free plants.

Vine fruits

GRAPE
Vitis vinifera

SIZE: Canes can grow 30 ft or more.
CLIMATE: Suitable for zone 5 and above. Some varieties are hardier than others so choose them to suit the climate. Commercially grapes are grown principally in California. High humidity is not helpful.
FROST TOLERANCE: Takes –10°F.
FLOWERING SEASON: Flowers in early spring.
FRUITING SEASON: Fruits appear in late summer and fall.
CROSS-POLLINATION: Not necessary; grapes are self-fertile.
WATERING: Water deeply but infrequently. Grapes take dryness but won't then produce good fruit.
FEEDING: Fertilize sparingly. If soil is deep and fertile, no feeding is needed. On poorer soils give a ration of complete plant food once in spring.
PROBLEMS: Grapes are attacked by several fungal diseases, especially where summers are humid, and also by aphids, mites and caterpillars. Birds eat the fruit unless vines are netted.

A GRAPE-COVERED pergola is beautiful, functional and productive.

IF YOU GROW kiwi fruit vines over a pergola, the fruit will hang down below.

KIWI FRUIT
Actinidia deliciosa, syn. A. chinensis

SIZE: Canes can grow to 30 ft.
CLIMATE: Kiwi fruit prefers no severe frosts and a mild to warm summer. However, they can be successfully grown in zone 8 and above. Grown commercially in New Zealand for their fruit.
FROST TOLERANCE: Accepts a low of 10°F.
FLOWERING SEASON: Flowers from middle to late spring.
FRUITING SEASON: Fruits in late fall and winter.
CHILLING REQUIREMENT: At least 500 hours below 50°F.
CROSS-POLLINATION: Grow a male and a female plant, and brush pollen from male flowers directly onto all the female flowers.
WATERING: Water very generously while the vine has leaves, less in winter. Soil must drain freely.
FEEDING: Feed with a high nitrogen complete plant food in early spring and again during summer.
PROBLEMS: Caterpillars, thrips and fruit fly will all attack kiwi fruit vines and the plants are also susceptible to gray mould during humid weather.

A HANDSOME VINE and very productive too, passionfruit requires a frost-free area.

PASSIONFRUIT

Passiflora edulis, P. caerulea

SIZE: Rampant. Can run to 50 ft.
CLIMATE: Grown for its fruits in zone 10 including southern California. A hardier species, *P. caerulea,* will grow in zone 7 and above.
FROST TOLERANCE: Takes the odd 30°F but prefers frost-free areas. *P. caerulea* will take 0°F.
FLOWERING SEASON: Flowers in early spring but rain then can reduce the fruit set.
FRUITING SEASON: Fruits in late spring to early fall.
CROSS-POLLINATION: Not needed but you may have to hand pollinate female flowers in the morning to get a good crop.
WATERING: Keep soil moist from the time flowers appear, increasing water as summer nears. Decrease water in fall. Excess water must drain freely or the plants will rot.
FEEDING: This is a very heavy feeder that needs extra rich soil. From spring to early fall (late summer in cool places) feed every 6 weeks with high nitrogen fertilizer.
PROBLEMS: Expect to replace diseased vines every 4–5 years. Bugs, scale, aphids and mites also attack vines but are not usually serious.

ROCK MELON

Also known as cantaloupe

Cucumis melo

SIZE: Varies with type: some are bushy but the traditional rock melon grows on a groundcovering vine.
CLIMATE: Grows best where there is a long, hot, not too rainy summer. Ideal for hot, dry inland gardens. In cold zones melons are too often grown as a summer crop under glass.
FROST TOLERANCE: None. Rock melons are annual, summer vines.
FLOWERING SEASON: Spring.
FRUITING SEASON: Fruits in summer and early fall.
CROSS-POLLINATION: Not necessary; rock melons are self-fertile.
WATERING: Keep the soil moist, gradually giving more water as summer nears. When fruits are fully formed, reduce the watering.
FEEDING: Grow in the fertile, well-drained soil found in a good vegetable patch. If soil has been enriched with rotted manure no feeding is necessary.
PROBLEMS: Vines are very susceptible to mildew, especially in humid weather, and should be sprayed with a suitable fungicide when the problem is first seen.

THE BEST rock melons are grown in hot, dry inland gardens. They need space.

■ *Pome and stone fruits*

APPLE

Malus sylvestris var. *domestica*

SIZE: From about 3 ft (trained) to about 30 ft.
CLIMATE: Suitable for zone 4 and up to zone 9. Apples do not grow well in zone 10 as there is not enough winter cold to induce dormancy.
FROST TOLERANCE: Depends on variety. The hardiest accept –30°F.
FLOWERING SEASON: Spring.
FRUITING SEASON: Varies with type from midsummer to midwinter.
CHILLING REQUIREMENT: 1,000 hours below 50°F but there are low-chill varieties for warmer areas.
CROSS-POLLINATION: Strongly recommended, as it increases fruit set. Always grow more than one variety and they should flower together.
WATERING: Keep soil evenly moist during the growing season. In warm areas with dry winters, water even leafless trees.
FEEDING: Apply high potassium fertilizer in spring. In fall mulch with rotted manure.
PROBLEMS: Codling moth, aphids, fruit fly, thrips and mites attack apples. Diseases include apple scab and mildew.

APPLES ARE a cool climate fruit.

PEACHES NEED some cold weather to fruit but can be grown in some frost-free areas.

PEACH AND NECTARINE

Prunus persica

SIZE: Reaches 10–15 ft tall.
CLIMATE: Zone 5 and above are suitable.
FROST TOLERANCE: Dormant trees take –10°F but frost at flowering or early fruiting time is very damaging.
FLOWERING SEASON: Flowers in early spring.
FRUITING SEASON: Fruits from late spring to early fall, depending on variety.
CHILLING REQUIREMENT: Varies with variety. Choose low-chill types if you live in a frost-free area.
CROSS-POLLINATION: Not usually necessary. Most peach varieties are self-fertile.
WATERING: Keep soil moist throughout the growing season. Peaches do not like to go dry.
FEEDING: Apply high nitrogen fertilizer in fall and mulch beneath and beyond the foliage canopy with compost or rotted manure or straw.
PROBLEMS: Brown rot, peach leaf curl, rust and bacterial canker are common diseases, while aphids, fruit fly, bugs and pear and cherry slugs are commonly encountered pests.

PLUM

Prunus domestica, P. salicina

SIZE: Reaches 16–20 ft tall, sometimes a little taller. With age, the trees develop a broad crown.
CLIMATE: Zone 5 and above for *P. domestica* (European plum) and zone 8 and above for *P. salicina* (Japanese plum). Where winters are mild, grow Japanese plums or low-chill varieties. European plums, and especially gages, are high-chill trees for cold areas only.
FROST TOLERANCE: European plum accepts a low of –20°F.
FLOWERING SEASON: Flowers in early spring but the exact timing of bloom varies with type. They are very ornamental in bloom.
FRUITING SEASON: Fruits in late spring and summer, depending on the variety grown.
CHILLING REQUIREMENT: At least 800 hours below 50°F are necessary for Japanese plums and you'll need at least 1,100 hours of cold for the Europeans.
CROSS-POLLINATION: Some plums are self-fertile enough for the home garden, but if you or your neighbor has another variety, fruit set and size will be improved. Check pollination needs when you are buying the plant.
WATERING: Water regularly from the time flowers appear until harvest. Don't completely neglect watering at other times, especially if your winters are fairly dry.
FEEDING: Mulch beneath and beyond the foliage canopy with well-rotted manure in fall but keep it away from the trunk. Give a ration of complete plant food at the same time. Water it in well.
PROBLEMS: Brown rot is a serious fungus disease of the fruit and is particularly common in humid, rainy weather. Plums are also attacked by insect pests, including fruit fly, scale, bugs and borers.

OVER TIME, plum trees develop a spreading crown that makes them good shade trees, and when covered with spring flowers they are as ornamental as trees can be.

Tropical fruits

AVOCADO

Persea americana

SIZE: Grafted plants reach 30 ft in height.
CLIMATE: Avocado is grown outside in the warmest parts of the USA, zone 10 and above. Most successful where frosts, if any, are light and infrequent.
FROST TOLERANCE: Takes 22°F. but that will damage the fruit. Best in frost-free gardens.
FLOWERING SEASON: Spring.
FRUITING SEASON: Fall, winter or spring, depending on type.
CROSS-POLLINATION: Not necessary for home fruit production in cooler areas but where winters are warm fruit set improves with a second tree. There are "A" and "B" class trees-have one of each.
WATERING: Water deeply, weekly in summer, less in spring and fall.
FEEDING: Apply complete plant food every six weeks from late spring to late summer. Mulch with rotted organic matter in winter.
PROBLEMS: Fruit fly, scale insects, and thrips will damage fruit but root rot (phytophthora fungus) is common and fatal. Grow trees in well-drained soil containing plenty of rotted organic matter.

AVOCADOES WON'T ripen on the tree. Pick them when fully formed.

FRUIT SET on mangoes is poor if rain falls during flowering or when fruits are small.

MANGO

Mangifera indica

SIZE: Reaches 65 ft or more in the tropics but only 10–15 ft at the cooler limit of its range.
CLIMATE: It is planted in southern Florida and the warmest parts of California. They will not fruit well in cooler areas.
FROST TOLERANCE: Will tolerate a low of 30°F. Any lower and the trees will be killed.
FLOWERING SEASON: Flowers in late winter and early spring.
FRUITING SEASON: Mid-spring to fall, depending on climate.
CROSS-POLLINATION: Not necessary. Mangoes are self-fertile.
WATERING: Start watering in late spring, giving plenty over summer, less in fall and none in winter and the first half of spring.
FEEDING: Grow in well-drained, not overly rich soil. Don't feed until plants are well established and then give a light ration of complete plant food two or three times in summer.
PROBLEMS: Fruit fly, fruit spotting bug and scale are common pests. The diseases anthracnose, mildew and bacterial black spot also attack.

PURPLE STRAWBERRY GUAVA

Psidium littorale var. *longipes*

SIZE: The purple strawberry guava is a large dense evergreen shrub that reaches up to 25 ft in height. It has small thick glossy leaves and makes an attractive and useful plant in frost-free gardens.

CLIMATE: The guava is native to tropical America and is widely grown in the tropics and subtropics for its fruits. However, it is about as hardy as the lemon, *Citrus limon*, so it can be grown, and indeed is frequently planted in gardens, in zone 10, in the southern parts of California and Florida. The purple strawberry guava would also make a good tub plant so in colder regions could be wintered under glass.

FROST TOLERANCE: It is suited only to frost-free gardens but will take a few degrees of frost occasionally.

FLOWERING SEASON: The white fragrant flowers appear in spring or early summer.

FRUITING SEASON: The fruits start to appear in early summer. It produces round, deep red fruits up to $1^1/2$ in in diameter. They are sweet, of very good flavor when ripe and are very high in vitamin C.

CROSS-POLLINATION: Not necessary as guavas are self-fertile.

WATERING: Give the most water from spring to early fall, decreasing as winter approaches. Watering this shrub should not be necessary throughout winter.

FEEDING: Use a complete plant food and feed lightly approximately once a month from mid-spring until the end of summer. Water the fertilizer well in after each application.

PROBLEMS: Compared to many other fruits, guavas are relatively free from pests and diseases, but the fruit can be attacked by fruit flies.

THE PURPLE STRAWBERRY GUAVA has sweet fruits that are high in vitamin C.

THIS PLANT is an attractive specimen for the garden or for a tub.

Other useful fruits

FIG

Ficus carica

SIZE: Usually reaches 20–25 ft tall but can be much bigger with great age.
CLIMATE: Figs can be grown in zone 8 and above. They are grown commercially in zone 9. It likes rainy winters and hot dry summers, typical of the natural habitats in the Mediterranean region. They do not like humid, rainy weather over summer.
FROST TOLERANCE: Accepts 10°F, possibly lower.
FLOWERING SEASON: Flowers in spring but flowers are never seen—they are inside the forming fruits.
FRUITING SEASON: Fruits appear in summer and fall.
CHILLING REQUIREMENT: It needs 300 hours under 50°F or fruit set, if any, will be poor.
CROSS-POLLINATION: Common figs do not need cross-pollination but the rarer Smyrna variety will not fruit without a pollinator.
WATERING: Give most water from mid-fall to mid-spring. In very hot, inland areas, the odd deep soaking in summer won't hurt.
FEEDING: Figs aren't heavy feeders and in suburban gardens, if they are grown in average, well-drained soil, little additional fertilizing is necessary. Mulching beneath and beyond the foliage canopy with rotted manure in fall is plenty of feeding.
PROBLEMS: Birds will peck the ripe fruit unless trees are netted, and fruit fly attack is certain in those areas it infests. Hang lures in trees to warn of their presence, then spray promptly. There are no major fig diseases.

FIGS PRODUCE luscious, unusual fruits and the trees themselves are relatively compact and attractive. Birds and fruit flies are the major pests of figs.

MULBERRY IS a great favorite with children and an easy fruit tree to grow.

MULBERRY

Morus nigra

SIZE: Reaches 30 ft or more.
CLIMATE: Originating from western Asia, the black mulberry, the species described here, can be successfully grown in zone 5 and above.
FROST TOLERANCE: Takes –20°F.
FLOWERING SEASON: Spring.
FRUITING SEASON: Fruits in mid-spring to early summer.
CROSS-POLLINATION: Not necessary as mulberries are self-fertile.
WATERING: Where rainfall is regular and reliable, little additional water seems necessary for the mulberry. Elsewhere, water deeply during dry times.
FEEDING: In average soil, feeding is not necessary. If you like, apply complete fertilizer once after harvest.
PROBLEMS: Birds compete for the mulberry fruit, but in the suburbs there is usually plenty of fruit left for human use.

OLIVE

Olea europaea

SIZE: Reaches 15–30 ft tall.
CLIMATE: It is a native of the Mediterranean region. It can be grown successfully in zone 9 and above. Grown commercially in Califonia and to a lesser extent in Arizona for its fruits. It has great ornamental value as well.
FROST TOLERANCE: Takes 20°F or perhaps a little lower.
FLOWERING SEASON: Early to mid-spring. Flowers will be damaged by late frosts.
FRUITING SEASON: Late summer and fall. Pick when fully formed, either green or when ripe and black.
CHILLING REQUIREMENT: At least 1000 hours (preferably more) below 50°F or fruit set will be poor.
CROSS-POLLINATION: Not necessary; olives are self-fertile.
WATERING: If watering is necessary, do so deeply and mostly during the cooler months. Olives are able to survive in very dry areas.
FEEDING: Not necessary. Olives grow on poor, stony soils.
PROBLEMS: Scale insects may attack plants but this is not very usual.

OLIVES GROW into attractive trees and in suitable climates the fruit is a bonus.

•CHAPTER TWENTY-NINE•

VEGETABLES

Nothing beats garden fresh vegetables and you don't need much space to grow them. Any sunny spot, even a pot, can produce a few favorites and with an area of just 14 x 14 ft you can grow an amazing range of the freshest food there is.

Choosing a site and settling on the size of your vegetable patch is the first task. The site must get full sun all day, and so choose a spot well clear of trees and big shrubs. How big an area you'll need depends on the size of your household and the number of different vegetables you want to grow, but an area of 14 x 14 ft is a good size for beginners. You can always expand it later but you'll be surprized at how much you can harvest from it.

GOOD SOIL IS ESSENTIAL

Fertile, free-draining soil is essential for good crops and you'll certainly have to improve what you have. Start by removing whatever is growing on the site and then dig the soil over, breaking up clods as you go. Work in plenty of well-rotted manure and compost and a small handful of complete plant food per square yard. The dug-over soil should end up dark, fine and crumbly.

If your soil is just sticky, heavy clay, don't dig. Instead, build a 10 in high retaining wall around the site and fill with good-quality soil brought in.

If your soil is very sandy, it will drain well and be easy to dig but you'll need to add lots and lots of organic matter to give it fertility and some body. In any type of soil, adding organic matter will increase its bulk, but don't worry about that. The raised soil level helps ensure good drainage. Rake over to level it and then water the area deeply.

CHOOSING THE CROPS

Let the site lie for a week or two while you decide what to plant. Select only varieties that you do or will eat and if you work out how many of each item your household currently consumes per week, you'll know how many of each to plant. As vegetables planted at the same time will mature at the same time, it's a good idea to plant small batches two or three weeks apart. The batches should yield no more than you can eat in two or three weeks. That way you will have a continuous supply without any wasteful and discouraging gluts. Few vegetables can be grown year round, and so be sure to choose varieties that are right for the season.

SEEDS OR SEEDLINGS?

Vegetables can be started from either seeds or seedlings. Seeds are far cheaper and there's a wider range of varieties available in seed packets than as seedlings. You can plant a few seeds now and save the rest for later sowings and most can be sown directly where they are to grow. You do have to pay attention to the directions on the pack, especially the sowing depth, and you must never allow the soil to dry out while the seeds are germinating (which may take two weeks). When the seedlings do appear the excess seedlings have to be thinned so that the spacing between each is correct.

Bought seedlings, being already several weeks old, are ready to eat that much sooner and they can be spaced correctly at the outset. On the down side, seedlings have to be planted all at once and you may not want a dozen of that variety maturing and ready to eat all together.

SINGLE OR WIDE ROWS?

Vegetables are usually grown in rows. Single rows are the traditional choice but some garden experts are now recommending wide rows, that is, three to five rows closely spaced to form one wide row. This increases the yield per square yard, but be careful not to produce gluts.

ROUTINE MAINTENANCE

All vegetables should be grown quickly, and so don't neglect to water them often—daily or even twice daily when it's hot and rainless. Frequent watering will wash the nutrients out of the soil and so you should also feed the vegetables at fortnightly intervals (but not in winter). You can use liquid or soluble fertilizer or sprinkle complete plant food alongside each row. If you have a good supply of rotted manure, mulching the vegetables with it will eliminate the need for fertilizer and will help conserve soil moisture as well.

Rich soil and plenty of water is a magnet for weeds and these mustn't be allowed to remain. Pull or hoe them out very regularly—well before they flower and set seed. If you turn the weeds upside down and don't water for a day or two, you can leave them to rot back into the ground.

CROP ROTATION

Crop rotation is the natural way to keep your garden soil and plants healthy.

Long before fungicides and pesticides came onto the scene, farmers discouraged pests and diseases by not planting the same crop or related crops in the same patch of soil two years in succession. Instead, they rotated their crops into different beds over a three- or four-year cycle. That way, those pests that fed on particular plants died when their food source was not replanted.

Here is a three-year crop rotation plan based on a vegetable garden divided into three beds.

- BED ONE. Grow all or some of these: any peas, any beans, peanuts, sweet corn, silver beet, spinach, lettuce.
- BED TWO. Grow all or some of these: cabbages, Brussels sprouts, cauliflower, broccoli, turnips, radishes, kohlrabi.
- BED THREE. Grow all or some of these: tomatoes, carrots, leeks, potatoes, cucumber, celery, beetroot, onions, zucchini, garlic.

The following year grow the contents of bed one in bed two; of bed two in bed three and of bed three in bed one. Repeat the process after every harvest.

Artichoke *Cynara scolymus* 	Zone 6 and above is the most suitable. It accepts –10°F but does not do well where summers are very hot. Good near the coast where sea breezes moderate temperatures.	Usually raised from shoots or suckers rather than from seed. In frost-free areas, these are planted in winter, elsewhere in spring after frosts have passed. Plant into soil previously enriched with rotted manure and a ration of complete plant food.	Keep evenly moist always and mulch around plants with compost, straw or rotted manure. Young plants are very susceptible to drying out. PROBLEMS Aphids attack and damage the developing flower buds and also spread plant diseases. Control at first sight. In humid areas, fungus diseases distort leaves, which should be promptly removed. HARVESTING Cut the flower buds before they begin to open.
Asparagus *Asparagus officinalis* 	The best climate has a cool to cold winter and warm, not very rainy summer. Asparagus grows well in zone 4 and above. Especially good in zones 9 and 10.	Prepare the planting site by digging a wide trench 14–18 in deep. Backfill to 10 in using a mix of the excavated soil and rotted manure or compost. In winter or early spring buy two-year-old crowns as growing it from seed is slow and tedious. If they are available, buy male plants only. Plant in the trench, 18 in apart, spreading the roots out all around. Cover with 2 in of the soil/organic matter mix. As the shoots appear, cover with more of this mix and continue to do this until the trench is overfull. An average family needs at least fifteen plants.	Keep the soil moist and sprinkle complete plant food over the bed once during late spring. Don't cut any spears in the first year, and when growth begins to yellow off in fall cut plants to the ground and mulch the bed with rotted manure. Repeat this process every year. PROBLEMS The disease rust can be avoided if rust-resistant varieties are grown. Otherwise the plant is largely trouble-free. HARVESTING You can take a small bunch in the second season after planting and begin harvesting in earnest in the third. Harvesting begins as soon as the spears appear and can continue until early summer. After that the plants must be left alone to grow leaves or next year's crop will be very poor.
Beans *Phaseolus vulgaris* 	Beans grow in all climate zones but do best where summers are humid. In zone 10 and anywhere else where winters are warm and frost-free, beans are grown year round or from fall to spring.	Sow seed directly where it is to grow, into soil that is warmer than 50°F. In cold areas, start seed indoors and plant out after frosts. A 6–10 ft row of beans feeds four people.	Beans have shallow roots and must not dry out. Feed by digging in complete plant food before sowing and give liquid or soluble fertilizer three times in summer. PROBLEMS Aphids and bean fly are common pests, and diseases such as anthracnose sometimes strike. Diseased plants and decaying plant matter are best removed from the bed. HARVESTING Pick beans when they are young and small—the more you pick, the more they produce. Harvesting begins about 10 weeks after seedlings appear.

VEGETABLE	CLIMATE	PLANTING	GROWING
Beetroot *Beta vulgaris* 	Grows in zone 5 and above.	Sow seed directly where plants are to grow, into soil that has had a small handful of lime dug in for each square yard (unless the soil is naturally alkaline). In cold zones start sowing when soil temperatures exceed 45°F. In zones 9 and 10 beetroot can be grown year round.	Thin seedlings to $1\frac{1}{2}$ in apart and later remove every second plant when they begin to crowd each other—these second thinnings are very tasty. Keep soil moist but don't feed the plants heavily. PROBLEMS Cutworm destroys seedlings. Leaf miners damage leaves. HARVESTING You can pull roots any time after about two months. Don't let the roots grow too big or they will be woody and tasteless.
Broad beans *Vicia faba* 	Good in all cool climates.	Sow seeds directly where they are to grow, 2 in deep and about 8 in apart. In cooler areas sow in early to mid-fall and again in late winter for a second crop. In frost-free places delay sowing until late fall. You'll need 16–26 ft of broad beans for a decent crop.	Keep the soil moist and do not feed the plants heavily. They will need supporting. PROBLEMS Aphids are sometimes a problem but the diseases rust and broad bean wilt are more serious. Remove infected plants at once. HARVESTING Either harvest the immature pods, or pick the mature pods for the shelled beans within.
Broccoli *Brassica oleracea* Italica group 	This cool season crop is best in zone 8 and above.	Sow seeds directly where they are to grow. In zones 8 and 9 sow from mid-spring to late summer. In frost-free or almost frost-free areas sow from early summer to late fall. In tropical areas sow in fall. Batches of six plants sown a month apart will feed four.	Thin seedlings to 6 in apart. When these begin to crowd each other, remove every second plant (which should have a small head). The remaining plants will grow much bigger and produce side heads. Feed once or twice with a low nitrogen fertilizer. Keep moist always. PROBLEMS Practice crop rotation to minimize diseases such as club root. Aphids and caterpillars are common pests that need prompt attention. HARVESTING Cut the central head with some stem attached when the buds are still tight. Side shoots will develop new heads.

VEGETABLE	CLIMATE	PLANTING	GROWING
Brussels sprouts *Brassica oleracea* Gemmifera group 	Zone 7 and above are suitable.	In frosty areas, sow seeds from mid-spring to midsummer. In frost-free places, summer sowing is recommended. Sow into pots, punnets or trays and transplant seedlings into very well-drained but moisture retentive soil when they are 1 in tall.	Keep the soil evenly moist always and feed Brussels sprouts plants with liquid or soluble plant food every three weeks after they have been transplanted. PROBLEMS Aphids and caterpillars are the main pests of this vegetable and can be controlled with insecticidal dusts or sprays. HARVESTING Pick Brussels sprouts from the bottom of the stem while the sprouts are still tight. The first sprouts will be ready for harvesting about four months after they have been transplanted out into the garden.
Cabbage *Brassica oleracea* Capitata group 	Grows in zone 8 and above.	Sow seed directly where it is to grow into soil that has been enriched with rotted manure and a ration of complete plant food. In the tropics, sow any time. Elsewhere, sow warm season growers in late winter or early spring, cool season growers in late summer or early fall. Sow cabbages in batches according to your family's needs.	Small types should be grown 12 in apart, full-size cabbages will need twice that spacing. Keep the soil moist always. If cabbage is planted in rich soil no further feeding will be needed. PROBLEMS Caterpillars are major pests, especially of warm season cabbages. Daily hand removal works, otherwise spray or dust with an insecticide. Never grow cabbages in the same soil two seasons running. HARVESTING Harvest whenever the head seems a good size. Compost the outer leaves.
Capsicum & chillies *Capsicum annuum* 	Suitable for zones 8 and above. They are frost tender.	Can be sown year-round in the tropics. Elsewhere sow seeds in spring when the weather has definitely turned warm. Sow seed into pots or trays and transplant the seedlings when they are 6 in tall.	Keep moist but increase watering as summer approaches. Soil must drain freely. Feed monthly with tomato food (a low nitrogen fertilizer). PROBLEMS Aphids and fruit fly are common pests and cutworms may destroy seedlings. Expect mildew diseases in warm, humid weather and treat promptly with fungicide. HARVESTING Pick capsicums when they are green or when they are fully ripe and colored. Ripe fruit is the sweetest. Leave some stem attached to the fruit when you pick it. Chillies may also be picked when they are green or when they are ripe, with the ripe fruit being the hottest.

VEGETABLE	CLIMATE	PLANTING	GROWING
Carrots *Daucus carota* 	This cool season crop can be successful in all zones.	Sow seed thinly directly where it is to grow. Begin sowing when soil temperature reads 45°F. For a continuous supply, sow 15 ft rows every six weeks. Globular and squat forms of carrots can be grown in containers.	Water seeds in well and thin seedlings to 1 in apart. As they grow, harvest baby carrots so that the remainder have room to develop. Don't overwater carrots—let the soil dry out between waterings. PROBLEMS Control carrot aphids at their first appearance. Root nematodes cause leaves to curl and turn red or yellow. Destroy affected carrots and treat the bed with nematicide. HARVESTING Pull the carrots whenever they are large enough to be eaten.
Cauliflower *Brassica oleracea* Botrytis group 	Best in zone 8 and above.	Sow directly where plants are to grow into warm soil, or start seeds in seedling trays and plant out when 6–8 weeks old. Sow small growing varieties (which are the best for home gardens) 16 in apart, twice that for full-size cauliflowers. Sow from late spring until midsummer. In zones 9 and 10 seeds can be sown in the fall. Plant in batches of six every 4–5 weeks.	Cauliflowers should be grown fast and strongly, so plant them into well-prepared, very fertile soil and never let it go dry. As the plants grow, if the white head (or curd) is visible, tie the outer leaves over it. PROBLEMS Caterpillars and aphids are serious pests during the warmer months especially. HARVESTING Harvest when the heads are big but still tightly packed. Cut out the entire head and compost the remains.
Celeriac Also known as turnip-rooted celery *Apium graveolens* var. *rapaceum* 	Suitable for zone 8 and above.	In cold areas sow seed from spring to early summer; late winter to late summer in frost-free areas. Sow into containers or trays and then transplant seedlings into small individual pots. When big enough, plant into fertile, free-draining soil that contains plenty of rotted manure and a ration of complete plant food.	Keep moist always. Plants must never want water and you may have to water daily in summer. After planting out, feed every three weeks with soluble or liquid fertilizer. PROBLEMS Slugs and snails will damage stems and a leaf-spotting fungus may attack the plant. It can be controlled with fungicide. HARVESTING Cut the whole plant at ground level or remove outside stems as needed.

VEGETABLE	CLIMATE	PLANTING	GROWING
Celery *Apium graveolens* 	Suitable for zone 8 and above.	In cold areas sow seed from spring to early summer; in frost-free areas late winter to late summer. Sow into trays and transplant seedlings into small pots. When big enough, plant in free-draining soil with lots of rotted manure and a ration of complete plant food.	Keep moist always. Plants must never want water and you may have to water daily in summer. After planting out, feed every three weeks with soluble or liquid fertilizer. PROBLEMS Slugs and snails will damage stems and a leaf-spotting fungus may attack the plant. It can be controlled with fungicide. HARVESTING Cut the whole plant at ground level or remove outside stems as needed.
Cucumber *Cucumis sativus* 	Suitable for zone 9 and above or under glass in cooler areas.	Sow seed in pots and plant out 30 in apart. Soil must be well enriched with rotted manure and/or compost and must drain freely.	Keep evenly moist, applying more water as summer approaches. Mulch with straw, compost or rotted manure. Feed every 3–4 weeks with liquid or soluble fertilizer, or complete plant food. PROBLEMS Pumpkin beetle, aphids and spider mite. Mildew strikes foliage in humid weather; control it with a suitable fungicide. HARVESTING Pick before the fruit becomes too big. Very large ones are tough and can be bitter.
Eggplant Also known as aubergine *Solanum melongena* 	Suitable for zones 8 and above. It is frost tender.	Sow year round in the tropics, spring to summer in warm zones and late spring only in cooler areas. Sow directly where it is to grow only if the soil temperature exceeds 68°F. If not, sow in pots and grow on until the soil temperature rises.	Keep lightly, evenly moist and remove weeds promptly. Feed once or twice with liquid or soluble fertilizer while growing and when fruit begins to set apply complete plant food. PROBLEMS Aphids, caterpillars and spider mites are the main pests of eggplant. An all-purpose insecticide will control the former two but an acaricide will be necessary for the latter. HARVESTING Pick as soon as fully colored but before the skin begins to wrinkle. Leave some stem attached to the fruit.
Florence fennel *Foeniculum vulgare var. dulce* 	Suitable for zone 5 and above.	Sow seed directly where it is to grow, in late summer in warm areas, spring in colder places. Soil must drain freely and be reasonably fertile and deeply dug over.	Water deeply, weekly (twice weekly in hot weather). Apply a ration of complete plant food once during the growing season. Keep the base of the plant covered with soil so that it remains white. PROBLEMS No particular problems. HARVESTING Harvest by lifting the whole plant when the base is swollen (3–4 months after sowing).

VEGETABLE	CLIMATE	PLANTING	GROWING
Leeks *Allium porrum* 	Suitable for zone 6 and above.	Leeks have a long growing season and are usually grown from seedlings. Drop each seedling into a hole 6 in deep so that the tops just protrude. Don't fill in the holes but do water well. This method helps develop the long, white stem. Make holes every 6–8 in along a 6–12 ft row (you can stagger the plantings for a longer season). Soil must be well-enriched. Sow seeds in early spring and plant out 8 in high seedlings.	Keep evenly moist and feed every two months with a ration of complete plant food. As the stems grow, mound soil around them to keep them white. PROBLEMS They may be troubled by onion thrips (hose them off) but are usually pest-free. HARVESTING Pull when the stems are of a suitable size. Don't let them get too fat or they become tough.
Lettuce *Lactuca sativa* 	Lettuces can be grown in zone 6 and above. Only some varieties are suited to warm climates. Seeds do not germinate above 77°F.	Except where winters are very cold, sow seeds directly, thinly, where they are to grow. In cold areas, sow indoors and transplant the seedlings when they are big enough. In hot areas, don't sow during summer. Everywhere, sow into friable, highly fertile soil that is well dug over and barely cover the seed. Keep the soil evenly moist. If you eat a lot of lettuces, a good way to keep them coming is to sow in 3 ft-long rows, sowing the next row when the previous has germinated. Lettuces grow very well in pots. Use wide containers for the best results.	Thin seedlings first to about 1 in apart. As they grow, continue to thin them, using the tender thinnings in salads. Don't overcrowd plants or they may become susceptible to fungus diseases in humid weather. Never allow them to dry out and keep competing weeds down. Feed them weekly or fortnightly with high nitrogen, soluble plant food. PROBLEMS Watch for caterpillars, grasshoppers, snails and slugs which eat holes in the leaves. Aphids can transmit diseases and stunt growth, and mildew can be a problem in humid weather. HARVESTING The outer leaves of loose-leaf lettuces can be picked as needed. Harvest hearting types when the size is satisfactory.

VEGETABLE	CLIMATE	PLANTING	GROWING
Marrow *Cucurbita* species 	Suitable for all climate zones but in the far north the growing season may be too short for the fruit to mature.	Sow seeds where they are to grow or, in cooler areas, in pots a few weeks before warm summer weather. Sow year round in tropical areas, spring to summer in warm zones and in early summer in cool ones.	Water well but try to keep water off leaves and stems. Pollinating flowers by hand may be necessary. PROBLEMS Mildew is a common disease controllable with a fungicide. Aphids can build up in spring: spray with a suitable insecticide. HARVESTING Start picking 2–3 months after planting and, in cooler areas, before frosts strike.
Mushroom *Agaricus* species 	Suitable for all climate zones. Grow under cover in cold climates.	Plant year-round in all climate zones. Use sterilized mushroom farm compost that has already been inoculated with mushroom spawn (this is sold as mushroom kits).	Kits contain everything necessary except water, which you add. Keep the kit indoors in a relatively even temperature. Keep the compost lightly, evenly moist, not sodden. PROBLEMS No problems if instructions are followed. HARVESTING Pick at any stage. Button mushrooms are picked before the cap opens, mature mushrooms when the cap opens flat, exposing the gills beneath. Discard compost when no more mushrooms appear.
Onions *Allium cepa* 	All climate zones are suitable but take care to plant the different types at the right time of year or results will be disappointing.	Sow seed where it is to grow or plant seedlings. Spacing for both is 3 in apart. Water seeds in and mulch with compost to conserve soil moisture and to prevent surface crusting. Plant a 20–30 ft long row of the long-keeping types, about half that for the others. You can plant the short-keeping types in batches. In zone 8 and above plant long-keeping onions in fall. Start spring onions and those not meant for storage any time except where frosts are sharp. In those areas avoid planting in coldest months. Don't plant in soil with a lot of recently added organic matter.	Keep the soil moist and feed plants every few months with low-nitrogen complete plant food. Stop watering long-keeping onions as they approach maturity. PROBLEMS Onion fly, which destroys the bulbs, is encouraged by excessive organic matter. Thrips may damage growth and downy mildew is a common disease. Don't allow weeds to establish around onions; pull them out when first seen. HARVESTING Pull spring or non-keeping onions as needed. Long-keeping onions are matured in the ground and pulled when the tops die back. Dry them thoroughly in the sun before storing them.

VEGETABLE	CLIMATE	PLANTING	GROWING
Parsnip *Pastinaca sativa* 	Suitable for all climate zones.	Sow seed where it is to grow, in fall and winter in southern states and from spring to summer in northern states. Soil must be dug over but not very rich—plant after another crop has been harvested.	Water deeply but not too frequently to encourage long roots. Pull weeds by hand and keep plants mulched in summer as hot soil is undesirable. PROBLEMS No serious diseases but aphids can cause leaves to distort—spray with soapy water or a mild insecticide. HARVESTING They are ready to harvest after 4–5 months. Lift the whole plant using a garden fork.
Peas *Pisum sativum* 	Peas may be grown in all climate zones but pea seeds won't germinate if the soil is colder than 50°F, and although the seedlings are frost resistant the flowers can be damaged. With that in mind, decide when it is best to sow in your area.	Sow seeds directly where they are to grow, 2 in deep and about 3 in apart. Plant into well-drained soil that has had a handful of complete plant food deeply dug into each yard of the row. Cover the fertilizer with soil and place the seeds on top so they don't touch it. Plant 10 ft of peas every three weeks for a continuous crop. In the north sow in early spring and onwards and in the south sow in fall and early winter.	Keep the soil moist and free from competing weeds. PROBLEMS Birds may pick the crop for you but otherwise peas are largely trouble-free. Don't plant peas in the same spot twice in succession. HARVESTING Pick garden peas and whole pod (sugar snap) peas as soon as they mature. Snow peas are picked when the pods are small and the peas just visible. Pick often as this will stimulate more flowers.
Potato *Solanum tuberosum* 	Grows in all zones.	Buy only certified, disease-free seed potatoes. Plant each 4 in deep into well-drained, fertile but not overly rich soil. Cover with soil and water them in. Start with six plants. Potatoes take 3–4 months to mature. In hot frost-free areas plant after the extreme heat of summer has passed, and in cold areas after frosts have finished in spring.	Keep moist but not wet, and as the plants grow, mound soil up around the stems so that none of the tubers is ever exposed to light. Remove weeds and stop watering as soon as the plants begin to die off. PROBLEMS Potato tuber moth leaves wiggly marks on the foliage and should be sprayed at first appearance. Aphids are another common pest and in humid weather leaf spotting or blighting diseases may occur. Control these with fungicides. HARVESTING Dig potatoes after the top growth has died.

VEGETABLE	CLIMATE	PLANTING	GROWING
Pumpkin *Cucurbita* species 	All zones but the growing season may be too short in the far north.	Pumpkin is a warm-season crop. Sow seed directly where it is to grow or, in cooler areas, in pots several weeks before the arrival of warm, late spring weather. Soil must be free-draining, fertile and rich in rotted organic matter.	Water deeply, weekly and mulch around plants with straw. Try to keep water off the foliage and flowers. Pull weeds promptly and to ensure good fruit set, brush pollen from male flowers onto stigmas of female flowers. Apply low nitrogen fertilizer when fruit begin to form. PROBLEMS Mildew is common in humid weather: control with a suitable fungicide. Aphids and pumpkin beetle will attack plants especially in spring and early summer: control when first seen or damage may be severe. HARVESTING Pick before frosts when the vine has died down. Leave a portion of the hard, dry stem attached to the pumpkin. Fruit is ripe when it sounds hollow.
Radish *Raphanus sativus* 	Suitable for all climate zones.	Sow seed directly where it is to grow any time of year except the coldest months. In zones 9 and 10, radishes can be sown year-round. Soil must drain freely and be friable and fertile.	Keep moist but not overwet. Feed with liquid or soluble plant food at fortnightly intervals. PROBLEMS Caterpillars and aphids are the main pests. Pick off and squash the former, spray the latter with soapy water or a mild, pyrethrum insecticide. HARVESTING Ready to pull anytime from about a month after seedlings emerge. Don't let plants get too big—they are sweetest and most tender when young.
Shallot *Allium cepa* Aggregatum group 	Grows in all zones.	Push the individual cloves just beneath the surface, pointy end up and about 8 in apart. Do this in early spring or in fall in warm climates. The bulbs form clumps like garlic and about a dozen plants is enough for starters. Plant into any well-drained, reasonably fertile soil.	Keep the soil moist while the plants are growing but stop watering when the plant is fully mature and the leaves are beginning to yellow. PROBLEMS No particular problems. HARVESTING Harvest when the tops of the plants die back. Lift the whole knob and dry it in the sun before storing.

VEGETABLE	CLIMATE	PLANTING	GROWING
Silver beet Also known as spinach, especially in warm areas *Beta vulgaris* var. *cicla* 	Grows in all zones.	Sow seeds directly where they are to grow, 14 in apart. Plant into soil enriched with rotted manure and a handful of high nitrogen complete plant food per square yard. Sow any time except in the heat of summer or when frosts are worst. Seedlings are able to withstand frost. About five plants is plenty. For year-round supplies of this vegetable, plant a batch in spring and another in fall. Silver beet grows well when planted in large containers.	Keep watered and give high nitrogen soluble fertilizer every 4–6 weeks (not in winter if frosty). PROBLEMS Aphids and leaf miners may distort or disfigure leaves and should be treated promptly. HARVESTING Pick the outer leaves as needed. Don't strip the whole plant.
Spinach *Spinacea oleracea* 	In mild climates can be grown through winter; in cold regions treat as a summer crop.	Sow seed thinly directly where it is to grow into cool soil that has been previously enriched with rotted organic matter. Sow a row 6 ft long every three weeks for a constant supply of this vegetable. Sow in spring in cold and cool climates and in fall in warm regions.	Keep moist and feed plants fortnightly with high nitrogen soluble fertilizer. Mulch around plants with straw to keep the area clean and always remove competing weeds. PROBLEMS Susceptible to fungus diseases in rainy or humid weather. HARVESTING Pull whole plants or remove the outer leaves. The harvesting season is short.

VEGETABLE	CLIMATE	PLANTING	GROWING
Swede *Brassica napus* Napobrassica group 	Very hardy. Will stand over winter in the north.	Sow seeds in spring where it is to grow or in fall in warm regions. Sow or thin to 9 in apart. Soil that has grown a previous crop is ideal for swedes (but not if that crop was cabbages, broccoli or Brussels sprouts).	Don't allow the seedlings or developing vegetables to dry out. Apply a ration of complete plant food about a month after planting. Keep weeds down and don't hill soil around the exposed top of the root. PROBLEMS Caterpillars and aphids are the main pests. Both can be controlled with pyrethrum-based insecticides. HARVESTING Pull the whole root before it gets too big and woody. Plants are usually ready for harvest 3–4 months after seedlings emerge.
Sweet corn *Zea mays* 	Possible in all zones except in regions with short summers.	Sow seeds about 2 in deep and 12 in apart in well-drained, fertile soil. Get more corn by sowing in a block (three rows of three is good). In frost-free zones sow from fall to early spring. In other zones sow from mid-spring to early summer.	Keep moist and give a ration of complete plant food when plants are about half grown. Remove weeds as they appear but don't dig around the roots. PROBLEMS Caterpillars attack the cobs and aphids suck sap and spread diseases. Control both pests with the one insecticide. Cobs may need netting against bird attacks. HARVESTING Pick corn when the silks have browned and the cobs stand at an angle. White, not clear, sap will ooze from a pierced kernel when it is ripe.
Sweet potato *Ipomoea batatas* 	Best in warm regions: zones 9 and 10 and above.	Grow from cuttings or from shoots from a purchased tuber. Plant the cuttings or shoots very shallowly into wide ridges of soil that has grown a previous crop. Space the cuttings or shoots 12 in apart and water them in well. Sweet potato plants run over the ground (6 ft or more in all directions) and all that space must be weed-free. Start them off in middle to late spring. Try planting about five of these plants to begin.	Keep moist. If planted into fertile soil, no feeding is needed. PROBLEMS Sweet potato is usually trouble-free in the home garden but don't plant it in the same spot twice. HARVESTING Harvest when the vine begins to die back (approximately 20 weeks after planting). Be careful, the tubers damage easily.

VEGETABLE	CLIMATE	PLANTING	GROWING
Tomato *Lycopersicon esculentum* 	Suitable for all zones but in regions with very short summers may not be successful.	Two to four plants are usually enough. Tall-growing types will need the support of at least one 6 ft tall stake but a teepee arrangement of three can be better. Place the stakes in the garden before planting. In the tropics and other frost-free areas, tomatoes can be grown year round. In cooler climates plant them out only when you're certain night temperatures are always above 45°F. Tomatoes are heavy feeders and require soil well enriched with rotted manure that has been dug in about a month before planting.	Keep the soil evenly moist and mulch around the plants with straw or compost. If weeds appear, pull rather than dig them out as tomatoes have roots at the surface. Feed the plants monthly with soluble tomato food (a low nitrogen, high phosphorus fertilizer that encourages flowering and fruiting). Pinching out most laterals (shoots that appear at leaf junctions) produces better sized fruit. PROBLEMS Fruit fly, caterpillars, aphids, thrips and mites may all attack tomatoes and the plants are also susceptible to a number of virus diseases and rots. Growing the plants in well-drained soil and in full sun is your best defence. HARVESTING Pick when ripe. In warm climates the fruiting season is quite long. The best flavored fruit is fully vine ripened.
Turnip *Brassica rapa* Rapifera group 	A temperate crop taking only light frosts.	Sow seed in spring and early summer directly where it is to grow. Sow or thin to 4 in apart. Soil that has grown a previous crop is ideal for turnips (but not if that crop was cabbages, broccoli or Brussels sprouts).	Don't allow the seedlings or developing vegetables to dry out. Apply complete plant food a month after planting. Keep weeds down and don't hill soil around the exposed top of the root. PROBLEMS Caterpillars and aphids are the main pests: control with pyrethrum-based insecticides. HARVESTING Pull the whole root before it gets too big and woody. Plants are usually ready for harvest 2–3 months after seedlings emerge.
Zucchini Also known as courgette *Cucurbita pepo* 	Suitable for all climate zones but frost sensitive.	Sow seeds directly where they are to grow into warm soil. In cooler areas, sow in pots and plant out when the soil temperature rises. Zucchini is a warm season crop that grows best when night temperatures are always over 50°F. Soil must be heavily fertilized and rich in rotted organic matter.	Keep free of weeds and water well but try to keep the leaves and stems dry. Hand pollination of the flowers may be necessary, especially in cooler areas. PROBLEMS Mildew strikes leaves in humid weather and must be controlled with a fungicide. Watch for aphids and pumpkin beetle: pick off by hand or spray with an all-purpose insecticide. HARVESTING Pick when fruits are 4 in long. Growth is rapid and large zucchini are woody and bitter. Constant picking prolongs production.

•CHAPTER THIRTY•

HERBS

No garden is complete without herbs. They're invaluable in the kitchen and can also be used in cosmetics, craft arrangements and natural remedies. Even if you never use them, most make delightful garden plants, some even repelling insect pests.

CHOOSING HERBS TO GROW

The herbs to grow are the ones you like best, those that feature in your favorite recipes or craft activities. (Chances are you'll already have them, dried, in your kitchen.) You will probably need several plants of these herbs to avoid harvesting them to death. However, don't let unfamiliarity stop you from trying out a plant or two of a herb with looks or fragrance that appeal to you. If you never use them, so what?

PLANTING HERBS

Herbs are traditionally grown in gardens of their own and a small, formal herb garden with its beds divided by paths arranged around a central feature, such as a statue or a sundial, can be a very pretty and appealing feature. Marshalling herbs into formal beds flatters them, and you can play their subtle foliage colors and textures off against one another. Not many herbs offer much in the way of flowers, although bergamot and pineapple sage are as bright as you could want: but there is nothing to stop you from adding a few annuals to the bed just for color, and heartsease is often used for this.

Conversely, you can plant herbs in flower beds where their subtle greens and grays will set off the bright flowers behind, as well as adding scent. If you plant them along the edges of paths, they will release aroma on the air as you brush past. A third way to use them is to be strictly utilitarian and plant them to edge the beds in the vegetable garden. Here they will give you something to look at when the vegetable beds are bare between crops, and they often help repel insect pests.

HERBS IN POTS

Most varieties grow very well in pots, which means that even if all the garden you have is an apartment balcony you can still have the pleasure of fresh herbs. You might even like to give them a box on the kitchen window-sill so that you can just reach out and harvest them as you need them—but only if the window gets the sun. It is preferable, too, for the box to be outside in the fresh air.

HARVESTING HERBS

Always gather herbs just as they are coming into flower (when the flavor is strongest). You can use them fresh or dry them for later use by spreading

HERB GARDENS are traditionally laid out in a geometric pattern, usually centered on a feature such as a statue, birdbath, sundial or fountain. The beds within are separated by gravel or brick-paved paths and a herb hedge may surround the lot.

them out on a table in the shade or hanging them upside down in bunches. Alternatively, use the microwave oven to dry them. Gather the herbs, spread them on a paper towel, cover them with another, and zap them with full power for a minute or two. If they aren't quite dry, give them some more time with the top towel off. The precise timing depends on what sort of herb it is and how dry the leaves were to start with.

MAINTENANCE

Growing herbs is easy. As a general rule, they love sunshine and don't need much water; indeed the flavor is richest if they aren't encouraged to grow too lush. They don't, however, appreciate being starved: give them good, well-drained soil and some fertilizer occasionally. The main exceptions to the rule are basil and chives, which do best with generous feeding and regular watering, and bergamot and the various mints, which are lovers of constantly damp soil. Most herbs have few or no specific pest or disease problems, in fact quite a few herbs will actually repel the very insects that would otherwise be attacking your ornamental plants and when rubbed onto the skin can act as a natural, personal insect repellant. You'll find more detail about the growing requirements of each in the description of each species.

ALOE VERA

Aloe vera, syn. A. barbadensis

FEATURES: A freely suckering, rosette-forming plant with thick, fleshy, pointy leaves. These are light green, streaked gray, often with a red tinge in cooler weather. Pendulous yellow and orange flowers appear in spring. Grows 24 in tall and wide.
CLIMATE: Zone 10 and above.
FROST TOLERANCE: None. In frosty areas grow in pots brought into a sunny room in winter.
ASPECT: Full sun gives the best results. As shade increases, plants lose their compactness.
PLANTING: In pots, grow in well-drained soil-based potting compost. Small plants can be planted anytime, except in very hot or very cold areas where spring is best. Plants prefer poor, sandy soils that drain fast and they will die suddenly in sodden soils.
GROWING: Water sparingly and don't feed garden grown plants at all. Give those in pots a ration of slow release granules once each spring. If more plants are wanted, remove young, rooted offsets in spring.
HARVESTING: Snap off leaves and rub gel over skin to soothe sunburn or moisturize dry skin.

ALOE VERA has long been valued for its soothing, cooling gel-like sap.

FOR BEST FLAVOR grow basil fast with lots of water. Harvest it while it's young.

BASIL

Ocimum basilicum, O. tenuiflorum

FEATURES: There are annual and perennial basil bushes and all have a strong and appealing aroma and flavor. Leaves may be yellow-green, dark green or purple and the plants range in height from 12 in to 30 in.
CLIMATE: Basils are very sensitive to frost and prolonged cold, damp weather. Suitable for growing out of doors all year round only in zone 10 and above. Elsewhere treat as a summer crop.
FROST TOLERANCE: None.
ASPECT: Full sun except in hot areas where afternoon shade is appreciated.
PLANTING: Plant in rich, moist, well-drained soil containing plenty of compost or old manure. Don't mulch until the soil has warmed up as basil roots need heat for growth.
GROWING: Keep evenly moist and feed monthly with a nitrogen-rich liquid fertilizer, fortnightly if plants are growing in pots. Keep the centers pinched to inhibit flowering and promote a bushier plant.
HARVESTING: Fresh leaves or sprigs can be picked at any time or harvested and dried during late summer. Leaves become bitter and too strong if plants are neglected or too old.

BAY TREE

Laurus nobilis

FEATURES: A slow-growing, aromatic, evergreen tree reaching 10–50 ft tall, the bay is often grown in pots to control its size. It is sometimes topiaried into formal shapes. The leaves are the edible part of the plant.
CLIMATE: This tree is not too hardy as it comes from southern Europe and the Canary Islands. However, it is suitable for zone 8 and above.
FROST TOLERANCE: Accepts a low of 10°F.
ASPECT: Where summers are mild, full sun is essential. Elsewhere, give afternoon shade in summer.
PLANTING: Plant in spring or fall into average, well-drained soil.
GROWING: Water generously from mid-fall to mid-spring. In summer, bays tolerate drier conditions and watering should be reduced. Mulch under and beyond the foliage in fall with rotted manure and apply a ration of complete plant food.
HARVESTING: Pick leaves early in the day throughout the year and use fresh or dried. Bay leaves are an essential component of the "bouquet garni" and are also used to flavor soups, stews and many other dishes.

BAY TREES do best where winters are cool and wet, summers hot and dry.

BORAGE FLOWERS are pretty and edible. Cut them off after bloom, before seeds drop.

BORAGE

Borago officinalis

FEATURES: Fast-growing, branching annual to about 24 in tall. Leaves are big, bristly and gray-green in color and the pretty spring flowers are a delicate sky blue with a deeper purplish center.
CLIMATE: A summer annual, borage is suitable for all zones.
ASPECT: Full sun or partial shade.
PLANTING: Seed is sown in early spring as the soil is warming up and drying out. Borage does not like transplanting, so thin out the seedlings. It prefers poor, sandy, well-drained soil.
GROWING: Water sparingly and don't feed or plants will grow lank and weak-stemmed. This plant seeds freely and can become a nuisance. Pull out unwanted seedlings promptly.
HARVESTING: Newly opened flowers can be picked for garnishing drinks or salads. Young leaves are edible and have a cucumber-like flavor. Use in drinks or salads.

CARAWAY
Carum carvi

FEATURES: Caraway grows to around 2 ft. The leaves are aromatic and finely cut and in summer the plant produces heads of small, white flowers. These are followed by dark brown seeds. All parts of the plant, including the roots, are edible.
CLIMATE: Zone 3 and above.
FROST TOLERANCE: Takes –40°F.
ASPECT: Full sun is best but caraway tolerates a few hours of afternoon shade. Shelter from wind is desirable.
PLANTING: Grow plants from seed sown in early spring or, where winters are mild, in fall. Sow shallowly, 6–8 in apart, or thin to that spacing after germination. Deeply dug, good quality, well-drained soil allows the roots to grow straight and long. In zones 9 and 10 grow it as a mild season annual.
GROWING: Water deeply during dry times and feed once or twice with a liquid or soluble fertilizer.
HARVESTING: Seed heads are picked when ripe. Young, spring leaves are picked as needed and the roots are dug in late spring. Seeds are used in baking. Leaves are added to salads, and roots can be steamed or boiled and eaten as a vegetable.

LIGHT AND AIRY caraway is an annual but it can be a biennial in some regions.

A POPULAR TEA, chamomile also makes a good lawn substitute.

CHAMOMILE
Chamaemelum nobile

FEATURES: A low, spreading plant about 12 in tall and 18 in across, chamomile has feathery, evergreen leaves topped in spring with small white daisies. Flowers have a spicy, sweet fragrance reminiscent of apples. They are attractive to bees.
CLIMATE: Suitable for zone 4 and above, through to Mediterranean climates, zones 9 and 10.
FROST TOLERANCE: Takes –30°F.
ASPECT: Full sun gives lowest, most compact growth. Tolerates partial shade where summers are hot.
PLANTING: Plant or sow seeds in spring. Existing plants can be divided into rooted sections then, too. Plants do best in moisture-retentive yet well-drained soil. Plant 8 in apart.
GROWING: Keep well watered in summer as it won't tolerate dryness for long. Apply liquid or soluble fertilizer 2–3 times in spring and summer. You can mow after flowering but don't cut too low.
HARVESTING: Pick the flowers in the morning and spread them out to dry in a warm place for a few days. Store in an airtight glass jar. Use as a garnish in salads or as a refreshing tea.

CHERVIL

Anthriscus cerefolium

FEATURES: Chervil is a ferny-leaved annual herb growing to 24 in tall with something of a liquorice flavor. It has tiny, white summer flowers that are produced in small, flat heads.
CLIMATE: Grows best in cooler climates—zone 6 and above—but does not thrive in intense summer heat.
FROST TOLERANCE: Takes –10°F.
ASPECT: It thrives in shade or partial shade. Avoid very hot sunny positions.
PLANTING: Sow seed in early spring or early fall in humus-rich, moisture-retentive, yet well-drained soil. A position among taller herbs, vegetables or flowers suits chervil.
GROWING: Keep moist at all times and always remove flower stems as they form as this will keep plants growing longer. Apply liquid or soluble fertilizer twice in spring and again in summer.
HARVESTING: Along with parsley, chives and tarragon, chervil leaves are an ingredient in *fines herbes*. Leaves can be picked anytime after about a month from germination.

CHERVIL IS one of the few herbs that do better in shade than sun.

AN EASY and useful herb to grow, chives are ideal for pots.

CHIVES

Allium schoenoprasum, A. tuberosum

FEATURES: Chives grow in grassy clumps from very small bulbs. The leaves have a mild onion flavor. Chinese or garlic chives (*A. tuberosum*) have bigger leaves that have a strong garlic taste. Both types grow well in small containers.
CLIMATE: Zone 5 and above, zone 7 for *A. tuberosum*.
FROST TOLERANCE: Chives tolerate – 20°F; garlic chives accept winter lows of 0°F.
ASPECT: These plants grow best in full sun but tolerate partial shade. In very hot, dry climates they may require a little shading and humidity.
PLANTING: A pot of garden center-bought chives can be planted any time although it is best to avoid the worst of summer and winter where those seasons are severe. Grow in average, well-drained soil or in pots.
GROWING: Keep the soil moist, especially if growing chives in pots. If clumps become overcrowded in pots or in the garden, lift them in fall or spring, break them into smaller clumps and replant them.
HARVESTING: Clip leaves close to the ground any time. Flowers are edible and look good in salads.

CORIANDER IS an essential ingredient in many Indian and Thai dishes.

CORIANDER

Coriandrum sativum

FEATURES: Also known as Chinese parsley or cilantro, this annual grows fast to about 20 in. The feathery, strongly flavored leaves, the seeds and roots are all edible. Coriander can be grown in pots.
CLIMATE: Likes hot, dry summers and wet winters but as it is an annual it can be grown in all climate zones.
FROST TOLERANCE: None. It is a warm season annual.
ASPECT: Prefers a sunny position but accepts partial shade in very hot areas.
PLANTING: Sow seeds directly where they are to grow in spring and, where winters are frost-free, in fall, too. Beds need to be well drained but not over-rich, as too much nitrogen lessens the flavor. Successive sowings several weeks apart extend the cropping period.
GROWING: Keep the soil evenly moist and do not allow weeds to compete with the plants.
HARVESTING: Pick fresh leaves as required, the smaller immature leaves having the better taste. Harvest seed when leaves and flowers turn brown. Use coriander sparingly in salads, in Asian recipes and in curries.

CURRY PLANT

Helichrysum italicum

FEATURES: This bushy, evergreen shrublet grows to 24 in tall and can spread wider. Its stems and narrow, 2 in long leaves are silvery gray and give off a distinct curry-like aroma. Small heads of golden flowers appear in summer and fall.
CLIMATE: Suitable for zone 8 and above. Dry climates are best—ideal for Mediterranean-type climates.
FROST TOLERANCE: Takes 10°F without damage. Provide winter protection in colder regions.
ASPECT: Full sun and an open, airy position are essential for optimum growth. Avoid an enclosed area with a humid atmosphere.
PLANTING: Best planted in early fall or spring in deep, free-draining sandy or gravelly soil. Roots easily from cuttings taken in early fall or spring.
GROWING: Although it takes dry conditions reasonably well, water weekly from spring to fall if it does not rain. Trim plants lightly in early spring to ensure compact growth. Remove dead flowers regularly.
HARVESTING: Flowers for drying are cut when opened. Cut leaves for potpourri. They don't taste like curry.

STRONGLY AROMATIC, curry plant scents the air after summer rain.

DILL

Anethum graveolens

FEATURES: Usually growing less than 3 ft tall, the annual dill is often mistaken for the similar looking, but taller growing, fennel. Dill has fine, dark green, feathery foliage and, in summer, flattened heads of small yellow flowers.
CLIMATE: Suitable for zone 8 and above.
FROST TOLERANCE: Dill is grown during the warmer months but it will take a low of 10°F.
ASPECT: Sun or, in hot areas, partial shade. Shelter from strong winds is essential as plants are weak.
PLANTING: Sow seeds in spring, after frosts, directly where plants are to grow. Dill prefers deep, fertile, moist, well-drained soil and plants or seeds should be spaced about 10 in apart.
GROWING: Keep moist always as dryness causes dill to go to seed. In good quality soil, do not feed but do sprinkle a little lime around plants and lightly work it in.
HARVESTING: Leaves can be cut fresh as needed. For preserving, cut leaves and dry in shade or freeze leaves in plastic bags for later use. Remove flowers as they form or dill will take over the garden.

DILL IS DECORATIVE as well as useful but it can be invasive if seeds fall.

A CLUMP of galangal can be grown from a rhizome purchased from the fruit shop.

GALANGAL

Alpinia galanga

FEATURES: This tall, tropical rhizomatous perennial produces a clump of upright stems similar to the ornamental gingers. Leaves are big, dark green and shaped like a spearhead. Flowers, which appear anytime, are greenish with white tips.
CLIMATE: Grow outside in zone 10 and above. Elsewhere grow in a warm humid glasshouse or conservatory, either in pots or in a soil bed.
FROST TOLERANCE: None.
ASPECT: In the tropics, galangal needs partial shade but in cooler areas it will take more sun.
PLANTING: Fresh, store-bought rhizomes can be planted in spring or fall or existing plants can be dug up and divided then. In cooler areas, don't start until late spring. Plant into rich, fertile, well-drained soil.
GROWING: Keep well watered whenever the plant has leaves. In cooler areas it dies back in winter when it should be left dry. Feed in spring and summer by mulching with rotted manure.
HARVESTING: In spring or fall harvest by lifting a rhizome, removing the amount wanted and replanting. Use as flavoring in Asian cuisines.

GARLIC
Allium sativum

FEATURES: Garlic is one of the world's most important foods and has a long list of medicinal uses, too.
CLIMATE: Suitable for zone 8 and above, garlic grows best in warm, dry climates. In colder regions grow this herb as a summer crop.
FROST TOLERANCE: Accepts a low of 10°F.
ASPECT: Full sun is essential.
PLANTING: Good drainage is essential but, given that, garlic is not fussy about soil. At mid-fall or in early spring, push cloves into the soil, pointy end up. Space about 8 in apart, cover with soil and water in well. Apply a small amount of fertilizer and then mulch lightly with compost or rotted manure.
GROWING: Newly planted garlic needs moisture but not wetness in fall and winter. If rain does not fall, water weekly. Gradually reduce watering in spring, as garlic needs a hot, dry summer.
HARVESTING: Harvest garlic when the leaves have yellowed (summer or fall). Don't cut the dead leaves off as they may be used to plait the bulbs together for storage. After harvest, wash the bulbs clean and then leave them in the sun for a few days to dry.

START YOUR OWN garlic from cloves broken from a knob of bought garlic.

EASY TO GROW in frost-free areas, fresh ginger has many culinary uses.

GINGER
Zingiber officinale

FEATURES: In the tropics, grows up to 10 ft tall as a clump of erect, leafy stems. Elsewhere, 5 ft is more usual. Yellow flowers are not showy.
CLIMATE: Suits zone 10 and above. In lower zones grow in a warm humid glasshouse or conservatory. Shelter plants from hot winds.
FROST TOLERANCE: None.
ASPECT: In tropical areas needs partial shade but in cooler places will accept more sun.
PLANTING: Plant fresh rhizomes, bought from food stores, in spring or dig existing plants up to divide them. Needs rich, well-drained soil and plenty of space as it will spread. Under glass, best grown in a bed.
GROWING: Keep moist whenever the plant has leaves. Out of the tropics, ginger dies back in winter and should be kept dry then. Feed by mulching with rotted manure in spring and summer. Out of the tropics, growth can be slow.
HARVESTING: In spring or fall harvest rhizomes by lifting the plant and removing the amount wanted. Replant immediately.

HORSERADISH

Armoracia rusticana

FEATURES: Horseradish is a clump-forming, wide-spreading perennial with spinach-like leaves and a long, deep tap root. In late spring or summer insignificant, white, cross-shaped flowers appear on long stems.
CLIMATE: It is very hardy and suitable for zone 5 and above, through to Mediterranean-type climates.
FROST TOLERANCE: Takes a low of –20°F.
ASPECT: Full sun, except where summers are very hot. There, some afternoon shade is helpful.
PLANTING: Horseradish is very invasive, a new plant springing from small sections of root left in the ground. If possible, grow it in a pot at least 18 in deep. Establish young plants in spring or plant sections of pencil-thick roots in fall. Space 12 in apart. Soil must be rich.
GROWING: When plants appear in spring, mulch around them with rotted manure. Keep moist and feed monthly with soluble plant food.
HARVESTING: Roots can be dug anytime. Grated root is used to give sauces and dishes a spicy heat.

IN THE GARDEN, plant horseradish only where it can be easily contained.

LEMON BALM is a desirable garden plant whether or not you use the aromatic leaves.

LEMON BALM

Melissa officinalis

FEATURES: A spreading, bushy perennial growing to 40 in high, lemon balm has small, serrated leaves with a lemon scent. The plants are very sensitive to frosts and may die back during winter but established plants will regenerate in spring.
CLIMATE: This is quite a hardy herb and will thrive in zone 4 and above. It will perform best where winters are frosty.
FROST TOLERANCE: Accepts a low of –30°F.
ASPECT: Full sun or partial shade.
PLANTING: Existing plants can be divided and established elsewhere in fall or a purchased specimen can be planted in spring. The best soil is well drained and fertile.
GROWING: Consistent moisture and a spring ration of complete plant food is all the care needed. Cut the plant to the ground in late fall.
HARVESTING: Pick fresh leaves as required. Whole stems may be cut when flowers begin to emerge and then dried. Leaves are most tender and full of flavor in spring. Fresh leaves and flowers are used in salads and the leaves also make a refreshing tea or can be added to cold drinks.

THE WHITE, lower stems of lemon grass are used in Asian recipes or to make tea.

LEMON GRASS

Cymbopogon citratus

FEATURES: Also known as citronella grass, lemon grass is a perennial tropical grass that grows in clumps 3 ft or more tall and wide. The white, succulent lower stems are the edible part and are strongly lemon flavored. It grows well in pots.
CLIMATE: Suitable for anywhere that is frost free. Zone 9 and above.
FROST TOLERANCE: None.
ASPECT: Prefers full sun or, in hotter areas, partial shade.
PLANTING: Existing plants can be divided in spring or a plant can be purchased from a garden center then. Plant into well-drained but fertile soil that contains plenty of organic matter.
GROWING: Needs plenty of water year round but be most generous from mid-spring to late summer. Feed occasionally with a high nitrogen plant food.
HARVESTING: Harvest a few stems at a time as needed. Scratch away some soil to expose the base of the section desired and pull the whole piece out. Replace the soil immediately. Chopped stems can be added to recipes or used to make a refreshing tea.

LEMON VERBENA

Aloysia triphylla

FEATURES: An attractive deciduous shrub with lemon-scented leaves and sprays of delicate, small white flowers in summer, this plant can grow up to 10 ft tall with a similar spread. It remains evergreen in the tropics.
CLIMATE: Zone 9 and above. In lower zones grow in a cool glasshouse or conservatory.
FROST TOLERANCE: Takes 23°F.
ASPECT: Under glass provide bright light. Full sun out of doors.
PLANTING: Plant or pot in spring. Under glass grow plants in pots of well-drained, loam-based potting compost. Out of doors plants will thrive in quite poor, well-drained, even dry soil.
GROWING: Under glass keep moist during the growing season but much drier in winter when the plant is resting. Plants under glass appreciate being fed monthly in the summer with a liquid fertilizer. Outdoor plants can be mulched in fall with rotted organic matter. Prune in spring to maintain a compact habit.
HARVESTING: Pick leaves any time for use in potpourri or as a refreshing tea. Finely chopped leaves can be added to dishes.

A SWEET LEMON aroma surrounds the decorative and useful lemon verbena.

MARJORAM AND OREGANO are related and are very similar in habit.

MARJORAM AND OREGANO

Origanum majorana,
Origanum vulgare

FEATURES: Marjoram and oregano are related and rather similar. These are bushy plants and both need the same treatment in the garden or they can be grown in pots.
CLIMATE: Best in cooler areas. Zone 7 and above for marjoram, zone 5 for oregano.
FROST TOLERANCE: Minimum of 0°F for marjoram, –20°F for oregano.
ASPECT: Full sun is essential.
PLANTING: Plant in spring into fairly rich but very well-drained soil. Both plants can be propagated by taking cuttings in mid-spring or by dividing existing plants in fall. Oregano stems root at intervals and rooted pieces can be detached.
GROWING: Water in early spring but reduce watering as summer approaches. In summer water only to prevent wilting. A ration of complete plant food sprinkled onto the plants in early spring is all the feeding needed.
HARVESTING: Leaves and flower buds are used fresh in spring and summer. Alternatively, cut stems down to 2 in above the ground and hang to dry in a cool, shady spot.

MINT

Mentha species

FEATURES: All varieties of mint have invasive runners that are best confined in pots. Different varieties have different aromas, including apple and eau-de-cologne as well as the more usual peppermint and spearmint.
CLIMATE: There are mints for most zones.
FROST TOLERANCE: Varies with species. The hardiest, such as *M. spicata* or spearmint take a low of -40°F.
ASPECT: Full sun or partial shade. In full sun it must be kept very well watered.
PLANTING: Rooted sections of existing mint or purchased plants can be established in spring or fall (any time in frost-free gardens). Soil should be moderately rich and well mulched to retain moisture. Too much organic matter or fresh manures will, however, encourage rust diseases.
GROWING: Mint must always have plenty of water.
HARVESTING: Young leaves or sprigs are picked any time. Fresh leaves can be chopped and frozen in small packages or ice cubes. Frequent picking of sprigs helps to keep the plants compact.

EAU-DE-COLOGNE MINT has the refreshing aroma of that famous perfume.

THE FLOWERS and young, tender leaves of nasturtium are both edible in salads.

NASTURTIUM

Tropaeolum majus

FEATURES: This fast-growing, groundcovering, warm season annual has round, aromatic leaves and funnel-shaped flowers in cream, yellow, orange and red shades. Given support, it can be induced to climb.
CLIMATE: Suitable for growing outdoors in all climate zones if sown when frosts are over.
FROST TOLERANCE: None. It is a warm season annual.
ASPECT: Full sun or, in very hot areas, dappled afternoon shade.
PLANTING: In frost-free areas, sow seed in late fall or early spring. In frosty areas, sow in spring. Start bought plants in early spring. Nasturtiums flower best and remain more compact in poor, sandy or gravelly soils. Fertile soil results in lush growth but fewer flowers. Plant 10 in apart in gardens or grow several plants in a hanging basket.
GROWING: Don't feed and water only during dry times.
HARVESTING: One or two chopped leaves add piquancy to salads. Use young, small leaves only. The flowers are also edible and add color to salads.

PARSLEY

Petroselinum species

FEATURES: Parsley lives for two years and grows from a strong taproot with erect stems bearing divided, small leaves that may be flattish or curly depending on variety.
CLIMATE: Suitable for zone 7 and above. In warm or hot regions it is grown as a mild season annual.
FROST TOLERANCE: Accepts 0°F if the roots are heavily mulched with straw in fall. This isn't necessary in areas of little or no frost.
ASPECT: Full sun or partial shade.
PLANTING: Seeds are slow to germinate and, as one plant is usually sufficient, most gardeners buy a small one. Plant any time in frost-free areas, in spring in cooler zones. Soil should drain freely but need not be especially rich. Established plants may self-seed if the plant is allowed to flower.
GROWING: Keep the soil evenly moist for faster growth and best flavor. A ration of complete fertilizer applied once in spring is sufficient.
HARVESTING: New growth comes from the center of the stem, and so always pick from the outside. Sprigs can be picked as needed. Curly-leaved parsley freezes well.

CURLY PARSLEY is one of the two varieties usually grown. The other is Italian parsley.

PYRETHRUM

Tanacetum cinerariifolium

FEATURES: A low-growing perennial perhaps 18 in tall and wide, pyrethrum is a daisy that produces a natural insecticide. Its leaves are finely cut and ferny, topped in summer by small, yellow-centered white flowers.
CLIMATE: Zone 6 and above are the most suitable.
FROST TOLERANCE: Takes a low of –10°F.
ASPECT: Full sun.
PLANTING: Needs well-drained soil and tolerates poor, stony or gravelly sites. Seed can be sown in fall or spring but most gardeners buy it as a small plant in early spring. Plant 12 in apart or scatter among other herbs or vegetables.
GROWING: Keep moist until flower buds appear, then water only to prevent wilting. Keep weeds away and replace plants every few years by cuttings or division. Don't replant in the same spot.
HARVESTING: The plant is not usually harvested. It is grown for its ornamental value and alleged insect repelling qualities.

PYRETHRUM IS the plant from which many insecticides are made.

THE YOUNG, small leaves of rocket are the sweetest. Keep sowing new batches.

ROCKET

Eruca sativa

FEATURES: Also known as arugula, this annual has lobed, dark green leaves with a pleasant peppery, nutty flavor. Except to save seed, don't let it flower or it may invade the garden.
CLIMATE: Zone 7 and above.
FROST TOLERANCE: 0°F.
ASPECT: In spring grow in full sun, in summer, afternoon shade helps.
PLANTING: Grow in fertile, well-drained soil. Sow seeds after frosts, 3/4 in deep and 15 in apart. As rocket grows fast and young leaves are the most palatable, make new sowings every four weeks until mid-fall. When the latest batch of seedlings is big enough to pick from, pull out the previous batch. In the tropics, start sowing in late fall and continue until the end of winter.
GROWING: Keep moist as dryness makes it bitter. Feed every two weeks with high nitrogen soluble fertilizer.
HARVESTING: Start picking young leaves when plants are a month old. Young leaves give green salads an appealing piquancy or they can be added late to stir frys. Ripe seedpods are also edible. Pick when plump.

ROSEMARY IS an attractive and useful shrub, especially in seaside gardens.

ROSEMARY

Rosmarinus officinalis

FEATURES: An evergreen shrub, rosemary has strongly aromatic leaves. There are several varieties, ranging in habit from upright to prostrate and in height from 18 in to over 6 ft.
CLIMATE: A native of the Mediterranean region, rosemary will be happy in zone 6 and above. Provide shelter from desiccating winds. In cold climates, rosemary does not enjoy prolonged winter wetness.
FROST TOLERANCE: Will accept –10°F if grown in a sunny, sheltered, well-drained spot.
ASPECT: Likes full sun and a reasonably dry position.
PLANTING: Plant in spring or fall into deep, well-drained soil. One bush is enough for culinary needs but several plants make a handsome, low hedge.
GROWING: Give average garden watering, a little more in winter than in summer. No feeding is necessary.
HARVESTING: Fresh leaves or sprigs 2–4 in long can be picked at any time of the year as required.

SAGE

Salvia species

FEATURES: Sage is a small, woody perennial—the various kinds include the ornamental purple sage (*S.* x *superba*) and pineapple sage (*S. rutilans*). The edible one is the common sage (*S. officinalis*), and its varieties such as the golden sage "Aurea".
CLIMATE: The common sage is quite hardy and will thrive in zone 5 and above.
FROST TOLERANCE: Varies with the species but the common sage will take a low of –20°F.
ASPECT: A sunny, sheltered, well-drained position suits all types.
PLANTING: Plant out in spring or fall (any time in frost-free areas) into very well-drained, quite rich soil.
GROWING: Water young plants often until established, and then reduce watering. Sage becomes rank and untidy if conditions are too good. Replace plants with rooted cuttings every three or four years.
HARVESTING: Leaves or flowers can be picked any time. For drying, harvest leaves before flowering begins. Fresh or dried leaves are used extensively as a food flavoring.

COMMON SAGE has gray or purple leaves and is aromatic on hot nights.

THE FRAGRANT LEAVES of scented geraniums come in many different aromas.

SCENTED GERANIUM

Pelargonium species

FEATURES: These plants may be sprawling perennials, shrublets or shrubs but all have furry or bristly, highly aromatic leaves. The range of fragrances is remarkable: peppermint, apple, citronella and rose to name a few. Flowers are not showy.
CLIMATE: Grow out of doors permanently only in frost-free climates. In areas prone to frost grow plants in pots in a frost-free glasshouse and plant outside for the summer. They prefer a dry atmosphere and are not suited to humid climates.
FROST TOLERANCE: None.
ASPECT: Grow in full sun for strongest aroma, or in partial shade.
PLANTING: Plant out only after frosts have finished in the spring. Space plants 18–24 in apart in moderately fertile but very well-drained soil. Cuttings root easily in summer.
GROWING: Water young plants to establish but when they are growing well water only sufficiently to prevent wilting. Keep plants on the dry side in winter. In spring cut back older plants to keep them compact.
HARVESTING: Pick leaves as needed to include in pot-pourri.

SORREL

Rumex acetosa

FEATURES: This is a perennial with many upright, oblong leaves somewhat like spinach in appearance. In summer, tall spikes of tiny, reddish flowers grow above the leaves. In bloom, sorrel may be 3 ft tall.
CLIMATE: Very hardy, suitable for zone 3 and above, but not for lowland tropical regions.
FROST TOLERANCE: Takes –40°F.
ASPECT: Full sun in cold or cool zones, but dappled or partial shade in warmer climates which prevents the leaves from becoming too bitter to be palatable.
PLANTING: Start young plants in spring or lift and divide an established plant in fall or spring. They can be started from seed collected in fall and sown in spring. Plants like deep, good quality, moist but well-drained soil.
GROWING: Small, succulent leaves have the best flavor and the plant should be grown fast with plenty of water and a couple of applications of high nitrogen soluble plant food.
HARVESTING: Pick young, fresh leaves often. Use one or two chopped leaves only in a salad. It can also be made into soup.

SORREL IMPARTS a tangy piquancy to salads and makes a delicious soup.

SUMMER SAVORY

Satureja hortensis

FEATURES: This strongly aromatic annual herb grows about 12 in tall. It is loosely branched, has long lanceolate leaves and small lilac flowers in summer.

CLIMATE: Zone 9 and above. But a summer annual, it is suitable for all climate zones.

FROST TOLERANCE: Takes 23°F.

ASPECT: Best grown in full sun.

PLANTING: Sow seeds in situ during spring. Can also be sown in fall in warm climates. For continuous cropping, make sowings every four weeks during the spring and summer. Grow in any reasonably fertile, well-drained soil.

GROWING: Keep moist until flowers appear. Apply a ration of complete plant food to the growing site once in spring.

HARVESTING: Pick leaves as needed. They are used to flavor meat, fish, vegetable and egg dishes. Unless seeds are wanted, pull plants out after flowering.

SUMMER SAVORY adds its own special flavor to a wide range of dishes.

FRENCH TARRAGON has a much finer flavor than the easier to grow Russian.

TARRAGON

Artemisia dracunculus

FEATURES: French tarragon is a perennial growing to 18 in. The leaves have an aniseed flavor.

CLIMATE: It needs a hot summer followed by a cool to cold winter. Tarragon is an extremely hardy herb—it comes from south-east Russia—and will be happy in zone 3 and above.

FROST TOLERANCE: Takes –40°F.

ASPECT: Full sun or partial shade.

PLANTING: Plant in spring into well-drained, sandy soils that contain some organic matter. Tarragon can be propagated by root division in late fall or winter, or by cuttings taken in late spring. Plant individual tarragon plants 2 ft apart.

GROWING: Water deeply, regularly so that the soil is damp but not soggy. A light ration of complete plant food applied in early spring is sufficient. Where winters are frosty, cover the roots with straw after cutting the plant to the ground in late fall.

HARVESTING: Pick leaves or sprigs as needed. For drying, harvest stems from early summer until fall, tie in bunches and hang upside down in a shady, airy place. Tarragon is one of the classic French *fines herbes*.

THYME

Thymus species

FEATURES: Most thymes are low, creeping plants but some will grow to 12 in. All have aromatic leaves.
CLIMATE: The culinary herb garden or common thyme *T. vulgaris*, comes from the western Mediterranean but is quite hardy and will be happy in zone 7 and above. Warm, dry climates best suit thyme. They are not happy in very warm humid climates.
FROST TOLERANCE: The garden or common thyme will take a low of 0°F but may need the protection of leaf litter or straw over winter.
ASPECT: Full sun is best.
PLANTING: Plant out in spring or fall (any time in frost-free areas) into well-drained, sandy soil. Existing plants can be lifted and divided in spring. Each division must have roots.
GROWING: Thymes prefer a dryish soil but not long periods of total dryness. Feeding is not necessary. To flatten growth, shear all over in spring.
HARVESTING: Fresh leaves can be picked as needed or the whole plant can be cut back to within 2 in of the ground in summer and the leaves dried. The fragrant blossoms can also be picked and eaten.

THYME BECOMES woody and sparse after a few years. Replace it with a new plant.

THE RHIZOMES of turmeric are the source of a bright yellow food coloring.

TURMERIC

Curcuma longa

FEATURES: A tropical perennial in the ginger family, turmeric grows 3 ft or more tall. Many straight stems are produced from the base and from these grow bright green, pleated leaves. The bright orange rhizome is used as food flavoring and coloring.
CLIMATE: Turmeric can be grown out of doors all the year round in zone 10 and above, otherwise grow it in a warm humid glasshouse, in pots or soil bed.
FROST TOLERANCE: None.
ASPECT: Provide good light under glass but not direct sun. Outdoors dappled or partial shade is preferred.
PLANTING: Fresh rhizomes from Asian food stores can be planted in late spring (anytime in the tropics). Existing plants can be lifted and divided in fall. It likes rich, well-drained soil with lots of rotted organic matter. Grows well in big pots.
GROWING: When the plant is growing keep it well watered and humid. Under glass allow it to die back in fall by gradually decreasing water, and keep almost dry in winter.
HARVESTING: In spring lift and divide the rhizomes and retain a few for culinary use.

• CHAPTER THIRTY-ONE •

FOLIAGE PLANTS

Flowers are beautiful, but if the garden is to look attractive all year it is a good idea to include some plants with ornamental leaves. Foliage is the wallpaper of the garden, providing a continuous vista of subtle colors and textures.

RED-LEAVED ACALYPHA and golden-foliaged euonymus look good year-round, despite their lack of showy blossom.

Leaves are not just a background for flowers. They are beautiful in their own right and, in fact, it is the leaves of the plant that provide most of the visual interest and all of the privacy, shade and shelter throughout the year. They are important to the overall look of the garden, and so it makes sense to choose for your garden plants that have attractive foliage, whether or not they also have a pleasing floral display.

It is not just the color or pattern of leaves that can be decorative, the shape and texture are also important. When you combine plants with leaves of different shapes and sizes in different colors and textures, you create a rich, finely detailed tapestry that is lovely to look at with or without flowers. In fact, by combining foliage patterns, you could easily create a beautiful and stylish garden without any showy flowers in it at all.

Many plants with pleasing foliage also have attractive flowers but some have blooms that could only be described as insignificant, and it is these that are often overlooked by gardeners who are unused to selecting garden plants for reasons other than for their flowers.

IRESINE, AMARANTHUS and alternanthera create a bold, abstract pattern in foliage. The effect lasts all year and simple clipping will keep the blocks of color separate.

COMBINING FOLIAGE WITH FLOWERS

Foliage colors have a role to play in the flower garden, too. Plants with colored leaves can be used to contrast or harmonize with particular flower colors. For example, if you have a bed of yellow flowers, golden foliage will add to the effect and there's nothing like a splash of burgundy leaves for adding impact to a red planting. In a bed of mixed colors, gray or silver foliage is a wonderful way to separate the drifts of different flowers. The neutral gray lifts the individual shades without altering the overall color combination.

FOLIAGE PLANTS FOR SHADE

It is, however, in shade that foliage plants really come into their own. The more shade there is in an area, the fewer plants there are that will flower there; but you can still have color and plenty of textural interest by choosing plants for their leaves. Many shade loving plants have striped, spotted or streaked leaves, and some, especially those from the tropics, are brightly colored as well. Most of these leaves are also big and impressive, to catch the maximum amount of light, and you can use their shapes to create pleasing patterns or make bold visual statements.

PATTERNS WITH FOLIAGE

Some modern gardeners use foliage plants to create abstract or regular patterns. Sloping ground is the ideal display site and for best effect make the individual blocks of color large. Plan the pattern to scale on graph paper first.

ANGEL WINGS

Caladium bicolor

TROPICAL HERBACEOUS PERENNIAL; PART-SHADE

ORIGIN: Tropical South America.
SIZE: Up to 30 in tall from a tuber.
CLIMATE: Zone 10. In lower zones grow in a warm humid conservatory or glasshouse. Can be bedded out for the summer, especially in areas with hot humid summers.
FROST TOLERANCE: None.
APPEAL: Magnificent heart-shaped leaves, brilliantly colored and patterned. Can be grown in pots or the garden. Out of the tropics, where summers are long and hot, angel wings are planted in late spring and the tubers lifted and stored when growth dies back in fall.
ASPECT: Dappled shade or morning sun are suitable. Hot sun will burn the foliage but leaves are most spectacular when backlit by early sun.
PRUNING: Cut leaves to the ground in fall when they are tatty. Lift the tubers and store dry until replanting time—this is spring in the tropics, late spring elsewhere.

MAGNIFICENT CALADIUMS can be grown as garden annuals or in pots in cool areas.

TO CREATE a dense bushy plant, pinch out the tips of bloodleaf when young.

BLOODLEAF

Iresine herbstii

EVERGREEN PERENNIAL; SUN OR PART-SHADE

ORIGIN: Brazil, Uruguay.
SIZE: Grows up to 6 ft tall with many lax stems forming a loose mass.
CLIMATE: Zone 10. In cooler zones grow as a pot plant under glass. Also use for summer bedding; for example, in subtropical bedding schemes. In cool zones take cuttings in late summer and overwinter under glass. Plant out in spring.
FROST TOLERANCE: It is not frost tolerant but may survive the odd light frost. In frost-prone areas overwinter young plants in a frost-free glasshouse.
APPEAL: Admired for its unusual purplish-red leaves and stems which are particularly striking when backlit. Use as a color contrast to flowers or foliage or mass over a broad area.
ASPECT: Full sun or part shade suits with the latter recommended where summers are very hot. Plants are weak and easily damaged by strong winds.
PRUNING: Young plants raised from cuttings are pinched out two or three times to promote low, bushy plants, which are better for bedding.

FRECKLE FACE

Hypoestes phyllostachya

PERENNIAL; SHADE OR PART-SHADE

ORIGIN: Madagascar.
SIZE: Grows about 18 in tall as a bushy, shrub-like perennial.
CLIMATE: Zone 10. In cooler zones grow as a pot plant in a cool glasshouse. Use as an annual for summer bedding—plant out in late spring or early summer when frosts are over. Take cuttings in late summer. Overwinter young plants under glass.
FROST TOLERANCE: None.
APPEAL: Gives a tropical look to summer plantings and looks good with ferns, impatiens, begonias and bromeliads. Leaves are dark green and spotted in either pink or rosy-red. Grows well in pots or the garden.
ASPECT: Shade or partial shade. Freckle face likes moist, humid conditions and the company of other plants. Suffers in hot, dry conditions.
PRUNING: Pinch out the growing tips periodically to promote bushiness. Remove the flower spikes as they form. Blooms are insignificant and removal encourages more leaves.

EASILY GROWN, freckle face makes a pretty, tropical-look groundcover in shade.

WONDERFUL BY water, giant rhubarb needs plenty of space.

GIANT RHUBARB

Gunnera manicata

HERBACEOUS PERENNIAL; SUN OR PART-SHADE

ORIGIN: Highlands of Colombia.
SIZE: This is a very big plant that needs plenty of room to spread. Leaves grow up to 10 ft tall and the plant can easily spread 15–18 ft across.
CLIMATE: Zone 8 and above. In areas prone to frosts, the crown needs to be protected over winter with a mound of dry straw or leaves.
FROST TOLERANCE: Takes a low of 10°F but it is essential to protect the crown and roots from severe frost.
APPEAL: Impressive and dramatic with its gigantic leaves and curious flower spikes, giant rhubarb is often grown by large ponds or streams where it thrives in the constantly moist soil. It will not tolerate dryness.
ASPECT: Prefers full sun where summers are mild but afternoon shade is advisable in hotter areas. The huge leaves are easily torn by strong winds so the plant is best positioned in a sheltered spot.
PRUNING: Remove tatty leaves and cut to the ground in late fall.

EVERGREEN gold dust plant makes a good screen or unclipped hedge.

GOLD DUST PLANT

Aucuba japonica "Variegata"

EVERGREEN SHRUB; PART-SHADE

ORIGIN: China, Japan, Taiwan.
SIZE: The gold dust plant is a low-growing shrub growing to 10 ft high with many upright stems from the base. Mature plants are broadly rounded in shape.
CLIMATE: It can be grown in zone 7 and above. In colder regions it can also be grown as a pot plant in a cool glasshouse.
FROST TOLERANCE: Takes 10°F.
APPEAL: Grown for its dense covering of glossy, leathery, bright green leaves, which are spotted and streaked in gold.
ASPECT: Bright full shade, dappled shade or morning sun suit this plant. It will take full sun in the coolest parts of zone 6.
PRUNING: None needed. It is a naturally neat and compact plant.

HELICHRYSUM

Helichrysum petiolare

EVERGREEN SHRUB; SUN

ORIGIN: South Africa.
SIZE: About 24–36 in tall, spreading to 3 ft or more wide. Forms a low, dense, rounded mound.
CLIMATE: Zone 10. In cooler zones, use for summer bedding, over-wintering young plants (take cuttings in summer) in a frost-free glasshouse.
FROST TOLERANCE: Will not tolerate frosts.
APPEAL: Helichrysum is grown for its light-reflective, whitish gray foliage. Although it grows quite large, young plants are often used as a component in mixed hanging baskets. The cultivar "Limelight" has light, lime-gray leaves.
ASPECT: Full sun keeps the plant compact but where summers are hot, afternoon shade is helpful.
PRUNING: Cut back hard in early spring to promote fresh new growth. To control size, shear lightly all over any time during the warmer months. Cut off flower stems as they arise. The tiny yellow flowers are not showy and make the plant look untidy.

BEAUTIFUL gray leaves let Helichrysum petiolare *complement any flower color.*

HOUTTUYNIA IS ideal by ponds or in wet soil but beware its fast-spreading habit.

HOUTTUYNIA

Houttuynia cordata "Chameleon", also known as "Variegata", "Tricolor" or "Court Jester"

HERBACEOUS PERENNIAL; SUN OR SHADE

ORIGIN: China, Japan.
SIZE: About 6 in tall but with an infinite spread. This groundcover for moist or wet soils can become invasive and should not be planted where it cannot be controlled easily.
CLIMATE: This plant is reasonably hardy, growing in zone 7 and above, but it is not recommended for tropical areas.
FROST TOLERANCE: Takes 0°–5°F.
APPEAL: Grown for its dense, weed suppressing, heart-shaped foliage which is streaked green, yellow and red. Very easy to grow but needs plenty of water in summer. Small white flowers are a pleasant bonus.
ASPECT: Takes anything from full sun to full shade. In sun, it is best grown in shallow water or in sodden soils. In shade, moist soil will do.
PRUNING: No pruning is needed except to remove rooted stems where they exceed their allotted space.

JAPANESE OLEASTER

Elaeagnus pungens

EVERGREEN SHRUB; FULL SUN

ORIGIN: Japan.
SIZE: About 10–12 ft tall and at least as wide, forming a broad, rounded shrub. Stems are somewhat spiny.
CLIMATE: This shrub is reasonably hardy and suitable for zone 7 and above. It is also a good shrub for coastal gardens as well as inland areas. Oleaster needs well-drained soil and regular summer watering.
FROST TOLERANCE: Very hardy. Tolerates 0°F.
APPEAL: Grown for its flowers, foliage and fruits. The white, late summer flowers are small but sweetly scented and are followed in fall by small, spotted fruits that ripen red. Most oleasters seen are named hybrids with showy, variegated leaves. "Aurea" has leaves with a golden edge, while "Maculata" has bright yellow leaves edged green. Other cultivars also have variously variegated leaves. All make good hedges or specimen shrubs.
ASPECT: Full sun.
PRUNING: None needed apart from tidying up or shaping if necessary.

OFTEN GROWN as a hedge, oleaster has pleasing flowers, fruits and foliage.

LEOPARD PLANT gives a tropical look to shady spots in cooler areas.

LEOPARD PLANT

Farfugium japonicum "Aureomaculatum"

EVERGREEN PERENNIAL; FULL SHADE OR PART-SHADE

ORIGIN: Japan.
SIZE: A low, spreading perennial, with a height and spread of about 24 in.
CLIMATE: Suitable for zone 9 and possibly milder parts of zone 8. Leopard plant prefers a mild, humid, rainy climate.
FROST TOLERANCE: It takes a temperature down to 23°F but where that may happen, mulch the plants in fall with straw.
APPEAL: Although the leopard plant does produce clusters of bright yellow daisies in summer, it is the big, gold-spotted, kidney-shaped leaves that are the chief attraction. This plant looks tropical but isn't, and it makes a startling edging along a shady path. It can also be grown in pots.
ASPECT: Bright full shade or dappled shade are ideal. In cooler areas, a few hours morning sun is acceptable but leaves will burn in hot sun.
PRUNING: None needed.

NEW ZEALAND FLAX

Phormium tenax

EVERGREEN PERENNIAL; SUN

ORIGIN: New Zealand.
SIZE: Several varieties are available, ranging in height from 3 to 10 ft. All form a fan of stiff, upright leaves.
CLIMATE: Suitable for growing in zone 8 and above. This is a good plant for coastal gardens as well as mild inland areas.
FROST TOLERANCE: Takes 20°F. Where temperatures fall lower, plants will, however, usually reshoot from the base in spring.
APPEAL: The stiffly upright fan of leaves makes a distinctive feature plant and there are several color varieties with leaves in shades of green, bronze and red, often with contrasting vertical stripes. Tall, branched flower spikes, which rise above the foliage, provide added interest.
ASPECT: Full sun or, in the hottest areas, afternoon shade.
PRUNING: None needed.

USE NEW ZEALAND FLAX for its strong, architectural shape.

THE SILVERY-PURPLE LEAVES of Persian shield lighten up shade in summer.

PERSIAN SHIELD

Strobilanthes dyeriana

EVERGREEN SHRUB; DAPPLED SHADE OR PART-SHADE

ORIGIN: Burma.
SIZE: About 3 ft tall and a little wider, as a loose, rounded, soft-stemmed shrub.
CLIMATE: Zone 10 and above. In cooler zones grow as a pot plant in a warm glasshouse or conservatory. It is also an unusual subject for summer bedding, especially in regions with hot and humid summers—plant out when frosts are over. Overwinter young cuttings-raised plants under glass.
FROST TOLERANCE: None.
APPEAL: Magnificent foliage shrub with leaves streaked silver, purple, green and red, It is an essential part of the tropical-look garden. In cool climates use as an outdoor summer display, especially in subtropical bedding schemes.
ASPECT: Protect from harsh summer sun and hot winds but don't position it in very dim light. In the tropics it will tolerate full shade but elsewhere a few hours morning sun is best.
PRUNING: Cut back to a framework of branches at the start of the new growing season.

ZEBRA PLANT

Calathea species

TROPICAL EVERGREEN PERENNIAL; SHADE OR PART-SHADE

ORIGIN: Tropical South America.
SIZE: Varies from 12 in to over 3 ft depending on species.
CLIMATE: Suitable for growing outdoors all year round in zone 10, but with winter protection. In cooler climates grow calathea species as pot plants in a warm humid glasshouse or conservatory. Also try bedding them out for the summer, especially in areas with hot humid summers—they make highly unusual subjects for a subtropical bedding scheme
FROST TOLERANCE: None.
APPEAL: They have big, bold leaves often horizontally striped or blotched. They may be slightly velvety to the touch and reddish-purple on the reverse. These are dramatic plants either in the garden or in pots.
ASPECT: Full shade, dappled shade or a little morning sun.
PRUNING: None needed but untidy leaves can be removed in spring.

THERE ARE many different leaf patterns and colors in Calathea *species.*

•CHAPTER THIRTY-TWO•

ORNAMENTAL GRASSES

There's more to grasses than just lawns, and in fact most grasses and grass-like plants are not suitable for lawns at all. They're grown as feature plants for their elegant, arching foliage and tall, feathery flowers.

The plants in this chapter are grasses or grass-like plants with long, strappy leaves, produced in dense clumps. They can be anything from small mounds 6–8 in tall, to fountains of foliage 6 ft and more tall with long flower spikes towering above that.

Smaller-growers can be massed as groundcover, used as edging along paths or flower beds, or grown in pots. Larger species can be grown in a mixed flower border or different types can be clumped together in a display of grasses. If you have the space, massing the bigger growers will create a prairie effect. Almost all types look and grow well beside water.

FLOWERS, FOLIAGE, SONG

The flowers are not showy in the traditional sense but their soft colors and feathery appearance are lovely. The leaves come in many shades of green or may be bluish, gray, golden, tan, red or even combinations of colors. In cooler areas, many grasses change color in fall.

An additional feature of grasses is their sound. Grasses rustle and sigh in the breeze and so can be a joy to both the eyes and ears.

EASY TO GROW

Some grasses are evergreen but many are herbaceous, dying down in winter for a few months and reshooting in spring. Herbaceous species are best suited to cooler areas while evergreens all grow in warm areas and some will grow in cooler places as well.

These are easy plants to grow. They need only average garden soil that drains well, but there are grasses that suit wet spots, too. Generally, true grasses do best in full sun but some grass-like plants tolerate partial shade. None demands a lot of feeding and if you water them regularly in the first year, almost all can live on rain in all but the driest areas.

GETTING GRASSES STARTED

Late winter or spring is the best time to plant although grasses purchased in pots may be planted anytime. If you buy grasses through the mail from a specialist grower, they come as small, rooted crowns. Grasses grow quickly and must be spaced according to the ultimate size of the plant or you'll have to replant them soon. Dig a wide planting hole and make a mound in the center. Spread the roots over

A GROUPING OF GRASSES makes an elegant, easy-care display but even a single specimen, prominently positioned, becomes a highlight of the garden.

the mound, backfill and water in. Plants need regular watering through the first spring and summer.

ROUTINE CARE

The on-going care of grasses is simple. In late fall or winter, cut the foliage mass to the ground, especially with herbaceous types, or the dead top growth will make the new spring growth look somewhat untidy.

Evergreen species don't have to be cut back but weather worn or old foliage can be sheared off at ground level in late winter.

New shoots appear in early spring and, at that stage, you can mulch around the plants with rotted cow manure or compost, or just give a ration of complete plant food and water it in thoroughly.

PROPAGATION

Grasses and grass-like plants can be propagated either by dividing the clump into smaller, rooted sections or by growing from seed. Divisions give a bigger plant sooner but you can raise many times more plants from seeds.

To divide the clump, use a garden fork to loosen the plant all round and then lift it from the ground. The best time to do this is in late winter when the plant is dormant or least actively growing. Pull smaller plants apart by hand but chop or saw larger grasses into pieces. If the roots are overlong, trim them back with sharp, clean pruners. Replant as soon as possible.

To grow from seed, collect seed as it ripens in fall and store it dry in an airtight jar in darkness until the next spring. When the weather is warm, sow the seed into small pots or a seedling tray and barely cover. Keep the pots moist and shaded and after germination move them into the sun. Continue to keep them moist and, when the plants are large enough to handle easily, plant them out.

Some species spread by seed and can become a nuisance. Watch for self-sown seedlings the following year and remove them promptly.

BLACK BAMBOO

Phyllostachys nigra

ORIGIN: China.
SIZE: Can grow up to 30 ft tall with an indefinite spread.
CLIMATE: It is a temperate species and suitable for cultivation in zones 8 and 9. As with all phyllostachys, it will not thrive in warm subtropical and tropical regions, however, it especially suits high-rainfall areas.
FROST TOLERANCE: Takes 10°F.
APPEAL: This is an elegant, lightly foliaged and extremely beautiful bamboo, the stems of which turn black and shiny after two or three years. It looks most effective in a grove but can also be grown in big, wide containers.
ASPECT: Full sun or partial shade. Needs shelter from sea winds.
FLOWERING SEASON: This plant is grown for its colored stems.
CARE: Grows best in moderately rich, moisture-retentive but well-drained soil. Feed in spring when new growth appears and don't neglect watering in the warmer months. Selectively remove older stems, but only if they become unattractive. This is a running bamboo that should be contained by a root control barrier.

BLACK BAMBOO is a most desirable grassy plant but it does need containing.

THE COLOR of the foliage of blue fescue makes a fine contrast with green plants.

BLUE FESCUE

Festuca glauca

ORIGIN: Europe.
SIZE: Grows about 12 in tall and 12 in wide, as a dense, rounded clump of fine, evergreen foliage.
CLIMATE: An extremely hardy grass suitable for zone 5 and above. It does not relish high summer rainfall, preferring dryish summers.
FROST TOLERANCE: Fully hardy. It will take a low of –20°F.
APPEAL: Blue fescue has attractive blue-gray foliage and a neat, compact habit. It looks very attractive massed or in small groups and is often used to line paths or drives, or as a pot plant. It is very easy to grow and is not known to be invasive.
ASPECT: Full sun is recommended but in hot arid areas it will take some shade.
FLOWERING SEASON: Summer, but flowers are not particularly showy. This is a foliage plant.
CARE: If plants look shabby after the winter cut the foliage to the ground. A flush of new growth then appears in the spring. To keep them young and vigorous and with good foliage color, lift and divide plants every two to three years.

THE BLUE OATGRASS is one of the bluest of the ornamental grasses.

BLUE OATGRASS

Helictotrichon sempervirens

ORIGIN: The blue oatgrass is a native of south-west Europe.
SIZE: Grows up to 4 ft in height. This perennial grass has a tufted habit, forming a rounded mound of very thin gray-blue leaves up to 8 in long.
CLIMATE: Despite its origins this grass is very hardy and is suitable for zone 5 and above. Blue oatgrass is also very wind resistant and suited to open, exposed situations.
FROST TOLERANCE: Will take a low of −10°F to −20°F.
APPEAL: This grass is grown primarily for its superb evergreen foliage but the straw-colored flowers are quite attractive. Ideal for mixed borders, and good in gravel or arid gardens.
ASPECT: This grass should be grown in full sun.
FLOWERING SEASON: Early and midsummer.
CARE: Soil should be well-drained, moderately fertile or even poor; chalky or limy soil preferred. Cut down dead flower stems and leaves in spring before new growth starts.

FOUNTAIN GRASS

Pennisetum species

ORIGIN: Asia, Africa, Australia.
SIZE: Species vary in height from about 24 in to 5 or 6 ft. They form a tufted, arching clump of narrow foliage and have foxtail-like flowers.
CLIMATE: Depends on species. The hardiest fountain grasses will grow in zone 7, others in zones 8 and 9.
FROST TOLERANCE: The hardiest take 10°F or a little lower.
APPEAL: Easy to grow and very effective in bloom, fountain grass is most attractive when backlit by early or late sun.
ASPECT: Full sun or partial shade suits this grass. It can be grown in coastal areas.
FLOWERING SEASON: Late spring to early fall.
CARE: Prefers moist soils and will even tolerate periodic wetness. These plants do best in better quality soils but grow just about anywhere. Cut to the ground in winter and be vigilant for unwanted seedlings. In areas prone to frost protect in winter with a mulch of organic matter.

ANOTHER OF the several fountain grasses is this Pennisetum setaceum.

GARDENER'S GARTERS is a handsome and popular grass best in cooler areas.

GARDENER'S GARTERS

Phalaris arundinacea var. *picta*

ORIGIN: North America, Europe.
SIZE: Grows about 3 ft tall with an indefinite spread. Very vigorous.
CLIMATE: An extremely hardy grass, suitable for zone 4 and above. It will not thrive in warm climates. The species itself is widespread, growing in varying conditions in the wild.
FROST TOLERANCE: Gardener's garters is incredibly frost tolerant, taking a low of –30°F.
APPEAL: This plant is grown for its strikingly variegated, green and white leaves which are often tinged pink. In frosty areas, the foliage turns an attractive papery beige in winter. Soft-textured, white flowers are also decorative. This is a lovely grass when grown near water.
ASPECT: Full sun or partial shade.
FLOWERING SEASON: Late spring to early summer.
CARE: Grow gardener's garters in moderately rich soil and keep it moist. It will grow in shallow water. It spreads fast by runners and can be very invasive unless contained. This plant is often grown in wide pots to control the spread.

JAPANESE BLOOD GRASS

Imperata cylindrica "Rubra"

ORIGIN: Japan.
SIZE: It is usually about 24 in tall and as wide or wider, as a clump of broad, stiffly upright leaves. It can grow taller in warmer climates.
CLIMATE: Suitable for zone 8 and above. In areas prone to frost protect plants over winter with a mulch of organic matter.
FROST TOLERANCE: Takes a low of 14°F.
APPEAL: This grass is grown for its colorful leaves which, soon after emerging, turn brilliant deep red. It is used as a feature or specimen grass, or as a color contrast with other grasses or with flowers. It also grows well in patio containers.
ASPECT: Full sun, except where summers are very hot. There, midday shade is appreciated.
FLOWERING SEASON: Blood grass is grown for its foliage.
CARE: Grow it in fertile, moisture-retentive soil. It is an easy plant that demands no special treatment. Foliage can be tidied up at any time.

BLOOD GRASS is the most spectacularly colored of all the ornamental grasses.

PALM GRASS will create a tropical effect if grown in the partial shade of taller trees.

PALM GRASS

Setaria palmifolia

ORIGIN: Africa, India.
SIZE: About 3 ft tall and wide, as an arching clump of broad leaves.
CLIMATE: This grass is suitable for zone 9 and above. It is grown in frost-free areas and enjoys plenty of water and high humidity in summer.
FROST TOLERANCE: Prefers a warm, frost-free climate but takes the odd light frost.
APPEAL: An impressive plant with dark green pleated leaves, it makes a bold statement on its own or when massed as a border. Leaves and flowers are used in indoor arrangements.
ASPECT: Tolerates full sun only where summers are mild. Elsewhere, afternoon shade keeps the leaves in top condition. In the tropics, it will take full shade. It grows in coastal areas but not with frontline exposure.
FLOWERING SEASON: Summer. The greenish flowers are pleasant enough but not dramatically showy.
CARE: Grow in reasonably fertile soil kept moist during the warmer months. Feed it in early spring and again in summer, and mulch around plants in spring with rotted manure.

SEDGES

Carex species

ORIGIN: Widely distributed, but common in temperate and cold regions.
SIZE: Varies with species from a few inches to over 3 ft.
CLIMATE: The sedges are generally most suited to cool and cold climates. Many species will thrive in zone 3.
FROST TOLERANCE: All take light frosts and some northern hemisphere species will accept –30°F to –40°F.
APPEAL: Grown for their grass-like, often colored or variegated leaves and their ease of growth in a wide range of conditions. Very attractive waterside plants. Sedges native to your region are recommended as imports can be weedy.
ASPECT: Full sun keeps the plants compact but many sedges are also happy to grow in shade.
FLOWERING SEASON: Summer.
CARE: Individual species have different needs. In general, sedges enjoy constantly moist soil and some will stand seasonal or permanent bogginess. Species from the southern hemisphere are very drought tolerant. Foliage can be cut to the ground in spring to tidy plants up.

SEDGES CAN become weedy so it is best to grow those native to your own region.

SPEAR GRASS

Stipa species

ORIGIN: Widely distributed in temperate and warm temperate regions.
SIZE: Varies with species from about 24 in to around 6 ft. All form clumps of arching or upright leaves.
CLIMATE: This depends on the species. There are many desirable spear grasses that are suited to zones 7 and 8.
FROST TOLERANCE: Depends on species. European and American species are more hardy than southern-hemisphere species.
APPEAL: These are easy-to-grow tussocky grasses, many with filamentous flowers that resemble spider webs. They are very useful in dry soil and, once established, will withstand droughts.
ASPECT: Full sun or partial shade.
FLOWERING SEASON: Late spring through to late summer.
CARE: Spear grasses are not fussy about soil so long as it drains freely. They won't tolerate prolonged wetness and cannot stand seasonal flooding. Cut them to the ground in late winter to encourage fresh new growth in spring. Remove flower heads before seeds set as they catch in clothing and can irritate.

UNUSUAL FLOWERS and tussocky foliage make spear grass a collector's item.

THE EVERGREEN tufted hair grass is valued for its light airy flower heads.

TUFTED HAIR GRASS

Deschampsia cespitosa

ORIGIN: Widely distributed in the USA and temperate Eurasia.
SIZE: Reaches 4 ft or more in height. This grass forms dense clumps or tussocks of stiff, upright and arching, very narrow leaves that are about 24 in long.
CLIMATE: This is an extremely hardy grass suited to zone 5 and above.
FROST TOLERANCE: It will take temperatures of –10°F to –20°F, or maybe even lower.
APPEAL: This is an evergreen grass with particularly attractive, light airy heads of purple, silver-tinted flowers. It is ideal for including in mixed or shrub borders and it looks especially good with plantings of perennials, particularly native species.
ASPECT: It will thrive in full sun or partial shade.
FLOWERING SEASON: The flowers are produced from early to late summer.
CARE: The hair grasses generally prefer neutral to acid (lime-free) soils. Moist or dryish conditions are acceptable. Cut down the dead flower heads in spring before new growth starts.

YELLOW-GROOVE BAMBOO

Phyllostachys aureosulcata

ORIGIN: China.

SIZE: Grows up to 30 ft high with an indefinite spread. This is a vigorous bamboo, producing clumps or thickets of branching canes, but is more restrained in cooler conditions.

CLIMATE: Widely grown in zone 8. Not suitable for warm subtropical or tropical regions.

FROST TOLERANCE: One of the hardiest phyllostachys, taking a low of at least 10°F.

APPEAL: Grown for its attractive canes which are brown-green with yellow grooves, and bearing pleasing 6 in long medium green leaves. Use as a specimen plant, grow it in patio containers, or include it in shrub borders or woodland gardens. Also, it makes a good screen.

ASPECT: Grow in full sun or dappled shade. Ensure shelter from cold, drying winds which will scorch the foliage.

FLOWERING SEASON: Not applicable—grown for its canes and foliage.

CARE: Soil should be moisture-retentive yet well-drained, reasonably fertile, and contain plenty of well-rotted organic matter.

THE YELLOW-GROOVE BAMBOO has handsome branching canes or stems.

VARIEGATED FOLIAGE makes zebra grass showy even without its feathery flowers.

ZEBRA GRASS

Miscanthus sinensis "Zebrinus"

ORIGIN: Eastern Asia.

SIZE: Grows about 4 ft tall and almost as wide, as a dense clump of long, narrow, arching leaves topped with tall flowers.

CLIMATE: This is a very hardy grass and will thrive in zone 4 and above. However, it is not suited to very warm climates.

FROST TOLERANCE: Takes –20°F to –30°F.

APPEAL: Zebra grass is a tall, graceful plant with yellow stripes across its mid-green leaves. It is a striking feature plant and, in a larger garden, impressive when massed. It looks particularly attractive near water. Its flowers are beautiful and long lasting when cut. Frosted foliage looks good.

ASPECT: Takes full sun or, in very hot areas, dappled afternoon shade. Shelter from strong or persistent winds.

FLOWERING SEASON: Late summer or early fall. Flowers are coppery pink and feathery.

CARE: Grow zebra grass in moist soil. Feed in early spring when new growth begins and once again in early summer. Cut plants to the ground in late fall or winter.

•CHAPTER THIRTY-THREE•

Container Gardening

Any plant will grow in a pot and that lets you enjoy them anywhere. You can have a garden on a verandah, in a bright room, on a window-sill or hanging overhead. You can also use container plants as eye-catching features in the garden itself.

To start a container garden, you can either choose an attractive pot and then select the plants to go in it or decide on the plants first. Either way, it is important to match the scale of the plants with the containers. Plants grown in pots that are too small quickly fill the pot with roots and need very frequent watering and feeding. Conversely, if the pot is too big, the match looks odd and, without roots to extract the water, much of the soil will remain permanently damp and stagnant and may lead to rotting of the roots. Shrubs and trees need relatively deep pots to accommodate their root systems but flowers, bulbs and other small plants look good and perform best in wide, shallow containers such as those shown below.

PLASTIC POTS come in realistic terracotta finishes as well as other colors and are sold in many modern and classical shapes. Wide dishes display small plants well.

TIMBER IS *one of the few materials from which you can make your own pots. This rustic box was knocked together in minutes from five pieces of planking.*

TYPES OF POT

Plastic pots

Plastic pots are cheap, durable, colorful and light to move around. Some look convincingly like terracotta. Being waterproof, they don't dry out as fast as porous containers and thus need less frequent watering and feeding. On the downside, they don't always look good, especially if you have a wide mix of colors and styles. If you are using a lot of plastic pots, stick to the one color.

Timber containers

Wooden pots usually look attractive, especially in rustic or natural-style gardens. Like plastic, they are waterproof and generally look best if you use one style throughout the garden. The disadvantages of wood include its weight and the fact that it eventually rots, although that takes a long time. Raise wooden pots off the surface to minimize rotting beneath.

Ceramic pots

Ceramic pots include unglazed terracotta and glazed earthenware or stoneware. Terracotta pots are the traditional containers for plants and

USE GLAZED CERAMIC *pots for special effects. In this miniature rock garden a bonsaied fig looks at home in a pot with an oriental appearance.*

PAINTING POTS

Water-based house paint that dries to a waterproof finish is useful for decorating pots, but if you want to completely paint a porous pot, it is advisable to paint it white first to ensure an even color. There are also verdigris finishes for brass and copper pots that will instantly give them the look of great age.

they will look good in most settings. Glazed pots are more showy in themselves but be careful in your choice as patterned pots will introduce a style that may or may not suit the rest of your garden.

Glazed pots and unglazed stoneware containers are waterproof, but terracotta pots are porous. This means that they can dry out fast and always require more frequent watering than waterproof pots. More frequent watering means more frequent feeding as watering washes some nutrients out of the soil with every application.

The disadvantages of ceramic pots include their fragility, weight and cost but they may still be right for you.

Concrete containers

Because of their weight, concrete pots are best placed permanently. They vary in size, some being big enough for quite large trees, and when sold with a matching pedestal can make impressive focal points in the garden. Weight and cost (especially of the bigger, more decorative pots) are the main disadvantages of concrete.

FOUNDATIONS FOR SUCCESS

Potting mixes

A good quality potting mix is essential for success with container-grown plants. Modern potting mixes are clean, weed-free and disease-free. They are designed to be fast draining yet moisture retentive, and because they are relatively lightweight too, they make it easier to move pots from place to place. There are specially formulated mixes for plants with specific needs, such as orchids, cacti and African violets, and also mixes for specific uses, such as hanging baskets or terracotta pots. These latter types of

USE STANDARD potting mixes for most shrubs, trees and flowers, but plants such as cacti and succulents do better in a more sandy mix. Specialist mixes for a number of plants are sold at garden centers.

INDOORS, SAUCERS are important in preventing spillages but always empty them after the pot has drained or you will encourage root-rotting diseases.

mixes are more moisture retentive to suit their particular purposes.

Drainage

Good-sized drainage holes are vital in pots as even the best potting mix won't drain if there is nowhere for the water to go. Avoid pots with drain holes that seem too small for the volume of soil they will contain unless you have the tools to drill more. If you want to be certain that drainage is adequate, fill the bottom of the pot with a layer of broken pots or coarse gravel. This used to be commonly advised and although it is not strictly necessary with today's free-draining potting mixes, it can't do any harm.

What can do harm, is standing pots in saucers of water. The practice is most dangerous with relatively small pots as these are easily waterlogged from below, but it is not a good idea with any pot. Good drainage is so important you should even raise the pot off the ground on bricks or stones or on pot feet which can be bought at garden centers. This allows excess water to run away freely, minimizes water damage to the bottom of the pot and the surface on which it is standing, and deprives slaters of a place to live.

Potting

You should always match the size of the pot to the size of the plants it will contain but, of course, plants grow and you should allow for this up to a point. If you are planting annuals from seedlings that are 2–3 in tall but will soon grow into flowers 16 in tall, choose a pot suitable for the mature size, not for the seedlings. But if you are planting a slower growing shrub or tree it is better to pot it up

IT IS NOT NECESSARY to have all of your pots exactly the same, but if you stick to the one material, terracotta in this case, your collection will have a more unified look.

progressively each year or two than to plant it into a very large pot at the outset. Small plants in big pots cannot use all the food and water available.

Potting mixes contain little or no plant foods and you should blend some into the mix at planting time. The amount to mix in varies with the size of the pot and the type of fertilizer but in all cases it is better to be stingy rather than generous, as too much fertilizer can kill plants. Not enough fertilizer just makes them grow slowly and is easily rectified. If you are unsure about this, read the directions on the fertilizer packets before buying one. The one to choose should explain how much to use in various size pots. Slow-release fertilizers are a good choice for containers so long as you remember when to replenish it.

Plants should be potted so that they are no deeper in the new potting mix than they were in the pot in which you bought them. To achieve this, partially fill the pot with potting mix and then sit the plant in it, adding or subtracting potting mix until the level is right. Unpot the plant and check that the roots are not spiralling around the base. If they are, gently tease them out. You can trim any that are overlong using sharp, very clean pruners. Place the plant into the new pot and fill it with potting mix to within 3/4 in of the rim. Gently firm the mix around the roots but don't compact it hard or you will lose aeration. Water the plant in well.

Watering

Don't water potted plants according to a schedule, say, every three days. Instead, water when they need it. This will be much more often in summer than in winter, in sun than in shade, in porous than in waterproof pots, in smaller than in bigger pots, in a windy than in a sheltered spot. Test whether or not water is needed by feeling down into the top 1 in of soil. If it is quite moist, don't water, but if it feels just damp, it is time to water. You'll soon get to know the watering needs of your different pots and won't have to feel the soil. Generally speaking, don't allow the potting mix to go completely dry as it can then be quite difficult to re-wet.

Over time, potting mixes can become water repellent and no matter how much water you apply, most runs straight through and the potting mix remains dry (although the surface looks wet). To test for this, water thoroughly and after it has drained from the surface, scratch the soil in several places. If it is dry underneath, apply a wetting agent (from garden centers) but do use the wetting agent strictly as directed as overdoses can be toxic to plants. Reapply it as needed.

Fertilizing

Only apply fertilizer during the growing season for that particular plant. Most plants grow most vigorously from spring to mid-fall and do not need or want fertilizer from the end of summer until early spring, although they still need water. Some plants are dormant or least active during the hot months and grow during the fall, winter and early spring. These should be fed in fall and early winter.

Always apply fertilizer to moist potting mix, never to dry, and always give it at the recommended rates—more fertilizer does not equal more growth; it makes the soil salty and toxic. Slow-release fertilizers are very convenient but you can also use complete plant food or soluble or liquid fertilizers, and it is a good idea to alternate between types.

Remember, the more you water, the more fertilizer you will have to apply and the best way to give it is in frequent but very small doses, say, a quarter strength four times as often.

Potting on (or up)

Plants that have outgrown their containers should be potted on (or potted up) and this is best done either in early spring or in early fall. You can check whether or not a plant needs potting on by removing the pot and examining the roots. If you see much more white (roots) than black (soil) it's time to pot on. Roots protruding strongly from drain holes is another good sign that potting on has become necessary.

To pot on, remove the plant from its existing pot. If you don't water it for a few days beforehand, the soil will shrink and the process will be easier. Tease out compacted or spiralling roots and trim any that are overlong. Replant into fresh potting

DECKS AND PATIOS cry out for color, and hanging baskets and dish planters are the perfect way to provide it. We grew this display from a packet of mixed seeds.

mix placed in a pot that is one size bigger than the existing pot. Water in well and place the plant in a bright but shady and sheltered spot for a week to recover before moving it to its original location.

If the plant is already in a big pot, scrape away about 1 in of potting mix all round and replace the plant in its original container with fresh potting mix poured around the outside. This is called repotting as it does not involve a bigger pot.

PLACES FOR POTS

In any garden there will be dozens of places that could be improved with a pot or, better still, a group of pots. Groups can be used for greater impact or to conceal an unattractive feature and pots of different shapes and sizes can look better when grouped together. They're easier to water, too.

For added height, upturn an empty pot and use it as a pedestal for another. Raised pots look great when trailing plants are allowed to cascade from them and one beautiful, well-planted urn on its own can make a stunning focal point.

With a little thought you can place pots with great effect. For a classically formal look, position a matched pair of pots either side of an entrance or steps, or you can add interest and beauty to a pergola by festooning it with hanging baskets bursting with flower and foliage.

MINI DESERT landscapes using cacti and succulents are just the thing for hot, sunny patios. They forgive the forgetful.

Avoid mishaps

Wind and weight are two important factors to consider when placing pots. Even quite heavy pots can be blown over by strong winds, especially if the plant within it is large, and you should consider what effect this would have should it happen. If the result would be dangerous, don't put the pot there—sooner or later a gale is a certainty. Hanging baskets are also severely affected by winds and they should never be placed in exposed locations.

Pots or baskets are heavy, doubly so when watered. Satisfy yourself that your deck, pergola or balcony will hold the wetted weight of the pots or baskets you have in mind.

IDEAS FOR IMPRESSIVE CONTAINERS

Planting up pots is one of gardening's most rewarding pastimes. It's fun to do and very creative, too, and by putting together several different plants in the one pot you can learn a lot about color and foliage combinations without tying up garden space. On the following pages you'll find planting ideas suitable for different locations, but you don't have to stick to our ideas: let your head go and come up with combinations that you really love.

BURSTING WITH color, this combination promises a summer-long display.

SPLENDOR IN THE SHADE

Here pink and white busy lizzie plants brighten a shady corner and the oval tin tub provides an effective contrast.

To re-create it you'll need 3 x busy lizzies (New Guinea *Impatiens*), 4 x floss flowers (*Ageratum houstonianum*), 3 x clumps lobelia seedlings, 4 x small-leaved variegated ivy, 1 oval tin tub, potting mix, slow-release fertilizer.

Planting and growing tips

- Plant in spring for spring and summer color.
- Punch twelve holes in the bottom of the tub for drainage.
- Blend a handful of slow-release fertilizer and some water-storing granules into the mix before planting.
- Place the tub in bright shade.
- Keep it moist but not wet.
- Feed monthly with soluble fertilizer.
- Remove spent flowers.
- Replace floss flowers when finished.
- Replace the lobelia when finished.
- Don't let the ivy take over. Prune it back regularly.

CASCADES OF COLOR

Wire baskets lined with sphagnum moss make really eye-catching hanging gardens that are also lightweight, a useful feature in any suspended container. If you prefer, you can use fiber liners instead of the sphagnum moss.

To create this basket you'll need 4 x petunia seedlings, 2 x verbena, 2 x moss verbena, 8 x alyssum seedlings, 1 wire basket, sphagnum moss or fiber liner, potting mix, slow-release fertilizer.

Planting and growing tips

- Plant in spring or summer for summer and fall flowers.
- Blend half a handful of slow-release fertilizer into the mix before planting.
- Hang the basket in full sun.
- Water often—once or twice daily during summer.
- Feed fortnightly with a measured quantity of soluble fertilizer.
- Pinch out young tips on petunias to encourage branching.

BASKETS OF FLOWERS look especially lovely and you'll be delighted with this one. All are long-blooming species that will eventually tumble over the edges in a cascade of color. Keep the faded flowers picked off to prolong bloom and cut back petunias when they become leggy.

THIS CONTAINER makes a pretty window-box or you can use one or several along the top of a balustrade.

A TOUCH OF CLASS

Centered on a small clipped box shrub, this combination of white and green plants creates a formal effect that suits the washed plaster container. It will look perfect in a formal setting, on a balcony or edging a patio.

To re-create this arrangement, you'll need 1 x dwarf box shrub, 2 x trailing white lantana plants, 2 x cineraria (dusty miller), 2 x white bedding begonia, 3 x star daisy seedlings, a 20 x 10 in trough, potting mix, slow-release fertilizer.

Planting and growing tips

- Plant in fall or spring.
- Blend half a handful of slow-release granules and water-storing crystals into the mix before planting.
- Place in a sunny position.
- Keep evenly moist but direct water onto the soil, not the plants.
- Begonias are susceptible to mildew on the leaves—spray with fungicide if it is seen.
- Cut back daisies when they become lanky or replace them with other white annuals.
- Lightly shear the box shrub often to preserve the tight, clipped shape.

PLANTER FOR A SUNNY SILL

This brilliant arrangement will brighten any window and is perfectly offset by a wire window-box.

To re-create this arrangement you'll need 2 x bush geraniums, 2 x ivy geraniums, 2 x perennial petunias, 2 x Swan River daisies, 2 x ivy, wire window-box and liner (16 x 9 in), potting mix, slow-release fertilizer.

Planting and growing tips

- Plant in spring for summer color.
- Blend half a handful of slow-release granules plus water-storing crystals into the mix before planting.
- Place the window-box in full sun.
- Keep it evenly moist always.
- Pinch out tips for bushier plants.
- Remove spent flowers promptly.
- Cut back geraniums and petunias when they become leggy.
- Don't let the ivy take over—prune it back regularly.
- Geraniums are susceptible to rust fungus—spray them with fungicide if you see any traces of it.

WINDOW-BOXES can dry out but this clever planting uses species that revel in heat and can take a little dryness, too. Pinch off the flowers as they fade and you'll keep more coming.

•CHAPTER THIRTY-FOUR•

PLANTS FOR EVERY SEASON

The plants from our directories are listed here according to the season in which they bloom. Some occur in several lists as variations in climate affect the timing of bloom—consult the particular plant entry (via the index) for more details.

PLANTS FOR SPRING DISPLAY

The plants listed here are decorative in spring. They may have flowers or attractive foliage then. Some may be decorative in spring only in certain climates.

Agapanthus
Alpine phlox
Alyssum
Anemone
Astilbe
Aurora daisy
Azalea
Baboon flower
Baby blue eyes
Baby's breath
Balsam
Beard tongue
Bedding begonia
Bellflower
Bergenia
Blue bugle flower
Blue poppy
Bluebell
Bottlebrush
Butterfly bush
Calendula
California poppy
Californian lilac
Camellia
Campion
Candytuft
Catmint
Checkered lily
Cherry pie
Chinese cherry
Clematis
Coleus
Columbine
Coral bells
Coreopsis
Cornflower
Cosmos
Crab apple
Daffodil
Darwin's barberry
Daylily
Delphinium
Dianthus
Dog-tooth violet
Dogwood
Dutch iris
English daisy
Epimedium
Euphorbia
Everlasting daisy
Floss flower
Flowering quince
Forget-me-not
Foxglove
Freesia
Fuschia-flowered gooseberry
Gaura
Gazania
Geranium
Geum
Gladiolus
Glory-of-the-snow
Godetia
Golden robinia
Grape hyacinth
Grevillea
Harlequin flower
Hawthorn
Honesty
Hosta
Hubei rowan
Hyacinth
Italian alder
Jade plant
Japanese crab apple
Japanese flowering cherry
Japanese maple
Japanese rose
Japanese spurge
Jelly beans
Jonquil
Judas tree
Juneberry
Kalanchoe
Kale
Lady's mantle
Lavender
Lenten rose
Lilac
Lily
Linaria
Livingstone daisy
Lobelia
Love-in-a-mist
Lungwort
Lupin
Mahonia
Maidenhair tree
Meadow rue
Meadowfoam
Mexican orange blossom
Monkey flower
Nemesia
Oleander
Orange browallia
Orchid cactus
Oriental poppy
Ornamental onion
Ornamental pear
Ox-eye chamomile
Pansy
Paper daisy
Pasque flower
Pelargonium
Peony
Petunia
Phlox
Photinia
Pieris
Pink
Plumbago
Polyanthus
Poppy
Potato vine
Primrose
Ranunculus
Red hot poker
Red valerian
Rhododendron
Rock rose
Rowan
Sage
Sargent cherry
Shasta daisy
Siberian crab apple
Snow-in-summer
Spiderwort
Spring starflower
Star jasmine
Statice

Stock
Sturt's desert pea
Sun rose
Sweet pea
Sweet William
Taiwan cherry
Tea tree
Thrift
Tulip
Verbena
Viburnum
Vinca
Wallflower
Warminster broom
Wedding bells
Weigelia
Whitebeam
Wisteria
Woolly willow
Zinnia

PLANTS FOR SUMMER DISPLAY

These plants are decorative in summer. They may flower then or have attractive fruit. Some may be decorative in summer only in certain climates.

Actinidia
Agapanthus
Alyssum
Amaranthus
Anemone
Angel's trumpet
Apple cactus
Aster
Astilbe
Aurora daisy
Baboon flower
Baby blue eyes
Baby's breath
Balsam
Beard tongue
Bear's breeches
Bedding begonia
Belladonna
Bellflower
Bergamot
Black cohosh
Blue bugle
Blue daisy
Blue poppy
Bluebeard
Box elder
Bramble
Butterfly bush
Calendula
Campion
Candytuft
Cardinal flower
Catmint
Cherry pie
Cinquefoil
Climbing hydrangea
Cockscomb
Coleus
Columbine
Coral bells
Coreopsis
Cosmos
Cranesbill
Crepe myrtle
Dahlia
Daylily
Delphinium
Dutch woodbine
English daisy
Escallonia
European red elderberry
Floss flower
Foxglove
Gaura
Gazania
Geranium
Geum
Gladiolus
Globe amaranth
Goatsbeard
Godetia
Golden barrel cactus
Golden hop
Grevillea
Hibiscus
Himalaya honeysuckle
Hollyhock
Honesty
Honey locust
Hosta
Hydrangea
Irish strawberry tree
Japanese anemone
Japanese hydrangea vine
Japanese spurge
Kaffir lily
Lady's mantle
Lily
Lobelia
Love-in-a-mist
Lupin
Mammillaria
Marigold
Meadow rue
Meadowfoam
Mealy cup sage
Mexican sunflower
Michaelmas daisy
Milfoil
Mock orange
Monkey flower
Mountain flax
Obedient plant
Oleander
Oriental poppy
Ornamental onion
Ox-eye chamomile
Pansy
Paper daisy
Peony
Perennial phlox
Perennial sunflower
Petunia
Phlox
Pink
Pittosporum
Plumbago
Poppy
Portulaca
Potato vine
Ranunculus
Red valerian
Rose-of-sharon
Sage
Salvia
Sea holly
Sedge
Shasta daisy
Shrubby cinquefoil
Shrubby groundsel
Small globe thistle
Snapdragon
Snow-in-summer
Spider flower
Spiderwort
St John's wort
Star jasmine
Statice
Stokes aster
Sun rose
Sunflower
Sweet pea
Sweet William
Thrift
Torenia
Tosa spiraea
Tree mallow
Tree of heaven
Trumpet creeper
Verbena
Whitebeam
Yellow spotted dead nettle
Zinnia

PLANTS FOR FALL DISPLAY

These plants look decorative in fall. They may flower then or have colorful fruits or fall foliage. Some may be decorative in fall only in certain climates.

PETUNIAS add color to fall gardens.

Alyssum
Amaranthus
Angel's trumpet
Aster
Autumn cherry
Balsam
Barberry
Beautyberry
Bedding begonia
Belladonna lily
Big blue lilyturf
Black birch
Bluebeard
Camellia
Cockscomb
Cockspur thorn
Coleus
Cosmos
Cotoneaster
Crab apple
Cranberry bush
Crepe myrtle
Cyclamen
Dahlia
Daphne
Dogwood
Fire thorn
Gazania
Globe amaranth
Golden robinia
Grevillea
Hibiscus
Himalaya honeysuckle
Hollyhock
Honey locust
Hubei rowan
Hydrangea
Irish strawberry tree
Japanese anemone
Japanese crab apple
Japanese fatsia
Japanese maple
Japanese rose
Jelly beans
Jonquil
Judas tree
Juneberry
Kaffir lily
Lily
Liquidambar
Maidenhair tree
Marigold
Mexican sunflower
Michaelmas daisy
Milfoil
Nerine
Obedient plant
Ornamental grape
Ornamental pear
Paper daisy
Paper-bark maple
Perennial phlox
Perennial sunflower
Petunia
Pin oak
Pittosporum
Plumbago
Portulaca
Potato vine
Red hot poker
Red valerian
Rowan
Sacred bamboo
Sage
Sallow thorn
Salvia
Sargent cherry
Siberian crab apple
Silver birch
Smoke bush
Snake-bark maple
Snapdragon
Sour gum
Spider flower
Spiderwort
Staghorn sumac
Stokes aster
Sunflower
Taiwan cherry
Torenia
Verbena
Viburnum
Virginia creeper
Wisteria
Zephyr lily

PLANTS FOR WINTER DISPLAY

The plants listed here are decorative in winter. Some may flower then or they may have attractive fruit or foliage. Some may be decorative in winter only in certain climates.

Alpine snow gum
Alyssum
Autumn cherry
Baboon flower
Bergenia
Black birch
Bluebell
Calendula
Camellia
Chinese cherry
Colchis ivy
Common snowdrop
Cyclamen
Daphne
Dianthus
Dragon-claw willow
English daisy
English holly
Euphorbia
Everlasting daisy
Fire thorn
Forget-me-not
Gazania
Grevillea
Heath
Holm oak
Hyacinth
Jonquil
Kalanchoe
Kale
Kuma bamboo grass
Lenten rose
Linaria
Livingstone daisy
Monterey cypress
Nemesia
Orange browallia
Pansy
Paper-bark maple
Pittosporum
Polyanthus
Poppy
Ranunculus
Sallow thorn
Siberian crab apple
Siberian dogwood
Silver birch
Snake-bark maple
Snapdragon
Spindle tree
Spring starflower
Star magnolia
Statice
Stock
Sturt's desert pea
Sweet pea
Taiwan cherry
Thorny elaeagnus
Viburnum
Wallflower
Winter jasmine
Witch hazel
Yulan

GLOSSARY

Accent plant A plant placed so as to draw attention to itself by contrasting with nearby plants in color, form, height or texture.

Acid soil Soil that does not contain lime and that has a pH of less than 7.

Aerial root Roots that appear on above-ground sections of stems.

Air-layering A way to induce woody plants to form roots on their stems with the aim of producing another plant or a plant that is relatively large.

Alkaline soil A soil that contains lime and has a pH greater than 7.

Annual A plant that germinates, grows, flowers, seeds and dies within a year.

Anther The pollen-bearing or male sex cells of a flower. Anthers are found at the tips of stalks called stamens.

Aspect The direction in which a garden faces.

Axil The point at which a leaf joins a stem.

Bed An area planted with flowers or shrubs and able to be seen from all sides.

Bedding out The complete covering of an area with annual flowers.

Bedding plant An annual flower used in a massed, temporary display.

Biennial A plant that germinates, grows, flowers, seeds and dies over two years.

Blanch To cause a plant to turn white by excluding light. Celery, leeks, witloof and asparagus are commonly blanched.

Bloom Usually a flower but can be a powder-like coating on plants, for example that on grape or blueberry fruits.

Bog garden Area without surface water where plants suited to constantly wet soil are grown.

Bolting An early rush to form flowers. Usually occurs in vegetables such as lettuces during hot weather.

Border An area planted with flowers and/or shrubs and seen primarily from one side.

Bottom heat The application of heat from below with an electric heating pad. It is a way of encouraging seeds to germinate or speeding the rooting of cuttings.

Bract A sometimes brightly colored modified leaf directly behind a flower or cluster of flowers. The display of both bougainvilleas and poinsettias is produced by bracts. The flowers are insignificant.

Broadcasting A way of sowing seeds or distributing fertilizer by throwing the seeds or fertilizer from the hands.

Broken shade Incomplete shade such as that under deciduous trees in winter or beneath the laths of a shadehouse. It is similar to dappled shade cast by thin overhead foliage.

Bud A swelling that is an unopened or embryonic flower or the beginnings of a growth shoot.

Budding A type of grafting used to propagate roses and fruit trees, whereby a growth bud from the desired plant is inserted into the stem of a related plant chosen for its strong root system. The two eventually grow as one, the bud forming the top growth.

Bulb An underground food storage organ from which leaves, flowers and roots emerge. It is composed of overlapping, fleshy scales such as those seen in a sliced onion.

Bulbil A small bulb attached to the stem. Lilies are bulbs that produce bulbils.

Callus The covering that forms over any wound suffered by a plant.

Calyx The covering that protects an unopened flower. The calyx consists of several petal-like structures called sepals. They may be colorful and decorative.

Cambium The green layer immediately below the bark, which is responsible for the thickening of branches and trunks.

Chlorophyll The green coloring in plants which, driven by light, turns water and carbon dioxide into food.

Chlorosis A lack of chlorophyll, which causes foliage to turn yellow. Nutrient deficiencies are a major cause of chlorosis.

Cloche A mini-greenhouse placed over a plant or row of plants as protection from cold.

Clone Plants produced vegetatively, that is, by cuttings, layers or division. They are identical to their parent whereas those grown from seed combine features from two parents.

Compost A fine, soil-like substance that is the end product of complete decomposition of plant or animal matter.

Compound leaf Any leaf made up of two or more leaflets.

Conifer Any cone-bearing tree, but including gingkos which are conifers without cones.

Conservatory A room of a house with glass walls or big windows and sometimes a glass ceiling. Conservatories are designed to trap light and heat to enable warm-climate plants to grow in a cold climate.

Copse A thicket or close planting of trees.

Corm An underground food storage organ from which leaves, flowers and roots emerge. Unlike a bulb, it is not composed of overlapping, fleshy scales.

Corolla The petals of a flower as a unit.

Crock A shard of pottery. A layer of crocks is often placed in the bottom of pots to improve drainage.

Crown That part of a plant where the stems meet the ground. It is usually applied to plants that die back each fall. New shoots arise from the top of the crown, roots from beneath the crown.

Cultivar A distinct variety of a plant that has some more desirable feature than the usual type. Cultivars are the result of deliberate breeding programs or they may arise in gardens but not in the wild.

Cutting A section of stem, root or leaf detached from a plant to induce it to form its own roots and grow into another plant.

Damping off A humidity-induced fungus disease that affects seedlings grown in too close conditions. The stems rot at ground level and the seedlings fall over.

Dappled shade Incomplete shade, usually cast by light foliage overhead through which the sky can be seen.

Dead-heading The removal of spent flowers in order to prevent seed formation and encourage more flowers to form.

Deciduous plant A tree or shrub that loses its leaves annually.

Disbudding The removal of some flower buds so that the plant's energies are directed into those remaining. Disbudding results in fewer but bigger flowers.

Division A way of propagating certain plants by separating a single clump into several smaller clumps. It is most often performed on perennials that are removed from the ground in winter, when dormant.

Double flower A flower that has many more than the usual number of petals.

Drill A shallow furrow into which seeds are sown or seedlings planted.

Edging plant A low-growing plant used to line the edges of paths or flower beds.

Epiphyte A plant that grows on another plant but is not a parasite.

Espaliered plant A plant trained in two planes, often flat against a wall but also free-standing on a framework of wires. It is a space-saving way to grow many types of fruit.

Evergreen plant A plant that retains its leaves year round.

Eye An inactive growth bud in plants such as a dahlia or potato, or the central, differently colored part of a flower.

Family A broad grouping of related plants. A plant family consists of several plant genera and usually many, even hundreds of species.

Fastigiate plant A tree or shrub with a narrow, upright habit of growth.

Filtered sunlight See "broken shade" and "dappled shade".

Floriferous The capacity to produce flowers.

Flush The appearance of more than just isolated flowers.

Forcing Making a plant flower before it normally would.

Formal garden A garden in which geometric patterns are produced by mass planting groups of the one species.

Friable soil Soil that is easily crumbled.

Frost-free Climate in which temperatures never fall below freezing point.

Fruit The seed-bearing structure of any plant.

Genus Related plants that display various similarities to each other. The individual members of a genus are called species. Related genera are grouped into families.

Germination The sprouting of a seed.

Grafting A way of joining two sections of plant together so that they grow as one. Used to fuse the desirable top growth and flowers of one species to the stronger, more disease-resistant roots of another.

Groundcover A usually but not necessarily low plant that is either spreading in habit or can be massed together to form a complete cover over the soil.

Growing season The period of the year during which plants actively grow. The length of this season usually depends on the climate with frosty weather signalling the end of the season for many plants. In the tropics, the onset of the dry season can be the end of the growing season.

Habit The usual form a plant takes.

Habitat The type of environment in which a plant or animal is found in nature.

Hardwood cuttings Cuttings taken from growths that are fully mature and "hard". Hardwood cuttings are usually taken in winter from growths that were produced the previous spring and summer.

Hardy plant A plant that is not damaged by frost. Hardiness is the degree of frost a plant will tolerate.

Heated pad An electric device placed beneath pots of seeds or cuttings to warm the soil and thereby speed germination or rooting.

Heel A strip of bark that remains attached to a cutting torn rather than snipped from a plant.
Herbaceous plant A plant with aboveground parts that are never woody. Many herbaceous plants die back to ground level in fall, reshooting in spring.
Herbicide A chemical that kills plants.
Hilling The mounding up of soil around the stems of plants, either to support the stems or to blanch them. Potatoes are hilled so that the tubers are not exposed to sunlight.
Humus The black, slightly sticky substance that is the final product from the decomposition of organic matter. It is a vital ingredient in fertile soils and its presence can be maintained with the regular addition of compost to soils.
Hybrid A plant with parents that are of different species or cultivars.

Inorganic matter Any matter that was never part of a living thing. Stone is inorganic.
Invasive plant A plant that is inclined to spread more widely and rapidly than the gardener would like.

Layer A layer is formed when a branch of a plant touches the ground and takes root at that point. It is possible to propagate plants by deliberately pegging down a branch and wounding the point where it touches the ground. Roots will form there and the plant can be detached from the parent and transplanted elsewhere.
Leaf litter Dry leaves and twigs that have fallen to the ground.
Leaf mould Partly decomposed or composted leaf litter.
Leggy plant A plant in which the spaces between leaves are overlong, resulting in a too tall appearance. Lack of light or overcrowding are common causes.
Legume A pea- or bean-producing plant. Legumes are important to soil fertility in that they have the ability to transfer the plant food nitrogen from the air into the soil.
Lift Dig up a plant with the aim of propagating it by dividing its roots or of storing the roots for later replanting.
Loam A type of fertile soil containing clay, sand and organic matter. Loam is crumbly, well-drained and an ideal garden soil.

Microclimate An area within a garden or region that has a combination of temperature and water different from the general climate. A microclimate can be the result of favorable or unfavorable landforms or the placement of structures. A warm microclimate could occur at the base of a wall that faces the sun. A cool microclimate may be found on the shady side.
Mixed border An area, designed to be seen from one side, that contains annual and perennial flowers, bulbs and shrubs.
Mulch Organic or inorganic matter spread over the soil with the aim of conserving soil moisture, suppressing weed growth and stabilizing soil temperature.

N:P:K The elemental symbols that stand for nitrogen (N), phosphorus (P) and potassium (K). They are used on fertilizer packets to indicate the proportions of each element contained. N, P and K are the three most important plant foods, and fertilizers that contain all three are designated "complete".
Naturalizing Placing a group of plants so that they appear to be "natural". Bulbs are often naturalized in lawns or under deciduous trees, the process involving the random planting of clumps of bulbs.
Near frost-free Describes a location where frosts are possible but not frequent.
Neck The narrow, top section of a bulb.
Node The part of a stem from which a leaf or bud grows.

Open-foliaged Describes plants (usually trees and shrubs) that can be seen through when fully leafed.
Organic matter Any substance that was once alive or part of a living thing.

Part-shade Describes an area that is shady for part of the day, sunny for the rest.
Parterre An area in which various plants are grown in patterns usually designed to be seen from above. Low, clipped hedges may form the outlines, with the spaces they contain being colored with foliage or flowers.
Perennial A plant that lives indefinitely. Strictly speaking, trees and shrubs are perennials but in gardening the term is usually applied to soft-wooded flowers.
Perennial border An area, designed to be seen from one side, planted with perennials.
pH A 14-point measure of the acidity or alkalinity of a substance. 1 is extremely acid, 7 is neutral and 14 is extremely alkaline.
Photosynthesis The process by which plants use light to convert water and carbon dioxide into carbohydrates.
Pinching out The removal of the growing tips of shoots by pinching between the thumb and forefinger. Pinching out results in the production of side shoots and thus a bushier plant.
Pollen Tiny, usually yellow grains that carry the male chromosomes. Pollen is produced by the anthers which are clustered in the center of flowers. When transferred to the female stigma by bees, birds, animals or wind, fertile seeds will be produced.

Pollination The transferral of pollen from anthers to stigmas.

Pot bound The condition of having too many roots for the size of the pot.

Potting on The transfer of a potted plant into a bigger pot.

Prick out Transfer seedlings from the pot in which they were germinated into a bigger pot so that they may have room to grow.

Propagation Any method of multiplying a single plant into two or more.

Pruning The removal of any part of a plant.

Remontant A term usually applied to roses which have the habit of repeat flowering within a single season.

Repotting Strictly speaking, the transfer of a plant from one pot into another of the same size. A proportion of soil is scraped from the rootball to make room for fresh potting mix. Many gardeners now use the term to mean "potting on" into a larger pot.

Rhizome An underground or above-ground food storage organ that grows horizontally, allowing the plant to spread outwards.

Rosette Literally means "resembling a rose" but is usually applied to leaves that are arranged in the pattern of rose petals. A loose-leaf lettuce has a rosette of leaves.

Salinity The amount of salt in soil or water.

Scion In grafting, the scion is the bud or cutting that will become the top growth and flowers of the new plant.

Self-seeding plant A plant that replaces itself, without the gardener's intervention, by the natural process of dropping seeds. Mostly applies to annual flowers.

Semi-ripe cutting Cuttings of stems that are beginning to mature but are not fully hard.

Sharp sand Washed sand that does not contain any clay. Sharp sand is gritty.

Shrub A woody plant with a short trunk or many stems arising from the ground.

Slow-release fertilizer Fertilizer that releases its nutrients over weeks or months as determined by temperature and/or moisture.

Soft-tip cuttings Cuttings made from the tips of fresh new growth.

Species A single type of plant. Different but related species make up a genus and several related genera are grouped into a family.

Sport A mutation within a single plant that gives rise to a branch with different characteristics than the rest of the plant. Its flowers or leaves may be different and, if desirable, the sport can be propagated to produce a new variety.

Standard A tree or shrub with a single, unbranched stem and a mop-like or weeping head of foliage. Standards are produced by grafting or by training a plant to a single stem.

Stock In grafting, the stock is the root-bearing plant onto which the scion is grafted.

Stolon A shoot that runs along or under the ground or emerges from the upper parts of a plant and that produces a new plant at its tip.

Subsoil The layer of infertile soil below the fertile topsoil. It is recognized by its different color and/or texture.

Succulent Any plant with juicy, water-storing leaves and stems.

Suckering The habit of spreading outwards by means of underground stems which shoot upwards at intervals.

Systemic A term applied to garden chemicals that work by being absorbed into the plant's sap stream and thereby distributed to all parts of the plant.

Tender plant A plant that is not able to withstand frost.

Terrestrial plant A plant that grows on the ground. The term is mostly used to differentiate between members of the same genus, some of which may be epiphytes (tree-dwelling) and others terrestrial.

Tilth Cultivated soil that is in good condition for the growing of crops.

Tip prune See "pinching out".

Topiary The art of shaping trees and shrubs into recognizable forms.

Trailing plant A plant with long, lax stems that grow over the ground or trail over walls or out of hanging baskets.

Transplant Move a plant from one location to another.

Tree A large woody plant with a distinct trunk or trunks and (usually) large, well-spaced branches.

Tuber An underground food storage organ, its surface randomly peppered with dormant growth buds or eyes.

Tussock A clump of grassy leaves.

Understock In grafting, the understock or stock is the root-bearing portion onto which is grafted the scion or future upper parts.

Variegated leaf A leaf that is spotted, striped, streaked or blotched with a different color or several colors.

Variety Like a cultivar, a variety has some more desirable feature than the usual type but it occurs naturally.

Viability The storage life of an ungerminated seed.

Vigor The speed and strength with which a plant grows.

Weeping The habit of having pendulous branches giving a drooping appearance.

Wetting agent A chemical that, when applied to dry soil, allows it to be rapidly rewetted.

INDEX

Published by Bay Books, an imprint of Murdoch Books Pty Limited.
Pier 8/9, 23 Hickson Rd, Millers Point NSW 2000.

This edition first published 2003. Reprinted 2005.

ISBN 0 681 18563 5

Authors: Margaret Hanks, Roger Mann, Denise Greig, Geoffrey Burnie
Managing Editor: Christine Eslick
Editorial Director: Diana Hill
Design concept: Marylouise Brammer
Designer: Norman Baptista
Cover design: Michelle Cutler
Design assistance: Wing Ping Tong, Michelle Cutler
Illustrators: Sonya Naumov (all except specified otherwise); Stephen Pollitt (10,11); Rod Scott (43, 44, 49 centre)
Photographers: Lorna Rose (all unless specified otherwise); Better Homes and Gardens® Picture Library (13, 18 top and bottom, 58, 59, 60, 69, 311, 384, 386LR, 387, 389): Geoffrey Burnie (85R, 89L, 104R, 105L, 159R, 174R, 211L, 220R, 228LR, 269L, 304, 305, 364R, 366L); Densey Clyne (51 centre); Jim Frazier/Mantis Wildlife (48 top); Denise Greig (34, 46, 47, 48 centre and bottom, 49 top and bottom, 50, 51 top and bottom, 52R, 53–6, 385 bottom); Phil Haley (3, 385 top, 390–2); Brian McInerney (24, 31, 35, 39, 41); Stirling Macoboy (89R, 174L, 213L, 214R, 222L, 235L, 284R, 309LR, 318R); Andre Martin (315); Luis Martin (29, 73); Reg Morrison (330–41); Murdoch Books Picture Library (93LR, 97R, 98R, 100L, 102R, 172R, 185L, 187R, 199R, 213R, 312L, 377R); Tony Rodd (345R, 346R, 349R, 355L, 357L, 358L, 359R, 365L)

CEO: Juliet Rogers
Publisher: Kay Scarlett

PRINTED IN CHINA
Produced by Phoenix Offset, Hong Kong